Roman remember to rule over the peoples with authority
These will be your skills; to impose the rule of peace.
To spare the conquered and to subdue the proud
—Vergil, Aeneid, vi 851-3

You have made one nation out of many different peoples
It was profitable for you to be captured while unjustly ruling
And you offer a sharing of your own rights to the conquered
You have made city that was previously the world.

apud ipses¹ fides obstinata²,³ misericordia in promptu;
adversus⁴ omnes alios hostile⁵ odium

1. apud: (preposition) + ipse (fem. acc of ipse): among
   themselves / within their own group
2. fides obstinata: fides (noun, nom. sing): faith/loyalty
   obstinata: (adj. nom sing fem.): resolute/stubborn ···
   /unyielding → resolute faith /unyielding loyalty
3. misericordia in promptu: (misericordia: noun, nom.
   sing.) compassion / mercy
   in promptu (prepositional phrase): at hand/readily available
   → compassion is readily available
4. adversus omnes alios > adversus (preposition):
   → against/towards
       omnes (adj. acc. pl.) → all
       alios (adj. acc. pl.) → others
       → towards all others
5. hostile odium
       hostile (adj. nom. sing. neuter): hostile
       odium (noun, nom sing): hatred
       → hostile hatred
translation:
   among themselves, faith is resolute, and compassion
   is readily available, but towards all others, there
   is hostile hatred.
       Tacitus— Historia V. 4.

'Tu regere imperio populos, Romane, memento;
Hae tibi'erunt artes; pacisque imponere morem.
Parcere subiectis, et debellare superbos.'

VERGIL, Aeneid, vi. 851 3

'Fecisti patriam diversis gentibus unam,
Profuit iniustis te dominante capi.
Dumque offers victis proprii consortia iuris,
Urbem fecisti quod prius orbis erat.'

RUTILIUS, i. 63-6

v

INTRODUCTORY NOTE

WHATEVER controversies may be astir as to the precise objects of a classical training, it will hardly be disputed that if that teaching has been successful the pupils will sooner or later be able to make out an ordinary passage of 'unseen' Latin or Greek. It is a test to which the purely linguistic teacher must obviously defer: while the master, who aims at imparting knowledge of the subject-matter must acknowledge, if his boys flounder helplessly in unprepared extracts, that they could have learnt about ancient life better through translations.

In, addition to the value of unseen translation, as a test of teaching it constitutes an admirable thinking exercise. But so numerous are the various books of extracts already published that I should have seen nothing to be gained from the appearance of a new one like the present volume were it not, as far as I know, different in two important respects from others. It contains six Demonstrations of *how* sentences are to be attacked: and further, the passages are chosen so that if a boy works through the book he can hardly fail to gain some outline knowledge of Roman Republican history.

As to the Demonstrations, their value will be evident if it is realised that failure in this sort of translation means failure to analyse: to split up, separate, distinguish the component parts of an apparently jumbled but really ordered sentence. A beginner must learn to trust the solvent with which we supply him; and the way to induce him to trust it is to show it to him at work. viThat is what a Demonstration will do if only the learner will give it a fair chance.

In regard to the historical teaching contained in the extracts, there can be little doubt that the present tendency of classical teaching is towards emphasising the subject-matter as well as the language. It is felt that as training in political principles the reading of Greek and Roman authors offers unique advantages, such as many English boys can appreciate, who are deaf to the literary appeal. The choice therefore of historical extracts in chronological order is an attempt to recognise both the two great aims of classical teaching at once. At any rate there is no reason to suppose that the linguistic exercise is in any way impaired by being combined with a little history.

I should like to direct attention also to the notes given on the extracts, and the purpose they are meant to serve. If no notes had been given some of the passages which are important or interesting historically would have been found too difficult for the boys for whom they are intended. Moreover, most of the notes concern the historical aspect of the extract to which they belong, and are part of the scheme by which the subject-matter of the passage is emphasised. Although the passages themselves are not strictly graduated, the help given in translation becomes less and less as the boy goes through the book; and it is obvious that those extracts which illustrate the later periods of Roman History will be found more difficult than the legends and stories which belong to an earlier age. In cases where no help at all is desired, the Miscellaneous Passages (which are without notes) may be used.

E. LYTTELTON.

ETON: *April 1908.*
vii

EDITOR'S PREFACE

THE aim of the present book is to help boys to translate at sight. Of the many books of unseen translation in general use few exhibit continuity of plan as regards the subject-matter, or give any help beyond a short heading. The average boy, unequal to the task before him, is forced to draw largely upon his own invention, and the master, in correcting written unseens, has seldom leisure to do more than mark mistakes—a method of correction almost useless to the boy, unless accompanied by full and careful explanation when the written work is given back.

Now that less time is available for Latin and Greek, new methods of teaching them must be adopted if they are to hold their own in our public schools. When Lord Dufferin could say,

'I am quite determined, so far as care and forethought can prevent it, that the ten best years of my boy's life shall not be spent (as mine were) in nominally learning two dead languages without being able to translate an ordinary paragraph from either without the aid of a dictionary;' and Dr. Reid could write, 'It is not too much to say that a large number of boys pass through our schools without ever dreaming that an ancient writer could pen three consecutive sentences with a connected meaning: chaos is felt to be natural to ancient literature: no search is made for sense, and the Latin or Greek book is looked upon as a more or less fortuitous concourse of words;' when Dr. Rouse can assert, 'The public schoolboy at nineteen is unable to read a simple Latin or Greek book with ease, or to express a simple series of thoughts without atrocious blunders: he has learnt from his classics neither accuracy viiinor love of beauty and truth'—it is obvious that, for the average boy, the system of perfunctorily prepared set-books and dashed-off unseens is a failure. The experience of every teacher who is also an examiner, and who has had to deal with public schoolboys, will confirm this; but during twenty-five years' teaching and examining of boys in almost every stage, I have found that translation at sight, taught upon the plan of this book, not only produces a good result, but teaches a boy how to grapple with the bare text of a Latin author better than the habitual practice of translating at sight without any help at all. If the average boy is to be taught how to translate, his interest must be awakened and sustained, and the standard of routine work made as high as possible. The clever boys are, as a rule, well provided for; but, even for them, the methods of this book have been found to be the shortest road to accuracy and style in translation. Moreover by this means they have gained a firsthand acquaintance with Latin literature and the sources of Roman history.

It is impossible here to enter into 'the question of the close and striking correspondence between the history, the literature, and the language of Rome. It was not until the history of Rome threw its mantle over her poetry that the dignity of the poet was recognised and acknowledged. . . . In the same way the life of the Roman people is closely bound up with the prose records, and the phenomena of the Roman Empire lend a human interest to all representative Roman writers.'1 Considerations of this kind form a sufficient justification of the method here adopted of employing the historical records of Rome as a basis of teaching.

In this book the Introduction (pp. 1-14) is written to teach a boy how to arrive at the meanings of words (*Helps to Vocabulary*, pp. 1-5); how to find out the thought of a sentence through analysis and a knowledge ixof the order of words in Latin (*Helps to-Translation*, pp. 5-12); how to reproduce in good English the exact meaning and characteristics of his author (*Helps to Style*, pp. 13-14).

In the Demonstrations (pp. 15-58) the boy is taught to notice all allusions that give him a clue to the sense of the passage, to grapple with the difficulties of construction, to break up sentences, and to distinguish between the principal and the subordinate thoughts both in prose and verse.

The Passages have been carefully selected, and contain accounts of nearly all the important events and illustrious men of the period of history to which they belong. They are chronologically arranged and divided into six periods, covering Roman history from B.C. 753 to B.C.44, leaving the Augustan and subsequent period to be dealt with in a second volume. The translation help given in the notes is carefully graduated. The notes to Parts I., II., III. (marked D, pp. 60-107) are thus intended to help younger boys to deal with passages which would in some cases be too difficult for them; less help in translation is given in Parts IV. and V. (marked C, pp. 108-159); while the notes to Part VI. (marked B, pp. 160-236) are mainly concerned with historical explanation, illustration, or allusion.

The Miscellaneous Passages (pp. 238-271), chosen for me by my brother-in-law, Mr. A. M. Goodhart (Assistant Master at Eton College), are added to provide occasional passages in which no help is given. It is hoped that these, which deal with subjects of general interest, and include a somewhat wide range of authors, may give variety to the book, and supply more verse passages than the historical character of the rest would admit. For the sake of variety, or to economise time, some of the passages may be translated *viva voce* at the discretion of the master.

The Appendices (pp. 274-363) may be referred to when a boy finds himself in doubt about the value of xa Conjunction (I.), the force of a Prefix (II.), the meaning of a Suffix (III.), the Life and Times of his Author (VI.), or the historical significance of a date (VII.). In Appendix V. a Demonstration is given to show how a boy, after sufficient practice in translation by the help of analysis, may to some extent learn to think in Latin, and so to follow the Latin order in arriving at the thought.

The important question of what maps should accompany the book will be best solved by providing each boy with a copy of Murray's Small Classical Atlas, edited by G. B. Grundy, which will be found to be admirably adapted to the purpose. By the kindness of Mr. John Murray, two

2

plans (Dyrrachium and Pharsalus), not at present included in the Atlas, have been specially drawn to illustrate passages on pp.216 and 218, and are placed opposite the text.

As far as possible I have acknowledged my indebtedness to the Editors whose editions of the classics have been consulted. For the historical explanations I am under special obligation to the histories of Ihne and Mommsen, to the 'Life of Cicero' by the Master of Balliol, and to the 'Life of Caesar' by Mr. Warde Fowler. I have also to thank Messrs. Macmillan for allowing me to quote from Dr. Potts' 'Aids to Latin Prose,' and from Professor Postgate's *Sermo Latinus*. For the prose passages the best texts have been consulted, while for Livy, Weissenborn's text edited by Müller (1906) has been followed throughout. As regards the verse passages, the text adopted is, ~~the collection of Latin poets~~ wherever possible, that of Professor Postgate's recension of the *Corpus Poetarum Latinorum*. For the Short Lives I have found useful 'The Student's Companion to Latin Authors' (Middleton and Mills), but I owe much more to the works of Teuffel, Cruttwell, Sellar, Tyrrell, and Mackail.

The Head Master of Eton, besides expressing his approval of the book, has kindly offered to write an Introductory Note. He has also given me an exceptional xiopportunity of testing more than half the historical passages by allowing them to be used in proof, until the book was ready, for the weekly unseen translation in the three blocks of fifth form, represented by the letters, B, C, D. The criticisms and suggestions made by Classical Masters at Eton, who have used the passages week by week, have been very valuable, and, in particular, my thanks are due to Mr. Impey, Mr. Tatham, Mr. Macnaghten, Mr. Wells, and Mr. Ramsay. My thanks are also due to the Lower Master, Mr. F. H. Rawlins, for kindly reading the MS. of the Introduction, Demonstrations, and Appendices I.-IV., and for giving me the benefit of his wide experience.

To my brother-in-law, Mr. A. M. Goodhart, I owe it that I undertook to write the book; without his advice it would never have seen the light, and he has given me most valuable help and encouragement at every stage.

As regards the choice of type and style of printing, I owe a special debt of thanks to Mr. W. Hacklett (manager of Messrs. Spottiswoode's Eton branch), whose unceasing care and attention has been invaluable in seeing the book through the press. I must also acknowledge the patience and skill of Messrs. Spottiswoode's London staff in carrying out the many alterations which I have found to be inseparable from the task of bringing each passage and its notes into the compass of a single page.

In conclusion I should like to say that it has been my aim throughout to adhere to what is best in Roman literature, and to omit passages the choice of which can only be justified by regarding their literary form apart from their moral value. Latin literature contains so much that is at once excellent in style and noble in thought that it seems a grave mistake to exalt the one at the expense of the other.

Maxima debetur puero reverentia.
the greatest respect is owed to a child — Juvenalis XIV. 4x

EDMUND LUCE.

WINDSOR: *April 1908.*
1. The late Professor Goodhart.
xiii

LIST OF PASSAGES FOR TRANSLATION.

DEMONSTRATIONS.

3

Part I.—The Regal Period, 753-509 B.C.

Part II.—The Early Republic, 509-366 B.C.

Part III.—The Conquest of Italy, 366-266 B.C.

5

Part IV.—The Contest with Carthage, 264-202 B.C.

7

Part VI.—Civil Strife in Italy, and Foreign Wars, ending in Revolution, 133-44 B.C.

48

8

9

10

Miscellaneous Passages.

11

13

		Plautus

I.

On Pacuvius — Domitius Marsus

II.

On Plautus — Ausonius, *Epit.* 36

Cicero, *Tusc.* i. 42.

V.   101

On Tibullus

:

In tumulo
I.   hominis felicis

Thermopylae

II.

2   Epilogue.

71

A. Horace — Horace, *Od.* iii. 30

B. Ovid — Ovid, *Met.* xv. 871

C. Martial — Martial iv. 89

xxiii

INDEX OF AUTHORS

Asinius Pollio, 223

Aulus Gellius, 63, 177, 179

Ausonius, 270

Caesar, 16, 196, 197, 198, 199, 200, 201, 202, 212, 214, 216, 218,220, 241, 265

Catullus, 231, 243, 247, 264, 267

Cicero, 54, 65, 79, 89, 97, 101, 102, 105, 111, 112, 113, 119, 127,136, 161, 163, 166, 169, 1
77, 181, 184, 185, 188, 190, 193, 204,205, 208, 225, 227, 230, 264, 265, 266, 270

Claudian, 235

Domitius Marsus, 270

Ennius, 270

Florus, 74, 103, 134, 149, 155, 157, 158, 164, 168, 169, 180, 183, 206

Frontinus, 123, 131, 146, 149, 172, 173

Horace, 86, 105, 106, 132, 133, 143, 152, 159, 182, 207, 238, 241,244, 246, 250, 261, 265, 2
71

Justinus, 100, 104, 109, 171

Juvenal, 105, 116, 163, 165, 168, 231, 244, 246, 250, 265

Livy, 32, 40, 61, 62, 64, 67, 68, 69, 70, 71, 72, 75, 76, 77, 78, 80, 81,82, 83, 85, 86, 87, 90, 9
1, 93, 94, 95, 96, 98, 99, 115, 117, 118,120, 121, 122, 124, 125, 128, 129, 130, 131, 133, 134, 135, 1
37,138, 139, 140, 141, 142, 144, 145, 147, 148, 150, 153, 154, 232,233, 246, 265

Lucan, 82, 165, 174, 175, 207, 211, 213, 214, 215, 217, 219, 221,222, 224, 227

Lucilius, 245

Lucretius, 246, 265

Manilius, 249

Martial, 69, 230, 243, 250, 251, 261, 265, 268, 269, 271

Naevius, 270

Nepos, 114, 151

Ovid, 24, 61, 64, 73, 74, 88, 169, 207, 241, 242, 247, 248, 250, 251,252, 260, 267, 271

Pacuvius, 242, 270

Persius, 245

Petronius, 263

Phaedrus, 258

Plautus, 254, 264, 265

Pliny the Elder, 256

Pliny the Younger, 256, 257, 260

Propertius, 79, 92, 132, 234, 253, 267

Prudentius, 236

Publilius Syrus, 265

Quintilian, 244, 250, 257, 264, 266

Sallust, 160, 162, 170, 177, 178, 194

Seneca, 240, 265

Silius Italicus, 114, 119, 123, 126

15

1

INTRODUCTION

1. Heading.—The selections in this book are in most cases intelligible apart from their context. In cases where this is not so, you will find it a valuable exercise to endeavour to arrive at the context for yourself. In all cases, however, you should pay attention to the **Heading**, which will give you a useful clue to the meaning of the passage,

2. Author.—When you see the author's name, try to remember what you know about him. For example, **Livy**, the historian of Rome and friend of Augustus, the contemporary of Vergil and Ovid. The short Lives, pp. 293-345, will tell you the chief facts about the authors from whom the selections are taken, and will give you a brief summary of their chief works. Also, if you refer to Appendix VII., pp. 347-363, you will gain some idea of the time in which the authors lived and of their contemporaries.

3. Read the Passage through, carefully.—As you read—

(1) Notice all **allusions** and **key-words** that may help you to the sense of the passage.

(2) **Pay special attention to the opening sentence.** In translating a passage much depends on getting the first sentence right.

(3) Notice especially the connectives which introduce sentences and clauses **marked off by commas.** In this way you will be able to distinguish between a **Principal Sentence** and a **Subordinate Clause.**

(For List of Conjunctions see Appendix I. pp. 274-276.)

HELPS TO VOCABULARY.

4. Through English Derivatives.—English derivatives, if used in the proper way, may give you valuable help in inferring meanings. The reason why you must generally **not** translate the Latin word by the derived English word is that, as 2you probably know, many English derivatives have come from Latin words which had wholly or in part lost their earlier classical meaning, or from Latin words not found at all in classical Latin. Yet in such cases the English word may be far from useless. You must take care to let it suggest to you the original or root-meaning, leaving the correct meaning of the Latin, whether the same as the English word or not, to be determined by the context.

For example, **sē-cūr-us** does not mean *secure*, but (like *secure* in Shakespeare and Milton) *care-less.*

'This happy night the Frenchmen are *secure,*
Having all day caroused and banqueted.'

SHAKESPEARE, *Hen. VI.* Part 1. II. i. 11.

In-crēd-ib-il-is, on the other hand, often cannot be better translated than by *incredible*, and **im-plācā-bilis** by *implacable.*

Notice, too, how often in the case of verbs the **supine stem** will suggest to you the meaning of the Latin through some English derivative, which the present stem conceals.

For example:—

	p	p	*p*	s	*to*
ingo	**ictum**	*icture*	uggests	*paint.*	
	c	c	*c*	,,	,,
aveo	**autum**	*aution*		*beware.*	
	c	c	*c*	,,	,,
olo	**ultum**	*ulture*		*till.*	
	f	f	*f*	,,	,,
allo	**alsum**	*alse*		*deceive.*	

5. Through French Derivatives.—Sometimes, when you cannot think of an English derivative, a French word that you know will help you to the meaning of the Latin.

For example:—

Latin	French		English
pontem	pont	suggests	*bridge.*
gustum	goût	,,	*taste.*
prātum	ré	,,	*meadow.*
tālem	el	,,	*such.*
bĭbĕre	oire	,,	*to drink.*

But, in order to make French derivatives a real help to you, you must know something of the origin of the French language and of the chief rules that govern the pronunciation (and therefore the spelling) of French. Without going too much into detail, it may help you to remember that—

3

(1) **French** has taken many words from **colloquial Latin**, which in the days of Cicero was very different from classical Latin.

For example:—

Literary Latin.	Popular Latin.	French.	
equus	caballus	cheval	*horse.*
pugna	batalia	bataille	*battle.*
os	bucca	bouche	*mouth.*

(2) **Unaccented** syllables are usually dropped.

For example:—

cérv-um	cerf	*stag.*
bonitátem	bonté	*goodness.*

(3) The general tendency of French is towards smoothness and contraction.

For example:—

Latin	French	English
bestiam	ête	*beast.*
factum	ait	*deed.*
spissum	pais	*thick.*
collum	ou	*neck.*

In fact, bearing in mind the caution given you, it is an excellent rule to try to think out the meaning of the Latin by the help of English and French derivatives.

6. Compound Words.—When you come to a word which you cannot translate, and in regard to which English and French derivatives do not help you, **break up the word**, if a compound, into its simple elements of **Prefix, Stem, Suffix**. Then from the meaning of its root or stem and from the force of the prefix and suffix, and by the help of the context, try to arrive at an English word to suit the sense.

In order to be able to do this you should have some knowledge of—

(1) A few simple rules for the **vowel changes of verbs in composition**. Thus:

a before two consonants (except **ng**) often changes to **e**.

E.g. sacr-o, con-**s**ecr-o; damn-o, con-**d**emn-o.

17

a before one consonant and before **ng** often changes to **i**.

E.g. fac-io, ef-fic-io; căd-o, ac-cid-o; tang-o, con-ting-o.

But grăd-ior, ag-grĕd-ior.

4

a before **l** and another consonant changes to **u**.

E.g. salt-are, in-sult-are.

ĕ changes to **ĭ** (but not **e** before two consonants) and **ae** to **i**.

E.g. ten-ere, ob-tin-ere; quaer-ere, in-quir-ere.

au changes to **u**.

E.g. claud-ere, in-clud-ere.

(2) **Prefixes:**—To help you to detach the prefix more readily, notice these simple euphonic changes, all of which result in making the pronunciation smoother and easier. Thus:—

(i.) **The last consonant of a Latin prefix is often made the same as, or similar to, the first consonant of the stem.**

E.g. **ad**-fero = affero; **ob**-pono = **op**-pono; **com**(=**cum**)-tendo =**con**-tendo.

(ii.) **The final consonant of a prefix is often dropped before two consonants.**

E.g. **ad**-scendo = a-scendo.

Notice also that the prepositional prefixes to verbs express different ideas in different combinations.

Thus, sometimes the prefix has a somewhat **literal prepositional** force.

E.g. **per**-currere = to run **through**.

But sometimes an **intensive** force.

E.g. **per**-terrere = to **thoroughly** frighten.

In all such cases you must be partly guided by the context.

(For List of Important Prefixes, see Appendix II. pp. 277—281.)

(3) **Suffixes** (other than grammatical inflexions).

A knowledge of the most important suffixes will often help you to the correct meaning of a Latin word, the root of which is familiar to you.

Thus from the √ag = *drive, move*, we have—

by addition of **tor** (= *agent or doer* of an action), **actor** = *a doer, agent.*

,, ,, **men** (= *acts or results of acts*), **agmen** = *a course, line of march*, &c.

,, ,, **ilis** (= *belonging to, able to*), **agilis** = *easily moved, agile.*

,, ,, **ito** (= *forcible or repeated action*), **agito** = *put in action, agitate.*

(For List of Important Suffixes, see Appendix III. pp. 282—286.)

5

(4) **Cognates**, that is, words **related in meaning** through a common root. You will find it very useful to make for yourself lists of cognate words.

Thus from the √**gna, gno** = *know*, we have—

gna-rus = *knowing.*

i-gnarus (= **in** + **gnarus**) = *ignorant.*

nos-co (= **gno-sco**) = *to get a knowledge of.*

i-gno-sco = *not to know, pardon.*

no-bilis (= **gno-bilis**) = *that can be known, famous, noble.*

no-men (= **gno-men**) = *a name.*

To group together in this manner words of common origin and words closely associated in meaning is one of the best ways in which you can increase your vocabulary.

(For additional Examples of Cognates, see Appendix IV. pp. 287-8.)

HELPS TO TRANSLATION.

You have now read the passage through carefully, and thought out the vocabulary to the best of your ability. Begin then to translate the opening sentence, and pay great attention to these

7. General Rules.—(1) Underline the **Principal Verb, Subject** (if expressed), and **Object** (if any).

(2) If the sentence contains **only one finite verb**, all you have to do is to group round Subject, or Verb, or Object the words and phrases that belong to each of the three.

(3) Translate the sentence literally. Do this mentally, without writing it down.

(4) Then write down the best translation you can.

For example:—

swiftly among the Germans, with their accustomed phalanx made, they received the attack of the swords

At GERMANI celeriter, consuetudine sua phalange facta, IMPETUS gladiorum **EXCEPERUNT.**

But the Germans quickly formed into a phalanx, as was their custom, and received the attacks of the swords (i.e. of the Romans with drawn swords).

(5) If the sentence contains one or more subordinate clauses, **consider each subordinate clause as if it were bracketed off separately**, and then deal with each clause as if it were a principal sentence, finding out its Subject, Verb, Object, and adding to each its enlargements. Then return to the sentence as a whole, and group round its Subject, Predicate, and Object the various subordinate clauses which belong to each.

6

8. Help through Analysis.—Very often analysis will help you to find out the **proper relation of the subordinate clauses** to the three parts of the Principal Sentence. You need not always analyse on paper, but do it **always in your mind**. You will find an example of a simple method of analysis at the close of Demonstrations I and IV, pp. 23, 47.

When analysing, notice carefully that:—

(1) An enlargement of a Noun may be

    (*a*) An adjective   **TERTIAM aciem.** *the third line*

    (*b*) A noun in apposition   **Publius Crassus ADULESCENS.** *(young man)*

    (*c*) A dependent genitive   **impetus GLADIORUM.** *the attack of the swords*

    (*d*) A participle or participial   **nostris LABORANTIBUS.**
phrase

    (*e*) An adjectival clause   **Publius Crassus QUI EQUITATUI** *who is calvary*
                                 PRAEERAT.

(2) An enlargement of a Verb may be

    (*a*) An adverb   **CELERITER exceperunt.** *(they swiftly welcomed)*

    (*b*) A prepositional   **EX CONSUETUDINE SUA exceperunt.** *(they welcomed as per their usual practice)*
phrase

    (*c*) An ablative   **PHALANGE FACTA exceperunt.** *(they welcomed [it] with a formed phalanx)*
absolute

    (*d*) An adverbial   **ID CUM ANIMADVERTISSET, Publius** *when he had noticed it,*
clause   **Crassus misit.** *Crassus sent.*

9. Help through Punctuation.—Though only the full-stop was used by the ancients, the punctuation marks which are now used in all printed texts should be carefully noticed, especially in translating long and involved sentences.

Thus in Demonstrations III and IV notice how the subordinate clauses are for the most part enclosed in commas.

10. Help through Scansion and Metre.—A knowledge of this is indispensable in translating verse. To scan the lines will help you to determine the grammatical force of a word, and a knowledge of metre will enable you to grasp the poet's meaning as conveyed by the position which he assigns to the various words, and the varying emphasis which results from variation of metre. For example:—

(1) *A grammatical help.*—You know that final -**a** is *short* in nom. and voc. sing. 1st Decl., and in neut. plural, and is *long* in abl. sing. 1st Decl. and 2nd Imperat. 1st Conj.

Thus in <u>Demonstration II</u> (p. 24) you can easily determine the grammatical form of finals in -**a**.

7

In Sentence IV **agnă**, in VI **cervă**, in VIII **iunctă columbă**, in IX**Cynthiă** are all short and nom. sing.

In Sentence V **umbrā unā** are long and abl. sing. in agreement.

(2) *A help to the poet's meaning.*—The more you know of the principles of scansion, the better able you will be to understand and appreciate the skill with which a great poet varies his metre and chooses his words.

11. Help through a Study of the Period in Latin.—One great difference between English and Latin Prose is that, while modern English is to a great extent a language of short, detached sentences, Latin **expresses the sense by the passage as a whole**, and holds the climax in suspense until the delivery of the last word. This mode of expression is called a **PERIOD** (a **circuĭtus** or **ambĭtus verborum**), because the reader, in order to collect together the words of the Principal Sentence, must make a *circuit*, so to say, round the inserted clauses,'[2] 'Latin possesses what English does not, a mode of expression by means of

19

which, **round one main idea are grouped all its accessory ideas**, and there is thus formed a single harmonious whole, called the **PERIOD.'**3

A **PERIOD** then is a sentence containing only one main idea (the Principal Sentence) and several Subordinate Clauses. The Periodic style is generally used for History and Description, and is best seen in Cicero and Livy.

The following is a good example of the PERIOD in Latin:—

4**VOLSCI exiguam spem in armis, alia undique abscissa, cum tentassent, praeter cetera adversa loco quoque iniquo ad pugnam congressi, iniquiore ad fugam, cum ab omni parte caederentur, ad preces a certamine versi, dedito imperatore traditisque armis, sub iugum missi, cum singulis vestimentis ignominiae cladisque pleni DIMITTUNTUR.**

The **VOLSCIANS** *found that now they were severed from every other hope, there was but little in prolonging the conflict. In addition to other disadvantages they had engaged on a spot ill-adapted for fighting and worse for flight. Cut to pieces on every side they abandoned the contest and cried for quarter. After surrendering their commander and delivering up their arms, they passed under the yoke, and with one garment each* **WERE SENT** *to their homes covered with disgrace and defeat.*

8

Notice here that

(1) There is only one main idea, that of *the ignominious return of the Volscians to their homes.*

(2) The rest describes the attendant circumstances of the surrender and of the causes that led to it.

(3) In English we should translate by at least four separate sentences.

(4) The Latin contains only forty-eight words, while the English contains eighty-one.

Professor Postgate ('Sermo Latinus,' p. 45) gives the following example of the way in which a Latin **PERIOD** may be built up:—

BALBUS vir optimus, dux clārissimus et multis mihi beneficiis carus, rogitantibus Arvernis ut populi Romani māiestātem ostentāret suīque simul imperi monumentum eis relinqueret, MŪRUM laterīcium, vīginti pedes lātum, sexāginta altitūdine et ita in immensum porrectum ut vix tuis ipse oculis crēderes tantum esse, nēdum aliis persuāderes, non sine adverso suo rūmore ut qui principātum adfectaret AEDIFICAVIT.

BALBUS, *an excellent man and most distinguished commander, who had endeared himself to me by numerous kindnesses, was requested by the Arverni to make a display of the power and greatness of Rome, and at the same time to leave behind him a memorial of his own government. He accordingly* **BUILT** *a* **WALL** *of bricks, twenty feet wide, sixty high, and extending to such a prodigious length that you could hardly trust your own eyes that it was so large, still less induce others to believe it. But he did not escape the malign rumour that he had designs upon the imperial crown.*

Here, as in the previous example,

(1) There is only one main idea,

BALBUS MURUM AEDIFICAVIT.

(2) The rest consists of—

(a) Enlargements of **BALBUS**—**vir optimus . . . carus**; placed, therefore, directly *after* **BALBUS**.

(b) Enlargements of **MURUM**—**laterīcium . . . persuaderes**; placed, therefore, directly *after* **MURUM**.

9

(c) Enlargements of **AEDIFICAVIT**

rogitantibus . . . relinqueret = the *cause* of the building of the wall.

(murum) non sine . . . adfectaret = the *attendant circumstances* of the building of the wall; placed, therefore, *before* **AEDIFICAVIT**.

(3) In English we must translate by at least three separate sentences, and, where necessary, translate participles as finite verbs, and change dependent clauses into independent sentences.

It has been well said: 'An English sentence does not often exhibit the structure of the Period. It was imitated, sometimes with great skill and beauty, by many of the earlier writers of English prose; but its effect is better seen in poetry, as in the following passage:—

"High on a throne of royal state, which far
Outshone the wealth of Ormuz and of Ind,
Or where the gorgeous East with richest hand
Showers on her kings barbaric pearl and gold,

20

Satan exalted sat."

MILTON, *Paradise Lost*, ii. 1-5.

12. Help through a Knowledge of the Order of Words in Latin.—If you study the examples already given of the Period you will see that the **Order of Words in English** differs very much from the **Order of Words in Latin.**

Dr. Abbott writes as follows: 'The main difference between English and Latin is that in English the *meaning* depends mainly on the *order* of words, and the *emphasis* mainly on the *voice*, while in Latin the *meaning* depends almost entirely on the *inflexions*, and the *emphasis* upon the *order*.'

Thus, if we take the English sentence, *Caesar conquered the Gauls*, we cannot invert the order of *Caesar* and *Gauls* without entirely changing the meaning. In Latin, however, we may write (since each Latin word has its own proper inflexion, serving almost as a label)

Caesar vicit Gallos: Gallos Caesar vicit: Caesar Gallos vicit, without any change of meaning except that of shifting the emphasis from one word to another.

The usual order of words in a Latin Prose Sentence may be said to be

(1) Particles, or phrases of connection (with some exceptions, *e.g.* **vero, autem, quidem, enim**, which stand second).

10

(2) Subject.

(3) Words, phrases, clauses, as enlargements of Subject.

(4) Adverbial enlargements of Predicate (though an Ablative Absolute must generally stand first).

(5) Indirect Object (if any) and its enlargements.

(6) Direct Object (if any) and its enlargements.

(7) The Principal Verb.

To take a simple example:—

5**LIVIUS, imperator fortissimus, quamquam adventus hostium non ubi oportuit nuntiatus est, PERICULUM illa sua in rebus dubiis audacia facile EVASIT.**

LIVIUS, *a most excellent commander, although the enemy's arrival was not reported when it should have been, easily* **ESCAPED** *the* **DANGER** *by his well-known daring in perilous positions.*

To take another example:—

6**Archimedis EGO quaestor ignoratum ab Syracusanis, cum esse omnino negarent, saeptum undique et vestitum vepribus et dumetis, INDAGAVI SEPULCRUM.**

When I was Quaestor, **I WAS ABLE TO TRACE OUT** *the* **TOMB** *of Archimedes, overgrown and hedged in with brambles and brushwood. The Syracusans knew nothing of it, and denied its existence.*

Notice here the following special points of order:—

(1) The two most important positions in the sentence are the beginning and the end.

(2) Special emphasis is expressed by placing a word in an unusual or prominent position. E.g. here, the unusual position of **Archimedis** and **sepulcrum**.

(3) In the middle of the sentence the arrangement is such that the words most closely connected in meaning stand nearest together.

E.g. here, **ignoratum . . . dumetis** is all logically connected with the object **sepulcrum**, which for the sake of emphasis is put in an unusual position at the end of the sentence.

13. Additional Hints.—(1) Remember that Latin is often **concrete** where English is **abstract**.

11

E.g.—

ingeniosi (men of genius) = *genius.*

eruditi
(learned men) = *learning.*
docti

viri summo ingenio praediti, saepe invidia opprimuntur.

The most exalted genius is frequently overborne by envy.

omnes immemorem benefici oderunt.

The world regards ingratitude with hatred.

(2) The same Latin word may stand for different English words. Take, for example, the various uses of the word **RES** in the following passage of Livy, xlv. 19:—

7Ut **RES** docuit . . . animo	*As the* **FACT** *showed . . . spirits running riot*
gestienti **REBUS** secundis . . .	*from* **PROSPERITY**. *. . to watch*
speculator **RERUM** quae a fratre	*the* **COURSE** *pursued by his brother . . . he restored what*
agerentur . . . **REM** prope prolapsam	*was almost a lost* **CAUSE** *. . . by saying that kingdoms grow*
restituit . . . aliis alia regna crevisse	*by various* **MEANS**.
REBUS dicendo.	

In translating **RES, avoid at all costs** the word **THING**, or **THINGS**, and let the context guide you to the appropriate English word.

(3) You may often translate a **Latin Active by an English Passive**. Latin prefers the Active because it is more direct and vivid.

For example:—

Liberas aedes coniurati

sumpserunt.

An empty house had been occupied by the

conspirators.

(4) Use great care in translating Latin **Participles**, and make clear in your translation the relation of the participial enlargements to the action of the main Verb.

For example:—

con	**Romani, non ROGATI, auxilium offerunt.**
cessive:	*The Romans,* **though they were not asked,** *offer help.*
fina	**Fortuna superbos interdum RUITURA levat.**
l:	*Fortune sometimes raises the proud, only* **to dash them**
	down.
12c	**S. Ahala Sp. Maelium regnum APPETENTEM**
ausal:	**interemit.**
	S. Ahala killed Sp. Maelius **for aiming at** *the royal power.*

Notice also:—

Pontem captum incendit = *He took and burned*

the bridge.

Nescio quem prope adstantem interrogavi.

I questioned someone who was standing by.

Haec dixit moriens = *He said this while dying.*

Nuntiata clades = *The news of the disaster.*

(5) In translating, try to bring out the exact force of the **Ablative Absolute**, by which a Latin writer shows the time or circumstances of the action expressed by the Predicate. The Ablative Absolute is an adverbial enlargement of the Predicate, and is not grammatically dependent on any word in the sentence. It is, therefore, called **absolutus** (i.e. *freed from* or *unconnected*). It should very seldom be translated literally. Your best plan will be to consider carefully what the Ablative Absolute seems to suggest about the action of the Principal Verb.

For example:—

Capta Troia, Graeci domum redierunt.

The Greeks returned home after the capture of Troy.

Regnante Romulo, Roma urbs erat parva.

When Romulus was reigning, Rome was a small city.

Exercitu collecto in hostes contenderunt.

They collected an army and marched against the enemy.

Nondum hieme confecta in fines Nerviorum contendit.

Though the winter was not yet over, he hastened to the territory of the Nervii.

Tum salutato hostium duce, ad suos conversus, subditis equo calcaribus,

Germanorum ordines praetervectus est, neque expectatis legatis, nec respondente ullo.

Thereupon, after saluting the enemy's general, he turned to his companions, and setting spurs to his horse,

rode past the ranks of the Germans, without either waiting for his staff, or receiving an answer from anyone.

13

HELPS TO STYLE.

Though Style cannot perhaps be taught, it can certainly be formed and improved. There are several ways of improving your Style. For example:—

14. Through the Best English Literature.—**Read good Literature**, the best English Authors in prose and verse. You will know something, perhaps, of Shakespeare and Scott, of Macaulay and Tennyson. Though you may not be able to attack the complete works of any great author, you ought not to have any difficulty in finding good books of selections from the English Classics.

15. Through good Translations.—Study a few **good English Versions** of passages from the best Latin writers. You may often have a good version of the passage you translate read to you in your Division after your mistakes have been pointed out to you, and to this you should pay great attention. You will thus learn eventually to suit your style to the Author you are translating, while at the same time you render the passage closely and accurately.

16. Be Clear.—Remember that the first characteristic of a good style is **clearness**—that is, to say what you mean and to mean what you say. Quintilian, the great critic, says that the aim of the translator should be, not that the reader may understand if he will, but that he *must* understand whether he will or not. The more you read the greatest Authors the more you will see that, as Coleridge says, 'there is a reason assignable not only for every word, but for the position of every word.'

17. Be Simple.—With clearness goes simplicity—that is, use no word you do not understand, **avoid fine epithets**, and do not choose a phrase for its sound alone, but for its sense.

18. Avoid Paraphrase.—You are asked to translate, not to give a mere general idea of the sense. What you have to do is to **think out the exact meaning** of every word in the sentence, and to express this in as good and correct English as you can.

19. Pay attention to Metaphors.—The subject of Metaphor is of great importance in good translation. You will find that every language possesses its own special Metaphors in addition to those which are common to most European languages. As you become familiar with Latin Authors you 14must try to **distinguish the Metaphors common** to English and Latin and those **belonging only** to English or to Latin.

For example:—

(1) Metaphors **identical** in Latin and English—

Progreditur res publica naturali quodam itinere et

cursu.

The State advances in a natural path and progress.

(2) Metaphors **differing** in Latin and English—

cedant arma togae	= *let the sword yield to the pen.*
ardet acerrime coniuratio	= *the conspiracy is at its height.*
rex factus est	= *he ascended the throne.*
conticuit	= *he held his peace.*

20. Careful Translation a Help to Style.—In conclusion. Nothing will help your style more than to **do your translations as well as you possibly can**, and to **avoid repeating the same mistakes**. The Latins themselves knew the value of translation as a help to style.

For example, Pliny the Younger says:—

'As useful as anything is the practice of translating either your Greek into Latin or your Latin into Greek. By practising this you will acquire propriety and dignity of expression, an abundant choice of the beauties of style, power in description, and gain in the imitation of the best models a facility of creating such models for yourself. Besides, what may escape you when you read, cannot escape you when you translate.'

2. Potts, *Hints*, p. 82.
3. Postgate, *Sermo Latinus*, p. 45.
4. Potts, *Hints*, p. 85.
5. Postgate, *Sermo Latinus*, p. 38.
6. Demonstration VI. Sent. 1. p. 55.
7. Postgate, *Sermo Latinus*, p. 34.
15

DEMONSTRATIONS
IN
UNSEEN TRANSLATION

NOTE

THE use of a personal mode of address in the following Demonstrations is explained by the fact that they are written primarily for the use of boys. It is hoped, however, that they may be found useful to masters also, and that the fulness with which each passage is treated may supply some helpful suggestions.

16

DEMONSTRATION I.
Fierce encounter with the Germans.

(*a*) Reiectis pilis cominus gladiis pugnatum est. |II| At Germani celeriter, ex consuetudine sua, phalange facta, impetus gladiorum exceperunt. |III| Reperti sunt complures nostri milites, qui in phalangas insilirent, et scuta manibus revellerent, et desuper vulnerarent. |IV| Cum hostium acies a sinistro cornu pulsa atque in fugam conversa esset, a dextro cornu vehementer multitudine suorum nostram aciem premebant. |V| Id cum animadvertisset Publius Crassus adulescens, qui equitatui praeerat, quod expeditior erat quam hi qui inter aciem versabantur, tertiam aciem laborantibus nostris subsidio misit. |VI| Ita proelium restitutum est. | |

CAESAR.

Fierce encounter with the Germans.

(*b*) Reiectis pilis cominus gladiis **pugnatum est**. II At **Germani** celeriter, ex consuetudine sua, phalange facta, **impetus** gladiorum **exceperunt**. III **Reperti sunt** complures nostri **milites** [*qui in phalangas insilirent, et scuta manibus revellerent, et desuper vulnerarent.*] IV [*Cum hostium acies a sinistro cornu pulsa atque in fugam conversa esset,*] a dextro cornu vehementer multitudine suorum nostram **aciem premebant**. V [*Id cum animadvertisset* **Publius Crassus** *adulescens,*] [*qui equitatui praeerat,*] [*quod expeditior erat quam hi qui inter aciem versabantur,*] tertiam **aciem** laborantibus nostris subsidio **misit**. VII ta proelium **restitutum est**.

CAESAR.

17

DEMONSTRATION I.

CAESAR, *B. G.* i. 52. *Reiectis pilis . . . restitutum est.*

Heading and Author.—This tells you enough for working purposes, even if you do not remember the outline facts of Caesar's campaign against Ariovistus, the chief of the Germans, called in by the Gauls in their domestic quarrels, who conquered and ruled them until he was himself crushed by the Romans.

Read through the passage carefully.—As you do this, notice all allusions and key-words that help you to the sense of the passage, *e.g.* **Germani**, **nostri milites**, **Publius Crassus**. The general sense of the passage should now be so plain (*i.e.* an incident in a battle between the Germans and the Romans) that you may begin to translate sentence by sentence.

I. Reiectis pilis cominus gladiis pugnatum est.

(i.) *Vocabulary.*—

Reiectis = **re** + **iacio** = *throw back* or *away*. The context will tell you which is the better meaning for **re-**. Notice the force of all prefixes in composition, whether separate or inseparable as here. For **re-**, see pp. 280, 281.

pilis = the **pīlum**, the distinctively *Roman* missile weapon.

cominus = **comminus**: *i.e.* **con** (= **cum**) + **manus** = *hand to hand*. N.B.—In composition *a* often becomes *i*, cf. **iacio**, **re-icio**; and cf. **e-minus** = *at a distance*.

(ii.) *Translation.*—

PUGNATUM EST. The only finite verb in the sentence, and the principal one. The form shows you it is a so-called impersonal verb, and therefore the subject must be sought from the verb itself in connection with the context. Here, clearly, you must translate *the battle was fought*.

cominus tells us *how*, i.e. *hand to hand*.

reiectis pilis. You will recognise this as an *ablative absolute* phrase. But do not translate this literally *their javelins having been thrown away*, for this is not English. Let the principal verb and the sense generally guide you to the force of the phrase. Thus you can see here that the Roman soldiers had no use for their javelins, and so threw them away as a useless 18encumbrance. (The context tells us that the Roman soldiers had no time to hurl their javelins against the foe.) You can now translate the whole sentence—*(and so) the Romans threw away their javelins and fought hand to hand with swords*.

II. *At Germani celeriter, ex consuetudine sua, phalange facta, impetus gladiorum exceperunt.*

(i.) *Vocabulary.*—

ex consuetudine sua = *according to their custom*. You will probably have met with **consuetudo**, or **consuesco**, or **suesco**. Our own word*custom* comes from it through the French *coutume*. For this use of ex*cf.* **ex sententia, ex voluntate**.

phalange = *phalanx*. If you learn Greek, you will readily think of the famous Macedonian phalanx.

impetus = *attacks* = **in** + **peto** (= *aim at*). Cf. our *impetus, impetuous*.

(ii.) *Translation.*—This sentence contains only one finite verb, the principal one.

EXCEPERUNT = *(they) received*. *Who* received? Clearly

GERMANI = *the Germans*. Received *what?*

IMPETUS = *the attacks*. **impetūs** must be Acc. Plur.

All you now have to do is to assign to their proper places the words and phrases that remain. Of these

1. **celeriter**

2. **ex consuetudine sua**   modify the action of **exceperunt**, telling us*when* and *how* they received, and

3. **phalange facta**

4. **gladiorum** belongs to **impetūs**.

Now translate the whole sentence. *But the Germans quickly formed into a phalanx, as was their custom, and received the attacks of the swords (i.e. of the Romans with drawn swords).*

III. *Reperti sunt complures nostri milites, qui in phalangas insilirent, et scuta manibus revellerent, et desuper vulnerarent.*

(i.) *Vocabulary.*—

insilirent = **in** + **salio** = *leap-on*. And cf. our *insult*. Notice the usual phonetic change of vowel from *a* to *i*. (English derivatives will often help you to the meaning of a Latin word, 19though, for reasons that are explained to you in the Introduction, pp. 1, 2, § 4, you must let them lead you up to the *root-meaning* of the Latin word rather than to an exact translation.)

revellerent = **re** + **vello** = *pluck-away*. If you forget the meaning of*vello*, the supine **vulsum** through some English derivative—e.g. *re-vulsion, con-vulsion*—will probably help you to the root-meaning.

(ii.) *Translation.*—This sentence contains four finite verbs. As you read it through, underline the principal verb, clearly **REPERTI SUNT**, and bracket **qui** to **vulnerarent**. You cannot doubt which verbs to include in your bracket, for **qui**, which is a subordinate conjunction as well as a relative pronoun, serves as a sure signpost. Also **revellerent** and **vulnerarent** are joined by **et**—**et** to **insilirent**, so your bracket includes all from **qui** to **vulnerarent**. The commas in the passage will often help you to the beginning and end of a subordinate clause. Now begin with the principal verb **REPERTI SUNT** and its subject **complures nostri MILITES**, *many of our soldiers were found*.

qui . . . vulnerarent. This subordinate clause describes, just as an adjective does, *the character* of these **complures nostri**, so that **qui** = *tales ut*—i.e. *brave enough to leap upon the phalanxes, and pluck away the shields (of the Germans) and wound them from above*.

IV. *Cum hostium acies a sinistro cornu pulsa atque in fugam conversa esset, a dextro cornu vehementer multitudine suorum nostram aciem premebant.*

(i.) *Vocabulary.*—

ăcies = *line of battle*.

√**ac** = *sharp* (cf. **ācer**), perhaps thought of as the *edge* of a sword.

cornu = *horn*; so, figuratively, *the wing of an army*.

(ii.) *Translation.*—This sentence contains three finite verbs. Underline **PREMEBANT**, clearly the principal verb, and bracket **cum to** **conversa esset**. Here the signpost is the subordinate conjunction **cum**. Next find the subject of **premebant**: obviously no word from **a dextro** to **aciem** can be the subject; it is implied in **premebant**—i.e. *they*, which as context shows = **Germani**. Now find the object = **nostram aciem** = *our line.*

20

Thus you have as the backbone of the whole sentence:—

They (the Germans) were pressing our line.

All the rest of the sentence will now take its proper place, as in some way modifying the action of **premebant**.

Thus:—

cum . . .		t	*wh*	they were pressing.
conversa esset	ells us	*en*		
a dextro cornu	,.	*wh*		,,
	,,	*ere*	,,	
vehementer	,.	*ho*		,,
	,,	*w*	,,	
multitudine	,.	*ho*		,,
suorum	,,	*w or why*	,,	

N.B.—**suorum**, reflexive, must be identical with the subject of **premebant**.

Now translate

T		the enemy's line had been routed and put to flight on their left
hough	wing,	
When		

on their right wing, owing to their great numbers, they were pressing hard upon

our line.

V. Id cum animadvertisset Publius Crassus adulescens, qui equitatui praeerat, quod expeditior erat quam hi qui inter aciem versabantur, tertiam aciem laborantibus nostris subsidio misit.

(i.) *Vocabulary.*—

animadvertisset = **animum** + **ad** + **verto** = *to turn the mind to, to observe.*

adulescens = here like our *junior*, to distinguish him from his father, Marcus Crassus the triumvir.

expeditior = *more free* (**ex** + **pes** = *foot-free*; so **impeditus** = *hampered, hindered*).

versabantur—(**verso** frequent. of **verto**) = *turn this way and that*; so **verso-r** dep. = *turn oneself, engage in, be*, according to the context.

(ii.) *Translation.*—This sentence is more involved, 'periodic' 8 in style. You will see on p. 23 how much help can be given by a more detailed analysis.

Now, as before, bracket the subordinate clauses thus:—

1. Id . . . adulescens

2. qui . . . praeerat

3. quod . . . versabantur

and then the only principal verb is **MISIT**. Underline this. Next underline the principal subject, clearly **P. CRASSUS**, 21 which is also the subject of clause 1. Then, *outside the brackets*, the only possible object is **ACIEM**: underline this.

Now analyse, as on p. 23.

(*a*) Write down **CRASSUS, MISIT, ACIEM**.

(*b*) Place alongside these their proper enlargements.

(*c*) If necessary, analyse separately all subordinate clauses—*e.g.* A₁, A₂, A₃ in example on p. 23.

You should now be able to translate without any difficulty; only take care to arrange the enlargements so as to make the best sense and the best English. Thus: *When Publius Crassus the younger, who was in command of the cavalry, had observed this, he sent the third line to the help of our men who were hard pressed, as he was more free to act than those who were engaged in action.*

VI. Ita proelium restitutum est. **In this way the battle was restored.**

Final Hints.

Remember that **one passage mastered** is worth a great many hurriedly translated. So before you leave this passage notice carefully in the

I. *Vocabulary.*—

(i.) Any words that are quite new to you. Look them out in the dictionary, and notice their derivation and use; if you do not do this you will find the same word new to you the next time you meet with it.

(ii.) *English Derivatives.*—As you have seen, these will often help you to the root-meaning of a word. Thus:—

reiectis = *reject, throw away*
insilirent = *insult, jump on*

and in the case of verbs, as these two examples show, derivatives are most easily found from the *supine* stem.

N.B.—This must be done very carefully, because many such English derivatives have come from Latin words after they had wholly, or in part, lost their classical meaning, or from Latin words not found at all in classical Latin.

A great many other English words are derived from the Latin of this passage— e.g. *pugnacious*, (with) *celerity*, *fact*, *except*, *military*, *manual*, *super*-sede, *vulnerable*, *hostile*, *sinister*, uni-*corn*, and many others.

22

(iii.) *Prefixes.*—Notice especially the force of prepositions and inseparable particles in composition, e.g.:—

re- in **re-iectis**, **re-vellerent**, **restitutum**.
in- in **impetus**, **insilirent**.
ex- in **exceperunt**, **expeditior**.

(iv.) *Simple Phonetic Changes in Composition*, e.g.:—

a to **i** in **insilirent**, **cominus** (**con** + **manus**).

(v.) *Groups of Related Words.*

Thus

acies √**ac** = *sharp*, is related to **ăc-er**, sharp; **ăc-ervus**, a heap; **ăc-utus**, sharp, &c.
expeditior √**ped** = *tread, go*, is related to **pes**, a foot; **impedio** = entangle; **impedimentum** = hindrance, etc.

II. *Historical and other Allusions.*—

(i.) Read a summary of Caesar's campaign against Ariovistus.

(ii.) *Terms relating to War.*—Thus notice:—

pilum, the distinctively *Roman* infantry weapon, and see a good illustration.
phalanx; cf. the Roman **testudo**.

tertiam aciem—*i.e.* the line of reserves, kept for just such emergencies. Read, if necessary, some short account of the **triplex acies**, the usual Roman order of battle.

III. *Some Authorities.*—

(i.) *Caesar*, Allen and Greenough, published by Ginn & Co. (an admirable edition).
(ii.) Froude's *Caesar*, p. 50.
(iii.) Mommsen's *History of Rome*, vol. iv. p. 295.
(iv.) Napoleon's *Caesar*, vol. ii. cap. 4, and vol. ii. p. 405.

23

DEMONSTRATION I.

CAESAR, B. G. i. 52: 'Reiectis pilis . . . restitutum est.'

SENTENCE	KIND OF SENTENCE	CONNECTIVE	SUBJECT			PREDICATE			OBJECT		
			SIMPLE	ENLARGED	IMPLE	ENLARGED	IMPLE	ENLARGED	IMPLE	ENLARGED	
A. Id cum animadvertisset Publius Crassus adulescens, qui	PRINCIPAL (complex)	CRASSUS	Publius	1. 2. adulescens 3. qui . . . praeerat	ISIT	Id cum . . . adulescens (= *when*) 1. 2. quod . . .	CIEM	tertiam 1. 2.			

27

equitatui praecerat, quod expeditior rat quam hi ui inter aciem versabantu r, tertiam aciem laborantib us nostris subsidio misit.						versaban tur (= *why*) 3. laboranti bus . . . subsidio (= *how*)		
A₁. Id cum animad- vertisset Publius Crassus adulescens	Subordinat e *adverbial* to **MISIT** in **A**	(um	C rassus	ublius	P	nima d- vertis set	— d —	
A₂. qui equitatui praecerat	Subordinat e *adjectival* to **CRASSUS** in **A**	(ui	q ui (= Cras sus)		—	raeera t	e quitatui	—
A₃. quod expeditior erat quam hi qui inter aciem versa- bantur	Subordinat e *adverbial* to **MISIT** in **A**	(uod	(Crassus)		—	rat exped itior	q uam . . . hi versa- bantur	—

8. See Introduction, pp. 7-9, § 11.

24

DEMONSTRATION II.
The Music of Arion.

(*a*) I
Quod mare non novit, quae nescit Ariona tellus?
II
Carmine currentes ille tenebat aquas.
III
Saepe, sequens agnam, lupus est a voce retentus;
IV
Saepe avidum fugiens restitit agna lupum;
V
Saepe canes leporesque umbra cubuere sub una,
VI
Et stetit in saxo proxima cerva leae:
VII
Et sine lite loquax cum Palladis alite cornix
VIII
Sedit, || et accipitri iuncta columba fuit.
IX
Cynthia saepe tuis fertur, vocalis Arion,
Tamquam fraternis obstupuisse modis.

The Music of Arion.

(*b*)I

Quod **mare** non **novit**, quae **nescit Ariona tellus**?

II

Carmine currentes **ille tenebat aquas**.

III

Saepe, sequens agnam, **lupus est** a voce **retentus**;

IV

Saepe avidum fugiens **restitit agna** lupum;

V

Saepe **canes leporesque** umbra **cubuere** sub una,

VI

Et **stetit** in saxo proxima **cerva** leae:

VII

Et sine lite loquax cum Palladis alite **cornix**

VIII

Sedit, et accipitri **iuncta columba fuit**.

IX

Cynthia saepe tuis **fertur**, vocalis Arion,

Tamquam fraternis **obstupuisse** modis.

25

DEMONSTRATION II.

OVID, *Fasti* ii. 83-92 (Hallam's Edition).

Heading and Author.—The heading will probably suggest to you the well-known story of Arion and the Dolphin, and the name of the author, Ovid, will lead you to expect a beautiful version of the legend.

Read the Passage carefully.—As you read, notice all allusions that help you to the sense of the passage. Thus the first line (which you can no doubt translate at once) tells of the fame of Arion, and the succeeding lines describe the charm of his music.

The Form of the Passage: Elegiac Verse.—Scan9 as you read, and mark the quantity in the verse of all finals in **-a**. You will see the value of this, as you translate.

You can now begin to translate, taking one complete sentence at a time.

I. Quod mare non nōvit, quae nescit Ărĭŏnă tellŭs?

(i.) *Vocabulary.*—You will know all the words here, but observe **nōvit**= *knows,* not *knew,* for **nōvi** means *I have become acquainted with, I have learned,* and [Symbol: therefore] *I know;* and notice also the important cognates from the √γνο-, γνω-, **-gna, -gno**, γι-γνώ-σκω = *I learn to know,* cf. our *know, ken, can, con*—νό-ος (*mind*), **-gna-rus** =*know-ing*; **no-sco** (= **gno-sco**).

(ii.) *Translation.*—This sentence contains no subordinates; the two finite verbs, **nōvit, nescit**, are both principal.

Next, the form of the sentence, with the question-mark at the end, shows that **mare** must be the subject of **nōvit**, and **tellus** of **nescit**. (**Ărĭŏnă** cannot be nominative, for the suffix **-a** is the usual Greek 3rd decl. Acc. Sing., where Latin has **-em**.) 26Also **quod** and **quae** are clearly interrogative and adjectival; so translate:—

What sea does not know, what land is ignorant of Arion?

N.B.—Try to render this line a little more poetically.

II. Carmine currentes ille tenēbat aquās.

(i.) *Vocabulary.*—You will know all these simple words.

(ii.) *Translation.*—Here again there are no subordinates. The principal verb is **tenebat**, the subject **ille**, and the object **aquas**; so translate:—

He used to stay the running waters by his song.

N.B.—Notice force of Imperfect in **tenebat**.

III. Saepe, sequens agnam, lupus est a voce retentus;

(i.) *Vocabulary.*—All you need notice here is the force of **re-** in**retentus** = *held back,* cf. our *re*-tain.

(ii.) *Translation.*—Before you translate, notice Ovid's frequent use of*parataxis, i.e.* placing one thought side by side with another thought,*without any connective,* even although one thought is, in sense, clearly subordinate to another. This is one of the ways in which all great poets*heighten the*

29

effect of what they say, and many examples of it are to be found in Ovid's best elegiac verse. As you look through this passage you will find:

(*a*) Lines 1, 2, 3, 4 each form a complete sentence.

(*b*) In the whole passage there is not *one* subordinate conjunction.

(*c*) The only expressed connective is the simplest link-word **et**.

The principal verb is **retentus est**, the subject **lupus**. **Sequens agnam**describes **lupus**, and **saepe** and **a voce** tell us *when* and *why* the wolf*was stayed.*

Often has the wolf in pursuit of the lamb been stayed at the sound.

(For this use of **a** or **ab** to express *origin* or *source* cf. Ovid, *Fasti*, v.655: *Pectora traiectus Lynceo Castor* **ab ense**.)

27

IV. *Saepe avidum fŭgiens restitit agnā lupum.*

(i.) *Vocabulary.*—

Restitit = *stood still;* **re + si-st-o**, *i.e.* from √sta-, strengthened by reduplication; cf. ῐ́-στη-μι. Contrast carefully meaning of **re-sto**, =*stand firm* or *be left.*

(ii.) *Translation.*—Again a very simple sentence. The principal verb is**restitit**, the subject **agnă**; **fugiens avidum lupum** enlarges the subject**ăgna**, and **saepe** tells us when the lamb *stood still.*

Often has the lamb, when fleeing from the hungry wolf, stood still(*stopped short in its flight*).

N.B.—Notice the *parallelism* in this couplet, where the parallel lines express the same idea. This is a characteristic feature of Hebrew poetry, e.g.:

'Seek ye the Lord while He may be found:
Call ye upon Him while He is near.'

Is. lv. 6.

and is frequently employed by Ovid.10

V. *Saepe cănes lepŏresque umbrā cŭbuēre sub unā.*

(i.) *Vocabulary.*—

Lepŏres = *hares.* As this is closely connected by **-que** with **cănes**, you are not likely to confuse it with **lĕpor** (**lepos**; cf. λάμπω) = *a charm,grace.*

Cubuere = *lay down.* Cp. **-cumbo** in composition, and our *recumbent,succumb,* and *cub*-icle.

(ii.) *Translation.*—Another simple sentence about which there can be no doubt. The metre shows that **umbrā** must be taken with **sub unā**:—

Often have the dogs and the hares reclined beneath the same shade.

VI. *Et stetit in saxo proximā cervā leae.*

(i.) *Vocabulary.*—

Leae = *lioness.* **Lea** (poetical form of **leaena**) suggests **leo**.

(ii.) *Translation.*—The metre shows **proximă** must be taken with**cervă**. But to translate *the nearest stag* (*hind*) makes 28nonsense, and renders **leae** untranslatable, while *the hind very close to the lioness*makes good sense.

And the hind has stood still on the crag close beside the lioness.

VII. *Et sīne līte lŏquax cum Palladis ālite cornix sēdit.*

(i.) *Vocabulary.*—

Līte = *strife.* To *litigate* = contest in law (**lit + agere**) may help you to the root-meaning.

Loquax = *talkative,* clearly connected with **lŏq-uor**, and *loq*-uacious.**Alite** = *a bird,* lit. *winged;* cf. **āl-a**, *a wing.*

Cornix = *a crow*, probably from √καρ; cf. our *croak*, and κόραξ,**cor-vus**, *a raven.*

Palladis. You have no doubt heard of Παλλὰς Ἀθήνη, the virgin goddess of war and of wisdom.

(ii.) *Translation.*—The force of the illustration lies in the strong contrast between the chattering, tale-bearing crow and the wise, silent owl sacred to the goddess of wisdom. Two such opposites, under the spell of Arion's music, forget to quarrel, though for the time in close company.

And the chattering crow has without strife sat in company with the bird of Pallas.

VIII. *Et accipitri iunctā cŏlumbă fuit.*

(i.) *Vocabulary.*—

Accipitri = *hawk* (a general name for birds of prey), probably from √πετ-, **pet-** = *move quickly;* cf. πέτ-ομαι = *fly about,* **pĕt-o** = *fall upon, attack, seek.*

So **accipiter** = **ac + pĕt-**, *swift + flying;* cf. ὠκύπτερος = *swift-winged.*

30

(ii.) *Translation.*—The metre shows that **columbă** and **iunctă** must be taken together:—
And the dove has-been-joined-to (has consorted with) the hawk.

IX. *Cynthia saepe tuis fertur, vōcalis Ărīōn,*

Tamquam fraternis obstŭpuisse mŏdis.
    (i.) *Vocabulary.*—
Cynthia = *Diana (Artemis)*, so called from Mt. Cynthus, in Delos, where she and Apollo were born.
29
Fertur = *is said, asserted*; cf. **fĕrunt** = *they say.*
Vōcalis = *tuneful*, clearly from same root as **vox**, **vŏc-o**, &c., of our*vocal*. For change of quantity cf. **rex**, **rēgis**, from **rĕgo**.
Obstŭpuisse = *to have been spell-bound*; **stŭp-eo**, **stŭp-idus**, and our*stupefy, stupid* will suggest the root-meaning.11
Mŏdis = *measures*, especially of verse, or, as here, of music.
    (ii.) *Translation.*—You will remember that Apollo, the god who brings back light and sunshine in spring, is also the god of music and of poetry. Ovid skilfully implies that Arion's playing was so beautiful that even Diana, Apollo's own sister, mistakes Arion's playing for her brother's.
    This sentence takes up a whole couplet, but is in form quite simple. Thus **fertur** is the incomplete predicate, and **obstupuisse saepe tuis modis tamquam fraternis** completes the predicate, *i.e.* tells us all that is said of the subject **Cynthia**.
    Vōcalis Ărīon is clearly vocative, or nominative of address.
O tuneful Arion, often is Cynthia said to have been spell-bound by thy strains, as by those of her brother (Apollo).

Final Suggestions.
    You have now learnt how to translate this passage, but you must do more before you can master it. Thus in these simple but beautiful lines notice:—
    (i.) *Vocabulary.*—This is easy and familiar, but even if you know the meaning of the words study their *cognates*—*i.e.* related words—as pointed out to you in the vocabulary, *e.g.* under **nōvit**, p. 25, sentence I.
    (ii.) *English Derivatives.*—Remember that often, where you cannot think of an English derivative, some very familiar *French* word will help you to the root-meaning of the Latin. Thus:—

L atin.	F rench.	Engl ish.
C armine	*C harme*	*Char m (Song)*
A gnam	*A gneau*	*Lamb*
L upus	*L oup*	*Wolf*
C erva	*C erf*	*Stag (Hind)*

30
and notice that where the English word, e.g. *charm*, differs in spelling from the Latin, it is because it comes to us through a French channel. Cf. *feat* from Fr. *fait* = L. *factum.*
    (iii.) *Allusions and Parallel Passages.*—In verse these are often numerous and important. Poetry is naturally full of imagery, and borrows from many sources. Thus, for ll. 1-8, compare Hor. *Od.* I. xii. 5:
    'Aut in umbrosis Heliconis oris
. . . .
Arte materna rapidos morantem
Fluminum lapsus . . .'
and Verg. *G.* iv. 510:
'Mulcentem tigris et agentem carmine quercus.'
Shakesp. *Hen. VIII.* III. i.:
'Orpheus with his lute made trees,
And the mountain-tops that freeze,
Bow themselves when he did sing';

or read Tennyson's poem 'Amphion.'

Lines 5, 6.—Cf. Isaiah xi. 6: 'The wolf also shall dwell with the lamb, and the leopard shall lie down with the kid; and the calf and the young lion and the fatling together; and a little child shall lead them.'

(iv.) *Hints for Verses.*—Ovid is the acknowledged master of elegiac verse. Therefore, whenever you have a passage of his elegiacs to translate, you should, if possible, learn it by heart. (The Arion story as told by Ovid is well worth a place in any collection of *Ediscenda*.) If you cannot do this, notice useful phrases and turns of expression, e.g.:—

Line 1.—A question, instead of a bare statement, where no answer is expected.

Cf. 'Quod crimen dicis praeter amasse meum?'

(Dido to Aeneas, Ov. Her. vii. 164.)

Lines 3, 4.—Parataxis and repetition of idea.

Line 9.—**Vocalis Arion**, apostrophe.

Line 2.—Simplicity; alliteration.

(v.) *The Poem as Literature.*—Ovid here depicts in language purposely exaggerated the power of music over the hearts of 31men, and even over nature, animate and inanimate. This gives point to the strong contrast in the lines which follow, where greed dominates all the feelings. Shakespeare refers to the love of music as a test of character:—

'The man that hath no music in himself,
Nor is not moved with concord of sweet sounds,
Is fit for treasons, stratagems, and spoils.'

9. See Introduction, pp. 6, 7, § 10.
10. E.g.:
Plena fuit vobis omni concordia vita,
Et stetit ad finem longa tenaxque fides.

Amores ii. 6. 13-14.

11. Notice this word, which is often employed to express the ideas of *entrance, enthrall, strike dumb, amaze*.

32

DEMONSTRATION III.
PART I.
A rash promise rashly believed.

Hannibali alia in his locis bene gerendae rei fortuna oblata est. |I| M. Centenius fuit cognomine Paenula, insignis inter primipili centuriones et magnitudine corporis et animo. |II| Is perfunctus militia, per P. Cornelium Sullam praetorem in senatum introductus, petit a Patribus, uti sibi quinque milia militum darentur: |III| se peritum et hostis et regionum, brevi operae pretium facturum et, quibus artibus ad id locorum nostri et duces et exercitus capti forent, iis adversus inventorem usurum. |IV| Id non promissum magis stolide, quam stolide creditum, tamquam eaedem militares et imperatoriae artes essent! |V| Data pro quinque octo milia militum; pars dimidia cives, pars socii. |VI| Et ipse aliquantum voluntariorum in itinere ex agris concivit, ac prope duplicato exercitu in Lucanos pervenit, ubi Hannibal, nequiquam secutus Claudium, substiterat. |VII|

LIVY.

A rash promise rashly believed.

Hannibali alia in his locis bene gerendae rei **fortuna oblata est.I M. Centenius fuit** cognomine Paenula, insignis inter primipili centuriones et magnitudine corporis et animo. IIIs perfunctus militia, per P. Cornelium Sullam praetorem in senatum introductus, petit a Patribus, [uti sibi quinque milia militum darentur]. III**Centenius dixit** *se peritum ethostis et regionum, brevi operae pretium facturum: et, [quibus artibus ad id locorum nostri et duces et exercitus capti forent], iis adversus inventorem usurum.* IV**Id** non **promissum** magis stolide, quam stolide**creditum:** [tamquam eaedem militares et imperatoriae artes essent!] V**Data** pro quinque octo **milia** militum; **pars** dimidia cives,**pars** socii. VIEt **ipse aliquantum** voluntariorum in itinere ex agris**concivit**, ac prope duplicato exercitu, in Lucanos **pervenit**, [ubi Hannibal, nequiquam secutus Claudium, substiterat].VII

LIVY.

33

DEMONSTRATION III.
LIVY, xxv. 19.

Read the passage through carefully. As you read—

(i.) Make all the use you can of your previous knowledge of History, Geography, and Antiquities.

Thus, **Hannibali** suggests an episode in the Second Punic War.

32

M. Centenius is clearly the unfortunate subject of the episode.

in Lucanos . . . substiterat helps to fix the date as later than **Cannae**, 216 B.C.

(ii.) Observe carefully all phrases that will require special care in translating—*e.g.* **bene gerendae rei**—**inter primipili centuriones**—**perfunctus militia**—**operae pretium**—**ad id locorum**.

You will now have a sufficient general idea of the form and general sense of the passage, and may begin to translate sentence by sentence.

I. Hannibali alia in his locis bene gerendae rei fortuna oblata est.

(i.) *Vocabulary.*—

oblata, cf. *ob-lation = an offering* and *of-fer.*

(ii.) *Translation.*—

oblata est shows that the subject must be **fortuna**, with which **alia** must agree, and **gerendae rei** is dependent genitive. So you may at once translate literally *Another fortune (chance) of carrying-on the matter well in these parts was offered to Hannibal.* But you must not be satisfied with this, for though literally correct it is neither good History nor good English. So render: *In this district Hannibal had another chance presented to him of achieving a success.*

Here notice especially the use of the word **res**,12 a remarkable example of the tendency of Roman writers to employ the ordinary and simple vocabulary wherever possible *instead of inventing a new word.* As a writer well says, '**Res** is, so to say, a blank cheque, to be filled up from the context to the requisite 34amount of meaning.' Cf. '**Consilium erat quo fortuna rem daret, eo inclinare vires,**' where **res** = *victory.*

II. M. Centenius fuit cognomine Paenula, insignis inter primipili centuriones et magnitudine corporis et animo.

(i.) *Vocabulary.*—

primipili = the chief centurion of the **triarii** (the third, veteran line of the legion), the **primipilus**, or **primus pilus**. So Livy vii. 41, '**primus centurio erat, quem nunc (centurionem) primi pili appellant.**'

cognomine, *i.e.* **co-nomen**, a name *added* to the **nomen**, a title, epithet, *e.g.*:

Publius = the distinctive **praenomen**.

Scipio = **nomen**, designating his **gens**.

Africanus = **cognomen**.

(ii.) *Translation.*—The form of this sentence is quite simple. The subject is **M. Centenius**, with which **insignis** agrees. *There was a certain M. Centenius, by surname Penula, distinguished among the first-rank* (or *chief*) *centurions* (of the Triarii) *both for his great bodily size and courage.*

III. Is perfunctus militia, per P. Cornelium Sullam praetorem in senatum introductus, petit a Patribus, uti sibi quinque milia militum darentur.

(i.) *Vocabulary.*—

perfunctus, cf. *function*, and notice force of **per** = discharge *completely.*

(ii.) *Translation.*—The principal verb is clearly **petit**, and **is** is the only possible subject (= **Centenius**), with which **introductus** agrees. There is one subordinate clause, introduced by **ut**, telling us the object of his request.

Translate, first literally, *He having discharged completely his military service, being introduced into the Senate by P. C. Sulla, the Praetor, asks the Fathers that 5000 soldiers should be given him.* Now improve this: get rid at all costs of the *having* and *being*, which are not English, and change the *asks* into the past tense of narration. Thus:—

After he had completed his term of service, and had been introduced to the Senate by P. Corn. Sulla, the Praetor, 35*he petitioned the Fathers that 5000 soldiers should be given him.*

IV. Se peritum et hostis et regionum, brevi operae pretium facturum: et, quibus artibus ad id locorum nostri et duces et exercitus capti forent, iis adversus inventorem usurum.

(i.) *Vocabulary.*—

peritum, cf. *ex-peri-enced.* √**par-**, **per-**, *pierce, go through;* so, **ex-per-ior**, **per-iculum**, in sense of a *trial.*

operae pretium = lit. '*what will pay for the trouble,*' *i.e. worth while, i.e.* worth the *time* (or *labour*) spent upon it.

artibus—ars. √**ar** = *fit, join* = skill in joining something, skill in producing; so, *artist, artisan, artifice,* etc.

ad id locorum13 = *to that point of time.* The ideas of *place* and *time* readily interchange; so, **in loco** = at the right *place* or *time.*

(ii.) *Translation.*—The form of the sentence shows that it is *reported speech*, and not the actual words of the speaker **Centenius**, who is still the principal subject, and **dixit**, *understood*, the principal verb, and **se peritum . . . usurum** the object of **dixit**. You should now be able to translate without any difficulty, and the logical common-sense rules for the conversion of Or. Recta into Or. Obliqua explain the mood of the verb **capti forent** in the subordinate clause introduced by **quibus**.

Literally: *Centenius said that he, experienced in both the enemy and the districts, would soon make it worth (their) while: and that he would use against their inventor those arts by which up to that time both our leaders and our armies had been overcome.* Notice that the long relative clause **quibus artibus . . . forent** is in Latin placed before the antecedent **iis**.

You will readily see that this must be improved in several points. Thus:—

(*a*) Use **Oratio Recta**—more graphic and better suited to our idiom.

(*b*) *arts*. Change this to some more suitable military term—e.g. *tactics.*

He was well acquainted (he said) both with the enemy and the country, and would shortly make it worth their while, and would 36*employ against their originator those very tactics by which both our leaders and our armies had up to that time been baffled.*

V. Id non promissum magis stolide, quam stolide creditum: tamquam eaedem militares et imperatoriae artes essent!

(i.) *Vocabulary.*—

stolide, cf. *stolid* = dull, foolish.

(ii.) *Translation.*—The finite copula **est** is, as often, omitted; the two principal verbs are **promissum (est)** and **creditum (est)** linked by the comparative particles **magis—quam**, and the subject is **id**; **tamquam—essent!** is a subordinate clause modifying the two principal verbs, and expressing contemptuous wonder.

Cf. 'tamquam clausa sit Asia, sic nihil perfertur ad nos.'

You can now translate

Literally: *That was promised not more foolishly than it was foolishly believed, just as if the arts of a soldier and of a general were the same.*

Here you can make several improvements; avoid the repetition of *foolishly*, and use a better term than *arts*, and perhaps break up the sentence into two short ones. Thus:—

The folly of the promise was not greater than that of the credit it received. Just as though the qualities of a soldier and of a general were the same!

VI. Data pro quinque octo milia militum; pars dimidia cives, pars socii.

(i.) *Vocabulary.*—

dimidia √med-, mid- = *middle*, so **dimidius** = **dis** + **medius**.

(ii.) *Translation.*—This sentence is very simple: notice that here, too, **sunt** and **erant** are omitted.

Eight thousand soldiers were given him instead of five: half were citizens, half allies.

VII. Et ipse aliquantum voluntariorum in itinere ex agris concivit, ac prope duplicato exercitu, in Lucanos pervenit, ubi Hannibal, nequiquam secutus Claudium, substiterat.

(i.) *Vocabulary.*—

aliquantum = *considerable*, used in the neuter as a noun, with a partitive genitive **voluntariorum**. Cf. use of **satis**, **parum**, etc.

37

concivit = *raised*, lit. roused, stirred up. Cf. **ci-eo**, and our *ex-cite*, *in-cite.*

substiterat = *had halted.* **si-st-o** is only a form of **sto** strengthened by reduplication (cf. ἵστημι) with a causal force. Cf. **restitit**, p. 27, sentence iv.

(ii.) *Translation.*—The principal subject is clearly **ipse**; there are two principal verbs, **concivit** and **pervenit**, coupled by **ac**, and one subordinate clause, **ubi . . . substiterat**, introduced by **ubi**, and modifying **pervenit**.

The sense is so clear that you may translate at once into good English:—

Moreover he himself raised a considerable number of volunteers in the country during his march; and so, with his numbers nearly doubled, he reached Lucania, where Hannibal, after his fruitless chase of Claudius, had halted.

The following version was shown up by a boy of fifteen in a recent scholarship examination:

'Hannibal in *carrying on his successful campaign met with some different luck in this district.* Marcus Centenius, whose cognomen was Penula, was famous among the centurions of the first rank for his huge limbs and great courage. This man, after having accomplished his years of military training, on being introduced into the Senate by the Prætor P. Cornelius Sulla, requested the Patricians to give him 5000 soldiers. He said that he was well acquainted both with the enemy's tactics and the district round about, and in a short time *would convert the engagement into a prize for the State*: moreover, he added, I will employ the same tactics against the *enemy* as those by which our generals and troops have been captured in these parts. This was *faithfully* believed as it was *faithfully* promised: the tactics of the soldiers and of the commanders were so much alike! He received 8000 men instead of 5000: half of them were Roman citizens, half allies: moreover he himself *got* some volunteers while on the march in the country districts and so almost doubled his army: he thus reached the territory of the Lucani, where Hannibal after a fruitless pursuit after Claudius, had taken up his position.'

This version is neither bad nor good. The style is, on the whole fair, knowledge of vocabulary very fair, and the rendering generally accurate. It will, however, be of use 38to you as an object lesson: so notice carefully the following points:—

I. *Style.*

Sentence IV.—

(i.) The Oratio Obliqua of the original he renders partly as Reported Speech and partly as Oratio Recta. This is, of course, to be avoided. Contrast the rendering given under Sentence IV.

Sentence III.—

(ii.) **Is perfunctus . . . darentur.** He uses too many participles. Contrast version under Sentence III.

Sentences VI., VII.—

(iii.) He translates **data pro quinque . . . substiterat** by one long sentence, instead of breaking it up into two at least.

II. *Vocabulary.*

Sentence IV.—

Se peritum . . . usurum. He confuses **pretium** with **praemium**, **operae** with **rei publicae** (?). He should have been familiar with the phrase **operae pretium**.

inventorem he renders by *enemy*; perhaps a careless mistake, as if the word were **inimicum** (which after all does not = **hostem**).

Sentence V.—

stolide he renders by *faithfully*. A moment's thought given to the English word *stolid* should have put him on the right track.

Sentence VII.—

concivit he renders by *got*, vague and inappropriate. He fails to bring out the root-meaning of **cieo** = *to stir up*.

III. *Construction.*

Sentence I.—

This is very bad. *Analysis* would at once have shown him that the logical order of the sentence was

Alia fortuna bene gerendae rei oblata est Hannibali in his locis,

though he might not see that **in his locis** must be closely connected with **oblata est.**
39

Sentence IV.—

brevi operae pretium facturum. Very bad: due probably to not carefully weighing the meaning of each word.

You will now see that a strict attention to analysis and to the root-meanings of words really familiar would have enabled this candidate to send up a good version.

12. Cf. Introduction, p. 11.

13. Cf. Sallust, *Jugurtha*, 63 *Tamen is* **ad id locorum** *talis vir*= *Such was his character up to this time*.

40

DEMONSTRATION IV.
PART II.
Rashness justly punished.

Haud dubia res est, quippe inter Hannibalem ducem et centurionem; exercitusque, alterum vincendo veteranum, alterum novum totum, magna ex parte etiam tumultuarium et semiermem. |I| Ut conspecta inter se agmina sunt, et neutra pars detrectavit pugnam, extemplo instructae acies. |II| Pugnatum tamen, ut in nulla pari re, duas amplius horas, concitata et, donec dux stetisset, Romana acie. |III| Postquam is non pro vetere fama solum, sed etiam metu futuri dedecoris, si sua temeritate contractae cladi superesset, obiectans se hostium telis cecidit, fusa extemplo est Romana acies. |IV| Sed adeo ne fugae quidem iter patuit omnibus viis ab equite insessis, ut ex tanta multitudine vix mille evaserint, ceteri passim alii alia peste absumpti sint. |V|

Rashness justly punished.

Haud dubia res est, [quippe inter Hannibalem ducem et centurionem; exercitusque, alterum vincendo veteranum, alterum novum totum, magna ex parte etiam tumultuarium et semiermem.]I[Ut conspecta inter se agmina sunt, et neutra pars detrectavit pugnam], extemplo **instructae acies**. II**Pugnatum** tamen, ut in nulla pari re, duas amplius horas, concitata et, [donec dux stetisset], Romana acie. III{Postquam is non pro vetere fama solum, sed etiam metu futuri dedecoris, [si sua temeritate contractae cladi superesset], obiectans se hostium telis cecidit}, **fusa** extemplo **est Romana acies**. IVSed adeo ne fugae quidem **iter patuit** omnibus viis ab equite insessis, [ut ex tanta multitudine vix mille evaserint, ceteri passim alii alia peste absumpti sint].V

41

DEMONSTRATION IV.
LIVY, xxv. 19.

Read through the Passage carefully.—The context will be familiar to you, as this piece is a continuation of Demonstration III; but, none the less, read the passage through very carefully. Notice, for example, the use of **quippe**, the various uses and meanings of **ut**, **alterum . . . alterum, alii alia**.

You can now begin to translate.

I. Haud dubia res est, quippe inter Hannibalem ducem et centurionem; exercitusque, alterum vincendo

veteranum, alterum novum totum, magna ex parte etiam tumultuarium et semiermem.

(i.) *Vocabulary.*—

quippe = **qui** + **pe**. **pe** = a form of **que** (cf. **nempe = nam-pe** = *indeed*) = *since of course.*
alterum (comparative of **al-ius**), cf. **alter**, *alternate, either, other.*
In distributive clauses, **alter—alter** = *the one, the other.*
tumultuarium (cf. **tumultus**), used of troops brought *hurriedly* together; so, *disorderly.*

(ii.) *Translation.*—This sentence is quite simple, consisting of one main statement, **Haud dubia res est**, and an explanatory subordinate statement of fact introduced by **quippe**. Notice that the influence of **inter** extends over the whole of the subordinate clause.

Literally: 'The affair was not doubtful, since, of course, it was between Hannibal as general and a centurion, and between armies, the one grown old in victory, the other wholly new, and for the most part also hurriedly raised and half-armed.'

There are several points in which this rendering must be improved. Thus:—

(*a*) *Affair* for **res** is too vague. You will remember what was said about **res** in Sentence I. of Part I. pp. 33, 34.

42

(*b*) You must try to express more strongly the contrast in generalship between Hannibal and a mere centurion. Thus:—

'The **result** *was not doubtful, considering that the contest was between a general such as Hannibal and a (mere) centurion; and between two armies, the one grown old in victory, the other consisting entirely of raw recruits, and for the most part undrilled and half-armed.'*

II. Ut conspecta inter se agmina sunt, et neutra pars detrectavit pugnam, extemplo instructae acies.
(i.) *Vocabulary.*—

neuter = **ne** + uter (**uter = eu-ter** or **quo-ter-us** = comparative in form of **quis**), *neither of two.*
detrectavit = *declined* (**de** + **traho**, draw-off).
extemplo = *immediately.* **Ex** + **templum** (dimin. **tempulum**).
templum √**tem** = cut; cf. τέμνω = prop. a *section.* So
(a) a *space marked* out, a consecrated place, a *temple.*
(b) a *portion of time*; cf. *extempore.*

(ii.) *Translation.*—This sentence again is quite simple (in form very similar to Sentence I.), consisting of one main statement, **extemplo instructae acies**, and an introductory subordinate statement of *time* introduced by **ut** = *when.*

'When the armies came in sight of each other, and neither side declined battle, the ranks were at once drawn up in fighting order.'

14III. Pugnatum tamen, ut in nulla pari re, duas amplius horas, concitata et, donec dux stetisset,

Romana acie.
(i.) *Vocabulary.*—

concitata = *stirred-up, roused.* **con + ci-eo**; cf. *ex-cite*, *incite*, **cĭ-tus** =*put in motion, swift,* &c.

(ii.) *Translation.*—This sentence is not quite so simple and needs care. Notice—

(*a*) **Pugnatum (est).** The Impersonal Pass. serves as the principal subject and predicate.

(*b*) **ut in nulla pari re. ut** is here not a *conjunction* but a relative*adverb* of manner, referring the assertion **pugnatum 43duas amplius horas** to the particular circumstance—*i.e.* of a battle fought under very unequal conditions. This use of **ut** = *considering* occurs frequently—*e.g.* **consultissimus vir ut in illa quisquam esse aetate poterat**(Livy). Cf. also p. 124, l. 19.

(*c*) **concitata Romana acie** is clearly ablative absolute. To make quite sure that you understand the logical connection of the thought conveyed by this sentence, you may consult the detailed analysis on page 47.

In spite of its being such an unequal match, the battle was maintained for more than two hours; the Roman army (as well as[et] *the enemy's) being roused (to great exertions) so long as their leader survived.*

IV. Postquam is non pro vetere fama solum, sed etiam metu futuri dedecoris, si sua temeritate contractae

cladi superesset, obiectans se hostium telis cecidit, fusa extemplo est Romana acies.

(i.) *Vocabulary.*—

dedecoris = *of dis-grace*, for **de** in composition = *separation,* and so*removal* of the fundamental idea. Cf. *un-, dis-, e.g.* **dis-par** = *un*-equal.

contractae = *brought on, caused.* **con + traho** = *bring about, cause.*

(ii.) *Translation.*—The meaning of this sentence should be quite plain to you if you notice carefully that

(*a*) the principal verb is **fusa est**, and the principal subject **Romana acies**, and

(*b*) that **Postquam . . . cecidit** is a subordinate clause of *time*modifying the action of the principal verb **fusa est**.

It would perhaps be well to translate at first literally:—

After that he, not only out of regard for (**pro**) *his old fame, but also from fear of future disgrace, if he should survive a disaster brought about by his own rashness, exposing himself to the weapons of the enemy fell, the Roman army was at once routed.*

You will see that this rendering, though verbally correct, is not English, and must be considerably altered before it can be called a good translation. Thus:—

44

(*a*) *It is too long.* You can remedy this by taking **postquam . . . cecidit**as one complete sentence, and **fusa . . . acies** as another.

(*b*) *Exposing himself.* Better *exposed himself to . . . and.* Notice here the strictly accurate use of the Pres. participle in Latin.

(*c*) 'future' may be omitted, as tautological15 in English. Cf. our inexact idiom '*he promised to come*' (Lat. '*that he would come*').

At last, both for the sake of his old renown and from the fear of disgrace should he survive a disaster brought on by his own rashness, he threw himself among the enemy's darts and was slain. The Roman army was routed in a moment. —Church and B.

V. Sed adeo ne fugae quidem iter patuit omnibus viis ab equite insessis, ut ex tanta multitudine vix mille

evaserint, ceteri passim alii alia peste absumpti sint.

(i.) *Vocabulary.*—

pătuit = *was open.* Cf. **păte-facio** = *to make open*; **păt-ulus** = *open,spread out*; **păt-era** = *a broad, flat dish.* English, *patent.*

insessis = *occupied*; **in + sed-eo** = *sit upon*—so, *occupy.*

passim = *hither and thither, far and wide,* formed from **passus**(pando), *expand.*

(ii.) *Translation.*—This sentence resembles in form Sentence IV., with one principal verb **patuit**, and a principal subject **iter**, and a subordinate clause of *result*, **ut . . . absumpti sint**, modifying the action of the principal verb **patuit**. You may conveniently break up this sentence into two, by beginning a new sentence with **Ceteri**. Thus:—

So completely closed against them was every chance of escape, all the roads being beset by cavalry, that out of so numerous a host hardly a thousand escaped. The rest perished as they fled, some by one death and some by another.

Before laying aside these two passages, you should pay attention to the following points:—

(i.) *Vocabulary.*—Besides carefully noticing *new* words, try to form groups of *cognates* (i.e. *related words*). One of the best ways to enlarge your vocabulary is to group together *words of* 45*common origin*, and to add to each, where you can, derivative and cognate English words. To take a few examples from this passage:—

Word.	Meaning.	English Derivative.
ALIUS	= *another* (of many).	
ali-enus	= *that belong to another*	alien, alienate.
ali-quot	= *some, several*	aliquot (parts).
al-ter	= *other of two*	alter, alternate.
ali-bi	= *elsewhere*	alibi.
etc.		
SENATUS	= *the Council of the Elders*	Senate.
sen-ex	= *old*	
sen-ior	= *older*	senior, sire, sir.
sen-ile	= *belonging to old people*	sen-ile.
sen-ectus	= *old age.*	
etc.		
ITER = (i-tiner)	= *a going*	itin-erant.
amb-it-io	= *a going round, canvassing*	ambition.
comes (cu m +eo)	= *a comrade.*	a Count (Fr. Comte).
in-it-ium	= *a going in, a beginning*	initial.
sed-it-io	= *a going apart, sedition*	sedition.
etc.		

(ii.) *Useful Phrases for Latin Prose.*—You should try gradually to put together your own phrase-book. You will find this much more useful to you than any ready-made collection. A good and simple plan is to have a special note-book for this purpose. Mark in the text as you read useful phrases, and in your note-book write the Latin on the right-hand page and a good idiomatic rendering on the left. For example, from this passage you might collect the following:—

English.	Latin.
A chance of achieving a success.	**fortuna bene gerendae rei.**
After completing his term of service.	**perfunctus militia.**
Would make it worth their while.	**operae pretium facturum.**
Up to that time.	**ad id locorum.**
The result was not doubtful.	**haud dubia res est.**
Though the fight was so unequal.	**ut in nulla pari re.**
Some by one death and some by another.	**alii alia peste.**

46

(iii.) **HANNIBAL.**—Read some good short estimate of Hannibal as a patriot, statesman, and soldier—such as may be found in Mommsen's or Ihne's *History of Rome.* If you have time, you will find much to interest you in the *Hannibal* ('Heroes of the Nations') by O'Connor Morris.

DEMONSTRATION IV.

S ENTENCE	KIND OF SENTENCE	C ON- NECTIVE	SUBJECT		PREDICATE		OBJECT	
			SI MPLE	E NLARGED	S IMPLE	E NLARGED	IMPLE	E NLARGED
Se ntence III.								
P ugnatum tamen, ut in nulla pari re, duas amplius horas; concitata et, donec dux stetisset, Romana acie.	Com plex	t amen	(THE BATTLE)	—	P UGNA TUM (EST)	1. duas amplius horas (*time*) 2. ut in nulla pari re (*manner*) 3. concitata . . . Romana acie (*manner*)		—
Se ntence IV.								
A. Postquam is non pro vetere fama solum, sed etiam metu futuri dedecoris, si sua temeritate contractae cladi superesset, obiectans se hostium telis cecidit, fusa extemplo est Romana acies.	Com plex	P ost- quam	A CIES	Ro mana	F USA EST	1. extemplo (*time*) 2. Postquam is . . . cecidit (*time*)		—
A₁	Subo	P	is	no	c	—		—

. Postqua m is . . . cecidit	rdinate *adv.* toFUS A EST in A	ost-quam			n pro vetere . . .OBIE C-TANSteli s	ecidit			
A₂ . si sua . . . superesse t	Subo rdinate *adv.* toOBI EC-TANS in A₁	s i	e)	(h	—	s uperess et	—	ladi	sua temeritate contrac-tae

14. Weissenborn and Müller read:—Pugnatum tamen, ut in nulla pari re, *diu*: duas amplius horas con*stitit pugna spe con*citante, donec dux stetit, Romana*m* acie*m*.

15. *i.e.* needless repetition (ταὐτὸ λέγειν = to say the same thing).

48

DEMONSTRATION V.
The Happy Life.

(*a*)I

Felix, qui potuit rerum cognoscere causas,
Atque metus omnes et inexorabile fatum
Subiecit pedibus, strepitumque Acherontis avari! | |

II

Fortunatus et ille, deos qui novit agrestes,
Panaque, Silvanumque senem, Nymphasque sorores! | |

III

Illum non populi fasces, non purpura regum
Flexit et infidos agitans discordia fratres,
Aut coniurato descendens Dacus ab Histro,

IV

Non res Romanae, perituraque regna; | | neque ille
Aut doluit miserans inopem aut invidit habenti. | |

VERGIL.

The Happy Life.

(*b*)I

Felix, (qui potuit rerum cognoscere causas,
Atque metus omnes et inexorabile fatum
Subiecit pedibus, strepitumque Acherontis avari!)

II

Fortunatus et **ille**, (deos qui novit agrestes,
Panaque, Silvanumque senem, Nymphasque sorores!)

III

Illum non populi **fasces**, non **purpura** regum
Flexit et infidos agitans **discordia** fratres,
Aut coniurato descendens **Dacus** ab Histro,

IV

Non **res Romanae, perituraque regna**; neque ille
Aut **doluit** miserans inopem aut **invidit habenti**.

VERGIL.

49

DEMONSTRATION V.
VERGIL, *Georg.* ii. 490-499.

Read the Passage carefully.—Notice as you read the many allusions and key-words in the passage, *e.g.* **Acherontis, Pana, Silvanum,Nymphas, Dacus ab Istro, res Romanae, rerum causas**, and **populi fasces**. These, taken in connection with the main predicates **felix,fortunatus, non flexit, neque doluit, aut invidit**, will readily suggest to you the main thought of the passage:—

Happy is Nature's bard who knows and fears not: happy he too who knows the gods of the country. He is not distressed by ambition, nor wars, nor pain, nor envy.

40

I. Felix, qui potuit rerum cognoscere causas,

Atque metus omnes et inexorabile fatum

Subiecit pedibus, strepitumque Acherontis avari!

    (i.) *Vocabulary.*—

    inexorabile = *relentless*; lit. *that cannot be moved by entreaty.* **in** (*not*) + **ex** (*easily*) + **orabilis** (*entreated*).

      For **oro** cf. **ōs** = *mouth*; **orator** = *speaker*; **oratio** = *speech*.

      fatum = *fate, i.e.* of *death*, as the common lot of all men, the decree of nature.

      fatum = *that which is said*, espec. prophetically. √**fa**, φα. Cf. **for** (**fā-ri**), *speak*; **fā-ma**, *report*; **fā-bula**, *a story*; **in-fans**, *that cannot speak*; **fā-cundus**, *eloquent.*

      strepitum = *roar*; lit. a wild, confused noise, din of any kind; cf.*obstreperous.*

      Acherontis = *Acheron* = (*a*) a river in the Lower World; (*b*) the Lower World itself. Perh. **Acheron** = ὁ ἄχεα ῥέων = the stream of woe; cf.Κωκυτός = *Cocytus*, river of *wailing.*

    (ii.) *Translation.*— You cannot be in doubt about the principal subject and predicate. **Felix** is the only word outside the subordinate clause from **qui . . . avari**. The sense, too, of these lines is clear, so you may translate at once; but you must take special care to use dignified and appropriate language:—

    50

    Happy the man who has availed to know the causes of things, and so trampled under foot all fears and fate's relentless decree, and the roar of insatiate Acheron.

    II. Fortunatus et ille, deos qui novit agrestes,

Panaque, Silvanumque senem, Nymphasque sorores!

    (i.) *Vocabulary.*—

    agrestes = *of the country*; cf. **ager** (ἀγρός), **agrarius**, *agrarian*;**peragro** (**per** + **ager**), *travel over.* Perhaps to be traced to the same root as **ag-o** = *drive*, **ager** and ἀγρός being so named **a pecore agendo** (cf. Germ. **trift** = *pasturage*, **treiben** = *drive*).

    Silvanum = *Silvanus* = Latin god of fields and woods (**silva**), *sylvan.*

    (ii.) *Translation.*—This sentence closely resembles in form Sentence I,**Ille Fortunatus** being the principal subject and predicate.

    He too is blest who knows the gods of the country, Pan, and old Silvanus, and the sisterhood of the Nymphs.

    III. Illum non populi fasces, non purpura regum

Flexit, et infidos agitans discordia fratres;

Aut coniurato descendens Dacus ab Histro,

Non res Romanae, perituraque regna;

    (i.) *Vocabulary.*—

    fasces = *fasces, i.e. honours*; **populi**, i.e. *conferred by the people.*

    fascis = a *bundle*, espec. of wood.

    fasces = *the lictors' rods* (*rods* + *axe* in certain cases) carried before the highest magistrates, as an emblem of authority.

    purpura, *i.e.* the *purple* robe worn by kings and magistrates.

    Cf. 16'**Purpura Pompeium summi velabit honoris.**'

OV. Ex Ponto IV. iv. 25.

    agitans = *driving*, i.e. *moving, impelling.*

    discordia = *discord.* Notice force of **dis-** = separation, negation; cf.**dis-crimen**, **dis-par.**

    coniurato = *united by oath, sworn confederate.*

    Dacus, the Dacians, akin to the Thracians, N. of Danube, conquered by Trajan. Cf. modern *Roumanians.*

    Histro = the Lower Danube.

    51

    (ii.) *Translation.*—You will see there is only one principal verb, **flexit**(or **flexerunt**), with several principal subjects, **fasces**, **purpura**,**discordia**, **res Romanae**, **perituraque regna**, and no subordinate clauses. You may therefore translate at once:—

    (*a*) *Him fasces of the people or purple of kings sway not, not maddening discord among treacherous brethren, nor the Dacians swarming down from the leagued Danube, not the Roman State, or realms destined to decay;*

41

OR

(b) He is not (1) moved by honours that the people confer, or the purple of empire, or civil feuds, that make (2) brothers swerve from brothers' duty; or the Dacian coming down from the Hister, his sworn (2) ally; no, nor by the great Roman State and the death-throes of subject kingdoms.

N.B.—*(b)* is superior to *(a)* in—

(1) the use of Passive for Active;

(2) the predicative use of **agitans, infidos, coniurato.**

IV.   *neque ille*

Aut doluit miserans inopem, aut invidit habenti.

(i.) *Vocabulary.*—You will probably know the meanings of the words in this sentence. Thus the meaning of—

do	is	**dolor.**
luit	suggested by	
m	,,	**miser.** Cf. *mis*
iserans	,,	*er-able.*
in	,,	**in + ops.** Cf.
opem	,,	*op-ulent.*
in	,,	**invidia.** Cf. *en*
vidit	,,	*vy.*

(ii.) *Translation.*—You have here two principal verbs, **doluit, invidit,** joined by **aut,** and a principal subject **ille.**

Notice that **inopem** must be the object of the participle **miserans,** and that **habenti** is used as a noun.

He never felt the pang of pity for the poor, or of envy for the rich.

Copy of a rendering shown up by a boy of fifteen in a recent scholarship examination:—

'Happy is the man who *is able* to discern the reason of things, and *controls* under his feet all changes and inexorable destiny, and the *groaning* of greedy Acheron! |I| Blessed also is he who knows the rustic gods, Pan and old Silvanus, and those sisters, the nymphs! |II| He is not moved by *the people's 52 axes,* nor by the regal purple, nor by discord that rouses brothers to *distrust* each other. He is not moved by *Dacus,* coming down from the *sacred* Danube, nor by *the affairs* of Rome, and the realms about to perish. |III| He neither *grieves for nor pities the helpless,* nor does he envy the rich.' |IV|

The above version is fair, but notice the following points:—

Sentence I.—

is able . . . and controls. The connection in thought is not shown: 'He is happy because he *knows* and ∴ fears not.'

groaning—i.e. **gemitum; strepitum** = *roar, din.*

Sentence III.—

by the people's axes. This suggests quite a wrong idea; contrast the version, 'by the honours that the people confer.'

sacred. This is quite wrong. **con-iurato** = *allied by oath.*

the affairs of Rome. A very weak, and inadequate rendering.

Sentence IV.—

grieves for nor pities. This quite obscures the point. Vergil says that a country life, with its absence of poverty, so commonly met with in a town, saves a man from the necessity of feeling a pang of pity for the poor.

Before you put aside this passage, try to avail yourself of some of the following suggestions. Thus:—

I. For the Poet *Vergil* 7 (70 B.C.-19 B.C.).—The chief facts of his life and the subject of his great poems are clearly and shortly given in the *Student's Companion to Latin Authors* (a useful and convenient book of reference).

II. For the *Georgics, Poems on Husbandry.* (The passage for translation is taken from *Georgic II.* lines 490-499.) See—

(i.) *Student's Companion to Latin Authors,* pp. 157-8.

(ii.) Nettleship's *Vergil,* pp. 37-45.

(iii.) Sellar's *Vergil,* pp. 174-198.

Notice especially the *political purpose* of the *Georgics*—to help the policy of Augustus, which aimed at checking the depopulation of the country districts. Compare the alarming migration from the country to the towns in England at the present day.

53

III. *Relation of Lucretius to the Georgics.*

(i.) Sellar's *Vergil*, pp. 199-243.

(ii.) Munro's *Lucretius*, Notes on Book i. line 78, and Book iii. line 449.

Notice in this connection the opening lines of the passage, **Felix qui potuit . . . Acherontis avari**, which may be summarised as follows: 'Happy he who knows the laws of Nature, and has therefore ceased to fear natural phenomena and has learnt to despise the fabled terrors of Hades.' Munro says: 'I feel that by his **Felix qui** Vergil does mean a poet-philosopher, who can only be Lucretius.'

Cf. also *Lucretius*, iii. 1-30. His address to Epicurus.

For the thought, cf. Wordsworth's *Happy Warrior*—

'He therefore does not stoop, nor lie in wait
For wealth, or honours, or for worldly state.'

16. 'The purple (the insignia) of the highest office shall clothe Pompeius.'

17. See Short Lives, p. 343.

54

DEMONSTRATION VI.
The Tomb of Archimedes.

I(*a*) Archimedis ego quaestor ignoratum ab Syracusanis, cum esse omnino negarent, saeptum undique et vestitum vepribus et dumetis, indagavi sepulcrum. |II| Tenebam enim quosdam senariolos, quos in eius monumento esse inscriptos acceperam: qui declarabant in summo sepulcro sphaeram esse positam cum cylindro. |III| Ego autem, cum omnia collustrarem oculis—est enim ad portas Agragantinas magna frequentia sepulcrorum—animadverti columellam non multum e dumis eminentem, in qua inerat sphaerae figura et cylindri. |IV| Atque ego statim Syracusanis—erant autem principes mecum—dixi me illud ipsum arbitrari esse quod quaererem. |V, VI| Immissi cum falcibus multi purgarunt locum. | | Quo cum patefactus esset aditus, accessimus: |VII| apparebat in sepulcro epigramma, exesis posterioribus partibus versiculorum, dimidiatis fere. | |

CICERO.

The Tomb of Archimedes.

I(*b*) Archimedis **ego quaestor** ignoratum ab Syracusanis, [cum esse omnino negarent,] saeptum undique et vestitum vepribus et dumetis, **indagavi sepulcrum**. II**Tenebam** enim quosdam **senariolos**, [quos in eius monumento esse inscriptos acceperam]: [qui declarabant in summo sepulcro sphaeram esse positam cum cylindro.] III**Ego** autem, [cum omnia collustrarem oculis|—est enim ad portas Agragantinas magna frequentia sepulcrorum—**animadverti columellam** non multum e dumis eminentem, [in qua inerat sphaerae figura et cylindri]. IV**Atque** **ego** statim Syracusanis—erant autem principes mecum—**dixi** me illud ipsum arbitrari esse [quod quaererem]. V, VI**Immissi** cum falcibus multi**purgarunt locum**. [Quo cum patefactus esset aditus],**accessimus**: VII**apparebat** in sepulcro **epigramma**, exesis posterioribus partibus versiculorum, dimidiatis fere.

CICERO.

55

DEMONSTRATION VI.
CICERO, *Tusc.* v. 23. 64.

Read the Passage through carefully.—As you read you will notice many allusions and key-words, *e.g.* **Archimedes, ego quaestor,Syracusanis, sepulcrum**, etc. These, taken in connection with the heading and the author, will suggest to you the main subject of the passage—the finding of the Tomb of Archimedes by Cicero.

I. *Archimedis ego quaestor ignoratum ab Syracusanis, cum esse omnino negarent, saeptum undique et vestitum vepribus et dumetis, indagavi sepulcrum.*

(i.) *Vocabulary.*—

Quaestor (contr. from **quaesītor**—**quaero**), i.e. *investigator,* originally two main functions:—

(*a*) The preparation of evidence in public prosecutions (this about 240B.C. transferred to the Tribunes).

(*b*) Treasurers of State. Of these the **Quaestores urbani** stayed at Rome, while the **Quaestores provinciales** or **militares** acted as financial assistants to the *Consuls* or *Praetors* for the provinces.

saeptum = *hedged in;* **saepes** = *a hedge, fence.*

vepribus = *with bramble-bushes.*

dumetis = *with brushwood.*

indagavi = *I traced out.* A metaphor from hunting. Cf.

43

'Dum trepidant alae, saltusque indagine cingunt.'

Verg. *Aen.* iv. 121.

'While the scouts (beaters) are all busy, and are encircling the coverts with nets.'

(ii.) *Translation.*—The form of the sentence is quite simple. The principal verb is **indagavi**, with subject **ego quaestor**, and object **sepulcrum**. From **ignoratum . . . dumetis** describes **sepulcrum**, and the subordinate clause **cum . . . negarent** emphasises **ignoratum a Syracusanis**. You may now translate

(*a*) literally: *I, when Quaestor, traced out the tomb of Archimedes, not known of by the Syracusans, for they said it was not there at all, hedged in on all sides and covered with brambles and brushwood.*

56

(*b*) A better rendering: *When I was Quaestor I was able to trace the tomb of Archimedes, overgrown and hedged in with brambles and brushwood. The Syracusans knew nothing of it, and entirely denied its existence.*

Notice here the improvement made by breaking up the one long sentence into two.

II. Tenebam enim quosdam senariolos, quos in eius monumento esse inscriptos acceperam: qui declarabant in summo sepulcro sphaeram esse positam cum cylindro.

(i.) *Vocabulary.*—

senariolos = *some lines, i.e.* of poetry—dimin. of **senarius** (**seni**) =*consisting of six each,* especially of the *iambic senarii.*

sphaeram = *a sphere, globe*—σφαῖρα.

cylindro = *a cylinder.* κύλινδρος.

(ii.) *Translation.*—The only principal verb is clearly **tenebam** (with subject contained in the verb), and the principal object **senariolos** (sc.**versus**). From **quos . . . cylindro** we have two subordinate adjectival clauses enlarging **senariolos**.

The fact is, I remembered some iambic lines which I had been told were inscribed on his monument, and which set forth that his tomb was surmounted by a sphere and a cylinder.

III. Ego autem, cum omnia collustrarem oculis—est enim ad portas Agragantinas magna frequentia sepulcrorum—animadverti columellam non multum e dumis eminentem, in qua inerat sphaerae figura et cylindri.

(i.) *Vocabulary.*—

collustrarem = *I was surveying on all sides;* **con** (**cum**) + **lustro.**

lustro, perhaps akin to **luc-eo, lu-men;** so, **il-lustris** = *lighted up,illustrious.*

frequentia = *a large number;* cf. **frequens,** √φρακ, **farc;** cf. φράγ-μα = *a fence,* **farc-io** = *pack close together;* so, **con-fer-tus** =*crowded,* **freq-uens** = *repeated, frequent.*

columellam = *a small column,* dimin. of **columen,** √cel; cf. **cel-sus** =*lofty;* cf. **ex-cello, col-umen** (= **cul-men**) = *the summit;* cf. *culminate.*

(ii.) *Translation.*—This sentence is apparently not quite so simple, but if you carefully bracket the subordinate clauses you will see that the only principal verb is **animadverti**, with subject **ego** and object **columellam**. Notice next that—

57

(*a*) **cum . . . oculis** modifies the principal verb **animadverti** and is an adverbial clause of *time.*

(*b*) The parenthetical clause **est enim . . . sepulcrorum** explains **collustrarem.**

(*c*) **in qua . . . cylindri** is an adjectival clause enlarging **columellam.**

You may now translate into your best English, following closely the thought and the order of the Latin:—

Well, as I was surveying the whole place (there is a large number of tombs at 18 *the Agrigentine gate) I perceived a small column just showing above the undergrowth, on which appeared the figure of a sphere and a cylinder.*

IV. Atque ego statim Syracusanis—erant autem principes mecum—dixi me illud ipsum arbitrari esse, quod quaererem.

(i.) *Vocabulary.*—The words of this sentence present no difficulty.

(ii.) *Translation.*—With the practice you have now had, you may translate at once; but notice carefully that—

(*a*) the parenthetical clause **erant . . . mecum** enlarges **Syracusanis;** and

(*b*) **quod quaererem** describes **illud ipsum.**

So I immediately said to the Syracusans who were with me (some people of importance) that I thought that was the very thing I was looking for.

V. Immissi cum falcibus multi purgarunt locum.

(i.) *Vocabulary.*—

44

falcibus = *with bill-hooks*; **falx** perh. akin to **flect-o** = *bend*, from its shape. Cf. *falcon* (from its *hooked* claws).

purgarunt = *cleared*; **purgo**, contr. from **pur-igo** = **purum** + **ago** =*purge*. Cf. **pur-us**.
(ii.) *Translation.—*
Some men sent in with bill-hooks cleared out the space.

VI. Quo cum patefactus esset aditus, accessimus.
(i.) *Vocabulary.—*
patefactus = *laid open*: **pateo** + **facio**. Cf. *patent*.
(ii.) *Translation.—*
As soon as the way was open, we went up to it.
58

VII. Apparebat in sepulcro epigramma, exesis posterioribus partibus versiculorum, dimidiatis fere.
(i.) *Vocabulary.—*
epigramma = *inscription*. Cf. *epi-gram*.
exesis = lit. *'eaten out'*; **ex** + **edo**. Cf. *ed-ible*.
dimidiatis = *halved* = **dis** + **medius**, i.e. *divided into halves*.
(ii.) *Translation.—There was the inscription on the tomb: the latter part of each line was gone, nearly half the verse.*
*Note.—*Notice here the rendering of the Lat. abl. absol., an idiom foreign to our language except for example in the so-called nom. absol. of Milton. Cf. Introduction, p. 12 (5).
Cicero adds the following reflection:—*'Ita nobilissima Graeciae civitas, quondam vero etiam doctissima, sui civis unius acutissimi monumentum ignorasset, nisi ab homine Arpinate didicisset.'*
*Thus it was that one of the most renowned of Greek cities, and in ancient times one of the most enlightened, would have remained ignorant of the monument of the greatest genius it ever produced, if it had not learnt it from a man born at Arpinum.*19

Some Suggestions and Authorities.

Before you leave this passage, try to notice some of the following points, and if possible consult *some* of these authorities:—

(i.) Read (*e.g.* in Church and Brodribb's translation) Livy's account of the siege of Syracuse by Marcellus, 214-212 B.C., Book xxiv. cap. 34; Book xxv. caps. 23-31.

(ii.) Freeman's *History of Sicily*. Notice especially the admirable plan of Syracuse illustrating the siege by Nicias.

Or *Sicily*—'Story of the Nations' Series.

(iii.) *Some good Life of Archimedes.* The *Encyclopaedia Britannica*supplies a good short life and refers to Cicero's finding the Tomb of Archimedes, and to the still extant work of Archimedes on the Sphere and the Cylinder.

(iv.) For *Cicero's Quaestorship in Sicily*, 75 B.C., consult some Life of Cicero, *e.g.* Forsyth's, pp. 38-58, where reference is made to this incident.

(v.) For the *Tusculanae Disputationes* (conversations between Cicero and a friend at his Tusculan villa, the subject of which is the chief essentials of happiness) consult the admirable introduction to the edition by T. W. Dougan, Camb. Press.

18. Var. lect. **ad portas Achradinas**.
19. Also the birthplace of Marius. Cf. p. 163.
59

PASSAGES
FOR
TRANSLATION AT SIGHT

In the original text, lines were numbered continuously on each page. For this e-text, verse selections have been renumbered to match the actual line numbers as cited in the text. Selections from the Hallam edition of Ovid's *Fasti*are numbered from 1 within each passage.

Line numbers in prose have been retained for completeness, except that markings of line 1 have been omitted. Since your browser's line breaks will not correspond to line breaks in the printed book, words mentioned in the linenotes have also been underlined.

In the "Miscellaneous Passages" section, which has no linenotes, line numbers were omitted in all prose and in the shorter verse passages. Longer verse passages have been renumbered as elsewhere.

60

REGAL PERIOD, 753-509 B.C.

D₁

45

The Vision of Anchises.—The Kings that are to be.

Quin et avo comitem sese Mavortius addet
Romulus, Assaraci quem sanguinis Ilia mater
Educet. Viden' ut geminae stant vertice cristae,
780
Et pater ipse suo superum iam signat honore?
En huius, nate, auspiciis illa incluta Roma
Imperium terris, animos aequabit Olympo,
Septemque una sibi muro circumdabit arces,
Felix prole virum.

      .   .   .   .   .

.   .

Quis procul ille autem ramis insignis olivae
Sacra ferens? Nosco crines incanaque menta
810
Regis Romani; primam qui legibus urbem
Fundabit, Curibus parvis et paupere terra
Missus in imperium magnum. Cui deinde subibit,
Otia qui rumpet patriae residesque movebit
Tullus in arma viros et iam desueta triumphis
815
Agmina. Quem iuxta sequitur iactantior Ancus,
Nunc quoque iam nimium gaudens popularibus auris.
Vis et Tarquinios reges animamque superbam
Ultoris Bruti fascesque videre receptos?

VERGIL, *Aen.* vi. 777-784, 808-818.

777 **Avo** = *grandsire*, i.e. Numitor, the father of the Vestal Rhea or Ilia.

    Mavortius = child of Mavors, old and poetic name for Mars.

778 **Assaraci**: King of Phrygia and grandfather of Anchises.

779 **geminae cristae.** The double-crested helm, a distinction of Mars.

780 **superum** = *for the world above*, i.e. as a god. Acc. Sing.

808 **ille** = Numa Pompilius (716-673 B.C.), a native of Cures (12) in Sabine country, whom the Romans regarded as the founder (**fundabit**, 12) of their religious and legal institutions.

813 **qui** = Tullus Hostilius (673-640 B.C.), a man of war, destroyed Alba.

    resides = *sluggish, lazy* (*re* + *sedeo*).

815 **Ancus Martius** (640-616 B.C.), conqueror of the Latins.

817 **Tarquinios reges** = (i.) Tarquinius Priscus (616-578B.C.) of Tarquinii in Etruria; (ii.) Tarquinius Superbus (534-509 B.C.), expelled by Brutus. Vergil omits Servius Tullius (578-534 B.C.).

817-818 **animamque . . . receptos.** Brutus, nephew of T. Superbus, roused Rome to expel the Tarquins and found the Republic: and thus the **fasces** (the sign of power) were *recovered* (**receptos**) by the people.—Sidgwick.

61

D₂

ROMULUS, 753-716 B.C.

A. The Passing of Romulus.

His immortalibus editis operibus cum ad exercitum recensendum contionem in campo ad Caprae paludem haberet, subito coorta tempestas cum magno fragore tonitribusque tam denso regemoperuit nimbo, ut conspectum eius contioni abstulerit; nec 5deindein terris Romulus fuit. Romana pubes, sedato tandem pavore, postquam ex tam turbido die serena et tranquilla lux rediit, ubi vacuam sedem regiam vidit, etsi satis credebat patribus, qui proxumi steterant, sublimem raptum procella, tamen velut 10orbitatismetu icta maestum aliquamdiu silentium obtinuit. Deinde a paucis initio facto deum deo natum, regem parentemque urbis Romanae salvere universi Romulum iubent; pacem precibus exposcunt, utivolens propitius suam semper sospitet progeniem.15

LIVY, i. 16.

2-3 **ad Caprae paludem** = *near the Goat's pool.*

4 **operuit** = *enveloped* (**ob** + **pario** = *get for, put upon,cover*), cf. opposite **a-per-io** = *get from, uncover.*

5 **abstulerit** = *auferret.* The event is regarded simply as past, without reference to other past events.

46

5-6 **nec deinde . . . fuit**, cf. 'Quirinus | Martis equis Acheronta fugit.' Hor. *Od.* iii. 3. 15.

7 **sēdato** = *settled, calmed.* **Sēd-o** = *cause to sit*, cf. **sēd-es**, and our *seat, settle.*

11 **orbitatis** = *of orphanhood*; cf. **orb-us** = *bereaved*, and our *orphan.*

15 **volens propitius**, an ellipse of *et*, cf. *optimus maximus.*

sospitet = *he may keep safe, preserve*, cf. **sospes** = *safe.*

B. The Mystery explained.

Pulcher et humano maior trabeaque decorus
Romulus in media visus adesse via,
Et dixisse simul: 'Prohibe lugere Quirites,
4
Nec violent lacrimis numina nostra suis.
Tura ferant placentque novum pia turba Quirinum,
Et patrias artes militiamque colant.'

OVID, *Fasti*, ii. 379-384. H.

1-6 Romulus appears as a god to Proculus Julius, an honourable man, bidding him tell his people not to mourn for him, but to worship him as Quirinus, and practise valour and all warlike virtues.

1 **trabea** = *in the (striped) robe of state.*

3-5 **Quirites** (cf. **Quirinus** = the deified Romulus) = lit.*spearmen.* Connected with *Cures* and *curis* (Sabine word for a *spear*), used of Roman *citizens* as opposed to Roman *soldiers.*

62

D₃

NUMA POMPILIUS, 716-673 B.C.

The Gate of Janus, open in war but shut in peace.

A.Qui regno ita potitus urbem novam, conditam vi et armis, iure eam legibusque ac moribus de integro condere parat. Quibus cum inter bella adsuescere videret non posse, quippe efferari militia animos, mitigandum ferocem populum armorum 5desuetudine ratus Ianum ad infimum Argiletum indicem pacis bellique fecit, apertus ut in armis esse civitatem, clausus pacatos circa omnes populos significaret.

LIVY, i. 19.

1 **Qui** = Numa Pompilius, the second king of Rome.

4-5 **quippe . . . animos** = *since* (he thought that) *men's tempers were made savage* (brutalised) *by warfare*.**efferari** = orat. obl. part of Numa's thoughts.

6 **desuetudine** = *by disuse*, i.e. by a cessation from the use of. Cf. *de-docēre* = *unteach.*

Ianum . . . Argiletum = (a temple of) Janus at the foot of the Argiletum, a slope to the N.E. of the Forum. (Prob. = the clayey ground, from *argilla* = white clay.)

8 **clausus.** It was closed for a short time, circ. 238 B.C., and again by Augustus 29-25 B.C.

B.

Sunt geminae Belli portae, sic nomine dicunt,
Religione sacrae et saevi formidine Martis:
Centum aerei claudunt vectes aeternaque ferri
610
Robora, nec custos absistit limine Ianus.
Has, ubi certa sedet patribus sententia pugnae,
Ipse Quirinali trabea cinctuque Gabino
Insignis reserat stridentia limina Consul;
Ipse vocat pugnas; sequitur tum cetera pubes,
615
Aereaque adsensu conspirant cornua rauco.

VERGIL., *Aen.* vii. 607-615.

609 **vectes** = *bolts or bars*, prob. from √veh = carry. Cf.*vect-īgal.*

612 **Quir. trabea** = *in the state robe of Romulus*, i.e. the striped robe of state, purple, with white stripes across.

cinctu Gabino = *with the Gabine girdle*, formed by girding the toga tight round the body by one of its loose ends.

613 **reserat** = *un-bars.* For *sēro* = *join*, cf. our *series.*

Parallel Passages. Ovid, *F.* i. 115-132. Cf. Hor. *Od.* iv. 15. 9. Verg. *Aen.* i. 293-4.

Numa Pompilius. 'The name of Numa is significant, and denotes an organiser or *lawgiver.* (For *Numa* cf. **numerus,nummus**, νόμος.) As Romulus was the founder of the State and of political and military order, so the legend regards Numa as the founder of the national religion.'—Ihne.

63

D₄

TARQUINIUS SUPERBUS, 534-509 B.C.

The Purchase of the Sibylline Books.

In antiquis annalibus memoria super libris Sibyllinis haec prodita est. Anus hospita atque incognita ad Tarquinium Superbum regem adiit, novem libros ferens, quos esse dicebat divina oracula: eos velle venundare. Tarquinius pretium percontatus 5est: mulier nimium immensum poposcit. Rex, quasi anus aetate desiperet, derisit. Tum illa foculum coram eo cum igne apposuit, et tres libros ex novem deussit; et, ecquid reliquos sex eodem pretio emere vellet, regem interrogavit. Sed enim 10Tarquinius id multo risit magis dixitque anum iam procul dubio delirare. Mulier ibidem statim tres libros alios exussit; atque id ipsum denuo placide interrogavit, an tres reliquos eodem pretio emat. Tarquinius ore iam serio, atque attentiore animo fit; eam 15constantiam confidentiamque non insuper habendam intelligit: libros tres reliquos mercatur nihilo minore pretio, quam quod erat petitum pro omnibus. . . . Libri tres in sacrarium conditi Sibyllini appellati. Ad eos, quasi ad oraculum, quindecimviri 20adeunt, cum dii immortales publice consulendi sunt.

AULUS GELLIUS (fl. 143 A.D.), i. 19.

1, 2 **libris Sibyllinis**, i.e. a collection of prophecies uttered by the legendary prophetess who lived at Cumae, near Naples.

5 **venundare** = *to sell.* Cf. *ven-eo* (= *venum* + *eo*), *ven-do*, and our *vendor.*

12 **delirare** = *to be out of her mind.* Lit. to make a crooked furrow in ploughing; *de* + *lira* (a furrow).

19 **sacrarium** = *the place for the keeping of holy things*, i.e. the Capitol. The original Sibylline Books were burnt in the fire on the Capitol, 82 B.C., but a fresh collection was made by Augustus, and deposited in the temple of Apollo on the Palatine.

20 **quindecimviri** (*sacris faciundis*), i.e. a college of priests who had charge of the Sibylline Books.

Parallel Passages. Verg. *Aen.* vi., espec. ll. 42-101, for the Cumaean Sibyl.

The Sibylline Books. 'There existed also Etruscan **libri fatales** (*Books of Fate*), and these, together with the Sibylline Books, were kept in the Temple of Capitoline Jupiter. Nothing seemed more natural than to suppose that Tarquin, who built that temple, purchased also the sacred books of the Sibyl.'—Ihne.

64

D₅

TARQUINIUS SUPERBUS, 534-509 B.C.

A. Sextus Tarquinius at Gabii.

Inde in consilia publica adhiberi. . . . Ita cum sensim ad rebellandum primores Gabinorum incitaret, ipse cum promptissimis iuvenum praedatum atque in expeditiones iret, et dictis factisque omnibus ad fallendum instructis vana accresceret fides, dux ad 5ultimum belli legitur. Ibi cum inscia multitudine, quid ageretur, proelia parva inter Romam Gabiosque fierent, quibus plerumque Gabina res superior esset, tum certatim summi infimique Gabinorum Sex. Tarquinium dono deum sibi missum ducem credere. 10Apud milites vero obeundo pericula ac laborespariter, praedam munifice largiendo tanta caritate esse, ut non pater Tarquinius potentior Bomam quam filius Gabiis esset.

LIVY, i. 54.

1 **Inde**, i.e. after the tale he told of his father's cruelty had gained credit with the men of Gabii.

adhiberi = *he was admitted.* Historic Infin.

2 **ad rebellandum** = *to renew the war.*

4-5 **ad fallendum instructis** = *were framed to deceive.*

8 **Gabina res** = *the cause of Gabii.* For **res** cf. .

11 **obeundo pariter** = *by facing alike* . . .

B. The Sequel: the Fall of Gabii.

Iamque potens misso genitorem appellat amico,
Perdendi Gabios quod sibi monstret iter.
Hortus odoratis suberat cultissimus herbis,
4
Sectus humum rivo lene sonantis aquae.

48

Illic Tarquinius mandata latentia nati
Accipit, et virga lilia summa metit.
Nuntius ut rediit, decussaque lilia dixit,
8
Filius 'Agnosco iussa parentis' ait.
Nec mora: principibus caesis ex urbe Gabina,
Traduntur ducibus moenia nuda suis.

OVID, *Fasti*, ii. 543-552. H.

1 **genitorem appellat . . .** = *he calls on his father (to tell him)* . . .
6 **virga** = *with a switch.*
  summa = *the tallest.*
10 **ducibus suis**, abl., after *nuda = deprived of.*
Reference. Hor. *Ep.* ii. 1. 23-27. Horace refers to the treaty made by Tarquinius with
Gabii.
Historic Parallel. Compare the extraordinary self-sacrifice of Zōpy̆rus, which enabled
him to betray Babylon to his master Darius. Herod, iii. 153-158.
65
D₆

The Position of Rome, the future Mistress of the World.

Urbi autem locum Romulus incredibili opportunitate delegit. Neque enim ad mare
admovit—quod ei fuit illa manu copiisque facillimum, ut in agrum Rutulorum Aboriginumve
procederet, aut in ostio Tiberino, quem in locum multis post annis rex 5Ancuscoloniam deduxit,
urbem ipse conderet,—sed hoc vir excellenti providentia sensit ac vidit, non esse
opportunissimos situs maritimos urbibus eis quae ad spem diuturnitatis conderentur atque imperi.
Itaque urbem perennis amnis et aequabilis et 10in mare late influentis posuit in ripa, quo posset
urbs et accipere ex mari, quo egeret, et reddere, quo redundaret: ut mihi iam tum divinasse ille
videatur, hanc urbem sedem aliquando et domum summo esse imperio praebituram: nam hanc
rerum tantam 15potentiam non ferme facilius alia in parte Italiae posita urbs tenere potuisset.
Urbis autem ipsius is est tractus ductusque muri cum Romuli tum etiam reliquorum regum
sapientia definitus ex omni parte arduis praeruptisque montibus. Locumque delegit 20et fontibus
abundantem et in regione pestilenti salubrem.

CICERO, *De Rep.* ii. 3. 5, 6 (selected).

3-6 **quod ei fuit . . .** = lit. which he might very easily have done with that band (of men)
and those forces, so that . . .
4 **Rutulorum.** S. of Rome. Turnus their King. Capital, Ardea.
6 **coloniam**, i.e. Ostia, the harbour of Rome and chief naval station.
7-8 **non esse opportunissimos**, e.g. as exposed to sudden attacks, and likely to contain a
too large foreign element.
12-13 **quo redundaret** = *its own superabundance.*
17-18 **is tractus ductusque** = *the plan and direction.*
19 **definitus** = *bounded.*
20 **arduis praeruptisque montibus.** 'The amphitheatre of seven hills which encloses the
meadows (afterwards the Campus Martius) in the bend of the Tiber, varying from 120 to 180 feet
above the stream, offered heights sufficiently elevated and abrupt for fortification, yet without
difficulties for the builder or cultivator.'
N.B.—In this passage be careful to translate Cicero's long, periodic sentences by two or
more separate sentences in English.
The Position of Rome. 'There was no place better fitted for an emporium of the Tiber
and sea traffic, and for a maritime frontier fortress than Rome. It combined the advantages of a
strong position and of immediate vicinity to the river.' Mommsen.
66
D₇

THE PRAISE OF ITALY.

'Salve, magna parens frugum, Saturnia tellus.'

Sed neque Medorum silvae ditissima terra,
Nec pulcher Ganges atque auro turbidus Hermus
Laudibus Italiae certent, non Bactra, neque Indi
Totaque turiferis Panchaia pinguis harenis.
140
Haec loca non tauri spirantes naribus ignem
Invertere satis immanis dentibus hydri,

49

Nec galeis densisque virum seges horruit hastis;
Sed gravidae fruges et Bacchi Massicus umor
Implevere; tenent oleae armentaque laeta.
145
Hinc bellator equus campo sese arduus infert;
Hinc albi, Clitumne, greges, et maxima taurus
Victima, saepe tuo perfusi flumine sacro,
Romanos ad templa deum duxere triumphos.
Hic ver assiduum atque alienis mensibus aestas;
150
Bis gravidae pecudes, bis pomis utilis arbor.
At rabidae tigres absunt et saeva leonum
Semina, nec miseros fallunt aconita legentes,
Nec rapit immensos orbis per humum, neque tanto
Squameus in spiram tractu se colligit anguis.

VERGIL, Georg. ii, 136-154.

136 **silvae ditissima** = *most rich in forests.*—Sidgwick.

137 **Hermus**, auriferous river of Lydia, cf. the R. Pactolus.

138 **Bactra**, modern Balk, N. of Afghanistan.

139 **Panchaia**, i.e. Arabia, the Eldorado of the Old World.

141 **satis . . . hydri** = *where the enormous dragon's teeth were sown.* **hydri** (ὕδρος), lit. *a water-snake.*

143 **Massicus umor** = *Massic juice*, i.e. of Mt. Massicus in N.W. Campania, famous for its wine, espec. the Falernian.

144 **implevere** (sc. **haec loca**) = *fill it all.*

146 **Clitumne.** R. of Umbria, famous for its white cattle.*

146-148 White cattle were required for the sacrifices of the Triumphs.

149 **alienis mensibus** = *in months not her own*, i.e. in months properly belonging to winter.

150 **bis gravidae pecudes** = *twice the cattle give increase*, Conington.

151, 152 **saeva leonum semina** = *the fierce lion-brood.*—Mackail.

  aconita, a deadly poison—*monkshood.*

153, 154 **neque—anguis** = *nor with so vast a sweep gather himself into a coil*, i.e. the snakes in Italy are not so large as elsewhere.

R. Clitumnus. Compare Pliny's beautiful letter (viii. 8) describing its source.

* Cf. the Chillingham 'Wild Cattle.'

67

D₈

EARLY REPUBLIC, 509-366 B.C.
ETRUSCAN INVASION UNDER PORSENA, 507 B.C. (1)

'How well Horatius kept the Bridge

In the brave days of old.'

A.
Nec non Tarquinium eiectum Porsenna iubebat
Accipere, ingentique urbem obsidione premebat;
Aeneadae in ferrum pro libertate ruebant.
Illum indignanti similem, similemque minanti
650
Aspiceres, pontem auderet quia vellere Cocles,
Et fluvium vinclis innaret Cloelia ruptis.

VERGIL, Aen. viii. 646-651.

Venus brings Aeneas his new armour: he gazes at the shield whereon were wrought scenes of the story of Rome to be.

646 **Porsenna.**
'Lars Porsena of Clusium
By the nine gods he swore
That the great house of Tarquin
Should suffer wrong no more.'—Macaulay.

648 **in ferrum ruebant** = *were flinging themselves on the sword.* C.

651 **Cloelia**, a Roman hostage, who escaped by swimming the Tiber.

B.Pons sublicius iter paene hostibus dedit, ni unus vir fuisset, Horatius Cocles. . . . Qui positus forte in statione pontis, cum captum repentino impetu Ianiculum atque

50

inde citatos decurrere hostes vidisset, 10trepidamque turbam suorum arma ordinesque relinquere, reprehensans singulos, obsistens obtestansque deum et hominum fidem testabatur nequiquam deserto praesidio eos fugere; si transitum pontem a tergo reliquissent, iam plus hostium in Palatio 15Capitolioque quam in Ianiculo fore. Itaque monere, praedicere, ut pontem ferro, igni, quacunque vi possint, interrumpant; se impetum hostium, quantum corpore uno posset obsisti, excepturum. Vadit inde in primum aditum pontis, insignisque inter 20conspecta cedentium pugnae terga, obversiscominus ad ineundum proelium armis, ipso miraculo audaciae obstupefecit hostes.

LIVY, ii. 10.

7 **Pons sublicius** = *the pile-bridge*, built by Ancus Marcius to connect Rome proper with the Janiculum-hill, or ridge.

8 **Cocles** = *the one-eyed*, from loss of an eye in battle.

10 **citatos** = *at full speed*. Adj. use of participle; cf. *citato equo*.

11 **trepidamque turbam** = *panic-stricken and in disorder*.

12 **reprehensans** = *seizing them by the arm one after another*.

14-15 **si transitum . . . reliquissent** = *if they left the bridge free for the enemy to cross by*. **transitum** = noun, in appos. to **pontem**.

21-22 **obversis armis** = *as he faced about*.

68

D₉

<h2 align="center">ETRUSCAN INVASION UNDER PORSENA, 507 B.C. (2)</h2>

<h3 align="center">'How well Horatius kept the Bridge</h3>

<h3 align="center">In the brave days of old.'</h3>

Duos tamen cum eo pudor tenuit, Sp. Larcium ac T. Herminium, ambos claros genere factisque. Cum his primam periculi procellam et quod tumultuosissimum pugnae erat, parumper sustinuit; deinde eos quoque ipsos, exigua parte pontis relicta, revocantibus, 5qui rescindebant, cedere in tutum coegit. Circumferens inde truces minaciter oculos ad proceres Etruscorum nunc singulos provocare, nunc increpare omnes: servitia regum superborum, suae libertatis immemores alienam oppugnatum venire. 10Cunctati aliquamdiu sunt, dum alius alium, ut proelium incipiant, circumspectant. Pudor deinde commovit aciem, et clamore sublato undique in unum hostem tela coniciunt. Quae cum in obiecto cuncta scuto haesissent, neque ille minus obstinatus ingenti 15pontem obtineret gradu, iam impetu conabantur detrudere virum, cum simul fragor rupti pontis, simul clamor Romanorum alacritate perfecti operis sublatus, pavore subito impetum sustinuit. Tum Cocles 'Tiberine pater,' inquit, 'te sancte precor, haec arma 20et hunc militem propitio flumine accipias.' Ita sic armatus in Tiberim desiluit, multisque superincidentibus telis incolumis ad suos tranavit, rem ausus plus famae habituram ad posteros quam fidei.

LIVY, ii. 10.

7 **ad proceres** = *on the chiefs*. For prŏcer cf. procērus = tall.

8-9 **provocare . . . increpare.** Historic Infinitives = Indic.

9 **servitia** = *the slaves* = *servos*. Abstract for concrete, freq. in Livy. Cf. Hor. *Od*. ii. 8. 18. (*servitus = servi*.)

14 **obiecto** = *presented*, i.e. to the enemy.

15-16 **ingenti gradu** = *with mighty (heroic) stand*. Cf. 'firm as a rock.'

18 **alacritate perfecti operis** = *from joy at the completion of the work*.

24 **plus famae . . . fidei** = *destined to win more fame than credit with posterity*.

'Oh Tiber! father Tiber!
To whom the Romans pray,
A Roman's life, a Roman's arms,
Take thou in charge this day!'
So he spake, and speaking sheathed
The good sword by his side,
And with his harness on his back,
Plunged headlong in the tide.—Macaulay.

69

D₁₀

<h2 align="center">ETRUSCAN INVASION UNDER PORSENA, 507 B.C. (3)</h2>

<h3 align="center">How C. Mucius lost his Hand, but won a Name.</h3>

A.Obsidio erat nihilo minus et frumenti cum summa caritate inopia,sedendoque expugnaturum se urbem spem Porsena habebat, cum C. Mucius, adulescens nobilis, . . . primo sua sponte penetrare in hostium castra constituit; dein metuens, ne, si consulum 5iniussu et

51

ignaris omnibus iret, forte deprehensus a custodibus Romanis retraheretur ut
transfuga, fortuna tum urbis crimen affirmante, senatum adit. 'Transire Tiberim,' inquit, 'patres,
et intrare, si possim, castra hostium volo, non praedo nec populationum 10in vicem ultor; maius,
si di iuvant, in animo est facinus.' Approbant patres; abdito intra vestem ferro proficiscitur. Ubi
eo venit, in confertissima turba prope regium tribunal constitit.

LIVY, ii. 12.

1 **cum summa caritate** = *involving* (**cum**) *a very high price.*

2 **sedendo** = *by sitting down before,* of a besieging army.

3 **Mucius.** From this incident surnamed Scaevola = *the left-handed.* After his time,
a frequent surname in the Gens Mucia.

7-8 **fortunā . . . affirmante** = *(a charge which) the present condition of the city would
confirm (substantiate).*

10-11 **non praedo . . . ultor** = *not to plunder nor to retaliate on* (lit. 'an avenger in turn on') *our
plunderers.*

B.

Cum peteret regem decepta satellite dextra
Ingessit sacris se peritura focis.
Sed tam saeva pius miracula non tulit hostis
4
Et raptum flammis iussit abire virum.
Urere quam potuit contempto Mucius igne,
Hanc spectare manum Porsena non potuit.
Maior deceptae fama est et gloria dextrae:
8
Si non errasset, fecerat illa minus.

MARTIAL, *Ep.* I. xxi.

1 **sătellite** = *the attendant,* i.e. the scribe or secretary of Porsena.

2 **ingessit** = *thrust into* (*in* + *gero*).

3 **tam saeva miracula** = *such a miracle of stern fortitude.*—S.

pius = *feeling,* as opposed to *unnatural.*

7-8 i.e. to have killed Porsena would have been less glorious than to display such
heroism.—Stephenson.

Porsena. Livy tells us that Mucius, in gratitude for the magnanimity of Porsena, revealed
to him that 300 Roman youths had sworn to attempt the same deed that he had undertaken.
Whereupon Porsena feared to distress the Romans any longer, and made peace with them.
70
D11

LATIN WAR. BATTLE OF LAKE REGILLUS, 498 B.C.

The Dictator and his Master of the Horse.

Ibi alia inter proceres coorta pugna. Imperator Latinus, ubi cohortem exulum a dictatore
Romano prope circumventam vidit, ex subsidiariis manipulos aliquot in primam aciem secum
rapit. Hos agmine venientes T. Herminius legatus conspicatus, interque5eos insignem veste
armisque Mamilium noscitans, tanto vi maiore, quam paulo ante magister equitum, cum hostium
duce proelium iniit, ut et uno ictu transfixum per latus occiderit Mamilium, et ipse inter
spoliandum corpus hostis veruto percussus, 10cum victor in castra esset relatus, inter primam
curationem exspiraverit. Tum ad equites dictator advolat obtestans, ut fesso iam pedite
descendant ex equis et pugnam capessant. Dicto paruere; desiliunt ex equis, provolant in primum,
et pro antesignanis 15parmas obiciunt. Recipit extemplo animum pedestris acies,
postquam iuventutis procceresaequato genere pugnae secum partem periculi sustinentes vidit.
Tum demum impulsi Latini, perculsaque inclinavit acies.20

LIVY, ii. 20.

1 **inter proceres.** The Battle of Lake Regillus was, in the main, a Homeric battle of single
combats between the opposing chiefs.

1-2 **Imperator Latinus,** i.e. Mamilius of Tusculum, son-in-law of Tarquin.

5 **T. Herminius,** one of 'the dauntless Three,' who kept the bridge.

7 **magister equitum,** i.e. T. Aebutius. The Master of the Horse, the second in command,
was nominated by the Dictator.

10 **veruto** = *with a javelin,* cf. *veru* = *a spit.*

11-12 **inter primam curationem** = *at the first attempt to dress his wound.*—Rawlins.

52

13 **dictator**, i.e. Aulus Postumius. The Dictator (*magister populi = master of the army*) was appointed by one of the two Consuls (= *colleagues*) in a time of national danger to avoid the possible want of unity between the two consuls in time of war.

15 **in primum = in primam aciem.**

antesignanis, i.e. the first line fighting *in front of the standards.*

17 **iuventutis proceres** = *the young noblemen*, i.e. the cavalry are not only the younger men (in Livy often =**iuvenes**) but also patricians.

Reference. Macaulay, *The Battle of Lake Regillus.*

71

D₁₂

FIRST SECESSION OF THE PLEBS, 494 B.C.

The Fable of the Belly and the Members.

Tribunes of the People.

Pavor ingens in urbe, metuque mutuo suspensa erant omnia. . . . Placuit igitur oratorem ad plebem mitti Menenium Agrippam, facundum virum et, quod inde oriundus erat, plebi carum. Is intromissus in castra prisco illo dicendi et horrido modo nihil 5aliud quam hoc narrasse fertur: Tempore, quo in homine non, ut nunc, omnia in unum consentientia, sed singulis membris suum cuique consilium, suus sermo fuerit, indignatas reliquas partes sua cura, suo labore ac ministerio ventri omnia quaeri, ventrem in 10medio quietum nihil aliud quam datis voluptatibus frui; conspirasse inde, ne manus ad os cibum ferrent, nec os acciperet datum, nec dentesconficerent. Hac ira dum ventrem fame domare vellent, ipsa una membra totumque corpus ad extremam tabem 15venisse. Inde apparuisse ventris quoque haud segne ministerium esse, nec magis ali quam alere eum, reddentem in omnes corporis partes hunc, quo vivimus vigemusque, divisum pariter in venas, maturum confecto cibo sanguinem. Comparando hinc, quam 20intestina corporis seditio similis esset irae plebis in patres, flexisse mentes hominum. Agi deinde de concordia coeptum concessumque in condiciones, ut plebi sui magistratus essent sacrosancti, quibus auxili latio adversus consules esset, neve cui patrum capere 25eum magistratum liceret. Ita tribuni plebei creati duo, C. Licinius et L. Albinus.

LIVY, ii. 32, 33.

1-2 **Pavor ingens . . . omnia.** One of the Roman armies (mainly recruited from Plebeians) refused to obey orders, entrenched itself on Mons Sacer, and threatened to secede from Rome altogether.

2 **oratorem** (i.e. *legatum*) = *spokesman*, charged with a*verbal* message.

4 **inde**, i.e. from the Plebs.

10-11 **ventrem . . . quietum** = *whereas the belly resting calmly in their midst.*—Rawlins.

13 **conficerent** = *grind*, and so aid digestion. Cf. **confecto**l. 20.

19-20 **maturum confecto cibo** = *brought to perfection only when the food is digested.*—R.

24 **sacrosancti** = *consecrated and inviolable.*

24-25 **quibus . . . esset**, i.e. as official protectors of the Plebs, by their right of veto on the official actions of all other magistrates.

For the Fable, cf. Seneca *de Ira* ii. 31, and 1 Corinthians, xii. 12-27.

72

D₁₃

WAR WITH THE VOLSCIANS, 493 B.C.

Veturia and her son Coriolanus.

Coriolanus prope ut amens consternatus ab sede sua cum ferret matri obviae complexum, mulier in iram ex precibus versa 'Sine, priusquam complexum accipio, sciam' inquit, 'ad hostem an ad filium venerim, captiva mater-ne in castris tuis sim. In 5hoc me longa vita et infelix senecta traxit, ut exulem te, deinde hostem viderem? Potuisti populari hanc terram, quae te genuit atque aluit? Non tibi, quamvis infesto animo et minaci perveneras, ingredienti fines ira cecidit? Non, cum in conspectu 10Roma fuit, succurrit: Intra illa moenia domus ac penates mei sunt, mater, coniunx liberique? Ergo ego nisi peperissem, Roma non oppugnaretur; nisi filium haberem, libera in libera patria mortua essem.' . . . Uxor deinde ac liberi amplexi, fletusque ab 15omni turba mulierum ortus et conploratio sui patriaeque fregere tandem virum. Complexus inde suos dimittit; ipse retro ab urbe castra movit. Abductis deinde legionibus ex agro Romano invidia rei oppressum perisse traduntalii alio leto.20

LIVY, ii. 40.

1 **Coriolanus.** Gaius Marcius received the cognomen of Coriolanus for his bravery at the capture of the Volscian town of Corioli (S.E. of Rome). After this, in a time of famine at Rome, C. advised that the corn obtained elsewhere should not be distributed, unless the Plebeians would

53

give up their Tribunes. For this he was impeached and went into voluntary exile among the Volsci.

consternatus = *in strong emotion*—lit. 'stretched on the ground.'

7 **potuisti** = *had you the heart to*—question indicated by *tone* of the voice.

10-11 **non . . . succurrit** = *did it not occur to you?*

19-20 **invidia rei oppressum** = *overwhelmed by the unpopularity of his action.*

20 **alii alio leto**, e.g. i. by a voluntary death; ii. put to death by the Volscians; iii. lived to old age in exile.

References. Cic. *Brutus* x. (compared to Themistocles). Plutarch, *Coriolanus.*

'The germ from which the whole legend sprang is the story of the filial love of Coriolanus, and of the great authority exercised in olden times by Roman matrons over their sons and husbands.' Ihne.

Shakespeare, *Coriolanus*, V. iii.

73

D₁₄

WAR WITH VEII, 483-474 B.C.

The Destruction of the Fabii at the Cremera, *477 B.C.*

Campus erat, campi claudebant ultima colles
Silvaque montanas occulere apta feras.
In medio paucos armentaque rara relinquunt,
4
Cetera virgultis abdita turba latet.
Ecce velut torrens undis pluvialibus auctus
Aut nive, quae Zephyro victa tepente fluit,
Per sata perque vias fertur, nec, ut ante solebat,
8
Riparum clausas margine finit aquas:
Sic Fabii vallem latis discursibus implent,
Quodque vident sternunt, nec metus alter inest.
Quo ruitis, generosa domus? male creditis hosti:
12
Simplex nobilitas, perfida tela cave.
Fraude perit virtus. In apertos undique campos
Prosiliunt hostes, et latus omne tenent.
Quid faciant pauci contra tot millia fortes?
16
Quidve, quod in misero tempore restet, adest?
Sicut aper longe silvis Laurentibus actus
Fulmineo celeres dissipat ore canes,
Mox tamen ipse perit: sic non moriuntur inulti
20
Vulneraque alterna dantque feruntque manu.
Una dies Fabios ad bellum miserat omnes;
Ad bellum missos perdidit una dies.

OVID, *Fasti*, ii. 175-196, H.

Context. To protect their territory from the constant raids of the Veientines, the noble house of the Fabii offered to undertake the war themselves. The consul Kaeso Fabius marched out of the city at the head of his clan, followed by the blessings and good wishes of the admiring people. He erected a fortified camp near the R. Cremera (a tributary of the Tiber), and from this spot plundered Veientine territory.

1 **campus.** 'Ovid here paints from fancy: there are, however, deep hollows admirably calculated to conceal an ambushed foe.'—Ramsay.

9 **discursibus** = *runnings to and fro*, of soldiers dispersing to plunder.

10 **metus alter** = *fear of a second enemy*, i.e. of one in ambush.

17 **silvis Laurentibus.** Laurentum on the coast of Latium between Ostia and Ardea. Wild boars are still found in the swampy thickets.

18 **Fulmineo ore** = *with flashing tusk.*—Hallam.

Parallel Passage. Livy, ii. 48, 49.

'The story probably came from the Chronicles of the Fabian Clan, perhaps through *Fabius* Pictor, the first Roman annalist.' Rawlins, Cf. Ihne, vol. i. cap. vi.

74

WAR WITH THE AEQUIANS, 458 B.C.

A. Cincinnatus called from the Plough.

Sed Aequos praecipue Quinctius Cincinnatus domuit, ille dictator ab aratro, qui obsessa et paene iam capta L. Minuci consulis castra egregia victoria recuperavit. Medium erat tempus forte sementis, cum patricium virum innixum aratro suo lictor in 5ipso opere deprehendit. Inde in aciem profectus, ne quid a rustici operis imitatione cessaret, more pecudum victos sub iugum misit. Sic expeditione finita redit ad boves rursus triumphalis agricola. Intra quindecim dies coeptum peractumque bellum, 10prorsus ut festinasse, dictator ad relictum opus videretur.

FLORUS, I. xi. 12-15.

1 **Aequos**, mountaineers (closely allied to the Sabines) who lived in the mountains forming the E. boundary of Latium.

Cincinnatus. 'The true type of primeval virtue, abstinence, and patriotism.'—Ihne.

2-4 **qui . . . recuperavit.** The Aequian general, Gracchus Cloelius, had defeated the consul, L. Minucius, and blockaded him in his camp on Mt. Algidus, the E. spur of the Alban range. Cincinnatus makes a wonderful night march from Rome of 20 miles, blockades in turn the investing Aequian force, and compels an unconditional surrender.

4 **sementis** = *of the seed-time*. Formed from *semen*, cf. *sero*.

B. 'In the brave days of old.'

Restat, ut inveniam, quare toga libera detur
2
Lucifero pueris, candide Bacche, tuo.

.   .   .   .

An quia, cum colerent prisci studiosius agros,
4
Et patrio faceret rure senator opus,
Et caperet fasces a curvo consul aratro,
Nec crimen duras esset habere manus,
Rusticus ad ludos populus veniebat in urbem:
8
Sed dis, non studiis, ille dabatur honor.

OVID, *Fasti*, iii. 729-742, H.

1 **toga libera** (or **virilis**), the man's dress of unornamented white wool. *Lībera* (*līber*), *free* from the restraints of boyhood.

2 **lucifero** = lit. *morning-star*. Here poet. for **die**.

5 **consul**, e.g. Cincinnatus, who was called to be *Dictator*.

8 **sed . . . honor**, i.e. in 'the good old days' worship, not amusement, was the chief object of the visit to Rome.

3-8 Ovid says one reason why the *toga libera* was assumed at the Liberalia (the Feast of Bacchus—the vintage, festival) was because it was the most crowded festival of the year.

References. Livy, iii. 26-28. Ihne, vol. i. cap. v.

75

THE DECEMVIRATE. THE TWELVE TABLES, 451-449 B.C.

Iam redierant legati cum Atticis legibus. Eo intentius instabant tribuni, ut tandem scribendarum legum initium fieret. Placet creari decemviros sine provocatione, et ne quis eo anno alius magistratus esset . . . Tum legibus condendis opera dabatur; 5ingentique hominum expectatione propositis decem tabulis populum ad contionem advocaverunt et, quod bonum, faustum felixque rei publicae, ipsis liberisque eorum esset, ire et legere leges propositas iussere. Se, quantum decem hominum ingeniis provideri 10potuerit, omnibus, summis infimisque, iura aequasse; plus pollere multorum ingenia consiliaque. Versarent in animis secum unamquamque rem, agitarent deinde sermonibus atque in medium, quid in quaque re plus minusve esset, conferrent. . . . Cum ad 15rumores hominum de unoquoque legum capite editos satis correctae viderentur, centuriatis comitiis decem tabularum leges perlatae sunt, qui nunc quoque in hoc immenso aliarum super alias acervatarum legum cumulo, fons omnis publici privatique 20est iuris.

LIVY, iii. 32, 34.

1 **cum Atticis legibus**, i.e. with a copy of the Laws of Solon (the great Athenian Lawgiver, 594 B.C.).

1-3 **Eo intentius . . . fieret**, because up to this time the knowledge of law and its interpretation was confined to the Patricians (cf. the Scribes of the N.T.). This could only be remedied by writng the laws down and making them public.

3-4 **sine provocatione** = *without appeal.* Lit. 'challenging.'

4-5 **ne quis . . . esset.** The Decemvirs were to supersede temporarily both Consuls and Tribunes.

14-15 **quid . . . conferrent** = '*Should point out in the interest of all* (lit. should contribute to the public good)*any faults of excess or defect in the several articles.*'—Stephenson.

15-17 **ad rumores hominum** = *in accordance with* (**ad**)*public opinion.*

17 **centuriatis comitiis.** Servius Tullius divided the people into five classes, according to the value of their property. The people (Patricians and Plebeians alike) voted by centuries; but as 98 centuries (and ∴ 98 votes) were allotted to the richest class and only 95 to the other four classes, the influence of wealth was decisive in the elections.

Parallel Passages. Cic. *De Republica* ii. 33-37, and *De Legibus* ii. 23.

The Twelve Tables. 'They were essentially only a written embodiment of the existing public and private law.'—Mommsen. Cf. Magna Carta.

76

D₁₇

SECOND SECESSION OF THE PLEBS, 448 B.C.

The Death of Verginia not in vain.

Concitatur multitudo partim atrocitate sceleris, partim spe per occasionem repetendae libertatis. In contionem Appius escendit; sequuntur Horatius Valeriusque. Eos contio audit; decemviro obstrepitur. Iam pro imperio Valerius discedere a privato 5lictores iubebat, cum fractis animis Appius vitae metuens in domum se propinquam foro insciis adversariis capite obvoluto recipit. M. Duillius deinde tribunus plebis plebem rogavit plebesque scivit, qui plebem sine tribunis reliquisset quique magistratum 10sineprovocatione creasset, tergo ac capite puniretur. Haec omnia ut invitis, ita non adversantibus patriciis transacta, quia nondum in quemquam unum saeviebatur. Fundata deinde et potestate tribunicia et plebis libertate tum tribuni aggredi singulos tutum15maturumque iam rati accusatorem primum Verginium et Appium reum deligunt. Spe incisa, priusquam prodicta dies adesset, Appius mortem sibi conscivit. M. Claudius assertor Verginiae, die dicta damnatus ipso remittente Verginio ultimam poenam 20dimissus Tibur exulatum abiit; manesque Verginiae, mortuae quam vivae felicioris, per tot domos ad petendas poenas vagati nullo relicto sonte tandem quieverunt.

LIVY, iii. 49, 55, 56, 58 (sel.)

Context. Verginius, seeing no way of saving his daughter from disgrace and dishonour at the hands of Appius Claudius, killed her before the judgment-seat of the tyrant and before the eyes of the people.

2 **per occasionem** = *by such a favourable opportunity.*—Rawlins.

3 **In contionem** = *to the rostra* (the platform for speakers).

3-4 **Horatius Valeriusque.** The first Consuls after the abolition of the Decemvirate in 449 B.C.

5 **pro imperio**, i.e. usurping the authority of a magistrate.

9 **plebesque scivit** (scisco) = *and the people approved* (i.e. voted for) it.

11 **provocatione** = *right of appeal.*

18 **prodicta** = *adjourned*, from the first hearing.—R.

19 **assertor V.** = *who claimed V. as his slave.*

Results of the Secession. 'The Valerian Laws, by the second of which it was ordained that in criminal trials, when the life of a citizen was at stake, the sentence of the Consul should be subject to an appeal to the people. This Valerian Law of Appeal was the Roman Habeas Corpus Act.'—Ihne.

77

D₁₈

WAR WITH THE ETRUSCANS OF FIDENAE AND VEII.

Cossus wins the Spolia Opima, *437 B.C.*

Erat tum inter equites tribunus militum A. Cornelius Cossus, eximia pulchritudine corporis, animo ac viribus par memorque generis, quod amplissimum acceptum maius auctiusque reliquit posteris. Is cum ad impetum Tolumni, quacumque se intendisset,5trepidantes Romanas videret turmas insignemque eum regio habitu volitantem tota acie cognosset, 'Hicine est' inquit 'ruptor foederis humani violatorque gentium iuris? Iam ego hanc mactatam victimam, si modo sancti quicquam in terris esse di10volunt, legatorum manibus dabo.' Calcaribus subditis infesta cuspide in unum fertur hostem; quem cum ictum equo deiecisset, confestim et ipse hasta innixus se in pedes excepit. Adsurgentem ibi regem umbone resupinat repetitumque saepius cuspide 15ad terram affixit. Tum exsangui detracta spolia, caputque abscisum victor spiculo gerens terrore caesi regis hostes perfudit. Ita equitum quoque fusa acies, quae una fecerat anceps certamen.Dictator legionibus fugatis instat et ad castra compulsos 20caedit.

LIVY, iv. 19.

3 **par** = *equally distinguished by*, equal, that is, to his beauty.—S.

5 **Tolumni** = Lars Tolumnius, King of the Veientos, in alliance with Fidenae (about 5 miles N.E. of Rome).

    quacumque se intendisset = *wherever he directed his charge.*

8-11 **Hicine . . . manibus dabo.** Fidenae had frequently been colonised by Rome, and had as frequently revolted. When the Romans sent four ambassadors to Fidenae to demand satisfaction for this last revolt, the people of Fidenae murdered them. Tolumnius is associated with their crime.

12 **infesta cuspide** = *with couched lance.*

13-14 **hasta . . . excepit** = *with the help of his spear leapt to the ground.* Lit. 'resting on his spear caught himself on his feet.'—Stephenson.

15 **umbone resupinat** = *he throws him back with the boss of his shield.*

    repetitum = *piercing him again and again.*—S.

19 **Dictator** = Mamercus Aemilius, a man of energy and ability.

The **spolia opima** (*spoils of honour*) were the arms taken on the field of battle by the victorious from the vanquished general. They were won on only three occasions:—

i. by **Romulus**, ii. by **Cossus**, iii. by **Marcellus** (the Conqueror of Syracuse), who in his first consulship, 222B.C., slew with his own hand Viridomarus, King of the Insubrian Gauls. Cf. Prop. V. x.

78

D₁₉

THE WAR WITH VEII, 405-396 B.C. (1)

First Pay given to Citizen Soldiers, *406 B.C.*

Additum deinde omnium maxime tempestivo principum in multitudinem munere, ut ante mentionem ullam plebis tribunorumve decerneret senatus, ut stipendium miles de publicoacciperet, cum ante id tempus de suo quisque functus eo munere esset. 5Nihil acceptum umquam a plebe tanto gaudio traditur. Concursus itaque ad curiam esse prensatasque exeuntium manus et patres vere appellatos, effectum esse fatentibus, ut nemo pro tam munifica patria, donec quicquam virium superesset, corpori10aut sanguini suo parceret. Cum commoditas iuvaret, rem familiarem saltem acquiescere eo tempore, quo corpus addictum atque operatum rei publicae esset, tum quod ultro sibi oblatum esset, non a tribunis plebis agitatum, non suis sermonibus efflagitatum, 15id efficiebat multiplex gaudium cumulatioremque gratiam rei. . . . Et lege perlata de indicendo Veientibus bello exercitum magna ex parte voluntarium novi tribuni militum consulari potestate Veios duxere.20

LIVY, iv. 59, 60.

1 **tempestivo** = *seasonable* (*timely*), in view of the coming struggle with Veii, and the necessity for winter campaigns.

2 **munere.** Livy tells us (cap. 60) that the Senate did *not*provide the pay as a present, but simply paid punctually their proper share of the *war-tax* (*tributum*)*in accordance with their assessment* (*cum senatus summa fide ex censu contulisset*).

4 **de publico** = *out of the Public Treasury.*

9 **fatentibus** = *while men admitted.*—R.

11-12 **Cum . . . acquiescere** = *While the comfortable thought* (*commoditas* = lit. *advantage*) *pleased them*(namely) *that their private property at least was undisturbed*— i.e. that they paid no war-tax while they were in the field.—Rawlins.

12-13 **quo corpus . . . esset** = *when they were impressed*(devoted to) *and actively employed in the public service.*—S. **addictus,** properly of an insolvent debtor made over to his creditor = a *bondman.*

16-17 **id . . . gratiam rei** in apposition to **quod . . . efflagitatum.**

19 **tribuni . . . potestate.** Military tribunes with consular power instead of Consuls were elected occasionally from 444 to 367 B.C.

20 **Veios.** The capture of Veii by Camillus (396 B.C.), in consequence of the introduction of military pay, was enormously important to Rome.

Reference. Ihne, *Hist.* vol. i. pp. 243-4.

79

D₂₀

57

A. Lament over Veii.

Heu, Veii veteres, et vos tum regna fuistis,
28
Et vestro posita est aurea sella foro:
Nunc intra muros pastoris bucina lenti
Cantat, et in vestris ossibus arva metunt.

PROPERTIUS, IV. (V.) x. 27-30.

27 **Veii** (Isola Farnese) on R. Cremera, about 12 miles N.W. of Rome.

28 **aurea sella**, i.e. the official seat of the King. Cf. the Sella Curulis at Rome, introduced from Etruria.

29 **bucina** = *horn*.

30 **et . . . metunt** = *and reapers gather the harvests from fields* (**metunt arva**) *enriched by the bones of your buried heroes* (**in ossibus vestris**).

B. The Rise of the Alban Lake.

Quid, quod in annalibus habemus, Veienti 5bello, cum lacus Albanus praeter modum crevisset, Veientem quemdam ad nos hominem nobilem profugisse, eumque dixisse, ex fatis, quae Veientes scripta haberent, Veios capi non posse, dum lacus is redundaret: et, si lacus emissus lapsu et cursu suo ad 10mare profluxisset, perniciosum populo Romano: sin autem ita esset eductus, ut ad mare pervenire non posset, tum salutare nostris fore? Ex quo illa admirabilis a maioribus Albanae aquae factadeductio est. Cum autem Veientes bello fessi legatos ad 15senatum misissent, tum ex his quidam dixisse dicitur, non omnia illum transfugam ausum esse senatu dicere: in iisdem enim fatis scriptum Veientes habere, 'Fore ut brevi a Gallis Roma caperetur:' quod quidem sexennio post Veios captos esse factum20videmus.

CICERO, de Divinatione, I. xliv. 100.

5 **in annalibus**, e.g. in Livy, v. 15.

6 **crevisset**, perh. partly due to the excessive snows of the preceding winter, 397 B.C.

7 **profugisse.** Livy says he was treacherously made prisoner.

8-9 **ex fatis . . . haberent**, i.e. the Etruscan **Libri fatales,***Books of fate*, cf. the **Libri Sibyllini** = the Roman Books of fate.

10 **lapsu et cursu suo** = *in its natural course and stream.*

14 **deductio** = *draining* (lit. *a leading off*). The tunnel then cut still carries off the superfluous waters of the lake.

20 **sexennio post** = *six years after*, i.e. 390 B.C. For the 10 years' siege of Veii, cf. the Trojan War.

Reference. Plutarch, *Camillus*, iii.-v. Livy, v. 15.
80
D21

The Conquest of Veii.

Veientes ignari se iam a suis vatibus, iam ab externis oraculisproditos, iam in partem praedae suae vocatos deos, alios votis ex urbe sua evocatos hostium templa novasque sedes spectare, seque ultimum illum diem agere, nihil minus timentes 5quam subrutis cuniculo moenibus arcem iam plenam hostium esse, in muros pro se quisque armati discurrunt mirantes, quidnam id esset, quod, cum tot per dies nemo se ab stationibus Romanus movisset, tum velut repentino icti furore improvidi currerent ad 10muros. . . . Cuniculus delectis militibus eo tempore plenus in aedem Iunonis, quae in Veientana arce erat, armatos repente edidit, et pars aversos in muris invadunt hostes, pars claustra portarum revellunt, pars, cum ex tectis saxa tegulaeque a mulieribus ac 15servitiis iacerentur, inferunt ignes. Clamor omnia variis terrentium ac paventium vocibus mixto mulierum ac puerorum ploratu complet. Momento temporis deiectis ex muro undique armatis patefactisque portis cum alii agmine irruerent, alii 20desertos scanderent muros, urbs hostibus impletur; omnibus locis pugnatur; deinde multa iam edita caede senescit pugna, et dictator praecones edicere iubet, ut ab inermi abstineatur.

LIVY, V. 21.

1 **a suis vatibus**, i.e. by the captured Etruscan soothsayer (*haruspex*).

1 2 **ab externis oraculis**, i.e. by the Delphic Oracle.

2-3 **iam in partem . . . (alios) deos.** Camillus had vowed to give to Apollo the tenth part of the spoils of Veii.

58

3-4 **alios . . . spectare**, i.e. Juno. 'It was a Roman practice to invite the patron deity of a place or country to leave it, and to promise a more honourable worship at Rome.'—Whibley.

5-6 **subrutis cunīculo** = *undermined.* Camillus had a tunnel (*cuniculum—rabbit-burrow*, cf. *cony*) cut from the Roman camp under the wall to the Temple of Juno on the citadel of Veii.

7 **discurrunt** = *run every man to his post*, cf. *ad arma discurritur.*

15 **tēgulae** = *tiles, roof-tiles* (*tēgo*).

23 **senescit** = *abates*, lit. *grows old, becomes exhausted.*

Results of the War. 'By the Conquest of Veii, Rome's territory, wealth, and population were largely increased. Rome was now emerging from the position of a federal capital of the Latins to become the mistress of a large country, when she was suddenly and unexpectedly overtaken by a disaster (**the Invasion of the Gauls**) which threatened not only her growth but her life.'—Ihne.

81

D₂₂

THE INVASION OF THE GAULS, 390 B.C. (1)

The Battle of the Allia.

Ibi tribuni militum non loco castris ante capto, non praemunito vallo, quo receptus esset, non deorum saltem, si non hominum, memores, nec auspicato nec litato instruunt aciem diductam in cornua, ne circumveniri multitudine hostium possent; 5nec tamen aequari frontes poterant, cum extenuando infirmam et vix cohaerentem mediam aciem haberent. Paulum erat ab dextera editi loci, quem subsidiariis repleri placuit; eaque res ut initium pavoris ac fugae, sic una salus fugientibus fuit. Nam Brennus, regulus10Gallorum, in paucitate hostium artem maxime timens, ratus ad id captum superiorem locum, ut, ubi Galli cum acie legionum recta fronte concurrissent, subsidia in aversos transversosque impetum darent, ad subsidiarios signa convertit, si eos loco depulisset, 15haud dubius facilem in aequo campi tantum superanti multitudinevictoriam fore; adeo non fortuna modo sed ratio etiam cum barbaris stabat. In altera acie nihil simile Romanis, non apud duces, non apud milites erat. Pavor fugaque occupaverat animos et 20tanta omnium oblivio, ut multo maior pars Veios, in hostium urbem, cum Tiberis arceret, quam recto itinere Romam ad coniuges ac liberos fugerent.

LIVY, V. 38.

4 **nec litato** = *without obtaining favourable omens* (=καλλιερεῖν).

4-5 **diductam in cornua** = *extended (drawn out) towards the wings.*

6-7 **cum . . . haberent** = *though they made*, concessive subjunctive.

8 **Paulum . . . editi loci** = lit. *a little piece of rising ground.*

10 **Brennus** = lit. *King of the army.* Cf. the Saxon *Heretoga.*

13 **recta fronte** = *front to front.*—Whibley.

14 **in aversos transversosque** = *on their rear and flank.*

16-17 **superanti multitudine** = i. (*the victory*) *would be*(*easy*) *to him superior* (**superanti**) *in point of numbers*, or ii. abl, of cause—*as he was so much superior in numbers.*

21-22 **Veios, in hostium urbem.** An exaggeration as Veii was in ruins.

22 **cum T. arceret** = *though the Tiber stood in their way.*

The Invasion of the Gauls. 'The most advanced tribe of the Gauls were the Senones who had settled on the Adriatic to the E. of Central Etruria. While the Romans reduced S. Etruria to a state of subjection, these Gauls suddenly crossed the Apennines, threatened Clusium, and then marched on Rome. **Thus for the first time the Gallic race was brought to the knowledge of the civilised world.** The two armies met on July 18 at the small R. Allia, only 15 miles from Rome.'—Ihne.

82

D₂₃

THE INVASION OF THE GAULS, 390 B.C. (2)

A. The Battle of the Allia *(cont.)*

Parumper subsidiarios tutatus est locus; in reliqua acie simul est clamor proximis ab latere, ultimis ab tergo auditus, ignotum hostem prius paene quam viderent, non modo non temptato certamine sed ne clamore quidem reddito integri intactique5fugerunt; nec ulla caedes pugnantium fuit; terga caesa suometipsorum certamine in turba impedientium fugam. Circa ripam Tiberis, quo armis abiectis totum sinistrum cornu refugit, magna strages facta est, multosque imperitos nandi aut invalidos, 10gravesloricis aliisque tegminibus, hausere gurgites. Maxima tamen pars incolumis Veios perfugit, unde non modo praesidii quicquam, sed ne nuntius quidem cladis Romam est missus. Ab dextro cornu, quod procul a flumine et magis sub monte steterat, 15Romam omnes petiere et ne clausis quidem portis urbis in arcem confugerunt.

LIVY, V. 38.

59

2-3 **simul (= simul ac) . . . auditus** = *as soon as the shout was heard, by those nearest on the flank, by the most distant in the rear.*

'**Proximi** denotes the Romans on the right wing, who were the first to be attacked; the Gauls after routing them pressed on to the rear of the Romans and attacked the centre and left wing (**ultimi**) from behind.'—Whibley.

7-8 **suomet . . . fugam** = *as they hindered their own flight by their struggling with one another in the crush.*

11 **graves** = *weighed down with,* equivalent to a pass. partic.

hausere gurgites = *the currents sucked down.*—W

15 **sub monte**, i.e. the Colles Crustumini, which run parallel to the South bank of the Tiber.

B. July 18th, a Dies Nefastus.

Pharsalia tanti
Causa mali. Cedant feralia nomina Cannae,
Et damnata diu Romanis Allia fastis.

LUCAN, Phars. vii. 407-9.

407 **Pharsalia**, Battle of, 48 B.C. Caesar signally defeated Pompey.

408 **feralia** = *fatal* (= **funesta**).

409 **fastis**, i.e. *Fasti consulares,* the registers of the higher magistrates. Cf. the Saxon Chronicle.

The Battle. 'The defeat of the Allia was never forgotten by the Romans. The panic (due to the strange appearance of the barbarians and their unwonted method of fighting) which alone had caused the defeat, struck so deep into their minds that for centuries afterwards the name and the sight of Gauls inspired them with terror.'—Ihne.

83
D24

THE INVASION OF THE GAULS, 390 B.C. (3)

Roman Dignity and Courage.

Romae interim satis iam omnibus ut in tali re ad tuendam arcem compositis turba seniorum domos regressi adventum hostiumobstinato ad mortem animo exspectabant. Qui eorum curulesgesserant magistratus, ut in fortunae pristinae honorumque ac5virtutis insignibus morerentur, quae augustissima vestis est tensasducentibus triumphantibusve, ea vestiti medio aedium eburneis sellis sedere. Galli autem ingressi postero die urbem patente Collina porta in forum perveniunt; ubi eos plebis aedificiis10obseratis, patentibus atriis principum, maior prope cunctatio tenebat aperta quam clausa invadendi; adeo haud secus quam venerabundi intuebantur in aedium vestibulis sedentes viros, praeter ornatum habitumque humano augustiorem maiestate etiam,15quam vultus gravitasque oris prae se ferebat, simillimos dis. Ad eos velut ad simulacra versi cum starent, M. Papirius, unus ex eis, dicitur Gallo barbam suam, ut tum omnibus promissa erat, permulcenti scipione eburneo in caput incusso iram 20movisse, atque ab eo initium caedis ortum, ceteros in sedibus suis trucidatos; post principum caedem nulli deinde mortalium parci, diripi tecta, exhaustis inici ignes.

LIVY, v. 41 (sel.)

1 **ut in tali re** = *considering the circumstances.*

3 **obstinato ad** = *firmly resolved on. . .*—Rawlins.

4-5 **curules magistratus** = *curule magistracies,* i.e. of Dictator, Censor, Consul, Praetor, Curule Aedile, who possessed the right of using *sellae curules (the ivory chairs of State),* originally an emblem of kingly power.

5-6 **in fortunae . . . insignibus** = *in the emblems of their old rank* (**fortunae**) *and office* (**honorum**) *and prowess*(**virtutis** i.e. prizes for valour; e.g. *phalerae* = *bosses,coronae* = *crowns*).

7 **tensas** = *state cars* in which the statues of the gods were drawn in solemn procession to the Circensian games.

11 **obseratis** = *shut up,* lit. *barred,* **ob** + **sera**, cf. *sĕro* = join.

14 **vestibulis** = *entrance-courts,* only found in large houses.

14-15 **praeter ornatum habitumque** = *not only in their garb and bearing.*—Whibley.

19 **ut tum . . . erat** = *worn long* (**promissa**) *as was then the custom with all,* or *worn long in accordance with the fashion of the time.*—R.

20 **scipione eburneo** = *the ivory staff,* one of the *insignia* of the *triumphator.*

23 **exhaustis** (sc. *aedibus*) = *when completely pillaged.*

Reference. Plutarch, *Camillus,* xxi. xxii.

84
D25

THE INVASION OF THE GAULS, 390 B.C. (4)

A. Manlius Capitolinus and the Sacred Geese.

In summo custos Tarpeiae Manlius arcis
Stabat pro templo et Capitolia celsa tenebat,
Romuleoque recens horrebat regia culmo.
655
Atque his auratis volitans argenteus anser
Porticibus Gallos in limine adesse canebat;
Galli per dumos aderant, arcemque tenebant,
Defensi tenebris et dono noctis opacae;
Aurea caesaries ollis, atque aurea vestis;
660
Virgatis lucent sagulis; tum lactea colla
Auro innectuntur; duo quisque Alpina coruscant
Gaesa manu, scutis protecti corpora longis.

VERGIL, Aen. viii. 652-662.

Context. Venus brings Aeneas his new armour: he gazes at the shield whereon were wrought scenes of the story of Rome to be.

652 **in summo** (sc. **clipeo**), *on the top of the shield*, as held in position.

654 **Romuleoque . . . culmo** = lit. *and the palace was stiff freshly covered* (**recens**) *with the thatch of Romulus*.

655-656 **auratis . . . porticibus** = *the gilded colonnades* of the Temple of Jupiter Capitolinus of Vergil's day, restored 69 B.C.

660 **virgatis sagulis** = *with striped cloaks*—**virgatus** = with bands or bars like shoots (*virgae*)—an effect produced by inlaying. C.

661-662 **Alpina gaesa** = *Alpine* (i.e. *native*) *javelins.*

B. The Fate of Manlius, *384 B.C.*

M. Manlius, unde Gallos depulerat, inde ipse praecipitatus est,quia fortiter defensam libertatem nefarie opprimere conatus fuerat. Cuius iustae ultionis nimirum haec praefatio fuit: 'Manlius eras15mihi, cum praecipites agebas Senones; postquam imitari coepisti, unus factus es ex Senonibus.' Huius supplicio aeternae memoriaenota inserta est: propter illum enim lege sanciri placuit ne quis patricius in arce aut Capitolio habitaret, quia domum eo loco20habuerat, ubi nunc aedem Monetae videmus.

VALERIUS MAXIMUS, vi. De Severitate.

13-14 **quia . . . fuerat.** Manlius in reality fell a victim to his sympathies with the Plebeians. Cf. the fate of Sp. Cassius 485 B.C.

18 **nota** = *a mark* (*brand*) *of infamy.*

20-21 **quia . . . habuerat.** His house on the Capitol was razed to the ground.

21 **aedem Monetae,** a surname of Juno, in whose temple on the Arx money was coined. Cf. our Mint.

'Thus ended the life of Manlius, the deliverer of Rome, the humane friend of an oppressed people, condemned by this very people to die the death of a traitor.'—Ihne.

85
D₂₆

THE INVASION OF ROME BY THE GAULS, 390 B.C. (5)

Camillus, Parens Patriae.

Sed diique et homines prohibuere redemptos vivere Romanos. Nam forte quadam, priusquam infanda merces perficeretur, per altercationem nondum omni auro appenso dictator intervenit auferrique aurum de medio et Gallos submoveri iubet. Cum 5illi renitentes pactos dicerent sese, negat eam pactionem ratam esse, quae, postquam ipse dictator creatus esset, iniussu suo ab inferioris iuris magistratu facta esset, denuntiatque Gallis, ut se ad proelium expediant . . . Instruit deinde aciem, ut 10loci natura patiebatur, in semirutae solo urbis et natura inaequali, et omnia, quae arte belli secunda suis eligi praepararive poterant, providit. Galli nova re trepidi arma capiunt, iraque magis quam consilio in Romanos incurrunt. Primo concursu haud 15maiore momento fusi Galli sunt, quam ad Alliam vicerant. Iustiore altero deinde proelioad octavum lapidem Gabina via, quo se ex fuga contulerant, eiusdem ductu auspicioque Camilli vincuntur. Ibi caedes omnia obtinuit; castra capiuntur, et ne 20nuntius quidem cladis relictus. Dictator recuperata ex hostibus patria triumphans in urbem redit, interque iocos militares, quos inconditos iaciunt, Romulus ac parens patriae conditorque alter urbis haud vanis laudibus appellabatur.25

61

Context. The Romans on the Capitol, despairing of outside help, agreed with Brennus that Rome should be redeemed by a ransom of 1000 pounds of gold. *Nondum omnni auro appenso*, Camillus appeared at the head of his troops.

3 **per altercationem** = *owing to the dispute*. When the Consular Tribune Sulpicius complained that the Gauls used unjust weights, Brennus in derision threw his sword into the scale and said *Vae victis!*

13-14 **nova re** = *at the change in their fortunes.*—Whibley.

15-16 **haud maiore momento** = *with no greater difficulty(effort).*

17 **Iustiore altero proelio** = *in a second and more regular engagement.*— W.

23 **inconditos** = *rough, unpolished.*

'The Gaul shall come against thee
From the land of snow and night:
Thou shalt give his fair-haired armies
To the raven and the kite.'—Macaulay.

86

D₂₇

THE INVASION OF THE GAULS, 390 B.C. (6)

A. **The Migration to Veii abandoned.**

Movisse eos Camillus cum alia oratione tum ea, quae ad religiones pertinebat, maxime dicitur; sed rem dubiam decrevitvox opportune missa, quod, cum senatus post paulo de his rebus in curia Hostilia haberetur, cohortesque ex praesidiis revertentes forte 5agmine forum transirent, centurio in comitio exclamavit: 'Signifer, statue signum; hic manebimus optime.' Qua voce audita et senatus accipere se omen ex curia egressus conclamavit, et plebs circumfusa approbavit. Antiquata deinde lege promiscue10urbs aedificari coepta.

1 **cum alia tum** = *especially*
ea = *ea parte orationis.*

3 **vox opportune missa** = *a phrase seasonably let fall.*

10 **Antiquata deinde lege** (= *rogatione*) = *the proposed law was then rejected*, **antiquare** = *to leave in its former state.*

B. **Juno forbids the Rebuilding of Troy.**

'Sed bellicosis fata Quiritibus
Hac lege dico, ne nimium pii
Rebusque fidentes avitae
60
Tecta velint reparare Troiae.
'Troiae renascens alite lugubri
Fortuna tristi clade iterabitur,
Ducente victrices catervas
64
Coniuge me Iovis et sorore.'

58 **hac lege** = *on this condition*, i.e. that Rome should always be the capital.
nimium pii = *too dutiful* to their mother-city Troy.

58-60 **ne . . . reparare Troiae.** There was a rumour, even in Caesar's time (v. Suet. *Iul. Caes.* 79) that he meant to migrate to Alexandria or Ilium. Horace, prob. with the sanction of Augustus, sets himself to discourage it. Cf. the Speech of Camillus, Livy, v. 51-54.

61-62 **Troiae . . . iterabitur** = the *fortunes of Troy, if with evil omen it is called to life again* (**renascens**), *shall be repeated in an overthrow as sad as before.*—Wickham.

'The Burning of Rome by the Gauls involved the destruction of all the existing records, and great loss of property. Yet in spite of all the damage done, the Romans set to work to establish the state anew, to rebuild the City, and to reassert their commanding position among their allies and neighbours.'—Ihne.

The Speech of Camillus. Its object was to show the growth of Rome under the guidance of Providence. Cf. the purpose of the *Aeneid*.

87

D₂₈

THE LICINIAN LAWS, 376-366 B.C. (1)

First Plebeian Consul, *366 B.C.*

Occasio videbatur rerum novandarum propter ingentem vim aeris alieni, cuius levamen mali plebes nisi suis in summo imperiolocatis, nullum speraret: accingendum ad eam cogitationem esse; conando agendoque iam eo gradum fecisse plebeios, unde, 5si porro annitantur, pervenire ad summa et patribus aequari tam honore quam virtute possent. In praesentia tribunes plebis fieri placuit, quo in magistratu sibimet ipsi viam ad ceteros honores aperirent. Creatique tribuni C. Licinius et L. Sextius promulgavere10leges omnes adversus opes patriciorum et pro commodis plebis, unam de aere alieno, ut deducto eo de capite, quod usuris pernumeratum esset, id, quod superesset, triennio aequis pensionibus persolveretur; alteram de modo agrorum, ne quis plus quingenta 15iugera agri possideret; tertiam, ne tribunorum militumcomitia fierent, consulumque utique alter ex plebe crearetur; cuncta ingentia et quae sine certamine maximo obtineri non possent. . . . Ita ab diutina ira tandem in concordiam redacti sunt ordines.20

LIVY, vi. 35.

1 **Occasio.** This, so Livy tells us, was the jealousy between the Fabian sisters, the one married to the patrician Sulpicius, the other to the plebeian Licinius Stolo.

1-2 **propter . . . alieni.** The old Roman law of debt was very harsh and severe.

3 **in summo imperio,** i.e. the Consulate.

4 **accingendum . . . esse** = *they must brace themselves to the execution of that idea.*— R. **accingendum,** reflexive here.

5 **iam eo,** i.e. to the office of Consular Tribune, created 444B.C.

6 **si porro annitantur** = *if they* **now** *make a further effort.* This use of Pres. Subj. in Or. Obl. frequent in Livy.

7 **tam honore quam virtute** = *in official rank as (they were already) in merit.*—Rawlins.

12-14 **ut deducto . . . persolveretur** = *'after deducting from the amount of the loan* (**capite** = *principal*) *what had been paid in interest, the balance should be paid in three equal instalments.'*—Cluer and Matheson.

15 **de modo agrorum** = *relating to the limitation of land-holding.*

16-17 **tribunorum militum** (sc. *cum consulari potestate*) created 444 B.C., but no plebeian obtained that honour till 400 B.C., and only two after that date.

17 **utique** = *one at any rate.*

Result. 'The principle was established that Patricians and Plebeians were both citizens of the State, and equally eligible to the honours and dignities of the Republic.'—Ihne.

88

D₂₉

THE LICINIAN LAWS, 376-366 B.C. (2)

The Origin of the Floralia, *238 B.C.*

'Dic, dea,' respondi, 'ludorum quae sit origo.'
Vix bene desieram; rettulit illa mihi:
'Cetera luxuriae nondum instrumenta vigebant:
4
Aut pecus, aut latam dives habebat humum;
Hinc etiam locuples, hinc ipsa pecunia dicta est.
Sed iam de vetito quisque parabat opes.
Venerat in morem populi depascere saltus;
8
Idque diu licuit, poenaque nulla fuit.
Vindice servabat nullo sua publica vulgus;
Iamque in privato pascere inertis erat.
Plebis ad aediles perducta licentia talis
12
Publicios: animus defuit ante viris.
Rem populus recipit: multam subiere nocentes:
Vindicibus laudi publica cura fuit.
Multa data est ex parte mihi, magnoque favore
16
Victores ludos instituere novos.
Parte locant Clivum, qui tunc erat ardua rupes:
Utile nunc iter est. Publiciumque vocant.'

OVID, *Fasti*, v. 237-254, H.

2 **illa**, i.e. *Flora*, the Roman goddess of Flowers and Spring.

3 **luxuriae instrumenta** = *appliance of luxury.*

5 **locuples** (*locus* + *plenus*) = *rich in lands.*

pecunia from **pecus**, *cattle* being in olden time the chief form of wealth and the chief medium of exchange. For**pecus**, cf. *fee, fief, feudal.*

7 **Venerat . . . saltus** = *it had grown into a custom to feed(cattle) on the public forest-pastures.* (Cf. the ager publicus.) H.

9 **sua publica** = *their common property*, i.e. their interest in the public land.

vulgus here = *the commons*, not the *plebs* as opposed to the *populus.*

10 **inertis erat** = *it was the mark of a man wanting in spirit.*

12 **Publicios.** L. and M. Publicius Malleolus,* plebeian aediles, B.C. 241.

animus . . . viris, i.e. information had before been given but no aedile dared to act upon it.

13 **recipit** = *takes up the charge at the Comitia.*

multam = *a fine.* Cf. to mulct = to fine.

14 **publica cura** = *their public spirit.*—H.

15 **multa . . . mihi**, i.e. a new Temple was built to Flora near the Circus Maximus.

16 **ludos novos** = *the Floralia.*

17 **Parte locant** (sc. *muniendum*) **Clivum** = *with the (other)part they contract for (the making of) the Clivus*, a sloping road, called the Clivus Publicius, which led up to the Aventine.

* For Malleolus, cf. Charles Martel of France, 'The Hammer' circ. 689-741 A.D.

89

D₃₀

THE CONQUEST OF ITALY, 366-266 B.C.
SECOND INVASION OF THE GAULS, 361 B.C.

Manlius and his son Torquatus.

L. Manlio, cum dictator fuisset, M. Pomponius tribunus plebisdiem dixit, quod is paucos sibi dies ad dictaturam gerendam addidisset; criminabatur etiam, quod Titum filium, qui postea estTorquatus appellatus, ab hominibus relegasset et ruri habitare5iussisset. Quod cum audivisset adulescens filius negotium exhiberi patri, accurrisse Romam et cum prima luce Pomponii domum venisse dicitur. Cui cum esset nuntiatum, qui illum iratum allaturum ad se aliquid contra patrem arbitraretur, surrexit e 10lectuloremotisque arbitris ad se adulescentem iussit venire. At ille, ut ingressus est, confestim gladium destrinxit iuravitque se illum statim interfecturum, nisi ius iurandum sibi dedisset se patremmissum esse facturum. Iuravit hoc terrore coactus Pomponius; 15rem ad populum detulit, docuit cur sibi causa desistere necesse esset, Manlium missum fecit. Tantum temporibus illis ius iurandum valebat. Atque hic T. Manlius is est, qui ad Anienem Galli, quem ab eo provocatus occiderat, torque detracto cognomen 20invenit,cuius tertio consulatu Latini ad Veserim fusi et fugati.

CICERO, de Officiis, iii. § 112.

1 **L. Manlio**, i.e. L. Manlius Capitolinus Imperiosus, appointed Dictator 363 B.C. 'to drive in a nail (*clavi figendi causa*) on the right side of the Temple of Jupiter, to mark the number of the year, because written documents were rare in those times.'

2 **diem dixit** = *named a day (for his trial before the Comitia).*

4-6 **quod Titum filium . . . iussisset.** Livy, vii. 4, says 'And for what offence? Because he was a little slow of speech and not ready with his tongue.'

4 **Torquatus**, Dictator 353 and 349 B.C., and three times Consul.

6 **negotium exhiberi patri** = lit. *that trouble was being brought upon his father*, i.e. *that his father was in trouble.*

9-10 **qui arbitraretur** = *inasmuch as he thought.* Adject. causal clause.—Holden.

11 **remotis arbitris** = *when he had put out of the room all witnesses.*—H. **arbiter*** = (ar = ad + bito = eo) = spectator, umpire.

14-15 **missum facturum** = *would set at liberty.*

19 **ad Anienem Galli.** On this, their second invasion, the Gauls advanced as far as the Anio. Livy tells us that after the death of their champion the Gauls fled under cover of night.

21-22 **cuius . . . fugati**, i.e. the great battle of Vesuvius fought 340 B.C. by the Veseris, a R. in Campania near Mount Vesuvius, which established for ever the supremacy of Rome over Latium.

Parallel Passage. Livy, vii. 4, 5, 9, 10.

* Cf. *arbiter pugnae, bibendi*, Horace.

90

D₃₁

64

FIRST SAMNITE WAR, 343-341 B.C. (1)

An Important Epoch in Roman History.

Maiora iam hinc bella et viribus hostium et longinquitate vel regionum vel temporum, quibus bellatum est, dicentur. Namque eo anno adversus Samnites, gentem opibus armisque validam, mota arma; Samnitium bellum ancipiti Marte gestum 5Pyrrhus hostis, Pyrrhum Poeni secuti. Quanta rerum moles! quoties in extrema periculoram ventum, ut in hanc magnitudinem, quae vix sustinetur, erigi imperium posset! Belli autem causa cum Samnitibus Romanis, cum societate amicitiaque iuncti essent,10extrinsecus venit, non orta inter ipsos est.

Samnites Sidicinisiniusta arma, quia viribus plus poterant, cum intulissent, coacti inopes ad opulentiorum auxilium confugere Campanis sese coniungunt. Campani magis nomen ad praesidium sociorum quam15vires cum attulissent, fluentes luxu ab duratis usu armorum in Sidicino pulsi agro, in se deinde molem omnem belli verterunt. Namque Samnites, omissis Sidicinis ipsam arcem finitimorum Campanos adorti, unde aeque facilis victoria, praedae atque gloriae 20plus esset, Tifata, imminentes Capuae colles, cum praesidio firmo occupassent, descendunt inde quadrato agmine in planitiem, quae Capuam Tifataque interiacet. Ibi rursus acie dimicatum; adversoque proelio Campani intra moenia compulsi, cum robore iuventutis 25suae acciso nulla propinqua spes esset, coacti sunt ab Romanis petere auxilium.

LIVY, vii. 29.

1 **iam hinc**, i.e. 343-266 B.C.

2 **longinquitate . . . temporum** = *the distance of the theatre of war* (**regionum**) *and the length of the campaign*(**temporum**).—Rawlins.

6-7 **quanta rerum moles** = *What stupendous exertions!*—R.

8 **in hanc magnitudinem**, i.e. in the reign of Augustus.

10 **cum societate**, i.e. from 354 B.C.

12 **Sidicinis**, a Sabellian people N.W. of Campania, on the Samnite border.

16 **fluentes (luxu)** = *enervated* (lit. *relaxed*) by luxury.

21 **Tifăta** (neut. Plur.), a mountain range N.E. of Capua.

22-23 **quadrato agmine** = *in regular order of battle*, so that the whole army formed a parallelogram.

The Cause of the War. 'The interference of Rome was a breach of the Treaty with the Samnites. Livy admits this, but asserts that Capua had formally surrendered to Rome, and as a subject state claimed her protection. The story is confessedly false, for Capua remained, what it had always been, an independent town.'—R.

91

D32

FIRST SAMNITE WAR, 343-341 B.C. (2)

Battle of Mt. Gaurus.

M. Valerius Corvus.

Non alias militi familiarior dux fuit, omnia inter infimos militumhaud gravate munia obeundo. In ludo praeterea militari, cum velocitatis viriumque inter se aequales certamina ineunt, comiter facilis; vincere ac vinci vultu eodem, nec quemquam aspernari5parem, qui se offerret; factis benignus pro re, dictis haud minus libertatis alienae quam suae dignitatis memor, et, quo nihil popularius est, quibus artibus petierat magistratus, iisdem gerebat. Itaque universus exercitus incredibili alacritate adhortationem10prosecutus ducis castris egreditur. . . . Primus omnium consul invadit hostem et, cum quo forte contulit gradum, obtruncat. Hoc spectaculo accensi dextra laevaque ante se quisque memorandum proelium ciet; stant obnixi Samnites, quamquam 15plura accipiunt quam inferunt vulnera. Aliquamdiu iam pugnatum erat, atrox caedes circa signa Samnitium, fuga ab nulladum parte erat; adeo morte sola vinci destinaverant animis. Itaque Romani, cum et fluere iam lassitudine vires sentirent et diei 20haud multum superesse, accensi ira concitant se in hostem. Tum primum referri pedem atque inclinari rem in fugam apparuit; tum capi, occidiSamnis; nec superfuissent multi, ni nox victoriam magis quam proelium diremisset.25

LIVY, vii. 33.

1 **familiarior** = *on better terms with.*—Cluer and Matheson.

2 **haud gravate** = *without reluctance (ungrudgingly)*. Compare Sallust's description of Marius and Sulla.

4 **aequales** = *competitors*, lit. *well-matched.*

  comiter facilis = *he was courteously good-natured.*

6-7 **pro re** = *to suit the occasion.*

9 **artibus iisdem** = *in the same spirit.*—Weissenborn.

11 **prosecutus** = *welcoming*, lit. *attending*.

12-13 **cum . . . gradum** = *with whom he happened to engage*. Cf. *collato pede* = *fighting foot to foot*.

15 **stant obnixi** = *stand their ground firmly*. **obnixus** (**ob** +**nitor**, *strive* + *against*), *resolute*.

23 **Samnis**, nom. sing.

capi, occidi, Historic Infinitives.

25 **diremisset** = *had broken off*. **dirimo** (*dis* + *emo*) = *take apart*.

The Battle of Mt. Gaurus. The battle was fought on the volcanic range of mountains between Cumae and Neapolis. The Consul in command, M. Valerius, obtained the surname of Corvus (Raven), because when serving as a military Tribune under Camillus in 349 B.C., he defeated the Gallic champion by the aid of a raven. See next page, A.l. 4.

92

D₃₃

THE LATIN WAR, 340-338 B.C. (1)

Self-Sacrifice of Decius Mus, *340 B.C.*

A. **Rome's Empire safe in the keeping of Augustus.**

Curtius expletis statuit monimenta lacunis;

64

At Decius misso proelia rupit equo;

Coclitis abscissos testatur semita pontes:

Est cui cognomen corvus habere dedit.

Haec di condiderunt, haec di quoque moenia servant:

68

Vix timeat, salvo Caesare, Roma Iovem.

PROPERTIUS, III. (IV.) xi. (x.) 63-68.

63 **Curtius . . . lacunis**, in allusion to the spot called *Lacus Curtius* (marked by a circular pavement) in the Forum which served as a memorial (*monimenta*) of his heroic sacrifice. Livy, vii. 6.

lacuna (cf. *lacus*) = *a hole, pool, chasm*.

65 **semita** (*sed* + *meo* = *go* + *aside*) = *a path, road*. Cocles, apparently, gave his name to the street running up from the bridge which he 'kept so well.'—Ramsay.

66 **cui**, i.e. M. Valerius Corvus, the hero of Mt. Gaurus. Seep. 91.

67-68 i.e. *with Caesar (Augustus) safe*, Rome has none to fear, nay, scarce Jove himself. Flattery can go no further than this!

B. **The Dream of the Consuls on the Eve of Battle.**

Illud etiam somnium et magnae admirationis et clari exitus, quod eadem nocte duo consules P. Decius Mus et T. Manlius Torquatus Latino bello gravi ac periculoso non procul a Vesuvi montis radicibus 10positis castris viderunt. Utrique enim quaedam per quietem species praedixit ex altera acie imperatorem, ex altera exercitum dis Manibus matrique Terrae deberi; utrius autem dux copias hostium superque eas sese ipsum devovisset, victricemabituram. Id 15luce proxima consulibus sacrificio vel expiaturis, si posset averti, vel, si certum deorum etiam monitu visum foret, exsecuturis, hostiarum exta somnio congruerunt, convenitque inter eos, cuius cornu prius laborare coepisset, ut is capite suo fata patriae lueret. 20Quae neutro reformidante Decium depoposcerunt.

VALERIUS MAXIMUS, i. *De Somniis*.

13 **Dis Manibus** = *the deified souls of the dead*, usually looked upon as beneficent spirits.

15 **victricem**, sc. *aciem*.

17 **deorum etiam monitu** = *by the warning of the gods also*, i.e. by the auspices as well as by the dream.

19-20 **cuius cornu . . . coepisset.** The left wing led by Decius was repulsed by the Latins, and Decius accordingly devoted himself to death.

Parallel Passage. Livy, viii. 6. 9.

93

D₃₄

THE LATIN WAR, 340-338 B.C. (2)

The Battle of Mt. Vesuvius, *340 B.C.*

Procedente deinde certamine cum aliis partibus multitudo superaret Latinorum, Manlius consul audito eventu collegae paulisper addubitavit, an consurgendi iam triariis tempus esset; deinde melius ratus integros eos ad ultimum discrimen servari,5Accensos ab novissima acie ante signa procedere iubet. Qui ubi subiere, extemplo Latini, tamquam idem adversarii fecissent, triarios suos excitaverunt; qui aliquamdiu pugna atroci cum et semet ipsi fatigassent et hastas aut

66

praefregissent aut hebetassent,10pellerent vi tamen hostem, debellatum iam rati perventumque ad extremam aciem, tum consul triariis 'Consurgite nunc' inquit 'integri adversus fessos, memores patriae parentumque et coniugum ac liberorum, memores consulis pro vestra victoria15morte occubantis.' Ubi triarii consurrexerunt, integri, refulgentibus armis, nova ex improviso exorta acies, receptis in intervalla ordinum antepilanis, clamore sublato principia Latinorum perturbant hastisque ora fodientes primo robore virorum caeso per alios manipulos 20velut inermes prope intacti evasere tantaque caede perrupere cuneos, ut vix quartam partem relinquerent hostium.

LIVY, viii. 10.

3-4 **an consurgendi . . . esset.** Livy says 'The Triarii were posted crouching by the standards, their left leg extended forwards, holding their shields resting on their shoulders, and their spears fixed in the ground with the points erect, so that their line bristled as if enclosed by a rampart.'

6 **Accensos.** The *Accensi* (*ad* + *censeo*), originally supernumeraries to take the place of those who fell in battle, = *levis armatura.*

ante signa, i.e. of the Hastati and Principes.

8 **excitaverunt** = *surgere iusserunt.*—Weissenborn.

10 **hebetassent** = *had blunted.*

18 **antepilanis** = *prop.* both the Hastati and Principes who were drawn up before the Pilani or Triarii who formed the third line.

19 **principia** = *the front line,* now the Triarii of the Latins.

22 **cuneos** = *columns* (lit. *wedges*), i.e. a body of soldiers drawn up in the shape of a wedge. Livy uses it of the phalanx.

The Cause of the War. The war was almost a civil one. The dispute was chiefly about a right to share in the privileges of the full Roman citizenship (espec. the right to vote and to hold office).

Result of the War. Rome broke up the Latin Confederation by making separate treaties with the Latin towns, and by prohibiting commercial intercourse between them.

94
D35

SECOND SAMNITE WAR, 326-304 B.C. (1)

The Dictator and his Master of the Horse.

Ea fortuna pugnae fuit, ut nihil relictum sit, quo, si adfuissetDictator, res melius geri potuerit; non dux militi, non miles duci defuit. Eques etiam, auctore L. Cominio tribuno militum, qui aliquotiens impetu capto perrumpere non poterat hostium agmen,5detraxit frenos equis atque ita concitatos calcaribus permisit, ut sustinere eos nulla vis posset; per arma, per viros late stragem dedere; secutus pedes impetum equitum turbatis hostibus intulit signa. Viginti milia hostium caesa eo die traduntur. Magister equitum, 10ut ex tanta caede, multis potitus spoliis congesta in ingentem acervum hostilia arma subdito igne concremavit, seu votum id deorum cuiquam fuit, seu credere libet Fabio auctori eo factum, ne suae gloriae fructum Dictator caperet nomenque ibiscriberet aut 15spolia in triumpho ferret. Litterae quoque de re prospere gesta ad senatum, non ad Dictatorem missae argumentum fuere minima cum eo communicantis laudes. Ita certeDictator id factum accepit, ut laetis aliis victoria parta prae se ferret iram tristitiamque.20

LIVY, viii, 30.

2 **Dictator** = L. Papirius Cursor, noted for the strictness of his military discipline. At this time he had gone to Rome to take the auspices anew (*ad auspicium repetendum*) and had given strict orders to his Master of the Horse, Q. Fabius Rullianus, to avoid all collision with the enemy during his absence.

7 **permisit** = *gave them their heads.* Cf. *immittere habenas.*

9 **turbatis . . . signa** = *attacked the enemy* (dative) *when in confusion.*

11 **spoliis,** i.e. the *arms* taken from the fallen.

13-14 **seu credere . . . factum** = lit. *or whether one prefer to credit the authority of Fabius that it was done on this account* (**eo**) . . . **Fabius Pictor**, the earliest Roman historian, wrote in Greek and served in the 2nd Punic War.

15 **ibi** (sc. *hostilia arma*) = *on them.* These, set up as a trophy with the victor's name inscribed, would have been borne in the triumphal procession.

19 **Ita certe . . . accepit** = *so* (**ita**) *no doubt the Dictator interpreted his* (Fabius') *action.*

The Cause of the War. The actual *casus belli* was a dispute between Rome and the Samnites for the possession of Palaeopolis (= *old city*) near Neapolis (= *new city*). Cf. the First Punic War, 241 B.C., due to the struggle for the possession of Messana, and the war with Pyrrhus, 281 B.C., for the possession of Tarentum.

67

Historic Parallel. Fabius Cunctator and Minucius.—Livy, xxii. 24-30.

95

D₃₆

SECOND SAMNITE WAR, 326-304 B.C. (2)

The Caudine Forks, *321 B.C.*

Duae ad Luceriam ferebant viae, altera praeter oram superi maris, patens apertaque, sed quanto tutior, tanto fere longior, altera perFurculas Caudinas, brevior; sed ita natus locus est. Saltus duo alti, angusti silvosique sunt, montibus circa perpetuis 5inter se iuncti. Iacet inter eos satis patens, clausus in medio, campus herbidus aquosusque, per quem medium iter est; sed antequam venias ad eum, intrandae primae angustiae sunt, et aut eadem, qua teinsinuaveris, retro via repetenda, aut, si ire 10porro pergas, per alium saltum, artiorem impeditioremque, evadendum. In eum campum via alia per cavam rupem Romani demisso agmine cum ad alias angustias protinus pergerent, saeptas deiectu arborum saxorumque ingentium obiacente mole 15invenere. Cum fraus hostilis apparuisset, praesidium etiam in summo saltu conspicitur. Citatiinde retro, qua venerant, pergunt repetere viam; eam quoque clausam sua obice armisque inveniunt. Sistunt inde gradum sine ullius imperio, intuentesque alii alios 20diu immobiles silent.

LIVY, ix. 2.

1 **ad Luceriam** = *in the direction of Luceria*, a town in Apulia on the borders of Samnium, and now threatened by the Samnites.

1-2 **praeter . . . maris** = *along the coast of the upper sea*, i.e. the Adriatic. Taking this route, they would go N. of Samnium, through the Peligni, and S. through the Frentani into Apulia.

3 **fere** = *just.*

3-4 **Furculas Caudinas**, two *fork-shaped* defiles near Caudium, the capital of the Caudine Samnites, between Beneventum and Capua on what was afterwards the *Via Appia.*

5-6 **montibus . . . iuncti** = *united by a continuous ring*(**perpetuis circa**) *of mountains.*

10 **insinuaveris** = lit. *have wound your way.*

11-12 **artiorem impeditioremque** = *more narrow and more difficult* (i.e. *steeper*).

13 **per cavam rupem** = *through an overhanging rocky defile.*

demisso agmine = *with their troops led down* (the descent).

14 **protinus** = *straightforward.*

14-15 **deiectu . . . mole** = lit. '*a barrier lying in the way*(*formed*) *by the throwing down of trees and large pieces of rock.*'

mole = an *abattis* (a *knocking down, felling*).—Rawlins.

16 **cum fraus . . .** = *no sooner had . . . when . . .*

17 **citati** = *hurriedly* (in hot haste). Partic. used adverbially.—Stephenson.

19 **sua obice** = *with a barrier of its own* (i.e. specially prepared).

96

D₃₇

SECOND SAMNITE WAR, 326-304 B.C. (3)

The Caudine Forks.

The Yoke.

Alii alios intueri, contemplari arma mox tradenda et inermes futuras dextras obnoxiaque corpora hosti; proponere sibimet ipsi ante oculos iugum hostile et ludibria victoris et vultus superbos et per armatos inermium iter, inde foedi agminis miserabilem viam5per sociorum urbes, reditum in patriam ad parentes, quo saepe ipsi maioresque eorum triumphantes venissent: se solos sine vulnere, sine ferro, sine acie victos: sibi non stringere licuisse gladios, non manum cum hoste conferre; sibi nequicquam animos datos. 10Haec frementibus hora fatalis ignominiae advenit, omnia tristioraexperiundo factura, quam quae praeceperant animis. Iam primum cum singulis vestimentis inermes extra vallum exire iussi, et primi traditi obsides atque in custodiam abducti. Primi 15consules propeseminudi sub iugum missi; tum ut quisque gradu proximus erat, ita ignominiae obiectus; tum deinceps singulae legiones. Ita traductisub iugum et, quod paene gravius erat, per hostium oculos, cum e saltu evasissent, etsi velut ab inferis 20extracti tum primum lucem aspicere visi sunt, tamen ipsa lux ita deforme intuentibus agmen omni morte tristior fuit.

LIVY, ix. 5, 6.

1-10 **intueri; contemplari . . .** = *There they are looking one on another.* . . . By a string of infinitives the picture of a series of actions is put before the reader without the actions being thought of singly.—Lee Warner.

2 **obnoxia** = *at the mercy of* . . .—Rawlins.

68

6 per sociorum urbes, e.g. *Capua.*

11 fatalis ignominiae = *destined for their disgrace.*

12 experiundo = *by experience*; **praeceperant** = *they had anticipated.*

16 seminudi = *with only their tunics on.*

17 gradu = *in rank.*

18 traducti, 'always used in this sense of *disgraceful*exhibition or parade.'—Stephenson.

22-23 ipsa lux . . . fuit = *the very light was to them as they gazed on so hideous a line of march more gloomy than any form of death.*

The Caudine Forks. Other writers state that the Romans were entrapped only after a severe defeat.

'By the side of those names (the Allia and Cannae) there was yet a third in the list of evil days—the name of the Caudine Pass.'—Ihne. Cf. p. 82, B.

Historic Parallels. Livy's account of Trasimene. The Kyber Pass, 1842. The Capitulation of Metz, 1870.

97

D₃₈

SECOND SAMNITE WAR, 326-304 B.C. (4)

Rome repudiates the Treaty.

At vero T. Veturius et Sp. Postumius, cum iterum consules assent, quia, cum male pugnatum apud Caudium esset, legionibus nostris sub iugum missis pacem cum Samnitibus fecerant, dediti sunt eis;iniussu enim populi senatusque fecerant. Eodemque 5tempore Ti. Numicius, Q. Maelius, qui tum tribuni plebis erant, quod eorum auctoritate pax erat facta, dediti sunt, ut pax Samnitium repudiaretur. Atque huius deditionis ipse Postumius, qui dedebatur, suasor et auctor fuit. Quod idem multis annis post10C. Mancinus, qui ut Numantinis, quibuscum sine senatus auctoritate foedus fecerat, dederetur, rogationem suasit eam, quam L. Furius, Sex. Atilius ex senatus consulto ferebant: qua accepta est hostibus deditus. Honestius hic quam Q. Pompeius, quo, 15cum in eadem causa esset, deprecante accepta lex non est. Hic ea, quae videbatur utilitas, plus valuit quam honestas, apud superioresutilitatis species falsa ab honestatis auctoritate superata est.

CICERO, De Officiis, iii. 109.

4 pacem . . . fecerant, i.e. *a military convention*, by which Rome and Samnium were to acknowledge each other as free peoples with equal rights and privileges, and Rome was to give up her conquests and colonies on Samnite territory.

5 iniussu . . . senatusque. 'The Senate considered it in the light of a *sponsio*, a convention made on personal responsibility, rather than a *pactio* or *foedus*, a public treaty.'—Holden.

6 tribuni plebis, prob. only tribunes-elect (= *designati*), for the tribunes could not leave Rome even for one night.

11 C. Mancinus commanded against Numantia in Spain, 137 B.C.

15 Q. Pompeius commanded against Numantia, 140 B.C.

16 cum in eadem causa esset = *though he was in the same case*, as Mancinus, i.e. had made a degrading peace with the Numantines.—H.

15-17 quo . . . deprecante . . . non est = *through his begging to be let off, the law* (i.e. for delivering him up to the enemy) *was not passed.*

17 Hic = *in this case*, i.e. that of Pompeius.

18 apud superiores, i.e. Veturius, Postumius, and Mancinus.

18-19 utilitatis species falsa = *the false semblance of expediency.*

The Repudiation of the Treaty. 'It is clear that Postumius and his brother officers could not bind the Roman Senate and people by the promise they had made in Caudium; but it is equally clear that they were bound by their promise to do what was in their power to cause the treaty to be ratified.'—Ihne.

98

D₃₉

SECOND SAMNITE WAR, 326-304 B.C. (5)

Battle of Bovianum, *305 B.C.* Peace made, *304 B.C.*

Eodem anno in campum Stellatem agri Campani Samnitium incursiones factae. Itaque ambo consules in Samnium missi cum diversas regiones, Tifernum Postumius, Bovianum Minuciuspetisset, Postumii prius ductu ad Tifernum pugnatum. Alii 5haud dubie Samnites victos ac viginti milia hominum capta tradunt, alii Marte aequo discessum, et Postumium, metum simulantem, nocturno itinere clam in montes copias abduxisse, hostes secutos duo milia inde locis munitis et ipsos consedisse. Consul ut 10stativa tuta copiosaque petisse videretur, postquam et munimentis castra firmavit et omni apparatu rerum utilium instruxit, relicto firmo praesidio de

vigilia tertia, qua* proxime potest, expeditas legiones ad collegam, et ipsum adversus alios sedentem, ducit. 15Ibi auctore Postumio Minucius cum hostibus signa confert, et, cum anceps proelium in multum diei processisset, tum Postumius integris legionibus defessam iam aciem hostium improviso invadit. Itaque cum lassitudo ac vulnera fugam
quoque praepedissent, 20occidione occisi hostes, signa unum et viginti capta.

LIVY, ix. 44.

* qua *duci* proxime potest.—W. and M.

1 **In campum Stellatem.** Stellas, a part of the Campanian plain, N. of Mt. Tifata (E. of Capua).

4 **Tifernum**, E. of Bovianum on the R. Tifernus.

Postumius . . . Minucius, Consuls 305 B.C.

Bovianum, in Samnium, W. of Luceria (in Apulia).

11 **stativa tuta** = *safe quarters.* Cf. *stativa castra = a stationary camp.*

15 **et ipsum . . . sedentem** = *also lying encamped*(**sedentem**) *in the face of another army.*— Stephenson.

20 **praepedissent** = *hampered,* lit. *to entangle the feet (prae + pes).*

21 **occidione occisi.** This has the force of *a superlative by the repetition,* a common idiom in Oriental† languages.—S.

† E.g. in Hebrew, Delivering I will deliver = I will surely deliver.

Results of the Second Samnite War. Roman influence became supreme in Campania and Apulia, and the Samnites were confined to their own mountains. In 304 B.C. the Romans renewed their ancient Treaty with the Samnites (as Livy tells us) by which they were left in possession of their independence.

Why the Romans conquered. (1) Their conduct of the war was more systematic. (2) By their plan of fortified colonies (e.g. Cales, Fregellae, Luceria) they retained their hold on the conquered territory. (3) The diplomatic skill of the Senate secured the friendship of the neighbours of the Samnites (e.g. the Apulians and Lucanians).

99

D40

THIRD SAMNITE WAR, 298-290 B.C.

Battle of Sentinum, *295 B.C.* 'Novum pugnae genus.'

Ferocior Decius et aetate et vigore animi quantumcunque virium habuit certamine primo effudit. Et quia lentior videbatur pedestris pugna, equitatum in pugnam concitat et ipse fortissimae iuvenum turmae immixtus orat proceres iuventutis, in hostem 5ut secum impetum faciant: duplicem illorum gloriam fore, si ab laevo cornu et ab equite victoria incipiat. Bis avertere Gallicum equitatum; iterum longius evectos et iam inter media peditum agmina proelium cientes novum pugnae conterruit genus: essedis10carrisque superstans armatus hostis ingenti sonitu equorum rotarumque advenit et insolitos eius tumultus Romanorum conterruit eqnos. Ita victorem equitatum velut lymphaticus pavor dissipat; sternit inde ruentes equos virosque improvida fuga,15turbata hinc etiam signa legionum multique impetu equorum ac vehiculorum raptorum per agmen obtriti antesignani; et insecuta, simul territos hostes vidit, Gallica acies nullum spatium respirandi recipiendique se dedit.20

LIVY, x. 28.

1 **Decius.** P. Decius Mus, Consul with Q. Fabius Maximus Rullianus, commanded the left wing at the Battle of Sentinum, where he was opposed to the Gauls, and when his troops began to give way before the Gaulish chariots (**essedae**) he, like his father at the Battle of Vesuvius, 340 B.C., devoted* himself with the hostile army 'to the gods of earth and of the grave.'

5 **proceres iuventutis** = *the flower of the young men.*

8 **avertere** (= **se avertere**) = *to retire* (lit. *turn away*).

10 **essedis** = *war-chariots*, on two wheels, open in front, but closed behind, and drawn by two horses; used also by the Britons.

14 **lymphaticus** = *mad, frenzied.*

16 **turbata . . . signa legionum** = *the ranks of the legions were thrown into disorder.* **Signa** is frequently used of military movement, as the most noticeable feature in an army.

* Cf. pp. 92, 93.

The Cause of the Third Samnite War. The democratic party among the Lucanians made overtures to the Samnites. The Romans peremptorily ordered the Samnites not to interfere in Lucania, an arrogant command which the Samnites declined to obey, and war broke out anew.

Results of the War. After an obstinate struggle peace was concluded in 290 B.C., the Samnites retaining their independence.

100

THE WAR WITH THE TARENTINES AND PYRRHUS, 281-275 B.C. (1)

The Aims of Pyrrhus.

Battle of Heraclea, *280 B.C.*

Pyrrhus rex Epiri cum iterata Tarentinorum legatione additis Samnitium et Lucanorum precibus, fatigaretur, non tam supplicum precibus quam spe invadendi Italiae imperii inductus venturum se cum exercitu pollicetur. In quam rem inclinatum semel 5animum praecipitem agere coeperant exempla maiorum, ne aut inferiorpatruo suo Alexandro videretur, quo defensore idem Tarentini adversus Bruttios usi fuerant, aut minores animos magno Alexandro habuisse, qui tam longa a domo militia Orientem subegerat. 10Igitur relicto custode regni Ptolemaeo filio annos xv nato exercitum in portu Tarentino exponit. Cuius audito adventu consul Romanus Valerius Laevinus festinans, ut prius cum eo congrederetur, quam auxilia sociorum convenirent, exercitum in15aciem educit. Nec rex, tametsi numero militum inferior esset, certamini moram fecit. Sed Romanos vincentes iam inusitata ante elephantorum forma stupere primo, mox cedere proelio coegit, victoresque iam nova Macedonum repente monstra vicerunt. 20Nec hostibus incruenta victoria fuit. Nam et Pyrrhus ipse graviter vulneratus est, et magna pars militum eius caesa, maioremque gloriam eius victoriae quam laetitiam habuit.

JUSTINUS, xviii. 1.

1 **iterata legatione** = *by a second embassy.*

3 **fatigaretur** = *was importuned.*

3-4 **non tam . . . inductus.** Pyrrhus aimed at founding a western Grecian Empire in Italy and Sicily.

7-9 **patruo suo Alexandro . . . fuerant.** Alexander of Epirus had almost succeeded in uniting the whole of Magna Graecia (332-326 B.C.) when he was cut off by the hand of an assassin.

9 **magno Alexandro.** Pyrrhus was acknowledged to be the first general of the school of Alexander, and Hannibal (so Plutarch tells us) considered him the greatest military genius.

18 **inusitata ante . . . forma** = *the unfamiliar appearance of.*

22-23 **magna pars militum.** Pyrrhus is said to have lost 4000 men, 'a serious matter to him in a foreign country, where he could not easily replace the loss of his tried old warriors.'— Ihne.

Cause of the War. By 282 B.C. Rome had taken possession of Magna Graecia, with the exception of Tarentum. In 282B.C. (in defiance of the treaty of 301 B.C.) a Roman fleet appeared before the Harbour of Tarentum. A naval battle ensued in which the Tarentines were victorious, and the war began.

101

THE WAR WITH THE TARENTINES AND PYRRHUS. (2)

Fabricius the Just.

Honesty before Expediency.

Cum rex Pyrrhus populo Romano bellum ultro intulisset, cumquede imperio certamen esset cum rege generoso ac potenti, perfugaab eo venit in castra Fabricii eique est pollicitus, si praemium sibi proposuisset, se, ut clam venisset, sic clam in Pyrrhi 5castra rediturum et eum veneno necaturum. Hunc Fabricius reducendum curavit ad Pyrrhum idque eius factum laudatum a senatu est.Atqui, si speciem utilitatis opinionemque quaerimus, magnum illud bellum perfuga unus et gravem adversarium imperi10sustulisset, sed magnum dedecus et flagitium, quicum laudis certamen fuisset, eum non virtute sed scelere superatum. Utrum igitur utilius vel Fabricio, qui talis in hac urbe qualis Aristides Athenis fuit, vel senatui nostro, qui numquam utilitatem a dignitate 15seiunxit, armis cum hoste certare an venenis? Si gloriae causa imperium expetendum est, scelus absit, in quo non potest esse gloria: sin ipsae opes expetuntur quoquo modo, non poterunt utiles esse cum infamia.20

CICERO, *De Officiis*, iii. 86, 87.

1-2 **bellum ultro intulisset** = *had begun an aggressive*(**ultro**) *war.*

ultro = lit. *to a place beyond*, hence = *beyond expectation, unprovoked.*

2 **de imperio** = *uter imperaret.*—Holden.

3 **perfuga** = *a deserter.* Aulus Gellius says the traitor was Nicias, a friend of Pyrrhus; Florus and Eutropius, a physician of Pyrrhus.

8 **atqui** = *and yet*, a more emphatic **at.**

8-9 **speciem utilitatis opinionemque** (sc. **utilitatis**) = *the semblance and (popular) opinion of expediency.*—H.

11-13 **sed magnum . . . superatum** = *but it would have been a lasting disgrace and scandal for a general, with whom the struggle lay for glory, to have been overcome by an act of wickedness and not by valour.*—H.

14 **Aristides Athenis.** Aristides the Just. 'Sans Peur et sans Reproche.'

19 **quoquo modo** = *in any way.* Cf. *quacumque ratione.*—H.

Parallel Passage. Eutropius ii. 7. 8. 14: *Tum Pyrrhus admiratus eum dixisse fertur: 'Ille est Fabricius, qui difficilius ab honestate quam sol a cursu suo averti potest.'*

Fabricius, like Cincinnatus and M'. Curius Dentatus, is the representative of the purity and honesty of the good old times.

102

D₄₃

THE WAR WITH THE TARENTINES AND PYRRHUS. (3)

Appius the Blind, *280 B.C.*

Ad Appi Claudi senectutem accedebat etiam ut caecus esset;tamen is, cum sententia senatus inclinaret ad pacem cum Pyrrho foedusque faciendum, non dubitavit dicere illa, quae versibus persecutus est Ennius:5

Quo vobis mentes, rectae quae stare solebant
Antehac, dementis sese flexere viai?

ceteraque gravissime, notum enim vobis carmen est, et tamen ipsius Appi exstat oratio. Atque haec ille egit septemdecim annis post alterum consulatum, 10cum inter duos consulatus anni decem interfuissent censorque ante superiorem consulatum fuisset, ex quo intelligitur Pyrrhi bello grandem sane fuisse. . . . Quattuor robustos filios, quinque filias, tantam domum, tantas clientelasAppius regebat et caecus 15et senex; intentum enim animum tamquam arcum habebat nec languescens succumbebat senectuti. Tenebat non modo auctoritatem, sed etiam imperium in suos:metuebant servi, verebantur liberi, carum omnes habebant; vigebat in illo animus 20patrius et disciplina.

CICERO, De Senectute, §§ 16, 37.

1 **Appi Claudi.** This was the Appius Claudius whose Censorship, 312 B.C., was famous for his great public works, the **Via Appia**, the great South road of Rome, and the **Aqua Appia**, an aqueduct which brought water to Rome a distance of eight miles; and also for his measure (corresponding to a Parliamentary Reform Bill) admitting freedmen as full citizens by enrolling them in Tribes.

2-9 **tamen is . . . exstat oratio.** When the Senate was about to yield to the persuasive eloquence of Cineas, the envoy of Pyrrhus, he had himself led into the Senate-house to make the speech which turned the scale against the invader.

4 **versibus persecutus est** = *has followed out in the lines.* J. S. R.

7 **viai** (= *viae* old genit.) = i. *quo viae*, cf. *ubi terrarum*, or ii. *sese flexere viae*, a Greek genitive.

9-10 **haec ille egit** = *he made this speech.*

14-15 **tantam . . . clientelas** = *a large household, a large number of dependents;* **clientelas = clientes.**

16 **intentum** (*in + tendo*) = *on the stretch.* Cf. opposite*remissus.*

19-21 **metuebant . . . disciplina** = *his slaves feared him, his children stood in awe of him, yet all held him dear; in him ancestral spirit and principles* (**disciplina**) *were strong.*—J. S. Reid.

The Speech of Appius Claudius. For the substance of the Speech, *see* Plutarch, *Pyrrhus,* xi.

103

D₄₄

THE WAR WITH THE TARENTINES AND PYRRHUS. (4)

A. The Battle of Asculum, *279 B.C.*

In Apulia deinde apud Asculum melius dimicatum est Curio Fabricioque consulibus. Iam quippe terror* beluarum exoleverat, et Gaius Numicius quartae legionis hastatus unius proboscide abscisa mori posse beluas ostenderat. Itaque in ipsas pila congesta sunt 5et in turres vibratae faces tota hostium agmina ardentibus ruinis operuerunt. Nec alius cladi finis fuit quam nox dirimeret, postremusque fugientium rex ipse a satellitibus umero saucius in armis suis referretur.10

* Cf. p. 100, ll. 17-20.

1 **Asculum**, a town in Apulia on the borders of Samnium, between Beneventum and Canusium.

3 **exoleverat** = *had grown less* (lit. *had grown out of use*).

6 **in turres vibratae faces** = *firebrands hurled against their towers.*

8 **dirimeret** = *separated* (the combatants).

The Battle of Asculum. It is clear that Pyrrhus was again victorious, but the Romans were able to retire into their fortified camp, and so lost fewer men than at Heraclea.

B. The Battle near Beneventum, 275 B.C.

Lucaniae suprema pugna sub Arusinis, quos vocant, campis ducibus isdem quibus superius; sed tum tota victoria. Exitum, quem datura virtus fuit, casus dedit. Nam provectis in primam aciem rursus elephantis unum ex his pullum adacti in caput teli15gravis ictus avertit; qui cum per stragem suorum recurrens stridore quereretur, mater agnovit et quasi vindicaret exsiluit, tum omnia circa quasi hostilia gravi mole permiscuit. Ac sic eaedem ferae, quae primam victoriam abstulerunt, secundam parem 20fecerunt, tertiam sine controversia tradiderunt.

FLORUS, I. xviii. 9-13.

11-12 **Lucaniae . . . campis.** The Battle was fought near Beneventum (orig. **Male-***ventum*, perhaps from *male* + *ventus* on account of its unwholesome air) in Samnium on the Via Appia, E. of Capua.

15-16 **unum ex his . . . avertit** = *the heavy stroke of a weapon driven home* (**adacti**) *into the head of a young elephant* (**pullum**) *made it turn aside.*

19 **gravi mole** = *with her unwieldy bulk.*

The Battle of Beneventum. Pyrrhus, in his attempt to storm the entrenched camp of Curius Dentatus, was obliged to fight on unfavourable ground. The result was a total defeat, and no choice was left him but to give up the unequal contest.

104

D₄₅

THE WAR WITH THE TARENTINES AND PYRRHUS. (5)

Death of Pyrrhus, 272 B.C.

In praise of a great General.

Repulsus ab Spartanis Pyrrhus Argos petit: ibi, dum Antigonum in urbe clausum expugnare conatur, inter confertissimos violentissime dimicans, saxo de muris ictus occiditur. Caput eius Antigono refertur, qui victoria mitius usus filium eius Helenum5cum Epirotis sibi deditum in regnum remisit, eique insepulti patris ossa in patriam referenda tradidit.

Satis constans inter omnes auctores fama est, nullum nec eius nec superioris aetatis regem comparandum Pyrrho fuisse, raroque non inter reges 10tantum, verum etiam inter illustres viros, aut vitae sanctioris aut iustitiae probatioris visum fuisse: scientiam certe rei militaris in illo viro tantam fuisse, ut cum adversus Lysimachum,Demetrium, Antigonum, tantos reges, bella gesserit, invictus15semper fuerit: Illyriorum quoque, Siculorum Romanorumque et Carthaginiensium bellis numquam inferior, plerumque etiam victor exstiterit; qui patriam certe suam angustam ignobilemque fama rerum gestarum et claritate nominis sui toto orbe 20illustrem reddiderit.

JUSTINUS, xxv. 5.

1-4 **Repulsus ab Spartanis . . . occiditur.** At the invitation of Cleonymus, who had been excluded from the throne of Sparta, Pyrrhus undertook and failed in a desperate attack on the city. He then turned against Argos, to wrest it from Antigonus Gonatas of Macedonia, and was hit *by a tile thrown from a roof by a woman.** As he lay helpless on the ground he was recognised and murdered.

8 **Satis constans fama** = *a tolerably unanimous opinion.*

12 **iustitiae probatioris** = *of more eminent* (lit. *tested*)*justice.*

14 **Lysimachum**, one of Alexander's generals. About 286B.C. King of Macedonia and Asia Minor.

Demetrium, surnamed *Poliorcetes* (*stormer of cities*), son of Antigonus, King of Asia (one of Alexander's generals).

16-17 **Siculorum bellis.** During the years 280-276 B.C.Pyrrhus made himself master of all Sicily with the exception of the Carthaginian stronghold of Lilybaeum.

* Cf. the death of Abimelech before Thebez, Judges ix. 53.

Character of Pyrrhus. 'He was not only one of the ablest generals and princes, but amiable also as a man, and worthy of our sympathy and respect.'—Ihne.

Why he failed. 'From lack of accurate information he wholly underestimated the power of Rome. Here was the great error in his calculation, an error for which he can hardly be held responsible.'—Ihne.

Reference. Plutarch, *Pyrrhus.*

105

D₄₆

THE WAR WITH THE TARENTINES AND PYRRHUS. (6)

Manius Curius Dentatus, an old-time Roman.

A.Possum persequi permulta oblectamenta rerum rusticarum, sed ea ipsa quae dixi sentio fuisse longiora. Ignoscetis autem, nam et studio rerum rusticarum provectus sum, et senectus est natura loquacior, ne ab omnibus eam vitiis videar vindicare. 5Ergo in hac vita M'. Curius, cum de Samnitibus, de Sabinis, de Pyrrho triumphavisset, consumpsit extremum tempus aetatis; cuius quidem ego villam contemplans, abest enim non longe a me, admirari satis non possum vel hominis ipsius continentiam 10vel temporum disciplinam. Curio ad focum sedenti magnum auri pondus Samnites cum attulissent, repudiati sunt: non enim aurum habere praeclarum sibi videri dixit, sed eis qui haberent aurum imperare.

CICERO, De Senectute, §§ 55-56.

Context. The speaker is Cato the Censor, 184 B.C., the founder of Latin Prose, whose manual of Agriculture, **de Re Rustica**, is still extant.

1 **Possum persequi** = *I might follow out.*
  oblectamenta = *amusements* (cf. *de-lecto, delight*).
4 **provectus sum** = *I have been carried away.*—J. S. Reid.
8 **extremum tempus aetatis** = *the closing season of his life.*
9 **a me** (= **a mea villa**) = *from my country-house.*
11 **disciplinam** = *morals* (lit. *teaching*).
11-13 After the close of the war Curius had become**patronus** of the Samnites, and they were bringing the customary offering of **clientes**.—J. S. R.

B.
Curius parvo quae legerat horto
Ipse focis brevibus ponebat holuscula.

JUVENAL., xi. 78-79.

78-79 Plutarch, *Cato* 2, tells the story. Curius was one of Milton's
'Men so poor | who could do mighty things.'—Duff.
79 **holuscula** (dimin. of **hŏlus**) = *small herbs or vegetables.*

C.
Hunc et incomptis Curium capillis
Utilem bello tulit et Camillum
Saeva paupertas et avitus apto
44
Cum lare fundus.

HORACE, Odes, I. xii. 41-44.

41 **Hunc** = Fabricius.
42 **paupertas** = *frugality*, not *poverty* (= *egestas*).
43-44 **apto cum lare** = *with its cottage home to match*(**apto**).—W.
'Hurrah! for Manius Curius
The bravest son of Rome,
Thrice in utmost need sent forth,
Thrice drawn in triumph home.'—Macaulay.
106
D47

THE WAR WITH THE TARENTINES AND PYRRHUS. (7)

In Praise of Tarentum.

Unde si Parcae prohibent iniquae,
Dulce pellītis ovibus Galaesi
Flumen et regnata petam Laconi
12
Rura Phalantho.
Ille terrarum mihi praeter omnes
Angulus ridēt, ubi non Hymetto
Mella decedunt viridique certat
16
Baca Venafro,
Ver ubi longum tepidasque praebet
Iuppiter brumas et amicus Aulon
Fertili Baccho minimum Falernis
20
Invidet uvis.

74

Ille te mecum locus et beatae
Postulant arces, ibi tu calentem
Debita sparges lacrima favillam
24
Vatis amici.

HORACE, Odes, II. vi. 9-end.

Subject. 'Septimius, my dear friend who would accompany me to the ends of the earth, let me spend the close of my life at Tibur (Tivoli), or if not there, then at Tarentum. Let us go there together, and live there till I die.'—Wickham.

9 **unde** = *from this place*, i.e. from Tibur.

10 **dulce pellitis ovibus** = *dear to the skin-clad* (**pellitis**)*sheep*, so clad to keep their fleeces clean.—Gow.

10-11 **Galaesi flumen**, flows into the Gulf of Tarentum, near the city.

12 **Phalantho**, an exile from Sparta, founded Tarentum, 708B.C.

13, 21, 22 **Ille** (13) . . . **ille** (21) . . . **ibi** (22) = *Tarentum*, emphatic guiding words. Cf. **te mecum** (21) . . . **tu amici** (22, 24) = *Septimius and Horace*.

14-15 **ubi non . . . decedunt** = *where the honey does not give way to (is not inferior to) that of Hymettus*.

15-16 **viridi Venafro** = *with the green (olive-groves of)Venafrum* (N. of Campania).

16 **Baca** = *the olive*, the noblest of berries.—Gow.

18 **Aulon** = *(the grapes of) Aulon*, a hill and valley near Tarentum.

19 **Fertili** = *who makes the vines fertile*.

22-24 **ibi tu . . . vatis amici.**

'There when life shall end,
Your tear shall dew my yet warm pyre,
Your bard and friend.'—Conington.

Reference. Polybius, x. 1. In 272 B.C. Milo with his garrison of Epirots marched out of Tarentum with all the honours of war.

Rome now ruled supreme over the whole of Italy from Ariminum in the North to the Sicilian Straits.

107

D48

THE PRAISE OF ITALY.

'Salve, magna parens frugum, Saturnia tellus,

Magna virum.'

155
Adde tot egregias urbes operumque laborem,
Tot congesta manu praeruptis oppida saxis,
Fluminaque antiquos subterlabentia muros.
An mare, quod supra, memorem, quodque alluit infra?
Anne lacus tantos? Te, Lari maxime, teque,
160
Fluctibus et fremitu adsurgens Benace marino?
.   .   .   .
165
Haec eadem argenti rivos aerisque metalla
Ostendit venis atque auro plurima fluxit.
Haec genus acre virum, Marsos pubemque Sabellam,
Adsuetumque malo Ligurem, Volscosque verutos
Extulit: haec Decios, Marios, magnosque Camillos,
170
Scipiadas duros bello, et te, maxime Caesar,
Qui nunc extremis Asiae iam victor in oris
Imbellem avertis Romanis arcibus Indum.
Salve, magna parens frugum, Saturnia tellus,
Magna virum: tibi res antiquae laudis et artis
175
Ingredior, sanctos ausus recludere fontes,
Ascraeumque cano Romana per oppida carmen.

VERGIL, Georg. ii. 155-176.

158 **mare quod supra alluit** = the *mare superum* = the Adriatic.

mare quod infra alluit = the *mare inferum* = the Tuscan or Tyrrhenian (Τυρρηνός = Tuscan) sea.

159 **Lari** = Lake Larius (= *Como*), N. of Milan.

160 **Benace** = Lake Benacus (= *Garda*), W. of Verona.

fremitu marino = *with roar as of the sea.*

168 **adsuetum malo** = *trained in hardship.*—Mackail.

Volscosque verutos = *and the Volscian spearmen (light infantry).* **verutos** = armed with the *verutum* (or *veru* = lit. a *spit*), a *javelin.*

170 **Scipiadas**, Greek patronymic form = Lat. *Sāpīōnēs.*

maxime Caesar = Augustus.

171-172 After Actium, 31 B.C., Augustus spent more than a year in reducing and settling the East (**imbellem Indum**) whose forces had been wielded by Antony.—Sidgwick.

173 **Saturnia tellus**, in allusion to Saturn's reign in Latium in the age of gold.

174-175 **tibi res . . . fontes** = *for thee I enter on themes of ancient glory and skill* (i.e. in agriculture) *and dare to unseal* (**recludere**) *the sacred springs*; **res laudis**, the theme of the *Aeneid*, **res artis**, of the *Georgics*.

176 **Ascraeum carmen** = *the song of Ascra*, i.e. the*Georgics*, because Hesiod (author of *Works and Days*to which Vergil is much indebted) was born at Ascra, near Helicon, in Boeotia.—S.

108

C₁

CONTEST WITH CARTHAGE, 264-202 B.C.

The Vision of Anchises.—Rome's Heroes.

'Ille triumphata Capitolia ad alta Corintho
Victor aget currum, caesis insignis Achivis.
Eruet ille Argos Agamemnoniasque Mycenas,
Ipsumque Aeaciden, genus armipotentis Achilli,
840
Ultus avos Troiae, templa et temerata Minervae.
Quis te, magne Cato, tacitum, aut te, Cosse, relinquat?
Quis Gracchi genus, aut geminos, duo fulmina belli,
Scipiadas, cladem Libyae, parvoque potentem
Fabricium, vel te sulco, Serrane, serentem?
845
Quo fessum rapitis, Fabii? Tu Maximus ille es,
Unus qui nobis cunctando restituis rem.'

.   .   .   .

855
'Aspice, ut insignis spoliis Marcellus opimis
Ingreditur, victorque viros supereminet omnes!
Hic rem Romanam, magno turbante tumultu,
Sistet, eques sternet Poenos Gallumque rebellem,
Tertiaque arma patri suspendet capta Quirino.'

VERGIL, Aen. vi. 836-846, 855-859.

836 **Ille** = L. Mummius Achaicus, destroyed Corinth, 146B.C.

838 **Ille** = L. Aemilius Paullus, crushed Perseus (= **Aeaciden**l. 839) at Pydna, 168 B.C.

841 **Cosse** = Cornelius Cossus, won Spolia Opima a second time, 428 B.C.

842 **Gracchi genus**, e.g. (i.) Tib. Sempronius Gracchus, twice Consul 215, 212 B.C., in 2nd Punic War; (ii.) T. S. G. distinguished in Spain; (iii.) the two great Tribunes, Tiberius and Gaius.

843 **Scipiadas** = (i.) Scipio Africanus Maior, victor at Zama, 202 B.C.; (ii.) Scipio Africanus Minor, destroyed Carthage, 146 B.C.

844 **Fabricium**, Consul 282 and 278 B.C. in war with Pyrrhus. Proof against bribes.

Serrane = Regulus, victor at Ecnomus, 256 B.C., a prisoner, 255 B.C. True to his word.

845 **Maximus** = Q. Fabius M. Cunctator, Dictator after Cannae. The Shield of Rome.

846 From the Annals of Ennius (239-169 B.C.), often quoted.

855 **Marcellus**, five times Consul. Took Syracuse 212 B.C.The Sword of Rome.

857 **magno . . . tumultu** = *when a great upheaving shakes it.*—Page.

Tumultus (as Cic. tells us) is specially used of a rising in Italy or in Gaul, as it was close to Italy. (Elsewhere =*bellum.*)

858 **Sistet, . . . sternet.** Notice the antithesis and alliteration (assonance).

The Vision of Anchises is the imperishable record of the national life, where the poet 'sums up in lines like bars of gold the hero-roll of the Eternal City.'—Myers.

109

C₂

FIRST PUNIC WAR, 264-241 B.C.

The Foundation of Carthage, *878 B.C.*

Pygmalion, cognita sororis fuga, cum impio bello fugientem persequi pararet, aegre precibus matris deorumque minis victus quievit. . . . Itaque Elissa delata in Africae sinum incolas eius loci adventu peregrinorum mutuarumque rerum commercio 5gaudentes in amicitiam sollicitat. Dein empto loco, qui corio bovis tegi posset, in quo fessos longa navigatione socios, quoad proficisceretur, reficere posset, corium in tenuissimas partes secari iubet atque ita maius loci spatium, quam petierat, occupat: unde10postea ei loco Byrsae nomen fuit. Confluentibus deinde vicinis locorum, qui spe lucri multa hospitibus venalia inferebant, sedesque ibi statuentibus ex frequentia hominum velut instarcivitatis effectum. est. . . . Itaque consentientibus omnibus Carthago 15conditur, statuto annuo vectigali pro solo urbis. In primis fundamentis caput bubulum inventum est, quod auspicium fructuosae quidem, sed laboriosae perpetuoque servae urbis fuit; propter quod in alium locum urbs translata. Ibi quoque equi caput repertum, 20bellicosum potentemque populum futurum significans, urbi auspicatam sedem dedit. Tunc ad opinionem novae urbis concurrentibus gentibus brevi et populus et civitas magna facta.

JUSTINUS, xviii. 5.

1 **Pygmalion**, King of Tyre, murdered Sychaeus, husband of Elissa (Dido).

4 **sinum** = Gulf of Tunis. (See Murray's Classical Atlas.)

5 **peregrinorum** = *of strangers*. **per** + **ager**. Cf. *pilgrim*. Fr.*pèlerin*.

    mutuarum rerum commercio = *barter*.

11 **Byrsae**, i.e., later, the Citadel quarter, as if from βύρσα = a *hide*, prob. corrupted from Phoen. *Bozra* (= a *fort*). So *Carthage* = *Kirjath* (*city*); cp. *Kirjath-Arba*(Hebron), and *Hannibal* (= Hanniel) = *the grace of Baal*.

14 **velut instar c.** = *as if the semblance of a state*; cf. 'instar montis equus,' Verg.—Post.

17 **bubulum** = *of an ox*, adj. from *bos*.

22 **auspicatam** = *auspicious*, in active sense.

Parallel Passages. Verg. *Aen.* i. 336-368, 418-438, and*Aen.* iv. 21-22.

References. Bosworth Smith, *Carthage and the Carthaginians.*—Ihne, *Hist. of Rome*, vol. ii. pp. 3-21.

110

C₃

FIRST PUNIC WAR, 264-241 B.C.

Aeneas views the Building of Carthage, circ. *878 B.C.*

Iamque ascendebant collem, qui plurimus urbi

420

Imminet adversasque aspectat desuper arces.

Miratur molem Aeneas, magalia quondam,

Miratur portas strepitumque et strata viarum.

Instant ardentes Tyrii pars ducere muros

Molirique arcem et manibus subvolvere saxa,

425

Pars optare locum tecto et concludere sulco;

Iura magistratusque legunt sanctumque senatum;

Hic portus alii effodiunt; hinc lata theatris

Fundamenta locant alii, immanesque columnas

Rupibus excidunt, scaenis decora alta futuris.

430

Qualis apes aestate nova per florea rura

Exercet sub sole labor, cum gentis adultos

Educunt fetus, aut cum līquentia mella

Stipant et dulci distendunt nectare cellas,

Aut onera accipiunt venientum, aut agmine facto

435

Ignavum fucos pecus a praesepibus arcent:

Fervet opus, redolentque thymo fragrantia mella.

'O fortunati, quorum iam moenia surgunt!'

Aeneas ait, et fastigia suspicit urbis.

419 **plurimus** = *in huge mass*, with the predicate **imminet.**

421 **magalia** = *huts*, a Carthaginian (Phoenician) word. Cf.μέγαρον.

422 **strata viarum** = *stratas vias* = *the paved roads.*—Sidgwick.

423, 424, 425 **ducere . . . moliri . . . subvolvere . . . optare . . . concludere**, dependent on the idea of *eagerness* or *striving* in **instant.**—S.

426 Vergil is thinking, as often, of Roman institutions, and not of what was appropriate to heroic times. Cf. *Aen.* i. 507-8.

430-436 This simile is a reproduction of *Georg.* iv. 162-169. Cf. Milton, *Par. Lost*, i. 768:

'As bees

In springtime, when the sun with Taurus rides,

Pour forth their populous youth about the hive.'

432 **līquentia** = *liquid*, from **līquor**, dep. Elsewhere Vergil uses **līquens** from **līqueo.**

433 **Stipant** = *pack*, the notion of *pushing* and *tightness* being given in the very sound of the heavy overhanging spondees in this line.—S.

435 **Ignavum . . . arcent** = *drive the drones, a slothful herd, from the enclosure.* Notice the order.—Page.

437 'The want of a city is the key-note of the *Aeneid.*'—Conington.

111

C₄

FIRST PUNIC WAR, 264-241 B.C.

A Roman Martyr.

Country before Expediency.

M. Atilius Regulus, cum consul iterum in Africa ex insidiis captus esset duce Xanthippo Lacedaemonio, iuratus missus est ad senatum, ut, nisi redditi essent Poenis captivi nobiles quidam, rediret ipse Carthaginem. Is cum Romam venisset, utilitatis5speciem videbat, sed eam, ut res declarat, falsam iudicavit: quae erat talis: manere in patria, esse domui suae cum uxore, cum liberis, quam calamitatem accepisset in bello, communem fortunae bellicae iudicantem tenere consularis dignitatis 10gradum. . . . Itaque quid fecit? In senatum venit, mandata exposuit, sententiam ne diceret recusavit: quam diu iure iurando hostium teneretur, non esse se senatorem. . . . Cuius cum valuisset auctoritas, captivi retenti sunt, ipse Carthaginem 15rediit neque eum caritas patriae retinuit nec suorum, . . . 'At stulte, qui non modo non censuerit captivos remittendos, verum etiam dissuaserit.' Quo modo stulte?etiamne, si reipublicae conducebat? potest autem, quod inutile reipublicae sit, id cuiquam 20civi utile esse?

CICERO, *De Officiis*, iii. 99, 100.

1 **consul.** Regulus was Consul 261 and 256 B.C., and Proconsul in Africa 255 B.C., when he was defeated and taken prisoner by Xanthippus.

6 **speciem** = the *specious* (*plausible*) *appearance*(*semblance*).

12, 13 **sententiam . . . recusavit** = *declined to give his own opinion on the case.*

13 **iure iurando** (sc. *dato*) = *by the oath sworn to his enemies.*

17 **'At stulte'** (sc. *fecit*) = *'But, it may be said, he acted like a fool.'*

19 **etiamne** (sc. *stulte fecit*) = *What, how did he act like a fool, if . . .*—Holden.

20, 21 **potest autem . . . utile esse.** Cf. Ὁ τῇ πόλει οὐκ ἔστι βλαβερὸν οὐδὲ τὸν πολίτην βλάπτει = that which is not harmful (βλαβερόν = **inutile**) to the State is not harmful to the citizen.

Parallel Passages. Polybius, i. 31-36 (he makes no mention of the embassy of Regulus); Pliny, *Ep.* vii. 2 (interesting letter on the death of Regulus); and espec. Hor. *Od.* III. v. 13-end.

'With counsel thus, ne'er else aread [*advised*],

He nerved the Fathers' weak intent,

And, girt by friends that mourn'd him, sped

Into illustrious banishment.'—C.

112

C₅

FIRST PUNIC WAR, 264-241 B.C.

A. First Roman Naval Victory near Mylae, *260 B.C.*

C. Duilius, primo Punico bello a Romanis dux contra Carthaginienses missus, cum videret eos multum mari valere, classem magis validam quam decoram aedificavit, et manus ferreas, quas corvos vocabant, instituit. His, quas ante pugnam hostes 5valde deriserant, in pugna ipsa ad Liparas insulas commissa naves hostium comprehendit, easque partim cepit, partim demersit. Dux classis Punicae Carthaginem fugit, et ex senatu quaesivit quid faceret. Omnibus ut

78

pugnaret succlamantibus:10'Feci,' inquit, 'et victus sum.' Sic poenam crucis effugit, nam hac poena dux, re male gesta, apud Poenos afficiebatur. Duilius autem victor primum triumphum maritimum Romae egit, et ad memoriam victoriae columna rostrata in foro posita est.15

(Adapted) Cf. FLORUS, I. xviii. 7-10.

4 **corvos** = *crows* (the κόρακες of Polybius), boarding-bridges. A broad movable ladder, fastened to the foremast, and held in position by a rope. When the rope was let go, the iron hook at the upper end of the ladder penetrated the deck of an enemy's ship.

6 **ad Liparas insulas** = Aeoliae Insulae (Lipari Islands), N.E. of Sicily. Mylae was on a promontory S.E. of these Islands.

8 **Dux**, i.e. Hannibal, the defender of Agrigentum 262 B.C.

B. Unique honour conferred on Duilius.

C. Duilium, qui Poenos classe primus devicerat, redeuntem a cena senem saepe videbam puer; delectabatur cereo funali et tibicine, quae sibi nullo exemplo privatus sumpserat: tantum licentiae dabatgloria.

CICERO, De Senectute, xiii. § 44.

18 **cereo funali**,* i.e. *torchlight*.

nullo exemplo = *without any precedent*.

18-19 **sibi . . . sumpserat.** Cicero is wrong: more probably the honour was conferred on Duilius by a vote of the Comitia Tributa.

19 **dabat** = *excused*; lit. *granted, allowed*.— J. S. Reid.

* The **funale** was a torch composed of twigs twisted into a rope (**funis**) and dipped in pitch or oil.—J. S. R.

References. Polybius, i. 22, for a description of the *corvi*,κόρακες. Sir Andrew Barton (Percy's *Reliques*). Lord Howard says:—

> 'Were twenty shippes, and he but one,
> I swear by kirke and bower and hall,
> He would overcome them every one
> If once his beames they do down fall.'

113

C₆

FIRST PUNIC WAR, 264-241 B.C.

Carthaginian Victory off Drepana, *249 B.C.*

Rashness of Claudius.

Praedictiones vero et praesensiones rerum futurarum quid aliud declarant nisi hominibus ea ostendi, monstrari, portendi, praedici? Ex quo illa ostenta, monstra, portenta, prodigia dicuntur. Quod si ea ficta credimus licentia fabularum, Mopsum, Tiresiam,5Amphiaraum, Calchantem, Helenum, quos tamen augures ne ipsae quidem fabulae adscivissent, si res omnino repudiaret, ne domesticis quidem exemplis docti numen deorum conprobabimus? Nihil nos P. Claudi bello Punico primo temeritasmovebit, qui 10etiam per iocum deos irridens, cum cavea literati pulli non pascerentur, mergi eos in aquam iussit, ut biberent, quoniam esse nollent? Qui risus, classe devicta, multas ipsi lacrimas, magnam populo Romano cladem attulit. Quid? Collega eius Iunius 15eodem bello nonne tempestate classem amisit, cum auspiciis non paruisset? Itaque Claudius a populo condemnatus est, Iunius necem sibi ipse conscivit.

CICERO, De Nat. Deorum, II. 3. 7-8.

3 **ostenta . . . dicuntur** = *are called in Latin* 'ostenta,' 'monstra,' etc.—Walford.

4 **prodigium** for *prodicium* = *pro* + √*dic*- δεικ- = *point out*.

5 **Mopsum**, etc. = *all those stories about Mopsus, etc.*, in apposition to **ea**: poetical construction.

Mopsum, the prophet who accompanied the Argonauts.

Tiresiam, the blind prophet of Thebes.

6 **Amphiaraum**, the seer of Argos. One of the Seven against Thebes.

Helenus, son of Priam. A seer of the *Iliad* and the *Aeneid*.

10 **P. Claudi temeritas.** P. Cl. Pulcher (son of Appius Claudius, the blind Censor) defeated by Adherbal off Drepana (N.W. corner of Sicily, between Eryx and Lilybaeum).

15 **Iunius.** L. J. Pullus, consul 249 B.C. His fleet was destroyed by a storm off Pachynus (C. Passaro) the same year.

Parallel Passage. Florus ii. 2 says that 'Claudius was overthrown, not by the enemy, but by the gods themselves, whose auspices he had despised.'

The Defeat off Drepana. 'The reason of the defeat lay in the superiority of the Carthaginian admiral and seamen, and the inexperience of Claudius and of his crews, consisting mainly of landsmen who knew nothing of the sea. This disaster and the destruction of the fleet of Junius crowned the series of misfortunes which befell the Romans in the year 249 B.C., the most dismal time of the whole war.'—Ihne.

114

C₇

FIRST PUNIC WAR, 264-241 B.C.

Victory of Lutatius off the Aegates Insulae, *241 B.C.*

Peace with Carthage.

A.Interim Carthaginienses classe apud insulas Aegates a C. Lutatio, consule Romanorum, superati statuerunt belli facere finem, eamque rem arbitrio permiserunt Hamilcaris. Ille, etsi flagrabat bellandi cupiditate, tamen paci serviendum putavit, quod 5patriam, exhaustam sumptibus, diutius calamitates belli ferre non posse intellegebat, sed ita, ut statim mente agitaret, si paulum modo res essent refectae, bellum renovare Romanosque armis persequi,donicum aut virtute vicissent aut victi manus dedissent.10

CORN. NEPOS, *Hamilcar*, i.

1 **apud insulas Aegates**, the Goat Islands, off the W. Coast of Sicily, between Drepana and Lilybaeum (Marsala).

3 **statuerunt belli facere finem.** This victory led to the close of the First Punic War.

5 **paci serviendum** = *to devote himself to (obtaining) peace.*

9 **donicum** (= *donec*), lit. '*at the time of day when* ——'

10 **virtute vicissent** = *they (the Romans) should have conquered by (superior) prowess.*

B.

Hic dum stagnosi spectat templumque domosque
Literni ductor, varia splendentia cernit
655
Pictura belli patribus monumenta prioris
Exhausti: nam porticibus signata manebant,
Quis inerat longus rerum et spectabilis ordo.

.   .   .   .   .   .

Addiderant geminas medio consurgere fluctu
685
Aegates: lacerae circum fragmenta videres
Classis et effusos fluitare in gurgite Poenos.
Possessor pelagi pronaque Lutatius aura
Captivas puppes ad litora victor agebat.

SILIUS ITALICUS, vi. 653-657, 684-688.

653-654 **stagnosi Literni.** Town and River on the coast of Campania, N. of Cumae. The River flows through a marsh = Literna palus.

654 **ductor** = Hannibal.

654-657 Silius (who closely imitates Vergil) makes Hannibal view the sculptured memorials of the First Punic War, just as Aeneas sees carved the tale of Troy. Verg. *Aen.* i. 445-493.

Parallel Passage. Polybius, i. caps. 59-63.

Terms of Peace. Carthage engaged to evacuate Sicily; not to make war upon Hiero of Syracuse; to give up all Roman prisoners without ransom, and to pay 2200 talents in twenty years.

Sicily the first Roman Province.

115

C₈

SECOND PUNIC WAR, 218-202 B.C.

A. Great Importance of the Second Punic War.

In parte operis mei licet mihi praefari bellum maxime omnium memorabile, quae unquam gesta sint, me scripturum, quodHannibale duce Carthaginienses cum populo Romano gessere. Nam neque validiores opibus ullae inter se civitates gentesque contulerunt 5arma, neque his ipsis tantum unquam virium aut roboris fuit, et haud ignotas belli artes inter sese, sed expertasprimo Punico conferebant bello, et adeo varia fortuna belli ancepsque Mars fuit, ut propius periculum fuerint, qui vicerunt. Odiis etiam prope 10maioribus certarunt quam viribus, Romanis indignantibus quod victoribus victi ultro inferrent arma, Poenis, quod superbe avareque crederent imperitatum victis esse.

3 **Hannibale duce.** Polybius called the war of which Hannibal was the life and soul the 'Hannibalian War.'

80

6 **his ipsis**, sc. *Romanis Poenisque*, with *validiores*.

6-7 **virium aut roboris** = *offensive or defensive strength*.—R.

8 **expertas** = *tested*, in a passive sense.

9 **ut propius . . . vicerunt**, e.g. after Cannae, 216 B.C.

12 **ultro inferrent arma** = *should presume to attack*.—Dimsdale.

13 **Poenis**, sc. *indignantibus*.

superbe avareque. 'When the war of the mercenaries broke out in Africa (241-238 B.C.) Rome availed herself of the distress of Carthage to extort the cession of Sardinia, and raised the war indemnity by 1200 talents.'—Ihne.

B. The Oath of the Boy Hannibal.

Fama est etiam, Hannibalem annorum ferme 15novem, pueriliterblandientem patri Hamilcari, ut duceretur in Hispaniam, cum,perfecto Africo bello, exercitum eo traiecturus sacrificaret, altaribus admotum, tactis sacris, iure iurando adactum, se, cum primum posset, hostem fore populo Romano.20

LIVY, xxi. 1.

16 **blandientem** = *coaxingly entreating*.—D.

17 **perfecto Africo bello**, i.e. between Carthage and her mutinous mercenaries, 241-237 B.C.

Parallel Passage. For Hannibal's Oath, Livy xxxv. 19.

Importance of the War. 'It was a struggle for existence, for supremacy or destruction. It was to decide whether the Graeco-Roman civilisation of the West or the Semitic (Carthaginian) civilisation of the East was to be established in Europe, and to determine its history for all future time.'—Ihne.

116

C9

SECOND PUNIC WAR, 218-202 B.C.

'The paths of glory lead but to the grave.'

147

Expende Hannibalem: quot libras in duce summo
Invenies?.   .   .   .

151

Additur imperiis Hispania, Pyrenaeum
Transilit. Opposuit natura Alpemque nivemque:
Diducit scopulos et montem rumpit aceto.
Iam tenet Italiam, tamen ultra pergere tendit:

155

'Actum,' inquit, 'nihil est, nisi Poeno milite portas
Frangimus et media vexillum pono Subura.'
O qualis facies et quali digna tabella,
Cum Gaetula ducem portaret belua luscum!
Exitus ergo quis est? O gloria! vincitur idem

160

Nempe et in exilium praeceps fugit, atque ibi magnus
Mirandusque cliens sedet ad praetoria regis,
Donec Bithyno libeat vigilare tyranno.
Finem animae, quae res humanas miscuit olim,
Non gladii, non saxa dabunt, nec tela, sed ille

165

Cannarum vindex et tanti sanguinis ultor,
Anulus. I, demens, et saevas curre per Alpes,
Ut pueris placeas et declamatio fias.

JUVENAL, *Sat.* x. 147-167.

147-148 **Expende . . . invenies** = *if you lay* (lit. 'weigh')*Hannibal in the scale, how many pounds will you find in the greatest of commanders?*—Duff. Cf. Ov. *Met.*xii. 615:

Iam cinis est: et de tam magno restat Achille
Nescio quid parvam quod non bene compleat urnam.

156 **media Subura**, i.e. in the heart of Rome. The Subura was one of the busiest and most populous quarters of Rome.

157 **O qualis facies . . . tabella** = *what a sight and how fit for caricature!* lit. 'worthy of what a picture' i.e. how ridiculous a picture it would have made.—Hardy.

81

158 **luscum** = *one-eyed*. Hannibal lost an eye from disease, while marching through the country flooded by the Arno, 217 B.C.

160 **in exilium**, i.e. first to Antiochus of Syria, and then to Prusias of Bithynia.

166 **anulus.** Hannibal took poison which he carried about in a ring (**anulus**) 183 B.C., aged 76.

167 **ut . . . fias** = *to suit the taste of schoolboys, and become the subject of their speeches.*—Duff.
For the thought, cf. Shak. Ham. V. i. 232:
Imperious Caesar, dead and turned to clay,
Might stop a hole to keep the wind away:
O, that that earth, which kept the world in awe
Should patch a wall to expel the winter's flaw!
117
C_{10}

SECOND PUNIC WAR, 218-202 B.C.

Character of Hannibal.

Nunquam ingenium idem ad res diversissimas, parendum atque imperandum, habilius fuit. Itaque haud facile discerneres, utrum imperatori an exercitui carior esset; neque Hasdrubal alium quemquam praeficere malle, ubi quid fortiter ac strenue agendum5esset, neque milites alio duce plus confidere aut audere. Plurimum audaciae ad pericula capessenda, plurimum consilii inter ipsa pericula erat. Nullo labore aut corpus fatigari aut animus vinci poterat. Caloris ac frigoris patientia par; cibi potionisque 10desiderio naturali, non voluptate modus finitus; vigiliarum somnique nec die nec nocte discriminata tempora: id, quod gerendis rebus superesset, quieti datum; ea neque molli strato neque silentioaccersita; multi saepe militari sagulo opertum humi iacentem 15inter custodias stationesque militum conspexerunt. Vestitus nihil inter aequales excellens; arma atque equi conspiciebantur. Equitum peditumque idem longe primus erat; princeps in proelium ibat, ultimus conserto proelio excedebat. Has tantas viri virtutes20ingentia vitia aequabant, inhumana crudelitas, perfidia plus quam Punica, nihil veri, nihil sancti, nullus deum metus, nullum ius iurandum, nulla religio.

LIVY, xxi. 4.

2 **habilius** = *better adapted*, lit. 'more easily handled'; cf. our *handy*.

7 **ad pericula capessenda** = *in incurring peril*.

12 **discriminata** = *regulated*, lit. 'divided off'; cf. *dis-cerno,dis-crimen*.

14 **accersita** (= *arcessita*) = *wooed*.

15 **sagulo** = *in his military cloak*: diminutive of *sagum*.

21 **inhumana crudelitas.** Polybius says that many of his alleged cruelties were to be set down to his namesake H. Monomachus.

21-23 **perfidia plus quam Punica.** 'This does not seem to have been anything worse than a consummate adroitness in laying traps for his enemies.'—Church and Brodribb. Cf. 'Perfidious Albion.'

23 **nulla religio** = *no scruples*, i.e. no force binding (*re* + *ligare*) or restraining from wrong-doing, no conscience.

Parallel Passages. Livy xxvi. 41 of Scipio Africanus Minor—Sallust *Cat.* 5 of Catiline—Polybius ix. 22-26 (important).

'Bitterly as the Romans hated, reviled, and persecuted Carthage, the most deadly poison of their hatred they poured upon Hannibal; they did not hesitate to blacken his memory by the most revolting accusations.'—Ihne.
118
C_{11}

SECOND PUNIC WAR, 218-202 B.C.

The Siege of Saguntum, *219 B.C.*

Angulus muri erat in planiorem patentioremque quam cetera circa vallem vergens; adversus eum vineas agere instituit, per quas aries moenibus admoveri posset. Sed ut locus procul muro satis aequus agendis vineis fuit, ita haudquaquam prospere, 5postquam ad effectum operis ventum est, coeptis succedebat. Et turris ingens imminebat, et murus, ut in suspecto loco, supra ceterae modum altitudinis emunitus erat, et iuventus delecta, ubi plurimum periculi ac timoris ostendebatur, ibi vi maiore obsistebant. 10Ac primo missilibus summovere hostem nec quicquam satis tutum munientibus pati; deinde iam non pro moenibus modo atque turri tela micare, sed ad erumpendum etiam in stationes operaque hostium animus erat; quibus tumultuariis certaminibus 15haud ferme plures Saguntini cadebant quam Poeni. Ut vero Hannibal ipse, dum murum incautius subit, adversum femur tragula graviter ictus cecidit, tanta circa fuga ac trepidatio fuit, ut non multum abesset, quin opera ac vineae desererentur.20

2 **quam cetera** (sc. *loca*) **circa** = *than the neighbouring country.*

4-5 **ut . . . ita** = lit. *as . . . so*, i.e. *although . . . yet . . .*

6 **postquam . . . ventum est** = *when they came to attack the wall in earnest.* **Effectum** (verbal noun in *us*) = *the completion of the work*, i.e. the bringing up of the ram.—Dimsdale.

8 **ut in suspecto loco** = *as (was natural) in a suspected* (i.e. weak) *spot.*—Capes.

11-12 **nec quicquam . . . pati** = *they allowed those engaged on the works no sort of safety*, lit. not (even) *moderate safety.*—D.

18 **adversum femur** = *in the front of the thigh.*

SAGUNTUM (Murviedro = muri veteres) in Hispania Tarraconensis (about 20 miles S. of Valencia) was supposed to have been founded by Greek colonists from Zacynthos (Zante). In 226 B.C. Rome made an alliance with Saguntum and Hasdrubal was informed of the fact. Hannibal attacked the city ostensibly on the ground of its having molested subject-allies of Carthage, but really because he was unwilling to leave a strong city in his rear, and wished to obtain funds. After an eight months' siege and a heroic defence, characteristic of Spanish towns, it was taken by storm 219 B.C.

> *Nec pavet hic populus (Massilia) pro libertate subire*
> *Obsessum Poeno gessit quod Marte Saguntum.*

> LUCAN, *Phars.* iii. 349-50.

Cf. also Juv. *Sat.* xv. 113-14, and the siege of Saragossa, 1808 A.D.

119

C₁₂

SECOND PUNIC WAR, 218-202 B.C.

A. **The Dream of Hannibal.**

Hannibalem Coelius scribit, cum cepisset Saguntum, visum esse in somnis a Iove in deorum concilium vocari; quo cum venisset, Iovem imperasse ut Italiae bellum inferret, ducemque ei unum e concilio datum: quo illum utentem cum exercitu progredi5coepisse; tum ei ducem illum praecepisse ne respiceret; illum autem id diutius facere non potuisse elatumque cupiditaterespexisse: tum visam belluam vastam et immanem, circumplicatam serpentibus, quacunque incederet, omnia arbusta, virgulta, tecta 10pervertere.

> CICERO, *De Divinatione*, i. 24, 49.

1 **Coelius**, i.e. L. Coelius Antipater (a contemporary of C. Gracchus 123 B.C.), wrote Annales, which contained a valuable account of the Second Punic War. Livy borrows largely from his narrative.

7 **id . . . non potuisse.** Cf. Livy 'temperare oculis nequivisse = he could not restrain his eyes.'

8 **cupiditate** = *from curiosity.* Cf. Livy 'cura ingeni humani = with the natural curiosity of the human mind.'

8-11 **visam belluam . . . pervertere** = *he thought he saw a monster overthrowing.*

B. **The Interpretation—Vastitatem esse Italiae.**

[200]

Hoc trepidus monstro . . . ardua quae sit,
Scitatur, pestis, terrasque urgentia membra
Quo ferat et quosnam populos deposcat hiatu.
Cui gelidis almae Cyllenes editus antris:
'Bella vides optata tibi: te maxima bella,
205
Te strages nemorum, te moto turbida caelo
Tempestas, caedesque virum, magnaeque ruinae
Idaei generis, lacrimosaque fata sequuntur.
Quantus per campos populatis montibus actus
Contorquet silvas squalenti tergore serpens,
210
Et late umectat terras spumante veneno:
Tantus, perdomitis decurrens Alpibus atro
Involves bello Italiam, tantoque fragore
Eruta convulsis prosternes oppida muris.'

> SILIUS ITALICUS, iii. 198-213.

202 **hiatu** = *with its wide-open mouth.*

203 **Cyllenes**, i.e. Mt. Cyllene (Zyria), the highest point in the Peloponnesus, on the borders of Arcadia and Achaia, where Hermes is said to have been born: hence styled *Cyllenius.*

209 **tergore** = **tergo**. poet. and post-Augustian.
Parallel Passage. Livy xxi. 22, and cf. Polybius iii. 47.
120
C₁₃

SECOND PUNIC WAR, 218-202 B.C.

From the Pyrenees to the Rhone.

Passage of the Elephants.

Elephantorum traiciendorum varia consilia fuisse credo, certevariat memoria actae rei. . . .
Ceterum magis constat ratibus traiectos esse elephantos. Ratem unam ducentos longam pedes
quinquaginta latam a terra in amnem porrexerunt, quam, ne5secunda aqua deferretur, pluribus
validis retinaculis parte superiore ripae religatam pontis in modum humo iniecta constraverunt, ut
beluae audacter velut per solum ingrederentur. Altera ratis aeque lata, longa pedes centum, ad
traiciendum flumen apta, 10huic copulata est; tum elephanti per stabilem ratem tamquam viam
praegredientibus feminis acti ubi in minorem applicatam transgressi sunt, extemplo resolutis,
quibus leviter annexa erat, vinculis ab actuariis aliquot navibus ad alteram ripam pertrahitur.
Ita 15primis expositis alii deinde repetiti ac traiecti sunt. Nihil sane trepidabant, donec continenti
velut ponte agerentur; primus erat pavor, cum soluta ab ceteris rate in altum raperentur. Ibi
urgentes inter se cedentibus extremis ab aqua trepidationis aliquantum 20edebant, donec quietem
ipse timor circumspectantibus aquam fecisset. Excidere etiam saevientes quidam in flumen; sed
pondere ipso stabilis deiectis rectoribus quaerendis pedetemptim vadis in terram evasere.25

LIVY, xxi. 28.

2 **variat . . . rei** = *the accounts of what was done differ*.—Dimsdale.
7 **parte superiore . . . pontis** = *fastened to the upper part of the bank*, i.e. to the bank at a
point higher up stream.—D.
9 **per solum** = *on firm ground*.
14 **ab actuariis** = *by some light craft*, lit. 'Easily moved' (*ago*).
17-18 **donec . . . agerentur** = *So long as they were being driven on what seemed a bridge connected
with the land*.—C. and B. *Agebantur* would be more usual, but*agerentur* may give the reason of *nihil
trepidabant*. Cf.*donec—fecisset* ll. 21-22.
19 **in altum** = *into mid stream*, usu. of the Sea.—D.
  inter se = *one on another, alii alios*.
24 **quaerendis pedetemptim vadis** = *feeling their way into shallow*
water. **pedetemptim** = *step by step*, lit. 'stretching out the feet' (*pes* + *tendo*). Cf. *paulatim,sensim*.
Reference. Polybius, iii. 46. Both Polybius and Livy thought that elephants could not
swim.
121
C₁₄

SECOND PUNIC WAR, 218-202 B.C.

From the Rhone to Italy.

Hannibal encourages his Soldiers.

Itaque Hannibal, postquam ipsi sententia stetit pergere ire atque Italiam petere, advocata
contione varie militum versat animos castigando adhortandoque: mirari se, quinam pectora
semper impavida repens terror invaserit. . . . Alpes quidem habitari, coli,5gignere atque alere
animantes; pervias fauces esse exercitibus. Eos ipsos, quos cernant, legatos non pinnis sublime
elatos Alpes transgressos. Ne maiores quidem eorum indigenas, sed advenas Italiae cultores has
ipsas Alpes ingentibus saepe agminibus cum10liberis ac coniugibus migrantium modo tuto
transmisisse. Militi quidem armato nihil secum praeter instrumenta belli portanti quid invium aut
inexsuperabile esse? Saguntum ut caperetur, quid per octo menses periculi, quid laboris
exhaustum esse! 15Romam, caput orbis terrarum, petentibus quicquam adeo asperum atque
arduum videri, quod inceptum moretur? Cepisse quondam Gallos ea, quae adiri posse Poenus
desperet. Proinde aut cederent animo atque virtute genti per eos dies totiens ab se victae, 20aut
itineris finem sperent campum interiacentem Tiberi ac moenibus Romanis.

LIVY, xxi. 30.

2-3 **varie . . . versat** = *works on their minds by different methods*, i.e. **castigando
adhortandoque**.—Dimsdale.
4-5 **repens terror.** Livy says that H.'s soldiers dreaded the Romans (victorious in the 1st
Punic War), but still more the exaggerated and unknown terrors of the Alps.
7 **Eos ipsos legatos**, i.e. of the Boii (Insubrian Gauls), long settled in Gallia Cisalpina
(round Mediolanum = Milan).
9 **advenas Italiae cultores** = *foreign settlers in Italy*.*advenas* = adj. here.—D.

84

11 **migrantium modo** = *as immigrants.*

16 **Romam caput orbis.** A rhetorical exaggeration, for Rome was not yet mistress even of all Italy (e.g. the Boii not subdued until 191 B.C.).

18 **Cepisse Gallos.** The Gauls sacked Rome 390 B.C.

20 **genti . . . victae,** e.g. at the Passage of the Rhone.

21 **campum,** i.e. the Campus Martius, N.W. of Rome, where the Tiber makes a wide curve. For the thought cf. p. 116, ll. 7, 8.

The Speeches of Livy. 'He does not intend in them to reproduce the substance of words actually spoken, or even to imitate the tone of the time in which the speech is laid. He uses them as a vivid and dramatic method of portraying character and motive.'—Mackail.

122

C₁₅

SECOND PUNIC WAR, 218-202 B.C.

From the Rhone to Italy.

The Descent of the Alps.

Natura locus iam ante praeceps recenti lapsu terrae in pedum mille admodum altitudinem abruptus erat. . . . Tandem nequiquam iumentis atque hominibus fatigatis castra in iugo posita, aegerrime ad id ipsum loco purgato: tantum nivis fodiendum atque5egerendum fuit. Inde ad rupem muniendam, per quam unam via esse poterat, milites ducti, cum caedendum esset saxum, arboribus circa immanibus deiectis detruncatisque struem ingentem lignorum faciunt, eamque, cum et vis venti apta faciendo igni10coorta esset, succendunt ardentiaque saxa infuso acetoputrefaciunt. Ita torridam incendio rupem ferro pandunt,molliuntque anfractibus modicis clivos, ut non iumenta solum sed elephanti etiam deduci possent. Quadriduum circa rupem consumptum 15iumentis prope fame absumptis; nuda enim fere cacumina sunt, et, si quid est pabuli, obruunt nives. Inferiora valles apricosque quosdam colles habent rivosque prope silvas et iam humano cultu digniora loca. Ibi iumenta in pabulum missa, et quies 20muniendo fessis hominibus data. Triduo inde ad planum descensum iam et locis mollioribus et accolarum ingeniis.

LIVY, xxi. 36, 37.

Context. At a short distance from the summit of the Pass (prob. the Little St. Bernard) Hannibal finds his passage barred by a break in the road, caused by a landslip or avalanche.

2-3 **in pedum . . . abruptus erat.** Polybius says that the precipice at the side of the road (leaving only a narrow ledge) extended for about 1000 ft. *in length.* Livy in mistake converts this into 1000 ft. *in depth.*

3-4 **Tandem . . . fatigatis,** i.e. after H.'s attempt to pass by a side-way over a glacier failed.

4 **in iugo,** i.e. on the higher level where the road was broken away.

6 **ad rupem muniendam** = *to cut a way through the rock.Munire* (cf. *moenia*) = lit. 'to wall,' 'to build.' So*munire viam* = *to make a road.* Hannibal widened the narrow ledge of road by making a sort of terrace.

9 **detruncatis** = *trimmed,* (lit. 'lopped off'), i.e. cleared of branches.

11-12 **infuso aceto.** Limestone rock might be softened by vinegar, which the *posca,* the soldiers' regular drink of vinegar and water, would supply. Polybius does not mention this.

13-14 **molliuntque . . . clivos** = *relieve the steepness of the descent by gently-sloping zigzag paths. Anfractus,* from *ambi + frango.*

References. Polybius, iii. 54-56; Ihne, i. 171-179.

123

C₁₆

SECOND PUNIC WAR, 218-202 B.C.

A. The Battle at the R. Trebia, *218 B.C.*

Hannibal, cum ad Trebiam in conspectu haberet Semproni Longi consulis castra, medio amne interfluente, saevissima hieme Magonem et electos in insidiis posuit. Deinde Numidas equites ad eliciendam Semproni credulitatem adequitare vallo eius 5iussit, quibus praeceperat, ut ad primum nostrorum incursum per nota refugerent vada. Hos consul et adortus temere et secutus ieiunumexercitum in maximo frigore transitu fluminis rigefecit: mox torpore et inedia adfectis Hannibal suum militem 10opposuit, quem ad id ignibus oleoque et cibo foverat; nec defuit partibus Mago, quin terga hostium in hoc ordinatus caederet.

FRONTINUS, *Stratagemata,* ii. 5. 23.

1 **ad Trebiam,** a small tributary S. of the Padus, which it joins 2 miles W. of Placentia (Piacenza).

85

2 **castra.** Ti. Sempronius Longus, with his army from Sicily, effected a junction with his colleague, Scipio, in his fortified camp on the W. or left bank of the Trebia.

8-9 **ieiunum . . . rigefecit,** i.e. Sempronius *made stiff*(**rigefecit**) with wading breast-high across the icy river his men *faint with hunger* (**ieiunum**).

11 **oleoque,** i.e. *ut mollirent artus* = *to make their limbs supple.*

12-13 **nec defuit . . . caederet.** The Romans kept their ground with the utmost courage till Mago burst out from his ambush and attacked them in rear.

B. The River bars the Retreat.

570
Et iam, dispersis Romana per agmina signis,
Palantes agit, ad ripas, miserabile! Poenus
Impellens trepidos, fluvioque immergere certat.
Tum Trebia infausto nova proelia gurgite fessis
Incohat, ac precibus Iunonis suscitat undas.
575
Haurit subsidens fugientum corpora tellus,
Infidaque soli frustrata voragine sorbet.
Nec niti lentoque datur convellere limo
Mersa pedum penitus vestigia: labe tenaci
Haerent devincti gressus, resolutaque ripa
580
Implicat aut caeca prosternit fraude paludis.

SILIUS ITALICUS, iv. 570-580.

574 **precibus . . . undas.** The poet, in his imitation of Vergil, makes Juno the devoted ally of Hannibal.

576 **soli frustrata** = *prevented from reaching firm ground.*

577 **lento** = *sticky.*

579 **resoluta** = *crumbling.*

References. Livy, xxi. 52-56; Ihne, ii. 187-191.

124
C₁₇

SECOND PUNIC WAR, 218-202 B.C.

The Battle of Lake Trasimene, *217 B.C. (1)*

Flaminius cum pridie solis occasu ad lacum pervenisset,inexplorato postero die vixdum satis certa luce angustiis superatis, postquam in patentiorem campum pandi agmen coepit, id tantum hostium, quod ex adverso erat, conspexit; ab tergo ac super 5caput*haud* detectae* insidiae. Poenus ubi, id quod petierat, clausum lacu ac montibus et circumfusum suis copiis habuit hostem, signum omnibus dat simul invadendi. Qui ubi, qua cuique proximum fuit, decucurrerunt, eo magis Romanis subita atque improvisa 10res fuit, quod orta ex lacu nebula campo quam montibus densior sederat, agminaque hostium ex pluribus collibusipsa inter se satis conspecta eoque magis pariter decucurrerant. Romanus clamore prius undique orto, quam satis cerneret, se circumventum 15esse sensit, et ante in frontem lateraque pugnari coeptum est, quam satis instrueretur acies aut expediri arma stringique gladii possent. Consul perculsis omnibus ipse satis, ut† in re trepida, impavidus turbatos ordines, vertente se quoque ad dissonos 20clamores, instruit, ut tempus locusque patitur, et, quacunque adire audirique potest, adhortatur ac stare ac pugnare iubet.25

LIVY, xxii. 4, 5.

* Var. lect. *decepere.*

† For this qualifying use of *ut* cf. p. 42, iii. (b) and p. 83 line 1.

1 **Flaminius** (Gaius), the chief of the popular party at Rome. Consul 223 B.C., conquered the Insubrian Gauls, Censor 220 B.C. Connected Picenum with Rome by the Via Flaminia. Consul (a second time) 217 B.C., defeated and killed at Trasimene.

2 **inexplorato** = *without reconnoitring.* 'This word expresses the whole blame attaching to Flaminius, and it is great.'—Dimsdale.

4 **pandi** (= *se pandere*) = *to deploy.*

13 **ipsa . . . conspecta** = *were sufficiently visible to each other.*

15 **prius quam satis cerneret** = *before he could clearly distinguish anything.*—D.

19 **ut in re trepida** = *considering the confusion of the moment.*—D.

The Scene of the Battle. At the N.W. end of the Lake the mountains of Cortona come right down to the lake, but a little further E. the pass expands and forms between the mountains and the lake a narrow plain from ½ to 1½ miles in width and about 4 miles in length. At the E.

end of the plain the mountains again close down upon the lake. Here Hannibal encamped with his Africans and Spaniards; posted his light-armed troops behind the crests of the hills which bounded the plain on the N., and his cavalry at the entrance to the pass on the W. to cut off the Roman retreat.

125

C₁₈

SECOND PUNIC WAR, 218-202 B.C.

The Battle of Lake Trasimene, *217 B.C. (2)*

Ceterum prae strepitu ac tumultu nec consilium nec imperium accipi poterat, tantumque aberat, ut sua signa atque ordines et locum noscerent, ut vix ad arma capienda aptandaque pugnae competeret animus, opprimerenturque quidam onerati magis iis5quam tecti. Et erat in tanta caligine maior usus aurium quam oculorum. Ad gemitus vulneratorum ictusque corporum aut armorum et mixtos *strepentium** paventiumque clamorescircumferebant ora oculosque. Alii fugientes pugnantium globo illati 10haerebant; alios redeuntes in pugnam avertebat fugientium agmen. Deinde, ubi in omnes partes nequiquam impetus capti, et ab lateribus montes ac lacus, a fronte et ab tergo hostium acies claudebant, apparuitque nullam nisi in dextera ferroque salutis15spem esse, tum sibi quisque dux adhortatorque factus ad rem gerendam et nova de integro exorta pugna est, non illa ordinata per principes hastatosque ac triarios, nec ut pro signis antesignani, post signa alia pugnaret acies; fors conglobabat et animus suus20cuique ante aut post pugnandi ordinem dabat; tantusque fuit ardor animorum, adeo intentus pugnae animus, ut eum motum terrae, qui multarum urbium Italiae magnas partes prostravit, nemo pugnantium senserit.25

LIVY, xxii. 5.

* Var. lect. *terrentium* = of those causing fear.

4 **ad arma capienda aptandaque** = *to seize and put on for the battle their arms*.—Dimsdale.

5 **onerati:** i.e. most were cut down in their full marching equipment.

8-9 **mixtos . . . clamores** = *the mingled shouts of noisy triumph* (**strepentium**) *or dismay*.

10 **pugnantium . . . haerebant** = *rushed upon a knot*(**globo**) *of combatants, and became entangled with it*.—Jebb.

14 **a fronte,** i.e. by Hannibal's African and Spanish infantry.

ab tergo, i.e. by Hannibal's cavalry and the Gauls.

18-19 **non illa . . . triarios** = *not in that well-known* (**illa**)*mode of fighting* (sc. **pugna**) *arranged according to*. . . . Livy refers to the old mode of formation (said to have been introduced by Camillus) of i. **hastati,** *of young men,* ii. **principes,** *of men at their prime,* iii.**triarii,** *of middle-aged men.*

References: Polybius, iii. 82-84; Ihne, *Hist.* vol, i. pp. 204-10.

126

C₁₉

SECOND PUNIC WAR, 218-202 B.C.

The Battle of Lake Trasimene, *217 B.C. (3)*

The Death of Flaminius.

Dumque ea commemorat densosque obit obvius hostes,
645
Advolat ora ferus mentemque Ducarius. Acri
Nomen erat gentile viro, fusisque catervis
Boiorum quondam patriis, antiqua gerebat
Vulnera barbaricae mentis, noscensque superbi
Victoris vultus, 'Tune, inquit, maximus ille
650
Boiorum terror? libet hoc cognoscere telo,
Corporis an tanti manet de vulnere sanguis.
Nec vos poeniteat, populares, fortibus umbris
Hoc mactare caput: nostros hic curribus egit
Insistens victos alta ad Capitolia patres.
655
Ultrix hora vocat.' Pariter tunc undique fusis
Obruitur telis, nimboque mente per auras
Contectus nulli dextra iactare reliquit
Flaminium cecidisse sua. Nec pugna perempto
Ulterior ductore fuit; namque agmine denso
660

Primores iuvenum, laeva ob discrimina Martis
Infensi superis dextrisque, et cernere Poenum
Victorem plus morte rati, super ocius omnes
Membra ducis stratosque artus certamine magno
Telaque corporaque et non fausto Marte cruentas
665
Iniecere manus. Sic densi caedis acervo
Ceu tumulo, texere virum.

SILIUS ITALICUS, v. 644-666.

644 **Dum . . . hostes**, i.e. after Flaminius' vain attempt to rally and form his men, and his consequent resolve to atone for his fault (*inexplorato* angustiis superatis*) with his life.

645 **Ducarius**—Livy, 'an Insubrian (Lombard) trooper.'

651 **mānet** = *will flow*. Cf. *emanate*.

652 **populares** = *fellow-countrymen*, but of Romans usu.*civis.*

658-666 Livy says more simply 'He (Ducarius) was trying to despoil the corpse, when some veterans screened it with their shields.'

660 **laeva** = *unfavourable*, lit. 'on the left side.' Cf. *sinister*.

* See p. 124, l. 2, note.

Parallel Passages.—Livy, xxii. 6; Polyb. iii. 84.

Character of Flaminius. 'The party feelings which have so coloured the language of the ancient writers (e.g. Livy, Polybius) respecting him need not be shared by a modern historian. Flaminius was indeed an unequal antagonist to Hannibal; but, in his previous life, as Consul and as Censor, he had served his country well; and if the defile of Trasimene witnessed his rashness, it also contains his honourable grave.' Arnold, *Hist. Rome*, iii. 110.

127

C₂₀

SECOND PUNIC WAR, 218-202 B.C.

Quintus Fabus Maximus Cunctator.

Ego Q. Maximum, eum qui Tarentum recepit, senem adulescens ita dilexi, ut aequalem. Erat enim in illo viro comitate condita gravitas, nec senectus mores mutaverat. . . . Hic et bella gerebat ut adulescens, cum plane grandis esset, et Hannibalem 5iuveniliterexsultantem patientia sua molliebat; de quo praeclare familiarisnoster Ennius:

Unus homo nobis cunctando restituit rem;
Noenum rumores ponebat ante salutem;
10
Ergo plusque magisque viri nunc gloria claret.

Nec vero in armis praestantior quam in toga; qui consul iterum, Sp. Carvilio collega quiescente, C. Flaminio tribuno plebis, quoad potuit, restitit agrum Picentem et Gallicum viritim contra senatus auctoritatem dividenti. . . . Multa in eo viro praeclara 15cognovi, sed nihil admirabilius quam quo modo ille mortem fili tulit, clari viri et consularis. Est in manibus laudatio, quam cum legimus, quem philosophum non contemnimus? Nec vero ille in luce modo atque in oculis civium magnus, sed intus 20domique praestantior.

CICERO, *De Senectute*, §§ 10-12.

1 **Ego**, i.e. M. Porcius Cato, the famous Censor of 184 B.C.

eum qui Tarentum recepit. Tarentum was betrayed to Hannibal 212 B.C. and *recovered* by Fabius 209 B.C.

2-3 **Erat . . . gravitas** = *that hero possessed dignity tempered by courtesy.*—J. S. R. **condita** (*condio*) = lit.*seasoned.*

5 **grandis**, sc. *natu*. He was consul for a first time in 233B.C.

6 **iuveniliter.** Hannibal was 29 when he crossed the Alps.

exsultantem = *wildly roaming*, of a horse galloping at will.

7 **noster Ennius**, circ. 239-169 B.C., famous espec. for his Annales in Hexameter verse. He was the first Latin writer to use this metre.

9 **Noenum** (*ne + oinum* = *not one thing*) = *non*. Cf. *nihil* =*ne + hilum* = not a whit, nothing.

12-14 Flaminius, when tribune 232 B.C., by a vote of the Comitia Tributa (i.e. by a *plebiscitum*) and against the expressed wish of the Senate (*contra senatus auctoritatem*) carried an agrarian law for the division of public land in Picenum amongst Roman citizens.

18 **laudatio**, sc. *funebris*, the funeral speech.

19-20 **in luce . . . civium** = *in public and under the gaze of his fellow-countrymen.*—J. S. R.

References. Polybius, iii. 89, 90; Livy, xxii. 12; Plutarch,*Fabius*, vi.

88

SECOND PUNIC WAR, 218-202 B.C.

Fabius and his Master of the Horse, *217 B.C.*

Ita per variam fortunam diei maiore parte exacta cum in castra reditum esset, Minucius convocatis militibus 'Saepe ego' inquit 'audivi, milites, eum primum esse virum, qui ipse consulat, quid in rem sit, secundum eum, qui bene monenti oboediat; qui 5nec ipse consulere nec alteri parere sciat, eum extremi ingenii esse. Nobis quoniam prima animi ingeniique negata sors est, secundam ac mediam teneamus et, dum imperare discimus, parere prudenti in animum inducamus. Castra cum Fabio iungamus; ad praetorium10eius signa cum tulerimus, ubi ego eum parentem appellavero, quod beneficio erga nos ac maiestate eius dignum est, vos, milites, eos, quorum vos modo arma ac dexterae texerunt, patronossalutabitis, et, si nihil aliud, gratorum certe nobis 15animorum gloriam dies hic dederit.' Signo dato conclamatur inde, utcolligantur vasa. Profecti et agmine incedentes ad dictatoris castra in admirationem et ipsum et omnes, qui circa erant, converterunt.20

LIVY, xxii. 29, 30.

Context. Fabius' policy of 'masterly inactivity' had become so unpopular at Rome that the command of the army was divided between Fabius and Minucius, who risked a battle, and was only saved from a destruction as complete as that of the Trebia by the timely aid of Fabius. **Minucius publicly and fully atones for his rashness.**

4 **consulat** = *can give counsel*—so *consulere* l. 6.

6-7 **extremi ingenii** = *has the meanest capacity.* gen. of quality.

7-8 **prima . . . sors est** = *the highest rank in the scale of spirit and intellect.*—Dimsdale.

14 **patronos** = *as the authors of your freedom.* **Patronus** = legal title used by a freed slave (*libertus*) of his former master. The soldiers of Minucius are to think of themselves as *liberti*, owing their freedom to those of Fabius, who are thus their **patroni.**

17 **ut colligantur vasa,** i.e. *impedimenta.* Cf. *signa movere.*

Fabius Cunctator. 'Fabius had to create a new army, to accustom it to war, and to inspire it with courage. He did this skilfully and persistently, and thus he rendered the most essential service that any general could at that time render to the State. It was probably at this time that the Senate voted him a crown of grass (*corona graminea*), the highest distinction which was awarded to a general who had saved a besieged town.'—Ihne.

SECOND PUNIC WAR, 218-202 B.C. CANNAE, 218 B.C. (1)

The Destruction of the Roman Infantry.

Sub equestris finem certaminis coorta est peditum pugna, primo et viribus et animis par, dum constabant ordines Gallis Hispanisque; tandem Romani, diu ac saepe conisi, obliqua fronte acieque densa impulere hostium cuneum nimis tenuem eoque parum 5validum a cetera prominentem acie. Impulsis deinde ac trepide referentibus pedem institere ac tenore uno per praeceps pavore fugientium agmen in mediam primum aciem illati, postremo nullo resistente ad subsidia Afrorum pervenerunt, qui utrimque reductis 10alis constiterant media, qua Galli Hispanique steterant, aliquantum prominente acie. Qui cuneus ut pulsus aequavit frontem primum, dein cedendo etiam sinum in medio dedit, Afri circa iam cornua fecerant irruentibusque incaute in medium Romanis circumdedere15alas; mox cornua extendendo clausere et ab tergo hostis. Hinc Romani, defuncti nequiquam proelio uno, omissis Gallis Hispanisque, quorum terga ceciderant, adversus Afros integram pugnam ineunt non tantum eo iniquam, quod inclusi adversus20circumfusos, sed etiam quod fessi cum recentibus ac vegetispugnabant.

LIVY, xxii. 47.

1 **Sub . . . certaminis,** i.e. *at the close of* (**sub**) the first stage in the battle, in which the Roman cavalry were defeated.

2-3 **constabant . . . Hispanisque.** These formed Hannibal's centre, the *convex* of his semicircular formation of his infantry, with the African troops on the horns of the semicircle to the right and left, but at some distance behind.

4 **obliqua fronte,** perh. = *concave,* so as to surround *the projecting part of the enemy's line* (**a cetera prominentem acie**).

5 **cuneum:** here = the *convex* formation of the Gauls and Spaniards.

8-9 **in mediam aciem** = *the centre of the line,* i.e. of the Gauls and Spaniards, who were intended to engage with the Romans first.

10 **subsidia** = *reserves,* i.e. the Africans, on the right and left.

14-16 **Afri circa . . . alas.** Hannibal's formation is now reversed.* The horns (**cornua**) of the semicircle (the Africans) are now advanced, and *outflanked*(**circumdedere alas**) the Romans, who rushed heedlessly *into the intervening space* (**in medium**, i.e. the *concave* part of H.'s line formed by the retirement of the Gauls and Spaniards).

21-22 **recentibus ac vegetis** = *fresh in body and mind.*

* i.e. the Africans now formed the horns of a *crescent* in relation to their centre, while it formed the *concave* part of the crescent.—D.

Results of the Battle. Hannibal becomes master of Magna Graecia, and the Romans lose (including 23,000 taken prisoners) about 70,000 men.

130

C₂₃

SECOND PUNIC WAR, 218-202 B.C. CANNAE, 216 B.C. (2)

'Paulus animae magnae prodigus.'

Cn. Lentulus tribunus militum cum praetervehens equo sedentem in saxo cruore oppletum consulem vidisset, 'L. Aemili' inquit, 'quem unum insontem culpae cladis hodiernae dei respiceredebent, cape hunc equum, dum et tibi virium aliquid superest, 5et comes ego te tollere possum ac protegere. Ne funestam hanc pugnam morte consulis feceris; etiam sine hoc lacrimarum satis luctusque est.' Ad ea consul: 'Tu quidem, Cn. Corneli, macte virtute esto; sed cave frustra miserando exiguum tempus e10manibus hostium evadendi absumas. Abi, nuntia publice patribus, urbem Romanam muniant ac, priusquam victor hostis advenit, praesidiis firment; privatim Q. Fabio L. Aemilium praeceptorumeius memorem et vixisse adhuc et mori. Memet in hac 15strage militum meorum patere exspirare, ne aut reus iterum e consulatusim aut accusator oollegae existam, ut alieno crimine innocentiam meam protegam.' Haec eos agentes prius turba fugientium civium, deinde hostes oppressere; consulem ignorantes, 20quis esset, obruere telis, Lentulum inter tumultum arripuit equus. Tum undique effuse fugiunt.

LIVY, xxii. 49.

1 **praetervehens equo** = *riding by.* **praetervehor** used here as a deponent.—Dimsdale.

2 **oppletum** (= *perfusum*) = *covered* (lit. *filled up*), or*drenched.*

4 **respicere** = *to look on with favour.*—D.

9 **macte virtute esto** = lit. *go on and prosper in your courage.*

mactus = i. *magis* + *auctus* = *increased, glorified,* or more prob. ii. = old partic. of obsolete *mago* (= *augeo*), from √μακ, e.g. in μάκ-αρ. Vocative used as nominative.

14 **praeceptorum.** His self-sacrifice was not in vain. The tactics of Fabius were again adopted after his death.

15 **et vixisse adhuc et mori** = *died as he had ever lived.*—D.

17 **reus iterum e consulatu** = *a second time to stand on my defence in consequence of my consulship,* i.e. on a charge that grew out of his acts as Consul (219 B.C.) with M. Livius Salinator of misappropriation of the spoils at the close of the Illyrian War.

18-19 **ut . . . protegam.** The two Consuls had the chief command of the army on alternate days. Varro was in command at Cannae.

'The overthrow of Cannae was so complete that every other nation but the Romans would have given up the idea of further resistance.'—Ihne.

131

C₂₄

SECOND PUNIC WAR, 218-202 B.C. CANNAE, 216 B.C. (3)

A. Maharbal urges Hannibal to march on Rome.

Hannibali victori cum ceteri circumfusi gratularentur suaderentque, ut tanto perfunctus bello diei quod reliquum esset noctisque insequentis quietem et ipse sibi sumeret et fessis daret militibus, Maharbal praefectus equitum, minime cessandum ratus, 'Immo 5ut, quid hac pugna sit actum, scias, die quinto' inquit 'victor in Capitolio epulaberis. Sequere: cum equite, ut priusvenisse quam venturum sciant, praecedam.' Hannibali nimis laetares est visa maiorque, quam ut eam statim capere animo posset. Itaque voluntatem 10se laudare Maharbalis ait; ad consilium pensandum temporis opus esse. Tum Maharbal: 'Non omnia nimirum eidem di dedere; vincere scis, Hannibal, victoria uti nescis.' Mora eius diei satis creditur saluti fuisse urbi atque imperio.15

LIVY, xxii. 51.

2-4 **diei . . . sumeret** = *he should take what remained of that day and the following night for rest.*— Church and Brodribb.

8 **venisse,** sc. **te,** suggested by **sequere.**—Dimsdale.

9 **res** = *the idea,* i.e. of such a rapid termination to the war.—D.

90

Hannibal was too far off (11 days' march) to take Rome by storm. Its population contained as many soldiers as his army, and the city was strongly fortified by its situation and by art.

B. Scipio forbids the Nobles to abandon Italy.

Post Cannensem cladem perculsis ita Romanorum animis, ut pars magna reliquiarum nobilissimis auctoribus descerndae Italiae iniret consilium, P. Scipio adulescens admodum impetu facto, in eo ipso in quo talia agitabantur coetu pronuntiavit manu se 20sua interfecturum, nisi qui iurasset non esse sibi mentem destituendae rei publicae: cumque ipse se primus religione tali obligasset, stricto gladio mortem uni ex proximis minatus, nisi acciperet sacramentum, illum metu, ceteros etiam exemplo coegit ad iurandum.25

FRONTINUS, Strat. iv. 7. 39.

18 **P. Scipio adulescens**, i.e. P. Corn. Scipio Africanns Maior, *fatalis dux huiusce belli*, the predestined champion in this war.

Parallel Passage. Livy, xxii. 53, and cf. Livy, v. 50-55, where Camillus dissuades the commons from migrating to Veii.

132

C₂₅

SECOND PUNIC WAR, 218-202 B.C.

A. Rome's Heroes.

Regulum et Scauros animaeque magnae
Prodigum Paulum superante Poeno
Gratus insigni referam Camena
40
Fabriciumque.
Hunc et incomptis Curium capillis
Utilem bello tulit et Camillum
Saeva paupertas et avitus apto
44
Cum lare fundus.
Crescit occulto velut arbor aevo
Fama Marcelli; micat inter omnes
Iulium sidus velut inter ignes
48
Luna minores.

HORACE, Odes, I. xii. 37-48.

37 **Scauros*** (= **Scaurum**) = *such men as Scaurus.* Censor, 100 B.C.

40 **Fabricium**, who despised the bribes of Pyrrhus. Censor 275 B.C. See p. 101, Fabricius the Just.

43-44 **apto cum lare** = *with homestead to match.*—Gow.

* Cf. in French, *Les Vergiles.*

B. The Dream of Propertius.

Visus eram molli recubans Heliconis in umbra,
Bellerophontei qua fluit umor equi,
Reges, Alba, tuos et regum facta tuorum,
4
Tantum operis, nervis hiscere posse meis;
Parvaque tam magnis admoram fontibus ora,
Unde pater sitiens Ennius ante bibit,
Et cecini Curios fratres et Horatia pila,
8
Regiaque Aemilia vecta tropaea rate,
Victricesque moras Fabii pugnamque sinistram
Cannensem et versos ad pia vota deos,
Hannibalemque Lares Romana sede fugantes,
12
Anseris et tutum voce fuisse Iovem.

PROPERTIUS, III. (IV.) iii. (ii.) 1-12.

Subject:—Propertius had tremblingly touched the mighty fount with his lips (l. 5): he dreamed that he essayed, in consequence, to follow the example of Ennius.

2 i.e. the Spring of Pirene near Corinth, where Pegasus was caught by Bellerophon. Its waters possessed inspiring properties.

4 **nervis . . . meis** = *that I had strength to gasp forth.*—Ramsay.

7 **Curios** = *Curiatios.*

Horatia pila: see pp. 67-68.

8 **Aemilia**, i.e. of L. Aemilius Paullus (son of the hero of Cannae), victor at Pydna 168 B.C. over Perseus of Macedon.

10 **versos . . . deos**, i.e. the solemn ordinances decreed by Fabius, Dictator after Trasimene, to which the gods *turned a ready ear* (**versos**).

12 **fuisse**, dependent on **cecini** l. 7.

Iovem, i.e. *Iovis Capitolini templum.* See p. 84.

133

C₂₆

SECOND PUNIC WAR, 218-202 B.C.

The Revolt of Capua, *216-211 B.C. (1)*

A. **Capua aspires to rival Rome.**

Altera iam teritur bellis civilibus aetas,
Suis et ipsa Roma viribus ruit.
Quam neque finitimi valuerunt perdere Marsi,
4
Minacis aut Etrusca Porsenae manus,
Aemula nec virtus Capuae nec Spartacus acer
Novisque rebus infidelis Allobrox,
Nec fera caerulea domuit Germania pube
8
Parentibusque abominatus Hannibal:
Impia perdemus devoti sanguinis aetas,
Ferisque rursus occupabitur solum.

HORACE, *Epod.* xvi. 1-10.

5 **Aemula virtus Capuae.** In 216 B.C. Capua was, after Rome, the richest and most powerful city in Italy. As the result of Cannae she aspired to dominion over Italy.

Spartacus acer, leader of the Servile War, 73-71 B.C.

6 **novis rebus infidelis** = *faithless to revolution*, because they assisted in betraying Catiline's plot 63 B.C.—Wickham.

9 **impia . . . aetas** = *we an impious generation whose blood is foredoomed* (i.e. there is a curse on us) *shall destroy*(Rome).

B. **Decius Magius defies Hannibal.**

Egressus curia Hannibal in templo magistratuum consedit, comprehendique Decium Magium atque ante pedes destitutum causam dicere iussit. Qui cum manente ferocia animi negaret lege foederis id cogi posse, tum iniectae catenae, ducique ante lictorem15in castra est iussus. Quoad capite aperto est ductus, contionabundus incessit ad circumfusam undique multitudinem vociferans: 'Habetis libertatem, Campani, quam petistis: foro medio, luce clara, videntibus vobis nulli Campanorum secundus vinctus ad mortem 20rapior. Quid violentius capta Capua fieret? Ite obviam Hannibali, exornate urbem diemque adventus eius consecrate, ut hunc triumphum de cive vestro spectetis.'

LIVY, xxiii. 10.

Context. After the Revolt of Capua, when Hannibal made a public entry into the city, the whole population, with the exception of Decius Magius and his son, poured out to meet him.

11 **in templo magistratuum** = *on the magistrates' bench*, (or *tribunal*).

12 **Decium Magium**, one of the few Capuan nobles faithful to Rome.

14-15 **negaret . . . posse** = *urged that by the terms of the treaty* (i.e. between the Capuans and H.) *this could not be insisted on.*—Church and Brodribb.

134

C₂₇

SECOND PUNIC WAR, 218-202 B.C.

The Revolt of Capua, *216-211 B.C. (2)*

A. **'Capua,' it is said, 'became Hannibal's Cannae.'**

Cum victoria Hannibal posset uti, frui maluit relictaque RomaCampaniam Tarentumque peragrare, ubi mox et ipse et exercitus ardor elanguit adeo ut vere dictum sit Capuam Hannibali Cannas fuisse. Si quidem invictum Alpibus, indomitum armis Campani—quis 5crederet?—soles et tepentes fontibus Baiae subegerunt.

FLORUS, II. vi. 21-22.

2 **Campaniam Tarentumque**, once the two most fertile districts in Italy.

4 **Capuam . . . fuisse.** Ihne says: 'Whatever may have been the pleasures and indulgences of Hannibal's troops in Capua, their military qualities cannot have suffered by them, as the subsequent history of the war sufficiently demonstrates.'

7-8 **tepentes fontibus Baiae**, on a small bay west of Naples and opposite Puteoli, abounded in warm mineral springs.

B. The Punishment of Rebel Capua, 211 B.C.

Ad septuaginta principes senatus interfecti, trecenti ferme nobiles Campani in carcerem conditi; alii per sociorum Latini nominisurbes in custodias 10dati variis casibus interierunt; multitudo alia civium Campanorum venum data. De urbe agroque reliqua consultatio fuit, quibusdam delendam censentibus urbem praevalidam, propinquam, inimicam. Ceterum praesens utilitas vicit; nam propter agrum, quem 15omni fertilitate terrae satis constabat primum in Italia esse, urbs servata est, ut esset aliqua aratorum sedes. Urbi frequentandae multitudo incolarum libertinorumque et institorum opificumque retenta; ager omnis et tecta publica populi Romani facta.20

LIVY, xxvi. 16.

10 **sociorum Latini nominis** = *sociorum* ac *Latini nominis*, which includes all the Italian allies. 'The *Nomen Latinum* were the members of the old Latin league whose rights were reduced in 338 B.C. after the Latin War.'—Rawlins.

13 **delendam.** Cf. Cato's *Delenda est Carthago.*

15-17 **agrum . . . in Italia esse.** Cf. Verg. *Georg.* ii. 224-5: 'Such is the tilth of wealthy Capua and the coast that borders the Vesuvian ridge.'—Mackail.

18 **frequentandae** = *for the purpose of peopling.*

19 **institorum** = *pedlars or dealers.* Cf. our 'commercial travellers.'

20 **publica . . . facta** = *confiscated.* 'This *ager publicus* was leased by the censors to farmers (*aratores*) who paid rent (*vectigal*) for it.'—R.

135

C₂₈

SECOND PUNIC WAR, 218-202 B.C.

Marcellus at Nola, 216 B.C.

Ad tres portas in hostes versas Marcellus tripertito exercitum instruxit. . . . Ita instructi intra portas stabant. Hannibali sub signis, id quod per aliquot dies fecerat, ad multum diei in acie stanti primo miraculo esse, quod nec exercitus Romanus 5porta egrederetur nec armatus quisquam in muris essent. Ratus deinde, prodita colloquia esse, metuque resides factos, partem militum in castra remittit iussos propere apparatum omnem oppugnandae urbis in primam aciem afferre, satis fidens, si cunctantibus 10instaret, tumultum aliquem in urbe plebem moturam. Dum in sua quisque ministeria discursu trepidat ad prima signa succeditque ad muros acies, patefacta repente porta Marcellus signa canere clamoremque tolli ac pedites primum, deinde equites, quanto15maximo possent impetu, in hostem erumpere iubet. Satis terroris tumultusque in aciem mediam intulerant, cum duabus circa portis P. Valerius Flaccus et C. Aurelius in cornua hostium erupere. . . .Ingens victoria eo die res ac nescio an maxima illo bello gesta 20est; non vinci enim ab Hannibale tunc diffcilius fuit quam postea vincere.

LIVY, xxiii. 16.

Context. The plebs in Nola (as in Capua) was in favour of joining Hannibal, and it was with difficulty that the nobles (who here, as elsewhere, favoured Rome) delayed the decision, thus gaining time to inform Marcellus, who was then stationed at Casilinum, of the danger of a revolt. Marcellus immediately hastened to Nola, and occupied the town with a strong garrison.

3-5 **Hannibali . . . primo miraculo esse** = *Hannibal, who . . . had his troops under arms till a late hour, was first of all astonished that.*—Church and Brodribb.

7 **colloquia esse**, i.e. his *communications* (**colloquia**) with the Carthaginian party in Nola.

8 **resĭdes** = *inactive*, lit. *that remains sitting* (**re** + **sedeo**).

10 **si cunctantibus instaret** = *if he met hesitation with prompt action.*—Church and Brodribb. Lit. *if he pressed upon those hesitating.*

12 **in sua . . . ministeria** = *to their several posts.*

19-21 **Ingens . . . gesta est** = *a great victory, the greatest, perhaps throughout the war, was achieved that day.*

Nola, an important town in Campania, S.E. of Capua. It remained faithful to the Romans, even after Cannae, when the other Campanian towns revolted to Hannibal.

93

Marcellus at Nola. 'It was the merit of Marcellus that he saved Nola from being taken.'—Ihne.

136

C₂₉

SECOND PUNIC WAR, 218-202 B.C.

Cicero's Description of Syracuse.

Urbem Syracusas maximam esse Graecarum urbium pulcherrimamque omnium saepe audistis, Est, indices, ita, ut dicitur: nam et situ est cum munito, tum ex omni aditu vel terra vel mari praeclaro ad aspectum: et portus habet prope in aedificatione5aspectuque urbis inclusos: qui cum diversos inter se aditus habeant, in exitu coniunguntur et confluunt. Eorum coniunctione pars oppidi, quae appellatur Insula, mari disiuncta angusto, ponte rursum adiungitur et continetur. Ea tanta est urbs, ut ex 10quattuor urbibus maximis constare dicatur: quarum una est ea, quam dixi,Insula: quae duobus portubus cincta, in utriusque portus ostium aditumque proiecta est: in qua domus est, quae Hieronis regis fuit, qua praetores uti solent. Altera autem est urbs 15Syracusis, cui nomen Achradina est: in qua forum maximum, pulcherrimae porticus, ornatissimum prytaneum, amplissima est curia, templumque egregium Iovis Olympii. Tertia est urbs, quae, quod in ea parte Fortunae fanum antiquum fuit, 20Tycha nominata est, in qua et gymnasium amplissimum est et complures aedes sacrae: coliturque ea pars et habitatur frequentissime. Quarta autem est urbs, quae quia postrema coaedificata est, Neapolis nominatur: quam ad summam theatrum est maximum.25

CICERO, *In Verrem*, ii. 4. 117-119.

5-6 **prope . . . inclusos**, a special feature of Syracuse, because many ancient cities were built at some distance from the sea, with a harbour detached from them (e.g. Ostia, the port of Rome), though sometimes joined by long walls, as at Athens.

7 **in exitu** = *at their outlet*, i.e. the narrow channel between Ortygia (= Insula) and the mainland which connected the two harbours.

9 **disiuncta** = *separated from the rest* (**dis**—).

12 **Insula**, i.e. Ortygia, the only part now inhabited.

14 **Hieronis regis**, King of Syracuse, 270-216 B.C., distinguished by his military ability and the wise policy of his reign. From 263 B.C. till his death, the faithful friend and ally of Rome.

16 **Achradina**, the mainland N. of Ortygia. At the time of the famous siege of Syracuse by the Athenians, 415-413 B.C., the city consisted only of Ortygia and Achradina.

18 **prytaneum** = *town-hall* (πρυτανεῖον = *the presidents' hall*).

25 **theatrum est maximum**, capable of holding 25,000 people. Of all the buildings described by Cicero as existing in Neapolis, the Theatre alone remains.

Reference. Freeman's *History of Sicily*.

137

C₃₀

SECOND PUNIC WAR, 218-202 B.C.

Engineering Skill of Archimedes.

Adversus hunc navalem apparatum Archimedes variae magnitudinis tormenta in muria disposuit. In eas, quae procul erant, naves saxa ingenti pondere emittebat, propiores levioribus eoque magis crebris petebat telis; postremo, ut sui vulnere intacti tela 5in hostem ingererent, murum ab imo ad summum crebriscubitalibus fere cavis aperuit, per quae cava pars sagittis parsscorpionibus modicis ex occulto petebant hostem. Quae propius quaedam subibant naves, quo interiores ictibus tormentorum essent, in 10eas tollenone super murum eminente ferrea manus, firmae catenae illigata, cum iniecta prorae esset graviquelibramento plumbi recelleret ad solum, suspensa prora navem in puppim statuebat; dein remissa subito velut ex muro cadentem navem cum 15ingenti trepidatione nautarum ita undae affligebat, ut, etiam si recta recideret, aliquantum aquae acciperet, Ita maritima oppugnatio est elusa omnisque spes eo versa, ut totis viribus terra aggrederentur. Sed ea quoque pars eodem omni apparatu tormehtorum instructa 20erat Hieronis impensis curaque per multos annos, Archimedis unica arte.

LIVY, xxiv, 34.

1 **adversus . . . apparatum**, i.e. to oppose the elaborate naval attack by Marcellus on the seaward defences of Achradina.

7 **cubitalibus fere cavis** = *with holes* (fr. **cavum** = noun)*about 1½ feet square*, **cubitalibus** (*cubitum*) = *a cubit long*. Polybius has a *palm* long, about 3 inches. This is more probable.

8 **scorpionibus** = *crossbows* or *manuballistae*.

94

10 **quo interiores . . . essent** = *so as to be too close in to be hit by* (**intertores ictibus**) *the engines.*

10-12 **in eas** (sc. **proras**) **iniecta** = *on their bows was dropped . . .*

11 **tollenone** = *from a swing beam,* supported at the centre of gravity by a strong fixed fulcrum.

12-13 **cum (ferrea manus) gravique . . . ad solum** = lit.*when (the grappling-iron) swung back* (**recelleret**) *to the ground by a heavyweight of lead.* 'This is incorrect; it was not the grappling-iron, but the other (*inland*) end of the lever which was brought down to the ground.'—Rawlins.

15 **remissa** (sc. **ferrea manus**) = *the grappling-hook was(then) suddenly let go.*

16 **ita undae affligebat** = *was dashed with such violence on the disturbed water* (**undae**).

Cause of the War. Soon after the death of Hiero in 216B.C., his whole family was murdered, and the supreme power in Syracuse fell into the hands of the two brothers, Hippocrates and Epicydes, Hannibal's agents.

138

C₃₁

SECOND PUNIC WAR, 218-202 B.C.

Marcellus laments over Syracuse.

Marcellus ut moenia ingressus ex superioribus locis urbem omnium ferme ilia tempestate pulcherrimam subiectam oculis vidit, illacrimasse dicitur partim gaudio tantae perpetratae rei, partim vetusta gloria urbis. Atheniensium classes demersae et duo5ingentes exercitus cum duobus clarissimis ducibus deleti occurrebant et tot bella cum Carthaginiensibus tanto cum discrimine gesta>, tot tam opulenti tyranni regesque, praeter ceteros Hiero cum recentissimae memoriae rex, tum ante omnia, quae virtus ei fortunaque 10sua dederat, beneficiis in populum Romanum insignis. Ea cum universa occurrerent animo subiretque cogitatio, iam illa momento horae arsura omnia et ad cineres reditura, priusquam signa Achradinam admoveret, praemittit Syracusanos, 15qui intra praesidia Romana fuerant, ut alloquio leni impellerent hostes ad dedendam urbem. . . . Achradina diripienda militi data est. Cum multa irae, multa avaritiae foeda exempla ederentur, Archimeden memoriae proditum est in tanto tumultu, quantum 20pavor captae urbis in discursu diripientium militum ciere poterat, intentum formis, quas in pulvere descripserat, ab ignaro milite, quis esset, interfectum; aegre id Marcellum tulisse sepulturaeque curam habitam, et propinquis etiam inquisitis honori praesidioque 25nomen ac memoriam eius fuisse.

LIVY, xxv. 24, 31.

1-2 **ex superioribus locis**, i.e. from the heights of Epipolae, which he had taken by a night attack, when the Syracusans were celebrating a three days' festival of Artemis.

6 **ducibus**, e.g. Lamachus, Eurymedon, Demosthenes.

7-8 **tot bella . . . gesta**, e.g. at Himera, 480 B.C., on the same day as Salamis.

8-9 **tot tam . . . regesque**, e.g. Gelo, 485 B.C.; Dionysius the Elder, 406 B.C.; Hiero II., the friend and ally of Rome, King of Syracuse, 270-216 B.C.

8 **tyranni**, i.e. *absolute rulers, despots,* with reference rather to the *irregular way* in which the power was gained, than the way in which it *was exercised.*

16 **qui . . . fuerant**, i.e. Syracusan deserters who kept up communication with the republican (pro-Roman) party in Syracuse.

22 **formis** = *diagrams.*

24 **sepulturae**. Cf. Demonstration VI, page 54.

The Treatment of Syracuse. It would have been the undying glory of Marcellus if, on obtaining possession, he had shielded the unhappy city from further miseries. The art-treasures of Syracuse were sent to Rome, a precedent afterwards followed.

139

C₃₂

SECOND PUNIC WAR, 218-202 B.C.

The Death of Marcellus, *208 B.C.*

Exiguum campi ante castra erat; inde in collem aperta undique et conspecta ferebat via. Numidis speculator, nequaquam in spem tantae rei positus, sed si quos vagos pabuli aut lignorum causa longius a castris progressos possent excipere, signum dat, ut5pariter ab suis quisque latebris exorerentur. Non ante apparuere, quibus obviis ab iugo ipso consurgendum erat, quam circumiere, qui ab tergo intercluderent viam. Tum undique omnes exorti et clamore sublato impetum fecere. Cum in ea valle 10consules essent, ut neque evadere possent in iugum occupatum ab hoste nec receptum ab tergo circumventi haberent, extrahi tamen diutius certamen potuisset, ni coepta ab Etruscis fuga pavorem ceteris15iniecisset. Non tamen omisere pugnam deserti ab EtruscisFregellani, donec integri consules hortando ipsique ex parte pugnando rem sustinebant; sed postquam vulneratos ambo consules, Marcellum etiam transfixum lancea prolabentem ex equo moribundum 20videre, tum et ipsi—perpauci autem supererant—cum Crispino consule duobus iaculis ieto et Marcello adolescente saucio et ipso effugerunt.

LIVY, xxvii. 27.

Context. Marcellus was Consul for a fifth time in 208 B.C.After the attempt to retake Locri (S.E. of Bruttium) was frustrated by Hannibal, Marcellus and his colleague Crispinus faced H. near Venusia in Apulia. Hannibal hoped to bring on a decisive action, but Marcellus adopted Fabian tactics, and himself headed a cavalry reconnaissance to explore the country between the Roman and the Carthaginian camps.

2-3 **Numidis speculator**. A wooded hill lay between the two camps: H. had posted here in ambush some Numidian horsemen.

4-5 **si quos possent excipere** = *on the chance of their being able to intercept.*—Stephenson.

6-8 **Non ante . . . circumiere** = *those who were to spring on the enemy* (lit. *those to whom it was necessary to rise in a mass confronting the enemy* **obviis**) *from the hill itself did not show themselves until a detachment had made their way round* (**circumiere**).—S.

10 **valle** = *a hollow*, i.e. a depression on the Roman side of the hill.

16 **Fregellani**. Fregellae, a town of the Volsci, on the Via Latina between Rome and Campania, colonised 328B.C.

17 **ipsique ex parte pugnando** = *taking their share in fighting.* S.

Character of Marcellus. 'He was a brave soldier, a firm intrepid patriot, and an unflinching enemy of the enemies of Rome, but as a general no match for Hannibal.'—Ihne.

140

C_{33}

SECOND PUNIC WAR, 218-202 B.C.

Character of Scipio Africanus Maior.

Fuit enim Scipio non veris tantum virtutibus mirabilis, sed arte quoque quadam ab iuventa in ostentationem earum compositus,pleraque apud multitudinem aut *ut* per nocturnas visa species aut velut divinitus mente monita agens, sive et ipse capti 5quadam superstitione animi, sive ut imperia consiliaque velut sorte oraculi missa sine cunctatione exsequerentur. Ad hoc iam inde ab initio praeparans animos, ex quo togam virilem sumpsit, nullo die prius ullam publicam privatamque rem egit, quam 10in Capitolium iret, ingressusque aedem consideret et plerumque solus in secreto ibi tempus tereret. Hic mos, quem per omnem vitam servabat, seu consulto seu temere vulgatae opinioni fidem apud quosdam fecit, stirpis eum divinae virum esse. Multa alia 15eiusdem generis, alia vera, alia assimulata, admirationis humanae in eo iuvene excesserant modum; quibus freta tunc civitas aetati haudquaquam maturae tantam rerum molem tantumque imperium permisit.

LIVY, xxvi. 19.

2-3 **in ostentationem earum compositus** = *he made a study*(**compositus**) *of displaying them*, implying artificiality.—R.

3-5 **pleraque . . . agens** = *in most of his dealings* (**pleraque agens**) *with the mob* (*representing his plans*) *as inspired* (**visa**) *by visions in the night or as matters of inspiration* (**divinitus mente monita**).

7 **sorte** = *by an oracular response* (which was often written on a little tablet or *lot*, **sors**).

11 **aedem**, i.e. the *cella* (*chapel*, the part enclosed within the four side-walls) of the Temple of Jupiter Capitolinus.

13-14 **seu consulto seu temere vulgatae** = *whether designedly or undesignedly spread abroad.*

17 **humanae** = *which one has for a mere man.*—Rawlins.

19 **tantam rerum molem** = *so stupendous a task.*—R. In 212 or 211 B.C. the two brothers, Publius and Gnaeus Scipio, were totally defeated by Hasdrubal and fell at the head of their troops. Scipio, son of this P. Scipio, was in 210 B.C. sent to Spain, at the age of 27, as proconsul in command of a reinforcement of 11,000 men.

Character of Scipio. 'He was a man far above the average of his contemporaries, and possessed a greatness of mind which could not fail to rivet attention. He differed from the majority of generals by not only daring to conceive bold plans, but by contriving to carry them out.'—Ihne.

141

C_{34}

SECOND PUNIC WAR, 218-202 B.C.

Scipio takes New Carthage, *210 B.C.*

Scipio ipse, ut ei nuntiatum est aestum decedere, quod per piscatores Tarraconenses nunc levibus cymbis, nunc, ubi eae siderent, vadis pervagatos stagnum compertum habebat, facilem pedibus ad murum transitum dari, eo secum armatos quingentos5duxit. Ubi urbem sine

96

certamine intravere, pergunt inde, quanto maximo cursu poterant, ad eam portam, circa quam omnecontractum certamen erat. In quod adeo intenti omnium non animi solum fuere, sed etiam oculi auresque pugnantium spectantiumque10et adhortantium pugnantes, ut nemo ante ab tergo senserit captam urbem, quam tela in aversos inciderunt et utrimque ancipitemhostem habebant. Tunc turbatis defensoribus metu et moenia capta, et porta intus forisque pariter refringi coepta; et mox15caedendo confectis ac distractis, ne iter impediretur, foribus armati impetum fecerunt. . . . Quoad dedita arx est, caedes tota urbe passim factae, nec ulli puberum qui obvius fuit parcebatur; tum signo dato caedibus finis factus; ad praedam victores versi, 20quae ingens omnis generis fuit.

LIVY, xxvi. 45, 46 (sel.)

3 **vadis pervagatos stagnum** = *made their way through the pool by wading* (**vadis**).

8 **contractum** = *concentrated (confined)*.

13 **ancipitem** = *double, twofold, on two opposite sides*.

15 **intus forisque** = *both within and without*.

foris, adv. (an abl. form from an obsolete nom. **fora**) =*out of doors, without*. Cf. **foras** = *out through the doors, forth*.

16-17 **caedendo . . . distractis foribus** = *when the doors were destroyed and broken up by blows*.

Carthago Nova (Carthagena) was founded by Hasdrubal (the uncle of Hannibal) 243 B.C. The city is situated on a promontory running out into the sea, and possesses one of the finest harbours in the world, protected by an island as by a natural breakwater. But it had a weak side, and this had been betrayed by fishermen to Scipio. During ebb-tide the water of the shallow pool W. of the town fell so much that it was fordable and the bottom was firm. Of this Scipio took advantage. He first made a feint attack on the N. wall and then led 500 men across the ford, who scaled the W. wall and opened the nearest gate from the inside.

Result of its Capture. 'New Carthage, the key of Spain, the basis of operations against Italy, and the Carthaginian arsenal, was taken, thus determining the issue of the Spanish War.'—Ihne.

142

C₃₅

SECOND PUNIC WAR, 218-202 B.C.

Nero's famous March to the Metaurus, *207 B.C.*

Praemissi (nuntii) per agrum Larinatem Marrucinum Frentanum Praetutianum, qua exercitum ducturus erat, ut omnes ex agris urbibusque commeatus paratos militi ad vescendum in viam deferrent, equos iumentaque alia producerent, ut 5vehiculorum fessis copia esset. Ipse de toto exercitu civium sociorumque quod roboris erat delegit, sex milia peditum, mille equites. . . . Et hercule per instructa omnia ordinibus virorum mulierumque undique ex agris effusorum, inter vota ac preces et 10laudes ibant: illos praesidia rei publicae, vindices urbis Romanae imperiique appellabant; in illorum armis dextrisque suam liberorumque suorum salutem ac libertatem repositam esse. Deos omnes deasque precabantur, ut illis faustum iter, felix pugna, matura 15ex hostibus victoria esset, damnarenturque ipsi votorum, quae pro iis suscepissent, ut, quem ad modum nunc solliciti prosequerentur eos, ita paucos post dies laeti ovantibus victoria obviam irent. Invitare inde pro se quisque et offerre et fatigare 20precibus, ut quae ipsis iumentisque usui essent, ab se potissimum sumerent; benigne omnia cumulata dare. Modestia certare milites, ne quid ultra usum necessarium sumerent; nihil morari, nec abscedere ab signis nec subsistere nisi cibum capientes: diem 25ac noctem ire; vix quod satis ad naturale desiderium corporum esset, quieti dare.

LIVY, xxvii. 43, 45 (sel.)

Context. Nero, on hearing from the captured Numidian horsemen of Hasdrubal's march and plans—to meet Hannibal in Umbria and then to march on Narnia and Rome—with 6000 picked foot and 1000 horse withdrew secretly from his camp before Hannibal at Canusium, and by a forced march joined his colleague Livius at the Metaurus.

1-2 **Larinatem**, etc., districts lying between Apulia and Umbria, but not given in their geographical order.

15 **faustum** (for *favostus, fav-eo*) = that which is done under the blessing of the gods: **felix** = that which succeeds in consequence of having this blessing upon it.—Stephenson.

16-17 **damnarentur . . . votorum** = *condemned (to pay)their vows*. Cf. Verg. *Voti reus* = *bound to my vow*, i.e. bound to fulfilment.

23 **Modestia certare** (sc. *cum iis*) **. . . sumerent** = *the soldiers were as moderate as they were pressing, refusing to take anything* . . .—S.

'Nero showed a resolution and a strategic ability which far surpassed the average qualifications of Roman generals.'—Ihne.

97

SECOND PUNIC WAR, 218-202 B.C.

The Metaurus, *207 B.C.*

Fortes creantur fortibus et bonis;
Est in iuvencis, est in equis patrum
Virtus, neque imbellem feroces
32
Progenerant aquilae columbam;
Doctrina sed vim promovet insitam,
Rectique cultus pectora roborant;
Utcumque defecere mores,
36
Indecorant bene nata culpae.
Quid debeas, o Roma, Neronibus,
Testis Metaurum flumen et Hasdrubal
Devictus et pulcher fugatis
40
Ille dies Latio tenebris,
Qui primus alma risit adorea,
Dirus per urbes Afer ut Italas
Ceu flamma per taedas vel Eurus
44
Per Siculas equitavit undas.
Post hoc secundis usque laboribus
Romana pubes crevit, et impio
Vastata Poenorum tumultu
48
Fana deos habuere rectos.

HORACE, *Odes*, IV. iv. 29-48.

29-36 The thought is: 'It is true that scions of a good stock must be good in men as well as in animals, but yet *education* (**doctrina** = *training* l. 33) *brings out the innate force*.'

29 **fortibus et bonis.** For the combined epithets cf. καλὸς κἀγαθός.

36 **Indecorant . . . culpae** = *faults disfigure* (**indecorant** = **dedecorant**) *scions of an honourable stock* (**bene nata**).

37 **Neronibus**, e.g. M. Claudius Nero (the hero of Metaurus), and the brothers Drusus and Tiberius (afterwards Emperor), stepsons of Augustus.

41 **alma adorea** = *with kindly (refreshing) success.*

43 **ceu flamma per taedas** = *like fire through a pine-forest.*—W.

44 **equitavit** = *galloped, careered*, used of Hannibal, and, by zeugma, with **flamma** and **Eurus**.

46-47 **impio tumultu** = *by the sacrilegious invasion* (or *riot,outrage*), possibly with reference to Livy's story (xxvi. 11) of the plundering of the Temple of Feronia.

48 **rectos** = *upright*, i.e. of the images supposed to have been thrown down by Hannibal, and not set on their pedestals again.

Results of the Battle. 'The war in Italy was to all appearances finished, and it was on the Metaurus that the Romans conquered Spain.'—Ihne. When Hannibal recognised the head of his brother Hasdrubal, he foresaw the doom of Carthage:—

'Lost, lost is all:
A nation's hope, a nation's name,
They died with dying Hasdrubal.'

C. (Hor. *Od.* IV. iv. 70-73).

SECOND PUNIC WAR, 218-202 B.C.

Hannibal leaves Italy, *203 B.C.*

Nihil certe ultra rei in Italia ab Hannibale gestum. Nam ad eum quoque legati ab Carthagine vocantes in Africam eis forte diebus, quibus ad Magonem, venerunt. Frendens gemensque ac vix lacrimis temperans dicitur legatorum verba audisse. 5Postquam edita sunt mandata, 'Iam non perplexe,' inquit, 'sed palam revocant, qui vetando supplementum et pecuniam mitti iam pridem trahebant. Vicit ergo Hannibalem non populus Romanus totiens caesus fugatusque, sed senatus Carthaginiensis10obtrectatione atque invidia; neque hac deformitate reditus mei tam P. Scipio exsultabit atque efferet sese quam Hanno, qui domum nostram, quando alia re non potuit, ruina Carthaginis oppressit.' Iam hoc ipsum praesagiens animo praeparaverat 15ante naves. Itaque inutili militum turba praesidii specie in oppida Bruttii agri, quae pauca magis metu quam fide continebantur, dimissa, quod roboris in exercitu erat in Africam transvexit. Raro quemquam alium, patriam exilii causa relinquentem, 20tam maestum abisse ferunt quam Hannibalem, hostium terra excedentem.

LIVY, xxx. 19, 20.

Context. Scipio (204 B.C.) landed in Africa and won such decisive victories over the Carthaginians under Hasdrubal, the son of Gisco, that ii was necessary in 203 B.C. to recall both Mago and Hannibal.

3-4 **ad Magonem.** Mago, H.'s youngest brother, had in 205B.C. been despatched from Carthage with considerable reinforcements for H. He took Genoa, again roused the Gauls against Rome, and in 203 B.C. fought an indecisive action with the Romans. Mago was severely wounded, and died at sea before he reached Africa.

6 **Iam non perplexe** = *now in no veiled manner* (lit. *not obscurely*).

8 **iam pridem trahebant** = *began long ago to try to pull me back.*—Rawlins.

11 **obtrectatione** = *by disparagement.*

13 **Hanno**, the leader of the aristocratic (peace) party at Carthage, and the persistent opponent of Hamilcar Barca and his sons.

Hannibal's Speech. ll. 6-15. This is purely imaginary and illustrates the bitter hatred of the Romans for H. They alleged that H. was personally responsible for the war, and that he undertook it for selfish and party ends. Also that Carthage, unable to prevent the war, withheld supplies and reinforcements. Ihne says 'The whole course of the war is a sufficient refutation of these charges.'

145

C38

SECOND PUNIC WAR, 218-202 B.C.

Zama, *202 B.C. (1)* Before the Battle.

Ita infecta pace ex colloquio ad suos cum se recepissent, frustra verba praelata renuntiant: armis decernendum esse habendamque eam fortunam, quam dei dedissent. In castra ut est ventum, pronuntiant ambo, arma expedirent milites animosque ad5supremum certamen, non in unum diem sed in perpetuum, si felicitas adesset, victores. Roma an Carthago iura gentibus daret, ante crastinam noctem scituros; neque enim Africam aut Italiam, sed orbem terrarum victoriae praemium fore; par 10periculum praemio, quibus adversa pugnae fortuna fuisset. Nam neque Romanis effugium ullum patebat in aliena ignotaque terra et Carthagini supremo auxilio effuso adesse videbatur praesens excidium. Ad hoc discrimen procedunt postero die duorum15opulentissimorum populorum duo longe clarissimi duces, duo fortissimi exercitus, multa ante parta decora aut cumulaturi eo dicaut eversuri. Anceps igitur spes et metus miscebant animos; contemplantibus modo suam modo hostium aciem, cum non oculis 20magis quam ratione pensarent vires, simul laeta simul tristia obversabantur.

LIVY, xxx. 31, 32.

1-2 **Ita infecta pace . . . renuntiant**, referring to Livy's picturesque account of the personal interview between Scipio and Hannibal, and the fruitless negotiations for peace.

7-10 **Roma an Carthago . . . praemium fore.** 'By the victory of Zama it was decided that the states of the ancient world should be welded into one great empire, and that this empire should be founded by Rome and not by Carthage.'—Ihne.

14 **effuso** = *dispersed*, i.e. *defeated.*

15 **discrimen** = *decisive point, decision.*

18 **aut cumulaturi aut eversuri** = *either to augment* (lit.*heap up*) *or overthrow.*

21 **pensarent vires** = *they estimated (weighed) their strength.*

The Battle of Zama. 'Here, too, the elephants proved disastrous to their own side. Some ran down the spaces between the Roman maniples (see C 39, B. note), and were of no further use; while others, driven aside by the Roman skirmishers, threw H.'s Carthaginian cavalry into such disorder that they were unable to resist the attack of Scipio's horse. The first Roman line threw H.'s mercenaries back upon their reserves of the second line, and in the confusion that ensued Scipio advanced with his second and third lines. The combat raged long and fiercely until Scipio's Roman and Numidian cavalry, returning from their pursuit of H.'s horse, fell upon the enemy's rear and decided the battle.'—Ihne.

146

C39

99

SECOND PUNIC WAR, 218-202 B.C.

Zama, *202 B.C. (2)*

The Order of Battle.

A.Hannibal adversus Scipionem, post elephantos lxxx, qui in prima fronte positi hostium turbarent aciem, auxiliares Gallos et Ligures et Baliares Maurosque posuit, ut neque fugere possent Poenis a tergo stantibus et hostem oppositi, si non infestarent, 5at certe fatigarent: tum suis et Macedonibus, qui iam fessos Romanos integri exciperent, in secunda acie collocatis, novissimos Italicos constituit, quorum et timebat fidem et segnitiam verebatur, quoniam plerosque eorum ab Italia invitos extraxerat.10

Hannibal's Army. It consisted broadly of five classes:

1. His veteran army of Italy, on which he could thoroughly rely, partly Carthaginian, partly Italian (mostly Bruttians).

These he placed in his *third* line.

2. A newly raised force of Carthaginian and Libyan militia.

These he placed in his *second* line.

3. Mercenaries, consisting of Moors, Gauls, Ligurians, the Balearic contingent, and the Spaniards.

These he placed in his *first* line.

4. Carthaginian and Numidian cavalry.

These he placed on his *wings*.

5. 80 elephants. These he placed on his *front*, to open the attack.

B.Scipio adversus hanc formam robur legionis triplici acie in fronte ordinatum per hastatos et principes et triarios opposuit: nec continuas construxit cohortes, sed manipulis inter se distantibus spatium dedit, per quod elephanti ab hostibus acti 15facile transmitti sine perturbatione ordinum possent. Ea ipsa intervalla expeditis velitibus implevit, ne interluceret acies, dato his praecepto, ut ad impetum elephantorum vel retro vel in latera concederent. Equitatum deinde in cornua divisit et dextro Romanis 20equitibus Laelium, sinistro Numidis Masinissam praeposuit: quae tam prudens ordinatio non dubie causa victoriae fuit.

FRONTINUS, Strategemata, ii. 3. 16.

Scipio's order of battle. Instead of drawing up his manipuli like the black squares of a chessboard—the usual order, so that, in advancing, the manipuli of the three lines could form one unbroken line—he placed them one behind the other, like the rounds of a ladder, so as to leave spaces in the lines, through which the elephants might pass without trampling down or throwing into confusion the infantry battalions, e.g.:

147
C40

FORMATION OF EMPIRE BEYOND ITALY.
SECOND MACEDONIAN WAR, 200-196 B.C. (1)

Battle of Cynoscephalae, *197 B.C.*

Non dubia res fuit; extemplo terga vertere Macedones, terrore primo bestiarum aversi. Et ceteri quidem hos pulsos sequebantur;unus e tribunis militum, ex tempore capto consilio, cum vigintisignorum militibus, relicta ea parte suorum, quae 5haud dubie vincebat, brevi circuitu dextrum cornu hostium aversum invadit. Nullam aciem ab tergo adortus non turbasset; ceterum ad communem omnium in tali re trepidationem accessit, quod phalanx Macedonum, gravis atque immobilis, nec 10circumagere se poterat, nec hoc, qui a fronte, paulo ante pedem referentes, tunc ultro territis instabant, patiebantur. Ad hoc loco etiam premebantur, quia iugum, ex quo pugnaverant, dum per proclive pulsos insequuntur, tradiderant hosti ad terga sua circumducto.15Paulisper in medio caesi, deinde omissis plerique armis capessunt fugam. Philippus cum paucis peditum equitumque primo tumulum altiorem inter ceteros cepit, ut specularetur, quae in laeva parte suorum fortuna esset; deinde, postquam fugam 20effusam animadvertit et omnia circa iuga signis atque armis fulgere, tum et ipse acie excessit.

LIVY, xxxiii. 9, 10.

Context. Philip V, King of Macedon, had made a treaty with Hannibal in 215 B.C., and provoked the first Macedonian War (214-205 B.C.) by an attack on Apollonia in Illyria, and the capture of the port of Oricum in Epirus. The Romans now resolved to make Philip suffer for the trouble he had caused them by interfering in the war with Hannibal. A *casus belli* was soon found in the Athenian Embassy to Rome (201 B.C.) asking for help against Philip.

3-4 **unus . . . militum.** Ihne says 'He seized the favourable opportunity to shape the battle which had begun without plan into a brilliant victory for Rome.'

5 **signorum** (= *manipulorum*) = *companies*, i.e. with some 3500 men.

13 **loco premebantur** = *they (i.e. the phalanx) began to feel the disadvantage of position.*— Rawlins.

16 **in medio caesi** = *cut down from both sides.*—R.

Cynoscephalae (*Dog's Heads*), a low chain of hills between Pherae and Scotussa in Thessaly.

Results of the Battle. 'The Romans lost only 700 men. That was the price paid for a victory which laid the Monarchy of Alexander the Great in the dust.'—Ihne.

Terms of Peace, 196 B.C. Macedonia to remain an independent state, but, like Carthage, to lose all her foreign possessions, and to be sunk to the level of a vassal state.

148

C₄₁

SECOND MACEDONIAN WAR, 200-196 B.C. (2)

Flamininus proclaims the Freedom of Greece, *196 B.C.*

Isthmiorum statum ludicrum aderat, semper quidem et alias frequens cum propter spectaculi studium insitum genti, quo certamina omnis generis artium viriumque et pernicitatis visuntur, tum quia propter opportunitatem loci, per duo diversa maria5omnium rerum usus ministrantis humano generi, concilium Asiae Graeciaeque is mercatus erat; tum vero non ad solitos modo usus undique convenerant, sed exspectatione erecti, qui deinde status futurus Graeciae, quae sua fortuna esset. Ad spectaculum10consederant, et praeco cum tubicine, ut mos est, in mediam aream, unde sollemni carmine ludicrum indici solet, processit et, tuba silentio facto, ita pronuntiat: 'Senatus Romanus et T. Quinctius imperator, Philippo rege Macedonibusque devictis, 15liberos, immunes, suis legibus esse iubet Corinthios, Phocenses,Locrensesque omnes et insulam Euboeam et Magnetas, Thessalos, Perrhaebos, Achaeos Phthiotas.' . . . Esse aliquam in terris gentem, quae sua impensa, suo labore ac periculo bella gerat pro 20libertate aliorum. Una voce praeconis liberatas omnes Graeciae atque Asiae urbes; hoc spe concipere audacis animi fuisse, ad effectum adducere et virtutis et fortunae ingentis.

LIVY, xxxiii. 32, 33 (scl.)

1 **Isthmiorum statum ludicrum** = *time fixed* (**statum**) *for the Isthmian Games* (celebrated at Corinth every two years).

3-4 **quo certamina . . . visuntur** = *which makes them go to see contests of every kind of artistic performance*(**artium**) *and of feats of strength and agility.*—Rawlins.

7 **concilium is mercatus erat . . .** = *that gathering was the general rendezvous* (**mercatus**) *of . . .* **mercatus** = i.*trade*, or *mart*; ii. *a festival assemblage* (πανήγυρις).

11 **in mediam aream** = *into the centre of the open space* (*of the stadium*).

17 **Locrensesque omnes**, i.e. E. & W. Locris.

18 **Perrhaebos**, N. of Thessaly.

Achaeos Phthiotas = the Achaeans who inhabited Phthiotis (S.E. of Thessaly).

19-24 **Esse aliquam . . . ingentis**: in these words the Greeks express their astonishment and gratitude at the greatness of the boon conferred upon them.

The Freedom of Greece. 'The Greeks believed with a childlike simplicity that the Romans really cared for their freedom, and that they had crossed the sea with no other object than to deliver Greece from a foreign yoke. . . . Flamininus was a skilful diplomatist, and particularly qualified to sift and settle the affairs of Greece; for he understood the Greek character, and was not inaccessible, like so many other Romans, to Greek views and opinions.'— Ihne.

149

C₄₂

WAR WITH ANTIOCHUS OF SYRIA, 191-190 B.C.

A. Battle of Thermopylae, *191 B.C.* Victory due to Cato.

Acilius Glabrio consul adversus Antiochi regis aciem, quam is in Achaia pro angustiis Thermopylarum direxerat, iniquitatibus loci non irritus tantum, sed cum iactura qnoque repulsus esset, nisi circummissus ab eo Porcius Cato, qui tum, iam 5consularis, tribunus militum a populo factus in exercitu erat, deiectis iugis Callidromi mentis Aetolis, qui praesidio ea tenebant, super imminentem castris regiis collem a tergo subitus apparuisset: quo facto perturbatis Antiochi copiis utrimque irrupere Romani 10et fusis fugatisque castra ceperunt.

Context. In 192 B.C. Antiochus the Great, king of Syria, accepted the invitation of the Aetolians, who, since the Peace of 196 B.C., had been snubbed by the Romans, to come to liberate Greece from the tyranny of Rome.

B. Battle of Magnesia, *190 B.C.*

Tum consule Scipione, cui frater, ille modo victor Carthaginis Africanus, aderat voluntaria legatione, debellari regem placet. Et iam toto cesserat mari, sed nos imus ulterius. Maeandrum 15ad amnem montemque Sipylum castra ponuntur. Hic rex, incredibile dictu quibus auxiliis, quibus copiis, consederat. Trecenta milia peditum, equitum falcatorumque curruum non minor numerus. Elephantis ad hoc immensae magnitudinis, auro purpura 20argento et suo ebore fulgentibus aciem utrimque vallaverat. Sed haec omnia praepedita magnitudine sua, ad hoc imbre, qui subito superfusus mira felicitate Persicos arcus corruperat. Primum trepidatio, mox fuga, deinde triumphus fuerunt.25

FLORUS, i. 24. 14-18.

Context. In 190 B.C. Lucius Scipio was appointed to carry the war into Asia. Scipio Africanus, who accompanied his brother as Chief of Staff, fell ill at Elaea, the port of Pergamum. His place was taken by Cn. Domitius, an experienced officer.

14-15 **Et iam toto cesserat mari,** as the result of the decisive defeat, in 190 B.C., of the Syrian fleet off**Myonnesus**.

15-16 **Maeandrum . . . ponuntur.** The battle was fought near Magnesia (N.W. of Lydia) at the foot of Mt. Sipylus.

Parallel Passage. Livy, xxxvii. 39-44, 'The **Battle of Magnesia** decided the fate of the Syrian Empire, as the battles of **Zama** and **Cynoscephalae** had decided the fate of Carthage and Macedonia.'—Ihne.

150

C₄₃

Deaths of Three Great Men, *183 B.C.*

Hannibal, postquam est nuntiatum milites regios in vestibulo esse, postico fugere conatus, ut id quoque occursu militum obsaeptum sensit et omnia circa clausa custodiis dispositis esse, venenum, quod multo ante praeparatum ad tales habebat casus, 5poposcit. 'Liberemus,' inquit, 'diuturna cura populum Romanum, quando mortem senis exspectare longum censent. Nec magnam nec memorabilem ex inermi proditoque Flamininus victoriam feret.' Exsecratus deinde in caput regnumque 10Prusiae, et hospitales deos violatae ab eo fidei testes invocans, poculum exhausit. . . . Trium clarissimorum suae cuiusque gentis virorum non tempore magis congruente comparabilis mors videtur esse, quam quod nemo eorum satis dignum splendore 15vitae exitum habuit. Nam primum omnes non in patrio solo mortui nec sepulti sunt. Veneno absumpti Hannibal et Philopoemen; exsul Hannibal, proditus ab hospite, captus Philopoemen in carcere et in vinculis exspiravit.Scipio etsi non exsul neque 20damnatus, die tamen dicta, ad quam non adfuerat reus, absens citatus, voluntarium non sibimet ipse solum sed etiam funeri suo exsilium indixit.

LIVY, xxxix, 51, 52 (sel.)

Context. After Zama Hannibal held the highest office (*Suffete* = L. *praetura*) at Carthage, and effected useful democratic reforms. However, his political enemies denounced him to Rome *as making plans for a new war*, and in 195 B.C. he was forced to flee from Carthage and took refuge with Antiochus. After Magnesia, H. found for seven years a safe asylum with Prusias, king of Bithynia; but the Romans could not be at ease so long as H. lived, and Flamininus the Liberator of Greece undertook the inglorious quest of demanding the surrender of Hannibal.

13-15 **non tempore magis congruente quam** = *not so much in coincidence of* (**congruente**, lit. *agreeing with*) *date as*.—R.

18 **Philopoemen**, the heroic chief of the Achaean League, was taken prisoner by Dinocrates, imprisoned in a dungeon at Messene (**in carcere**, l. 19), and compelled to drink poison.

20-23 **Scipio** was accused, at the instigation of Cato, by the tribune Naevius (185 B.C.) of having been bribed by Antiochus to procure for him favourable conditions of peace. Too proud to defend himself against such a charge, Scipio retired to his country-seat at Liternum, where *by a voluntary act he consigned both himself and his grave to exile* (**voluntarium . . . indixit**).

'Ingrata patria, ne ossa quidem mea habes.'

Epitaph of Scipio, written by himself.

151

C₄₄

M. Porcius Cato, *234-149 B.C.* *(1)*

At Cato, censor cum L. Valerio Flacco, severe praefuit ei potestati. Nam et in complures nobiles animadvertit et multas res novas in edictum addidit, qua re luxuria reprimeretur, quae iam tum incipiebat pullulare. Circiter annos octoginta, usque ad extremam 5aetatem ab adolescentia, rei publicae causa suscipere inimicitias non destitit. A multis tentatus non modo nullum detrimentum existimationis fecit, sed, quoad vixit, virtutum laude crevit.

In omnibus rebus singulari fuit industria: nam 10et agricola sollers et peritus iuris consultus et magnus imperator et probabilis orator et cupidissimus litterarum fuit. Quarum studium etsi senior arripuerat, tamen tantum progressum fecit, ut non facile reperiri posset neque de Graecis neque de 15Italicis rebus, quod ei fuerit incognitum. Ab adulescentia confecit orationes. Senex historias scribere instituit. Earum sunt libri vii. Primus continet res gestas regum populi Romani, secundus et tertius unde quaeque civitas orta sit Italica, ob quam rem omnes 20Origines videtur appellasse.

NEPOS, Cato, ii., iii.

1 **Censor**, 184 B.C., with L. Valerius Flaccus, his great friend and patron, by whom he was introduced to political life.

3 **in edictum.** The Censors, on their entrance upon office, issued a *proclamation* or *edict*, setting forth the principles upon which they intended to act. Cato set forth in his edict that he intended to use his power for the suppression of luxury.

5 **pullulare** = *to spread, increase*; lit. *to put forth*, of plants and animals. Cf. *pullus* (our *pullet*), *pu-er*, πῶλος (= *a foal*).

octoginta. This is an exaggeration. He was only eighty-five when he died 149 B.C.

6-7 **rei publicae . . . non destitit.** Seneca says: *Scipio cum hostibus nostris bellum, Cato cum moribus gessit.*

7-9 Cato was accused no less than 44 times, but each time acquitted.

11 **iuris consultus** = *lawyer.*

12 **magnus imperator**, e.g. in the 2nd Punic War, and the decisive victory at Thermopylae (191 B.C.) was mainly due to Cato.

probabilis orator = *a tolerable, acceptable orator.* Oscar Browning.

17-21 His two great works were his treatise **De Re Rustica**(or **De Agri Cultura**), the earliest extant work in Latin prose, and his **Origines**, or accounts of the rise and growth of the Italian nation, the earliest history in Latin prose. 'It was Cato's great merit that he asserted the rights of his native language for literary prose composition.'—Ihne.

Cato the Censor. 'He deserves our highest respect for the defiant and manly spirit that animated him in his untiring contest with the vices of the age.'—Ihne.

152

C45

M. Porcius Cato. *(2)*

Iam pauca aratro iugera regiae
Moles relinquent, undique latius
Extenta visentur Lucrino
4
Stagna lacu platanusque caelebs
Evincet ulmos: tum violaria et
Myrtus et omnis copia narium
Spargent olivetis odorem
8
Fertilibus domino priori;
Tum spissa ramis laurea fervidos
Excludet ictus. Non ita Romuli
Praescriptum et intonsi Catonis
12
Auspiciis veterumque norma.
Privatus illis census erat brevis,
Commune magnum: nulla decempedis
Metata privatis opacam
16
Porticus excipiebat Arcton.
Nec fortuitum spernere caespitem
Leges sinebant, oppida publico
Sumptu iubentes et deorum

20

Templa novo decorare saxo.

HORACE, *Odes*, II. xv.

Argument. 'Our palaces and fish-ponds and ornamental gardens are supplanting the cultivation of corn and vines and olives. **This is not the spirit of Romulus or of Cato.**Their rule was private thrift, public magnificence; private houses of turf, public buildings and temples of hewn stone.'—W.

1 **Iam** = *presently.*

1-2 **regiae moles** = *princely piles.* **moles**, lit. *masses, of huge buildings.*

2-4 **undique . . . lacu** = *and fish-ponds* (**stagna**) *of wider extent than the L. lake will be sights to see* (**visentur**).—Wickham.

4 **platanus caelebs** = *the bachelor plane*, so called because vines were not *wedded to it* (i.e. trained upon it).—Gow.

6 **omnis copia narium** = *all that is sweet to smell.* Lit. *all the fulness of the nostrils.*

10 **ictus** (sc. *solis*). The point is that formerly trees were stripped to admit the sun to the vines and olives: nowadays the sun is excluded.—Gow.

11 **intonsi** (= *antiqui*) = *old-fashioned.* Cf. Cic.'s use of *barbatus.*

13 **census erat brevis** = *list of property was short.*

14 **commune** (= τὸ κοινόν) = *the common* (*public*) *stock.*

14-15 **decempedis metata privatis** = *measured with ten-foot rods for private owners.* In old days the **porticūs**were always *publicae.*

17 **fortuitum caespitem** = *the chance-cut* (*handy*) *turf.*

20 **novo saxo** = *with fresh-hewn stone*, i.e. hewn on purpose.—W.

Parallel Passages. Livy xxxix. 6. 40. 41; Sallust, *Catiline*12, 13.

'Cato saw the greatness of Rome in the olden time, and he endeavoured without success to bring this old time back.'—Ihne.

153

C₄₆

THIRD MACEDONIAN WAR, 171-168 B.C.

Pydna *(Aemilius Paulus)*, 168 B.C. *(1)*

Movebat imperii maiestas, gloria viri, ante omnia aetas, quod maior sexaginta annis iuvenum munia in parte praecipua laboris periculique capessebat. Intervallum, quod inter caetratos at phalanges erat, implevit legio, atque aciem hostium interrupit. A5tergo caetratis erat, frontem adversus clipeatos habebat:chalcaspides appellabantur. Secundam legionem L. Albinus consularis ducere adversus leucaspidem phalangem iussus; ea media acies hostium fuit. In dextrum cornu, unde circa fluvium10commissum proelium erat, elephantos inducit et alas sociorum; et hinc primum fuga Macedonum est orta. Nam sicut pleraque novacommenta mortalium in verbis vim habent, experiendo, cum agi, non quemadmodum agatur edisseri oportet, sine ullo 15effectu evanescunt, ita tum elephantorum impetum sustinere non poterant, et commenta Macedonum nomen tantum sine usu fuerunt. Elephantorum impetum subsecuti sunt socii nominis Latini, pepeleruntque laevum cornu.20

LIVY, xliv. 41.

Context. Perseus, son of Philip, became King of Macedonia on the death of his father in 179 B.C. He did all he could to prepare for the inevitable struggle with Rome by strengthening Macedonia, posing as the Liberator of Greece, and forming marriage alliances with Seleucus of Syria (the successor of Antiochus), and Prusias of Bithynia. In 174 B.C., the Romans were informed that Perseus was secretly negotiating with Carthage, and after fruitless embassies war was declared. The Senate, after three years of unsuccessful warfare (171-168 B.C.), appointed L. Aemilius Paulus (son of the hero who died at Cannae) to the supreme command in Macedonia.

4 **caetratos** = *Targeteers*, armed with the *small* round shield.

5-7 **A tergo . . . habebat** (sc. **legio prima**) = *the (first)Legion thus took the Targeteers in the rear, while it faced towards the Shieldmen.*—Rawlins.

6 **clipeatos** = *Shieldmen*, armed with the *large* round shield.

7 **chalcaspides** = *Brazen Shields*, Right Division of phalanx.

9 **leucaspidem** = *White Shields*, Left Division of phalanx.

10 **in dextrum cornu** (sc. **Romanum**), i.e. nearest to the sea.

13-15 **commenta . . . oportet** = lit. *the contrivances of men, though in theory* (**in verbis**) *they had some importance*(**vim**)*yet upon trial* (**experiendo**) *when there is need of action and not of discussion* (**edisseri**) *how to act.* . . .

104

17 commenta Macedonum. Perh. with reference to Perseus' contrivances (e.g. by the use of *dummy* elephants) to prepare his men and horses to make a stand against*real* elephants.

154

C₄₇

THIRD MACEDONIAN WAR, 171-168 B.C.

Pydna *(Aemilius Paulus), 168 B.C. (2)*

In medio secunda legio immissa dissipavit phalangem; neque ulla evidentior causa victoriae fuit, quam quod multa passim proelia erant, quae fluctuantem turbarunt primo, deinde disiecerunt phalangem, cuius confertae et intentis horrentes 5hastis intolerabiles vires sunt; si carptim aggrediendo circumagere immobilem longitudine et gravitate hastam cogas, confusa strue implicantur: si vero aut ab latere aut ab tergo aliquid tumultus increpuit, ruinae modo turbantur. Sicut tum adversus catervatim 10incurrentes Romanos et interrupta multifariam acie obviam ire cogebantur, et Romani, quacumque data intervalla essent, insinuabant ordines suos. . . . Diu phalanx a fronte, a lateribus, ab tergo caesa est; postremo, qui ex hostium manibus elapsi erant, 15inermes ad mare fugientes, quidam aquam etiam ingressi, manus ad eos, qui inclasse erant tendentes, suppliciter vitam orabant; et cum scaphas concurrere undique ab navibus cernerent, ad excipiendos sese venire rati, ut caperent potius quam occiderent, 20longius in aquam, quidam etiam natantes, progressi sunt. Sed cum hostiliter e scaphis caederentur, retro, qui poterant, nando repetentes terram, in aliam foediorem pestem incidebant. Elephanti enim, ab rectoribus ad litus acti, exeuntes obterebant 25elidebantque.

LIVY, xliv. 41, 42.

1 **In medio . . . immissa** = *On the centre the second legion charged* (**immissa**), i.e. into the interstices of the phalanx, which was not preserving its usual close order.—Rawlins.

4-6 **fluctuantem . . . vires sunt** = *first demoralised the phalanx so as to make it waver,* (**fluctuantem**), *and then shattered it. Its (aggressive) force, so long as it keeps close order and bristles with couched (**intentis**)spears, is irresistible (**intolerabiles**).*

6 **carptim aggrediendo** = *by repeated harassing attacks.*

10 **ruinae modo** = *in hopeless confusion.*—R.

17 **classe.** The Roman fleet under Octavius was co-operating with the army.

Results of the Battle. Perseus was captured, and his kingdom was divided into four independent parts. The Macedonian phalanx had fought its last great battle.

Character of Paulus. 'He was a model of the Roman of the best time. He was not, like his contemporary Cato, a onesided worshipper of everything old; but he was a Conservative in the best sense of the word, anxious to preserve old institutions, but at the same time to improve them.'—Ihne.

155

C₄₈

THIRD PUNIC WAR, 149-146 B.C.

Destruction of Carthage, *146 B.C.*

Manilio deinde consule terra marique fervebat obsidio. Operti portus, nudatus est primus et sequens, iam et tertius murus, cum tamen Byrsa, quod nomen arci fuit, quasi altera civitas resistebat. Quamvis profligato urbis excidio tamen fatale Africae nomen5Scipionum videbatur. Igitur in alium Scipionem conversa respublica finem belli reposcebat. Sed quem ad modum maxime mortiferi morsus solent esse morientium bestiarum, sic plus negoti fuit cum semiruta Carthagine quam cum integra. Compulsis 10in unam arcem hostibus portum quoque mari Romanus obstruxerat. Illi alterum sibi portum ab alia urbis parte foderunt, nec ut fugerent; sed qua nemo illos nec evadere posse credebat, inde quasi enata subito classis erupit, cum interim iam diebus, 15iam noctibus nova aliqua moles, nova machina, nova perditorum hominum manus quasi ex obruto incendio subita de cineribus flamma prodibat. Deploratis novissime rebus triginta sex milia virorum se dederunt quod minus credas—duce Hasdrubale.20

FLORUS, II. xv. 11-17 (sel.).

Context. An Embassy was sent from Rome in 157 B.C. to inquire into the affairs of Africa. Among its members was M. Porcius Cato, who, astonished and alarmed at the flourishing condition of Carthage, returned to Rome with the firm conviction that Carthage must be destroyed—*delenda est Carthago.* A pretext was soon found in the war (151 B.C.) between Carthage and Masinissa, King of Numidia, the ally of Rome. Though the Carthaginians surrendered all their arms and munitions of war, Rome declared that they would have to leave their city and settle ten miles from the sea. The Carthaginians resolved to die rather than give up the sacred soil of their country.

5 **profligato** = *almost finished.*

6 **in alium Scipionem**, i.e. P. Corn. Scipio Aemilianus Africanus Minor, the younger son of Aemilius Paulus (of Pydna) and adopted by P. Scipio, the son of the conqueror of Hannibal.

12 **alterum portum**, i.e. they pierced the narrow strip of land separating the round naval port (Cothon) from the sea.

18 **deploratis** = *was looked upon as lost*, lit. *wept for bitterly*.

20 **duce Hasdrubale:** 'Hasdrubal seems to have deserved the name of *the last Carthaginian* in the best sense of the word, as a representative of the intensity of the strength, endurance, and patriotism of his race.'—Ihne.

'The plough was drawn over the site of destroyed Carthage, and a solemn curse was pronounced against anyone who should ever undertake to build a new town on that spot.'—Ihne.

Africa made a Roman Province.

156

C₄₉

WAR WITH ANDRISCUS AND THE ACHAEANS, 148-146 B.C.

Destruction of Corinth *(L. Mummius Achaicus), 146 B.C.*

Eodem anno, quo Carthago concidit, L. Mummius Corinthum post annos DCCCCLII, quam ab Alete Hippotis filio erat condita, funditus eruit. Uterque imperator devictae a se gentis nomine honoratus, alter Africanus, alter appellatus est Achaicus; nec5quisquam ex novis hominibus prior Mummio cognomen virtute partum vindicavit. Diversi imperatoribus mores, diversa fuere studia: quippe Scipio tam elegans liberalium studiorum omnisque doctrinae et auctor et admirator fuit, ut Polybium Panaetiumque,10praecellentes ingenio viros, domi militiaeque secum habuerit. Neque enim quisquam hoc Scipione elegantius intervalla negotiorum otio dispunxit semperque aut belli aut pacis serviit artibus: semper inter arma ac studia versatus aut corpus periculis15aut animum disciplinis exercuit. Mummius tam rudis fuit, ut capta Corintho cum maximorum artificum perfectas manibus tabulas ac statuas in Italiam portandas locaret, iuberet praediciconducentibus, si eas perdidissent, novas eos reddituros.20

VELLEIUS PATERCULUS, i. 13.

Context. In 149 B.C. an adventurer named Andriscus claimed to be Philip, the son of Perseus, and mastered Macedonia and part of Thessaly. He totally defeated the praetor Juventius, but in 148 B.C. his army was routed and himself taken prisoner by Q. Caecilius Metellus. The Romans, *no longer needing the help of Greek troops*, determined to break up the Achaean League. A last desperate struggle for freedom ensued, but the Greeks were easily defeated (146 B.C.) by L. Mummius on the Isthmus, and Corinth itself was plundered and destroyed.

2-3 **quam . . . condita.** Aletes, son of Hippotes and a descendant of Heracles, is said to have taken possession of Corinth by the help of the oracle of Zeus at Dodona, and therefore named the city Διὸς Κόρινθος.

10 **Panaetium**, a native of Rhodes and a celebrated Stoic philosopher, settled in Rome, where he became the intimate friend of Laelius and Scipio Africanus Minor.

13 **dispunxit** = *he devoted, gave up* (lit. *marked off*).

19 **locaret** = *he hired* (lit. *place out*, i.e. *give out on contract*).

conducentibus = *to the contractors.*

The Destruction of Corinth. 'The flames which consumed Miletus (destroyed by the Persians 494 B.C.) and Athens (burnt by Xerxes 480 B.C.) were the signal for the great rising of the people, the dawn of a magnificent day of Greek splendour: after the fall of Corinth came the long dark night.'—Ihne.

Macedonia made a Roman Province. Greece placed under the control of the Roman governor of Macedonia.

157

C₅₀

WAR WITH VIRIATHUS IN SPAIN, 149-140 B.C.

The Lusitanian Hannibal.

Sed tota certaminum moles cum Lusitanis fuit et Numantinis. Quippe solis gentium Hispaniae duces contigerunt. Lusitanos Viriathus erexit, vir calliditatis acerrimae. Qui ex venatore latro, ex latrone subito dux atque imperator et, si fortuna 5cessisset, Hispaniae Romulus, non contentus libertatem suorum defendere, per quattuordecim annos omnia citra ultraque Hiberum et Tagum igni ferroque populatus, castra etiam praetoria et praesidia aggressus Claudium Unimanum paene ad internecionem 10exercitus cecidit et insignia trabeis et fascibus nostris quae ceperat in montibus suis tropaea fixit. Tandem eum iam Fabius Maximus consul oppresserat; sed a successore Popilio violata victoria est. Quippe qui conficiendae rei cupidus, fractum ducem et extrema15deditionis agitantem per fraudem et insidias et domesticospercussores aggressus hanc hosti gloriam dedit ut videretur aliter vinci non posse.

106

Context. After the defeat of Perseus (168 B.C.) and before the outbreak of the third Punic War (149 B.C.) a suitable opportunity seemed to present itself to Rome for continuing the interrupted conquest of Spain; but 'for eight long years Viriathus, although a barbarian and of humble origin, defied the armies of Rome, and thereby secured for himself a position in history almost equal to that of Hannibal and Mithridates.' Ihne.

1 **cum Lusitanis.** The Lusitani (S. of the R. Tagus = mod. Portugal, and part of Estremadura and Toledo) were not finally subdued till after the capture of Numantia by Scipio in 133 B.C.

6 **cessisset** (= *concessisset*) = *had permitted.*

10-12 **Claudium Unimanum . . . fixit**, i.e. in 147 B.C. 'The captured fasces of the lictors were exhibited, with other trophies (e.g. **trabeis**, l. 11), far and wide on the Spanish mountains.'—Ihne.

13 **Fabius Maximus consul**, i.e. Quintus Fabius Maximus Servilianus, who allowed himself to be decoyed into an ambush 141 B.C., and was compelled to grant an honourable peace, which Rome soon found a pretext for breaking.

17 **percussores** = *assassins*, lit. *strikers* (*per* + *cutio* =*quatio*). Cf. the fate of Sertorius, 72 B.C.

The War with Viriathus. 'It was sad and disgraceful for the Roman arms, but in a far higher degree for Roman morals. It sowed, moreover, the seeds of the Numantine War, in which both the warlike ability and the moral virtues of the Roman nation appear more deteriorated than even in the war with Viriathus.'—Ihne.

158
C$_{51}$

NUMANTINE WAR, 143-133 B.C.

Destruction of Numantia, *133 B.C.*

Tanti esse exercitum quanti imperatorem vere proditum est. Sic redacto in disciplinam milite a Scipione commissa acies, quodque nemo visurum se umquam speraverat, factum ut fugientes Numantinos quisquam videret. Dedere etiam se volebant, 5si toleranda viris imperarentur. Cum fossa atque lorica quattuorque castris circumdatos fames premeret, a duce orantes proelium, ut tamquam viros occideret, ubi non impetrabant, placuit eruptio. Sic conserta manu plurimi occisi, et cum urgueret 10fames, novissime consilium fugae sedit; sed hoc quoque ruptis equorum cingulis uxores ademere, summo scelere per amorem. Itaque deplorato exitu in ultimam rabiem furoremque conversi, postremo Rhoecogene duce se suos patriam ferro veneno 15subiecto igne undique peregerunt. Macte fortissimam et meo iudicio beatissimam in ipsis malis civitatem! Asseruit cum fide socios, populum orbis terrarum viribus fultum sua manu aetate tam longa sustinuit. Novissime maximo duce oppressa civitas nullum de 20se gaudium hosti reliquit. Unus enim vir Numantinus non fuit qui in catenis duceretur; praeda, ut de pauperrimis, nulla: arma ipsa cremaverunt. Triumphus fuit tantum de nomine.

Context. In 143 B.C. the Celtiberians (of Middle Spain), encouraged by the successes of the Lusitanians, took up arms once more. Their most important town was Numantia, situated near the sources of the R. Durius (Douro), strongly fortified by nature and by art. Consul after consul failed to take it, until in 134 B.C. Scipio Africanus Minor, the conqueror of Carthage, was sent out to Spain to reduce the stubborn city.

2-3 **Sic redacto . . . a Scipione.** 'Scipio's first task, when he arrived in Spain, was to accustom the army which he found there, once more to Roman discipline. Luxury and indulgence were rife, and cowardice—the most unroman of all vices—had begun to creep in.'—Ihne.

7 **lorica** = *a breastwork*, serving as *a screen*. Usu. = *a cuirass*.

11 **sedit** = *was decided on*, lit. *settled.*

16 **Macte** = *a blessing on* or *hail to thee*. **Mactus** prob. from $\sqrt{μακ}$, e.g. in μάκ-αρ = *blessed*, but cf. *mag-nus.*

18 **Asseruit** = *it protected*. **assero** (*ad* + *sero*) = lit. *join-to.*

Destruction of Numantia. Scipio, of his own accord, razed the town to the ground, and received the added surname of**Numantinus**.

Roman Province in Spain.

159
C$_{52}$

Rome the Invincible.

Dixitque tandem perfidus Hannibal:
'Cervi, luporum praeda rapacium,
Sectamur ultro, quos opimus

107

52
Fallere et effugere est triumphus.
Gens, quae cremato fortis ab Ilio
Iactata Tuscis aequoribus sacra
Natosque maturosque patres
56
Pertulit Ausonias ad urbes,
Duris ut ilex tonsa bipennibus
Nigrae feraci frondis in Algido,
Per damna, per caedes ab ipso
60
Ducit opes animumque ferro
Non Hydra secto corpore firmior
Vinci dolentem crevit in Herculem,
Monstrumve submisere Colchi
64
Maius Echioniaeve Thebae.
Merses profundo: pulchrior evenit;
Luctere: multa proruet integrum
Cum laude victorem geretque
68
Proelia coniugibus loquenda.'

HORACE, Odes, IV. iv. 49-68.

51 **ultro** = *aggressively, needlessly.*—Wickham.

51-52 **opimus triumphus** = *a rare* (lit. *rich, noble*) *triumph.* Cf. *spolia opima.*

53-56 'This stanza is a *résumé* of the story of the *Aeneid.*'—W.

53 **gens** (sc. **illa**), i.e. the Roman stock.

57-60 'The idea of this stanza is that their very calamities only gave them fresh heart and vigour. They rise like the Phoenix from its pyre.'—W.

58 **frondis** with **feraci**. Cf. *fertilis frugum.*

59-60 **ab ipso . . . ferro** = *from the very edge of the steel itself, the holm-oak* (= *the Roman stock*) *draws fresh power and spirit.*

61-62 Cf. the saying of Pyrrhus, recorded by Floras i. 18, 'I see that I was born under the constellation of Hercules, since so many heads of enemies, that were cut off, arise upon me afresh out of their own blood, as if from the Lernaean serpent.'

63-64 i.e. of the armed warriors which sprang from the dragon's teeth sown by Jason at Colchis or by Cadmus at Thebes.

63 **submisere** = *produced, raised.*

64 **Echioniae Thebae.** Echion was one of the five survivors of the Σπαρτοί (sown men). He helped Cadmus to found Thebes.

65 **Merses** (= **si mersaris**) = *plunge it if you will.*
evenit = *it emerges (comes forth).*

66-67 **multa cum laude** = *amid loud applause,* of a feat in a wrestling match.—W.

68 **coniugibus** = i. *by Roman wives* or ii. *by Carthaginian widows.* So Conington, 'Whose story widow'd wives shall tell.'

160
B₁

CIVIL STRIFE IN ITALY, AND FOREIGN WARS,
ENDING IN REVOLUTION 133-44 B.C.

THE GRACCHI.

Nam postquam Tiberius et C. Gracchus, quorum maiores Punico atque aliis bellis multum rei publicae addiderant, vindicare plebem in libertatem et paucorum celera patefacere coepere, nobilitas noxia atque eo perculsa, modo per socios et nomen Latinum,5interdum per equites Romanos, quos spes societatis a plebe dimoverat, Gracchorum actionibus obviam ierat, et primo Tiberium, dein paucos post annos eadem ingredientem Gaium, tribunum alterum, alterum triumvirum coloniis deducendis, cum10M. Fulvio Flacco ferro necaverat. Et sane Gracchis cupidine victoriae haud satis moderatus animus fuit. Sed bono vinci satius est quam malo more iniuriam vincere. Igitur ea victoria nobilitas ex lubidine sua usa multos mortales ferro aut fuga exstinxit plusque 15in reliquum sibi timoris quam potentiae addidit. Quae res plerumque magnas civitates pessum dedit, dum alteri alteros vincere quovis modo et victos acerbius ulcisci volunt.

SALLUST, Jugurtha, 42.

1-3 **quorum maiores . . . addiderant**, e.g. their grandfather P. Scipio Africanus Maior, and their father Tib. Sempronius Gracchus (in Spain and Sardinia).

3-4 **paucorum scelera . . . coepere.** (i) Tib. Gracchus by his Agrarian Law tried to counteract the selfish land-grabbing of the ruling class (in excess of the 500*iugera* limit of the Licinian Laws, 367 B.C.). (ii) C. Gracchus exposed the corrupt Senatorian Courts, transferred their judicial power to the Equites, and carried the Sempronian Law, 'one of the cornerstones of individual liberty.'

5 **per socios . . . Latinum**, by working on Roman jealousy against the Italians, for whom equality was claimed.

6 **spes societatis**, i.e. the hope of sharing with the nobility in office, and in provincial appointments.

10 **triumvirum c. d.**, one of the three Commissioners for establishing Colonies of Roman citizens on the *ager publicus*.

11 **Fulvio Flacco**, slain with C. Gracchus, 121 B.C.

17 **pessum dedit** = *has destroyed*. *pessum* (prob.) = *pedis* +*versum* = *towards the feet, to the ground*, cf. *pessum ire*.

The aim of the Gracchi. 'Their object was to reduce the excessive power of the nobility, and to make the sovereignty of the people, which had become merely nominal, a reality.'—Ihne.

Their political mistake. 'Their error consisted in the belief that such a change was possible by returning to the simple forms of the old Comitia. They overlooked the necessity of remodelling the Roman people itself by giving the popular assemblies a form which would in reality make them represent the people.'—Ihne.

161

B$_2$

CICERO ON THE GRACCHI.

A. On the Death of Tiberius Gracchus, *133* B.C.

Nec plus Africanus, singularis et vir et imperator, in exscindendaNumantia rei publicae profuit quam eodem tempore P. Nasicaprivatus, cum Ti. Gracchum interemit.

De Off. i. 76.

2 **Numantia**, destroyed by P. Scipio Africanus Minor Numantinus, 133 B.C.

3 **P. Nasīca**, a partisan leader of the Senate. **privatus** = *not in office*. Cicero speaks very differently of the Gracchi when it suits his purpose, e.g. in *de lege agraria*, ii. §
10, *duos* (*Gracchos*) *clarissimos, ingeniosissimos, amantissimos plebei Romanae viros . . . quorum consiliis, sapientia, legibus multas esse video partes constitutas.*

B. On the Lex Frumentaria of C. Gracchus, *123* B.C.

Et quidem C. Gracchus, cum largitiones maximas 5fecisset et effudisset aerarium, verbis tamen defendebat aerarium. Quid verba audiam, cum facta videam? L. Piso ille Frugi semper contralegem frumentariam dixerat. Is lege lata consularis ad frumentum accipiendum venerat. Animum advertit 10Gracchus in contione Pisonem stantem: quaerit audiente populo Romano qui sibi constet, cum ea lege frumentum petat, quam dissuaserit. 'Nolim' inquit 'mea bona, Gracche, tibi viritim dividere libeat, sed si facias, partem petam.' Parumne declaravit vir 15gravis et sapiens lege Sempronia patrimonium publicum dissipari? Lege orationes Gracchi, patronum aerari esse dices.

Tusc. Disput. iii. 20, 48.

8 **L. Piso ille Frugi** = L. Calpurnius Piso Frugi (the man of*worth*), a convinced and honourable opponent of C. Gracchus.

8-9 **legem frumentariam**, by which corn was sold to Roman citizens at about half the market price. 'One of the worst measures ever proposed by a well-meaning statesman.'—Ihne.

12 **qui** = *how*, old abl. of *qui*.

C. On C. Gracchus as an Orator.

Sed ecce in manibus vir et praestantissimo ingenio et flagranti studio et doctus a puero, C. Gracchus. Noli enim putare quemquam. Brute, pleniorem et uberiorem ad dicendum fuisse.

Brutus, 125.

20 **doctus a puero.** CORNELIA MATER GRACCHORUM (inscribed upon her statue erected by the Roman people), the daughter of the Conqueror of Zama, was mainly responsible for their training and education; so Cic.*Brut.* 104 *Fuit Tib. Gracchus diligentia matris a puero doctus et Graecis literis eruditus.* 'From her they had received that sensitive nature and that sympathy with the weak and suffering, which animated their political action.'—Ihne.

162

B$_3$

109

THE JUGURTHINE WAR, 111-106 B.C.

The Betrayal of Jugurtha, *106 B.C.*

Postea, tempore et loco constituto, in colloquium uti de pace
veniretur, Bocchus Sullam modo, modo Iugurthae legatum appellare, benigne habere, idem
ambobus polliceri. Illi pariter laeti ac spei bonae pleni esse. Sed nocte ea, quae proxuma fuit
ante5diem colloquio decretum, Maurus, adhibitis amicis ac statim immutata voluntate remotis,
dicitur secum ipse multa agitavisse, voltu et oculis pariter atque animo varius: quae scilicet tacente
ipso occulta pectoris patefecisse. Tamen postremo Sullam accersi10iubet et ex illius sententia
Numidae insidias tendit. Deinde ubi dies advenit et ei nuntiatum est Iugurtham haud procul
abesse, cum paucis amicis et quaestore nostro quasi obvius honoris causa procedit in tumulum
facillumum visu insidiantibus. Eodem15Numida cum plerisque necessariis suis inermis, uti
dictum erat, accedit; ac statim signo dato undique simul ex insidiis invaditur. Ceteri
obtruncati, Iugurtha Suilae vinctus traditur et ab eo ad Marium deductus est.20

SALLUST, *Jugurtha*, 113.

2 **Bocchus**, King of Mauretania, and father-in-law of Jugurtha, coveted the West of
Numidia, and was ready to accept it either from the Romans or from Jugurtha, as the price of his
alliance.

Sullam, appointed Quaestor 107 B.C. by Marius, who superseded Metellus in the
conduct of the Jugurthine War.

9 **quae scilicet . . . patefecisse**, i.e. the external signs of his irresolution,—the calling and
then dismissing his people (**adhibitis . . . remotis**, ll. 6, 7), and the changes of his countenance
(**voltu . . . varius**, ll. 8, 9). **Scilicet**is here used with the Infinitive **patefecisse**, the verbal sense of
the word (= *scire* + *licet*) being prominent.

10 **accersi** (= *arcessiri*), frequent in Sallust.

16 **necessariis** (*necesse*) = *friends*. Cf. ἀναγκαῖοι(ἀνάγκη).

19 **Iugurtha Sullae . . . traditur.** Sulla is said to have been so proud of this stratagem that
he had the scene engraved upon a signet-ring, an act of vainglory which estranged Marius from
him. (Plutarch, *Sulla*, 3.)

Jugurtha. 'Having resisted the whole power of the great Republic for six years, having
kept his ground against the best generals of the time, against a Metellus, a Marius, and a Sulla, he
was deluded by treacherous promises of peace and betrayed by his own ally and father-in-law.'—
Ihne.

163
B₄

A. Arpinum—Birthplace of Cicero and Marius.

237
Hic novus Arpinas, ignobilis et modo Romae
Municipalis eques, galeatum ponit ubique
Praesidium attonitis et in omni monte laborat.
243
. . . . Sed Roma parentem,
Roma patrem patriae Ciceronem libera dixit.
245
Arpinas alius Volscorum in monte solebat
Poscere mercedes alieno lassus aratro,
Nodosam post haec frangebat vertice vitem,
Si lentus pigra muniret castra dolabra;
Hic tamen et Cimbros et summa pericula rerum
250
Excipit et solus trepidantem protegit urbem.

JUVENAL, *Sat.* viii. 237-239, 243-250.

239 **in omni monte**, i.e. in every part of Rome, on each of the seven hills.

244 **patrem patriae:** under the Empire the title *pater patriae* became a formal one, always
accorded to the new Emperor.

libera = *while yet free*, emphatic. The State was no longer free when Augustus received
this title, 2 B.C.—Duff.

247 **frangebat vertice vitem** = *he had the vine-switch(rattan) broken on his head*, i.e. served as a
common soldier.—D.

248 **dolabra** = half-hatchet for cutting stakes, and half-pickaxe for digging the fossa.
For **dolabra**, cf.*Dolabella*.

249 **Cimbros**, annihilated by Marius and Catulus near Vercellae, 101 B.C.

250 **Excipit** = *faced* (lit. *is ready to receive*); metaphor from field-sports.—D.

B. From a poem by Cicero on his fellow-townsman Marius.

Hic Iovis altisoni subito pinnata satelles
Arboris e trunco serpentis saucia morsu
Surrigit ipsa feris transfigens unguibus anguem
Semianimum et varia graviter cervice micantem.

.   .   .   .

Hanc ubi praepetibus pennis lapsuque volantem
Conspexit Marius, divini numinis augur,
Faustaque signa suae laudis reditusque notavit,
Partibus intonuit caeli pater ipse sinistris:
Sic aquilae clarum firmavit Iuppiter omen.

1 **Iovis pinnata satelles**, i.e. the Eagle. Cf. Pindar, *Pyth.* i. 6:εὕδει δ' ἀνὰ σκάπτῳ (=
σκήπτρῳ) Διὸς αἰετός, *and sleeps on the staff of Zeus his eagle.*

3 **Surrigit** (= *surgit*) = *raises up*; very rare in this sense. The *v.l.* **Sūbigit** (for *sŭbigit*) = *carries
aloft.*

Compare Plutarch's story of the eagle's nest, with seven young ones in it, which fell into
the lap of Marius when a boy, predicting (so the diviners said) that Marius would be seven times
Consul.

164

B₅

The Annihilation of the Teutones at Aquae Sextiae, *102 B.C.*

Cimbri et Teutones ab extremis Germaniae profugi, cum terras eorum inundasset
Oceanus, novas sedes toto orbe quaerebant, exclusique et Gallia et Hispania cum in Italiam
demigrarent, misere legatos in castra Silani, inde ad Senatum 5petentes ut populus Martius aliquid
sibi terrae daret. Sed quas daret terras populus Romanus, agrariis legibus inter se dimicaturus?
Repulsi igitur, quod nequiverant precibus, armis petere coeperunt. Sed nec primum impetum
barbarorum Silanus, nec 10secundum Mallius, nec tertium Caepio sustinere potuerunt: omnes
fugati, exuti castris.Actum erat, nisi Marius illi saeculo contigisset. . . . Ille mira statim velocitate
occupatis compendiis praevenit hostem, prioresque Teutones sub ipsis Alpium
radicibus 15adsecutus in loco quemAquas Sextias vocant, proelio oppressit. Vallem fluviumque
medium hostes tenebant, et nostris aquarum nulla erat copia. Consultone id egerit imperator an
errorem in consilium verterit, dubium; certe necessitate acta virtus 20victoriae causa fuit. Nam
flagitante aquam exercitu, 'Si viri estis' inquit, 'en, illic habetis.' Itaque tanto ardore pugnatum est,
ea caedes hostium fuit ut victor Romanus cruento flumine non plus aquae biberit quam sanguinis
barbarorum.25

FLORUS, III. iii. 1-9 (sel).

5 **Silani** = M. Junius Silanus, defeated by Cimbri, 109 B.C.

11 **Mallius—Caepio**, defeated by Cimbrians at Arausio, on the Rhone, 105 B.C.

Plutarch, *Lucullus* 27, says: 'The 6th Oct., on which day the battle was fought, was
marked in the calendar as a black day, like the fatal day of the Allia, 390 B.C.'

12 **Actum erat**, sc. *de republica.*

14 **compendiis** = *short ways*; cf. our *compendium* = *an abridgement.*

16 **Aquas Sextias**, founded by Sextius Calvinus 122 B.C. = Aix, 18 miles N. of Marseilles.

23 **caedes hostium.** 150,000 (Vell.) and 200,000 (Liv. Ep. lxviii.).

'By the great victories of Aquae Sextiae and of Vercellae (over the Cimbri, 101 B.C.), the
movement of the German races southward was for the present stopped. Rome was saved, and
the saviour of Rome was Marius, the champion of the people.'—Ihne.

Parallel Passages. Propert. IV. iii. 41-44; Livy Ep. lxviii.

References. Plutarch, *Marius*, 15. Ihne, *Hist. Rome*, vol. v. pp. 98-105.

165

B₆

MARIUS, 157-86 B.C.

A. His Flight from Sulla: Consul for the 7th time.

Atque aliquis magno quaerens exempla timori,
'Non alios,' inquit, 'motus tum fata parabant,
Cum post Teutonicos victor Libycosque triumphos
70
Exsul limosa Marius caput abdidit ulva.
Stagna avidi texere soli laxaeque paludes

Depositum, Fortuna, tuum: mox vincula ferri
Exedere senem longusque in carcere paedor.
Consul et eversa felix moriturus in urbe
75
Poenas ante dabat scelerum. Mors ipsa refugit
Saepe virum, frustraque hosti concessa potestas.
Sanguinis invisi: primo qui caedis in ictu*
Deriguit ferrumque manu torpente remisit;
Viderat immensum tenebroso in carcere lumen
80
Terribilesque deos scelerum Mariumque futurum
Audieratque pavens: "Fas haec contingere non est
Colla tibi: debet multas his legibus aevi
Ante suam mortes: vanum depone furoremi."
Si libet ulcisci deletae funera gentis,
85
Hunc, Cimbri, servate senem.'

LUCAN, *Pharsalia*, ii. 67-85.

* Postgate, *actu.*
67 **exempla timori** = *precedents to hear out his fears.*—Haskins.
70 **Exsul.** 88-7 B.C. For details see Plut. *Marius*, caps. 38-40.
72 **Fortuna**, i.e. the *evil* destiny of Rome, protecting him because the gods were angry with Rome. Cf. 82-83*debet . . . mortes.*
73 **in carcere**, i.e. at Minturnae, S.E. of Latium. There were extensive marshes in the neighbourhood.
    paedor = *filth.*
82 **legibus aevi** = *the laws that govern time* = *fatis.*—H.

B. Marius outlived his fame.
Quid illo cive tulisset
Natura in terris, quid Roma beatius umquam,
280
Si circumducto captivorum agmine et omni
Bellorum pompa animam exhalasset opimam,
Cum de Teutonico vellet descendere curru?

JUVENAL, *Sat.* x. 278-282.

Marius outlived his powers and his reputation.
'Had he now died, he would have gone down to posterity as one of the greatest men of his people, as a second Romulus or Camillus, unstained with any blood save that of foreign foes.'—Ihne.
Parallel Passages. Ov. *P. Ep.* iv. 3. 45-48; Juv. x. 276-278.
References. Plut. *Marius*, caps. 38-end. Ihne, vol. iv. pp. 336-7, vol. v. pp. 111-12.
166
B₇

Cicero on Civil Strife.
Etenim recordamini, Quirites, omnes civiles dissensiones, non solum eas quas audistis, sed et has quas vosmetipsi meministis atque vidistis. L. Sulla P. Sulpicium oppressit: ex Urbe ciecit C. Marium, custodem huius urbis, multosque fortes viros partim5eiecit ex civitate, partim interemit. Cn. Octavius consul armis ex Urbe collegam suum expulit: omnis his locus acervis corporum et civium sanguine redundavit. Superavit postea Cinna cum Mario: tum vero, clarissimis viris interfectis, lumina civitatis 10exstincta sunt. Ultus est huius victoriae crudelitatem postea Sulla: ne dici quidem opus est, quanta deminutione civium et quanta calamitate reipublicae. . . . Atque illae tamen omnes dissensiones, quae non ad delendam, sed ad commutandam rempublicam 15pertinebant—non illi nullam esse rempublicam, sed in ea quae esset se esse principes, neque hanc urbem conflagrare, sed se in hac urbe florere voluerunt—eius modi fuerunt, ut non reconciliatione concordiae, sed internecione civium diiudicatae sint.20

CICERO, *In Cat.* iii. 10.

4 **P. Sulpicium**, distinguished orator, bought over by Marius. As Tribunus Plebis 88 B.C. carried the Leges Sulpiciae.
6 **Cn. Octavius**, one of Sulla's chief supporters. Consul 87B.C. Expelled his colleague Cinna. Murdered in his curule chair.

9-11 **Superavit . . . exstincta sunt**, i.e. 87-6 B.C. The Reign of Terror. Marius Consul for the 7th time. Cf. Vell. Pat. ii. 22 'Nihil illa victoria fuisset crudelius, nisi mox Sullana esset secuta.'

10 **lumina civitatis**, e.g. the Consuls Cn. Octavius and L. Merula; Q. Catulus, the conqueror (with Marius) in the Cimbric War; the orator M. Antonius; the brothers L. and C. Caesar.

11-13 The victims of the Sullanian proscriptions. Cf. Vell. Pat. ii. 28 'Primus ille (Sulla), et utinam ultimus, exemplum proscriptionis invenit.'

Parallel Passages. Horace, *Epodes* vii. and xvi. 1-14.

The Sullanian Proscriptions. Sulla was not like Marius swayed by feelings of revenge alone. His main object was the public good, which in his conviction was to be realised by a return to the older institutions of the republic. This he believed could be accomplished only by the utter annihilation of his opponents. The Proscriptions were not however intended to be an encouragement to indiscriminate murder, but rather a barrier against the rage of over-zealous partisans.

167

B₈

Tribunate of M. Livius Drusus, *91 B.C.*

Deinde interiectis paucis annis tribunatum iniit M. Livius Drusus, vir nobilissimus, eloquentissimus, sanctissimus, meliore in omnia ingenio animoque quam fortuna usus. Qui cum senatui priscum restituere cuperet decus et indicia ab equitibus ad 5eum transferre ordinem . . . in eis ipsis, quae pro senatu moliebatur, senatum habuit adversarium non intellegentem, si qua de plebis commodis ab eo agerentur, veluti illiciendae multitudinis causa fieri, ut minoribus perceptis maiora permitteret. Denique 10ea fortuna Drusi fuit, ut malefacta collegarum quamvis optime ab ipso cogitatis senatus probaret magis. . . . Tum conversus Drusi animus, quando bene incepta male cedebant, ad dandam civitatem Italiae: quod cum moliens revertisset e foro, immensa 15illa et incondita, quae eum semper comitabatur, cinctus multitudine in area domus suae cultello percussus, qui affixus lateri eius relictus est, intra paucas horas decessit. Sed cum ultimum redderet spiritum, intuens circumstantium macrentiumque 20frequentiam, effudit vocem convenientissimam conscientiae suae: ecquandone, inquit, propinqui amicique, similem mei civem habebit res publica? Hunc finem clarissimus iuvenis vitae habuit.

VELLEIUS PATERCULUS, ii. 13-14.

3-4 **Drusus.** 'Generous and free from all selfishness and meanness, but without political experience, adroitness and knowledge of men, he aspired to a task which surpassed his strength.'—Ihne.

4-6 By the Sempronian Laws of C. Gracchus 123 B.C.*exclusive judicial rights had been given to the Equites*, as a counterpoise to the power of the Senate. The corruption of the Equites (as Judices) was flagrant, and Drusus proposed to transfer the judicial functions to a mixed body of 300 Senators and 300 Knights, the selected Knights to be included in the now attenuated ranks of the Senate.

14 **ad dandam civitatem Italiae.** The claims of the Italians to the franchise were just and pressing, but the overbearing pride and self-sufficiency of the Roman citizens proved too strong.

Parallel Passages. Cic. *de Oratore* iii. 1, and *pro Cluent.*56, 153. Florus, iii. 18.

Reference. Ihne, *Hist.* vol. v. pp. 176-189.

'Drusus was the Mirabeau of the social revolution of Rome, and had his measures been carried Rome might have been spared the most terrible of her civil wars.'

168

B₉

THE SOCIAL OR MARSIC WAR, 91-88 B.C. (1)

A. Cause and Outbreak of the War at Asculum.

Cum ius civitatis, quam viribus auxerant, socii iustissimepostularent, quam in spem eos cupidine dominationis Drusus erexerat, postquam ille domestico scelere oppressus est, eadem fax, quae illum cremavit, socios in arma et in expugnationem urbis5accendit. . . . Primum fuit belli consilium ut in Albano monte festo die Latinarum Iulius Caesar et Marcius Philippus consules inter sacra et aras immolarentur. Postquam id nefas proditione discussum est, Asculo furor omnis erupit, in ipsa quidem ludorum10frequentia trucidatis qui tum aderant ab urbe legatis. Hoc fuit impii belli sacramentum. Inde iam passim ab omni parte Italiae duce et auctore belli discurrante Poppaedio diversa per populos et urbes signa cecinere.15

FLORUS, III. xviii. 3-10 (sel.).

2 **iustissime.** 'The final issue of the war confirmed the justice and the wisdom of the reforms planned by the Gracchi and by Livius Drusus.'—Ihne.

113

7 **Latinarum**, sc. *Feriarum*, the solemn festival conducted by the Consuls on the Alban Mount.

10 **Asculo.** Asculum (Ascoli), chief town of Picenum. The opening and closing scene of the war.

B. Advice of the Sabellian father to his sons.

'Vivite contenti casulis et collibus istis,
180
O pueri,' Marsus dicebat et Hernicus olim
Vestinusque senex, 'panem quaeramus aratro,
Qui satis est mensis: laudant hoc numina ruris,
Quorum ope et auxilio gratae post munus aristae
Contingunt homini veteris fastidia quercus.
185
Nil vetitum fecisse volet, quem non pudet alto
Per glaciem perone tegi, qui summovet Euros
Pellibus inversis; peregrina ignotaque nobis
Ad scelus atque nefas, quaecumque est, purpura ducit.'

JUVENAL, *Sat.* xiv. 179-188.

179 **collibus istis**, i.e. in the central mountain range of Italy. The Federals chose Corfinium (E. of Lake Fucinus) to be the Italian rallying-point, and the seat of a new State.

180-181 **Marsus . . . Hernicus . . . Vestinus**, Sabellian peoples noted for their bravery and simplicity; the backbone of Rome's army.

182 **numina ruris**, e.g. Ceres, Liber and Priapus.

185-186 **alto perone** = a high rustic boot of raw hide.

187 **pellibus inversis** = skins with the hair turned inwards.—Duff.

169
B₁₀

THE SOCIAL OR MARSIC WAR, 91-88 B.C. (2)

A. Defeat and Death of Rutilius.

Hanc tibi, 'Quo properas', memorant dixisse 'Rutili?
Luce mea Marso consul ab hoste cades.'
Exitus accessit verbis, flumenque Toleni
566
Purpureum mixtis sanguine fluxit aquis.

OVID, *Fasti*, vi. 563-566.

563 **Hanc**, sc. *Leucothea*, goddess of the sea and of harbours.

Rutili. Rutilius, consul 90 B.C., defeated and slain at the R. Tolenus (Turano) by the Marsian Vettius Scato.

B. The Lex Plautia Papiria of *89 B.C.*

Data est civitas Silvani lege et Carbonis: si qui 5foederatis civitatibus ascripti fuissent, si tum, cum lex ferebatur, in Italia domicilium habuissent et si sexaginta diebus apud praetorem essent professi.

CICERO, *pro Archia*, 4, 7.

5 **lege**, i.e. the Lex Plautia Papiria of the tribines M. Plautius Silvanus and C. Papirius Carbo. The Lex Julia of L. Julius Caesar 90 B.C., granting the *civitas* to the Latins and to all the other Italian States not in rebellion, had weakened the resistance. The Lex Plautia Papiria 'scattered among the Italian ranks the seeds of discord and dissolution.'

C. Cicero's first and only Campaign.

Memini colloquia et cum acerrimis hostibus et cum gravissime dissidentibus civibus. Cn. Pompeius, 10consul me praesente, cum essem tiro in eius exercitu, cum P. Vettio Scatone, duce Marsorum, inter bina castra collocutus est. . . . Quem cum Scato salutasset, 'quem te appellem?' inquit: 'voluntate hospitem, necessitate hostem.' Erat in colloquio aequitas: 15nullus timor, nulla suberat suspicio; mediocre etiam odium. Non enim, ut eriperent nobis socii civitatem, sed ut in eam reciperentur petebant.

CICERO, *Phil.* xii. 11, 27.

D. The battle near Asculum, and capture of the city.

Strabo vero Pompeius omnia flammis ferroque populatus non prius finem caedium fecit quam Asculi 20eversione manibus tot exercituum consulum direptarumque urbium dis litaretur.

FLORUS, III. xviii. 14.

114

20 **Asculi eversione.** The siege was memorable for the desperate patriotism of the besieged under their leader Judacilius, cf. siege of Saguntum.

Reference. Ihne, *Hist.* vol. v. pp. 190-220.

170

B₁₁

L. CORNELIUS SULLA, 138-78 B.C.

His Character and Bearing.

Igitur Sulla gentis patriciae nobilis fuit, familia prope iam exstincta maiorum ignavia, litteris Graecis et Latinis iuxta atque doctissimi eruditus, animo ingenti, cupidus voluptatum sed gloriae cupidior: tamen ab negotiis numquam voluptas remorata; 5facundus callidus et amicitia facilis, ad simulanda negotia altitudo ingeni incredibilis, multarum rerum ac maxumae pecuniae largitor. Atque illi, felicissumo omnium ante civilem victoriam, numquam super industriam fortuna fuit, multique dubitavere fortior 10an felicior esset. Nam postea quae fecerit, incertum habeo pudeat an pigeat magis disserere. Igitur Sulla, uti supra dictum est, postquam in Africam atque in castra Mari cum equitatu venit, rudis antea et ignarus belli, solertissumus omnium in paucis 15tempestatibus factus est. Ad hoc milites benigne appellare, multis rogantibus aliis per se ipse dare beneficia, invitus accipere, sed ea properantius quam aes mutuum reddere, ipse ab nullo repetere, magis id laborare utilli quam plurimi deberent, ioca atque 20seria cum humillumis agere, in operibus in agmine atque ad vigilias multus adesse neque interim, quod prava ambitio solet, consulis aut cuiusquam boni famam laedere, tantum modo neque consilio neque manu priorem alium pati, plerosque antevenire.25

SALLUST, *Jug.* 95, 96.

1 **nobilis**, i.e. of a patrician family which had held curule offices.

1-2 **familia . . . exstincta.** The Cornelii were a distinguished *gens* in early times and included 7 patrician families (e.g. the Lentuli and Scipios). Of these the Sullae were the least known.

2-3 **litteris Graecis . . . eruditus.** Contrast the proud boast of Marius:—'I have learnt no Greek: in the knowledge, however, which is far the most important for the State, I am a master.'—Sall. *Jug.* 85.

9 **ante civilem victoriam**, i.e. before 81 B.C.

10-11 **fortior an felicior.** Sulla assumed the name Felix on the death of the younger Marius 82 B.C. Cf. Plut. *Sulla*, cap. vi.

11-12 **Nam postea . . . disserere.** Cf. Vell. Patere. II. xvii. 2: 'Sulla vir qui neque ad finem victoriae satis laudari neque post victoriam abunde vituperari potest.'

20 **illi** more strictly *sibi*—'a negligence not unfrequent.'—Merivale.

22 **multus adesse** = *frequently visited,* **multus** = *saepe.*

For **character of Sulla** cf. Plut. *Sulla*, and Mommsen, iv. pp. 139-142: 'One of the most marvellous characters in history.'

171

B₁₂

MITHRIDATES THE GREAT, 130-63 B.C.

A. His Youth and Early Training.

Huius futuram magnitudinem etiam caelestia ostenta praedixerant. Nam et eo, quo genitus est, anno, et eo, quo regnare primum coepit, stella cometes per utrumque tempus LXX diebus ita luxit, ut caelum omne conflagrare videretur. Puer tutorum insidias5passus est, qui eum fero equo imposito equitare iacularique cogebant: qui conatus cum eos fefellissent, supra aetatem regente equum Mithridate, veneno eum appetivere. Veritus deinde, ne inimici, quod veneno non potuerant, ferro peragerent, venandi10studium finxit, quo per septem annos neque urbano neque rustico tecto usus est, sed per silvas vagatus, diversis montium regionibus pernoctabat ignaris omnibus, quibus esset locis; adsuetus feras cursu aut fugere aut persequi, cum quibusdam etiam viribus15congredi. Quibus rebus et insidias vitavit, et corpus ad omnem virtutis patientiam duravit.

1 **Huius.** Mithridates (*Mithras* = Persian sun-god) 'second only to Hannibal in inextinguishable, life-long hostility to Rome, as also in military genius.' Ihne.

5 **tutorum** = (*at the hands*) *of his guardians.* Cf. *tueor.*

17 **ad omnem virtutis patientiam** = *to all manly endurance.*

B. His Preparations for Conquest.

Ad regni deinde administrationem cum accessisset, statim non de regendo, sed de augendo regno cogitavit. Itaque Scythas invictos antea ingenti 20felicitate perdomuit. Hieme deinde appetente, non in convivio, sed in campo, nec in avocationibus, nec inter sodales, sed inter acquales, aut equo aut cursu aut viribus contendebat.Exercitum quoque suum ad parem laboris patientiam cotidiana exercitatione 25durabat, atque ita invictus ipse inexpugnabilem exercitum fecerat.

JUSTINUS, xxxvii. 2, 3, 4.

19 **de augendo regno.** He subdued all the coast districts of the Euxine, East, North and West, as far as the Hister (Danube).

22 **avocationibus** = *in diversions* (very rare).

24 **exercitum.** At the outbreak of the War with Rome, 88B.C., he had collected a motley force of 250,000 foot and 40,000 horse.

Mithridates. 'With one blow he overthrew the Roman dominion in Asia, carried the war into Europe, united almost the whole Eastern world in an attack on the Republic, and resisted for 25 years the first generals of his time,—a Sulla, a Lucullus, and a Pompeius.'—Ihne.

Historic Parallels. Alexander, Hannibal, Peter the Great.

172

B$_{13}$

FIRST MITHRIDATIC WAR, 88-84 B.C. (1)

The Battle of Chaeronea, *86 B.C.*

Brilliant Tactics of Sulla.

Archelaus adversus L. Sullam in fronte ad perturbandum hostemfalcatas quadrigas locavit, in secunda acie phalangem Macedonicam, in tertia Romanorum more armatos auxiliares, mixtis fugitivis Italicae gentis, quorum pervicaciae plurimum fidebat; 5levem armaturam in ultimo statuit; in utroque deinde latere equitatum, cuius amplum numerum habebat, circumeundi hostis causa posuit. Contra haec Sulla fossas amplae latitudinis utroque latere duxit et capitibus earum castella communiit: qua 10ratione, ne circuiretur ab hoste et peditum numero et maxime equitatu superante, consecutus est. Triplicem deinde peditum aciem ordinavit relictis intervallis per quae levem armaturam et equitem, quem in novissimo conlocaverat, cum res exegisset, emitteret.15Tum postsignanis qui in secunda acie erant imperavit ut densos numerososque palos firme in terram defigerent, intraque eos appropinquantibus quadrigis antesignanorum aciem recepit: tum demum sublato universorum clamore velites et levem armaturam20ingerere tela iussit. Quibus factis quadrigae hostium aut implicitae palis aut exterritae clamore telisque in suos conversae suntturbaveruntque Macedonum structuram: qua cedente, cum Sulla instaret et Archelaus equitem opposuisset, Romani equites 25subito emissi averterunt eos consummaverantque victoriam.

FRONTINUS, *Strategemata*, ii. 3. 17.

1 **Archelaus** (and his brother Neoptolemus) 'trained in the traditions and experience of Greek and Macedonian masters.'

2 **falcatas quadrigras.** Archelaus had 60 of these chariots armed with scythes projecting. Cf. Livy xxxvii. 41.

5 **pervicaciae** = *steadfastness (per + vic;* cf. *vinco).*

11-12 **qua ratione . . . consecutus est.** Sulla had about 30,000 men (15,000 Romans only) against 120,000.

23 **turbaverunt.** 'The war-chariots on this as on other occasions (e.g. at Magnesia) had not only proved a failure, but had actually led to a partial disaster.'—Ihne. Cf. use of war elephants, e.g. at Beneventum 275B.C. and at Zama 202 B.C.

27 **victoriam.** It was a great victory, but the results were trifling, partly because Sulla had no fleet, and partly because his political enemies at Rome were bent on crippling him.

Historic Parallel. The Battle of Magnesia 190 B.C.

173

B$_{14}$

FIRST MITHRIDATIC WAR, 88-84 B.C. (2)

A. Capture of Athens and the Piraeus, *86 B.C.*

Sulla interim cum Mithridatis praefectis circa Athenas ita dimicavit, ut et Athenas reciperet et plurimo circa multiplicesPiraei portus munitiones labore expleto amplius CC milia hostium interficeret nec minus multa caperet. . . . Nam oppressi (Athenienses) 5Mithridatis armis homines miserrimae condicioniscum ab inimicis tenerentur, oppugnabantur ab amicis et animos extra moenia, corpora necessitati servientes intra muros habebant.

VELLEIUS PATERCULUS, ii. 23.

2 **ut Athenas reciperet.** Sulla reduced the city by starvation.

3 **Piraei portus.** This was strongly held by Archelaus, and was taken only after a most obstinate defence.

7 cum . . . tenerentur. The contemptible adventurer Aristion, with his bodyguard of 2000 men and the bribe of Delos and its treasure, had made himself master of Athens.

B. Battle of Orchomenus, *85 B.C.*

Sulla restores the Fight.

L. Sulla, cedentibus iam legionibus exercitui 10Mithridatico ductu Archelai, stricto gladio in primam aciem procucurrit appellansque milites dixit, si quis quaesisset, ubi imperatorem reliquissent, responderent pugnantem in Boeotia: cuius rei pudore universi eum secuti sunt.15

FRONTINUS, Strategemata, ii. 8. 12.

10-15 = 'The great victory at Orchomenus was the turning-point in the War.'—Ihne.

C. Peace of Dardanus.

End of the First Mithridatic War, *84 B.C.*

Transgressus deinde in Asiam Sulla parentem ad omnia supplicemque Mithridatem invenit, quem multatum pecunia ac parte navium, Asia omnibusque aliis provinciis, quas armis occupaverat, decedere coegit, captivos recepit, in perfugas noxiosque 20animadvertit, paternis, id est Ponticis finibus contentum esse iussit.

VELLEIUS PATERCULUS, ii. 23.

16-22 **The terms of peace** were (i) Restoration of all conquests, (ii) Surrender of 80 ships and of all prisoners, (iii) Indemnity of 3000 talents. Florus says 'Non fregit ea res Ponticos, sed incendit.' Sulla was anxious to secure peace, because his presence was needed at Rome.

Sulla's Conduct of the War. 'No previous general had shown so great a mastery of the art of war and such care and interest for the welfare of the State, as distinguished from the success of a party.'—Ihne.

174

B₁₅

SECOND CIVIL WAR, 83-82 B.C. (1)

Battles of Sacriportus and the Colline Gate.

A.

Iam quot apud Sacri cecidere cadavera Portum
135
Aut Collina tulit stratas quot porta catervas,
Tum cum, paene caput mundi rerumque potestas
Mutavit translata locum, Romanaque Samnis
Ultra Caudinas speravit volnera Furcas.

LUCAN, Pharsalia, ii. 134-138.

134 **apud Sacriportum**, near Praeneste, where Sulla totally defeated the Marians, under the younger Marius, 82B.C.

135 **Collina Porta**, i.e. N.E. gate of Rome near the *Collis*Quirinalis.

138 **paene**, with *mutavit*, l. 137.

B.At Pontius Telesinus, dux Samnitium, vir animi bellique fortissimus penitusque Romano nomini infestissimus, contractis circiter XL milibus fortissimae pertinacissimaeque in retinendis armis iuventutis Kal. Novembribus ita ad portam Collinam cum Sulla 10dimicavit, ut ad summum discrimen et eum et rempublicam perduceret, quae non maius periculum adiit Hannibalis intra tertium miliarium conspicata castra, quam eo die, quo circumvolans ordines exercitus sui Telesinus dictitansque adesse Romanis ultimum 15diem vociferabatur eruendam delendamque urbem, adiciens numquam deluturos raptores Italicae libertatis lupos, nisi silva, in quam refugere solerent, esset excisa. Post primam demum horam noctis et Romana acies respiravit et hostium cessit. Telesinus 20postera die semianimis repertus est, victoris magis quam morientis vultum praeferens, cuius abscisum caput ferro figi gestarique circa Praeneste Sulla iussit.

VELLEIUS PATERCULUS, ii. 27.

6 **Pontius Telesinus**, 'a kinsman in name and temper of the hero of 321 B.C.'

12-14 **quae . . . castra.** 'As Hannibal had tried to relieve the closely pressed Capua by a direct attack on Rome, Pontius Telesinus thought to draw off the besieging army from Praeneste by threatening the Capital.'—Ihne.

20 **Romana acies respiravit.** Sulla, with the left wing, was driven back by the Samnites to the walls of Rome, but Crassus with the right wing was completely victorious, and to him the final victory was due.

'The issue of the whole war, at least on Italian ground, was decided by the battle of the Colline Gate.'—Ihne.

117

SECOND CIVIL WAR, 83-82 B.C. (2)

A. Death of the Younger Marius.

Sulla Felix.

Tum demum desperatis rebus suis C. Marius adulescens per cuniculos, qui miro opere fabricati in diversas agrorum partes fuerunt, conatus erumpere, cum foramine e terra emersisset, a dispositis in id ipsum interemptus est. . . . De quo iuvene quid5existimaverit Sulla, in promptu est; occiso enim demum eo Felicis nomen adsumpsit, quod quidem usurpasset iustissime, si eundem et vincendi et vivendi finem habuisset.

VELL. PAT. ii. 27.

1 **Tum**, i.e. after Sulla's victory at the Colline Gate, 82 B.C.

C. Marius. 'He possessed his father's martial spirit, courage and unyielding perseverance.'—Ihne.

2 **per cuniculos** = *through subterranean passages.*

B. The Sullan Proscriptions.

139

'Sulla quoque immensis accessit cladibus ultor.
Ille quod exiguum restabat sanguinis urbi
Hausit: dumque nimis iam putria membra recidit,
Excessit medicina modum, nimiumque secuta est,
143
Qua morbi duxere, manus . . . .
145
Tum data libertas odiis, resolutaque legum
Frenis ira ruit. Non uni cuncta dabantur,
Sed fecit sibi quisque nefas: semel omnia victor
Iusserat . . .
221
Hisne Salus rerum, Felix his Sulla vocari,
His meruit tumulum medio sibi tollere Campo?
Haec rursus patienda manent: hoc ordine belli
224
Ibitur: hic stabit civilibus exitus armis.'
232
.   .   .   .   Sic maesta senectus
Praeteritique memor flebat metuensque futuri.

LUCAN, *Pharsalia*, ii. 139-148, 221-224.

139 **Sulla . . . ultor** = *Sulla too in his vengeance came to crown these fearful disasters.*—Haskins.

141-143 **dumque . . . manus.** Sulla is compared to a surgeon who in too great haste to remove the mortified flesh cuts away the sound flesh also.

146 **non uni . . .** = *all crimes were not committed for one man's sake,* i.e. to please Sulla.

223-224 **hoc ordine belli ibitur** = *in this course of war events will move.*—H. i.e. History will repeat itself.

232 **sic maesta senectus.** An old man, who had lived through the Marian and Sullan times, predicts similar horrors of the Civil War between Caesar and Pompey.

The Proscriptions. 'They were the product not of passion or thirst of blood, but of a cool political calculation, and the conviction of its inevitable necessity.'—Ihne.

A. Sulla appointed Dictator, *81 B.C.*

Dictator creatus (cuius honoris usurpatio per annos centum et viginti intermissa; nam proximus post annum quam Hannibal Italia excesserat, uti appareat populum Romanum usum dictatoris haud metu desiderasse tali quo timuisset potestatem) imperio, 5quopriores ad vindicandum maximis periculis patriam usi erant, eo in immodicae crudelitatis licentiam usus est.

VELLEIUS PATERCULUS, ii. 28.

1-2 **cuius honoris . . . intermissa.** The last real Dictator (M. Junius Pera) was appointed after Cannae 216 B.C.

5-8 **imperio quo . . . usus est.** 'The Dictator of the first age of the Republic down to the Punic Wars had always a*well-defined special duty to discharge in a given time.* Sulla's task was of *a general* *nature and all-comprehensive range*, and he had the most essential of all monarchical attributes, which is *the unlimited duration of office.*'—Ihne.

B. Sulla lays down his Dictatorship, *79 B.C.*

Nec minoris impotentiae voces propalam edebat, ut Titus Ampiusscribit, 'Nihil esse rempublicam, 10appellationem modo sine corpore ac specie. Sullam nescisse litteras, qui dictaturam deposuerit.'

SUETONIUS, Divus Iulius, 77.

9 **impotentiae** = *arrogance* (lack of self-restraint).
10 **Ampius.** Titus Ampius Balbus, a Pompeian general.
11-12 **Sullam nescisse litteras** = (i) S. had not profited by the teachings of History, or (ii) S. was without a liberal education.

C. Death of Sulla, *78 B.C.*

Puteolis enim ardens indignatione, quod Granius, princeps eius coloniae pecuniam a decurionibus ad refectionem Capitolii promissam cunctantius daret, 15animi concitatione nimia atque immoderato vocis impetu convulso pectore, spiritum cruore ac minis mixtum evomuit, nec senio iam prolapsus, utpote sexagesimum ingrediens annum, sed alita miseriis reipublicae inpotentia furens. Igitur in dubio est 20Sullane prior an iracundia Sullae sit extincta.

VALERIUS MAXIMUS, ix. 3. 8.

13 **Granius**, the chief magistrate of Puteoli, had kept back money destined for the building of the new temple of Jupiter Capitolinus. The old one was destroyed by fire 83 B.C. 'It was Sulla's great desire that his name should be recorded on the front of the new temple, for it was to be the symbol of the Republic, restored as he fondly hoped by him to its pristine purity.'—Ihne.
177
B₁₈

THE LEGES CORNELIAE, 81 B.C.

A. Limitation of the Tribune's Right of Veto.

In ista quidem re vehementer Sullam probo, qui tribunis plebis sua lege iniuriae faciendae potestatem ademerit, auxili ferendireliquerit.

CICERO, de Legibus, iii. 9. 22.

2 **iniuriae faciendae**, e.g. by their abuse of the right of veto.
3 **auxili ferendi.** 'Sulla limited the office of tribune to the original functions for which it was established, *the legal protection of the people from the abuse of magisterial power.*'—Ihne.

B. Abolition of Corn Distributions.

Populus Romanus, paullo ante gentium moderator, exutus imperio gloria iure, agitandi inops despectusque ne servilia quidem alimenta relicua habet.

SALLUST, Hist., Orat. M. Lepidi.

5 **agitandi inops** (i.e. *vitam sustentandi*) = *without means of livelihood.*
6 **servilia alimenta** = *a slave's allowance of food.* Sulla abolished the largesses of corn.

C. Restoration of Judicial Functions to the Senators.

Iudicandi munus quod C. Gracchus ereptum senatui ad Equites, Sulla ab illis ad Senatum transtulerat.

VELLEIUS PATERCULUS, ii. 32.

8-10 Sulla filled up the gaps in the Senate from the ranks of the Equites, and to the new Senate thus constituted he entrusted the administration of justice.

D. A Sumptuary Law, Limiting the Expense of the Table.

L. Sulla dictator, cum plerique in patrimoniis amplis eluerentur et familiam pecuniamque suam prandiorum conviviorumque gurgitibus proluissent, legem ad populam tulit, qua cautum est, ut Kalendis, Idibus, Nonis diebusque ludorum et feriis quibusdam15sollemnibus sestertios trecenos in cenam insumere ius potestasque esset, ceteris autem diebus omnibus non amplius tricenos.

AULUS GELLIUS, ii. 24, 11.

12 **eluerentur** = *had squandered* (lit. 'washed away').
Leges Corneliae. 'Sulla's legislation was an attempt to revive what was dead and gone. The time had arrived when the old republican institutions could last no longer. The transformation of the state into a monarchy was inevitable.'—Ihne.
The Sultan Constitution. It had as little endurance as that of Cromwell, and was finally destroyed in 70 B.C. during the consulship of Pompeius and Crassus.

Speech of Lepidus against Sulla, *78 B.C.*

Nam praeter satellites commaculatos quis eadem volt? aut quis non omnia mutata praeter victorem? Scilicet milites, quorum sanguine Tarulae Scyrtoque, pessumis servorum, divitiae partae sunt! Itaque maxumam mihi fiduciam parit victor exercitus, cui5per tot volnera et labores nihil praeter tyrannum quaesitum est. Nisi forte tribuniciam potestatem evorsum profecti sunt, per arma conditam a maioribus suis, utique iura et iudicia sibimet extorquerent, egregia scilicet mercede, cum relegati in paludes et10silvam contumeliam atque invidiam suam, praemia penes paucos intellegerint. Quare igitur tanto agmine atque animis incedit? Quiasecundae res mire sunt vitiis obtentui; quibus labefactis, quam formidatus est, tam contemnetur; nisi forte specie 15concordiae et pacis, quae sceleri et parricidio suo nomina indidit; neque aliter rempublicam et belli finem ait, nisi maneat expulsa agris plebes, praeda civilis acerbissima, ius iudiciumque omnium rerum penes se, quod populi Romani fuit. Quae si vobis 20pax et concordia intelleguntur, maxuma turbamenta reipublicae atque exitia probate, annuite legibus impositis, accipite otium cum servitio et tradite exemplum posteris ad populum Romanum suimet sanguinis mercede circumveniundum.25

SALLUST, Hist, Orat. M. Lepidi.

1 **Nam**, sc. 'His luck is not so great as he supposes, for. . .'

7-8 **tribuniciam . . . evorsum**, i.e. by the Leges Corneliae 81 B.C.

9 **iudicia.** Sulla restored the judicial functions to the Senate (from the Equites).

10 **relegati in paludes.** Sulla established 120,000 soldiers in military colonies in different parts of Italy, but their roaming adventurous life had unfitted them for agricultural pursuits.

13-14 **Quia . . . obtentui** = *because prosperity serves in a marvellous manner to cover a man's faults of character.*—Holden. For **obtentui** cf. *draw a veil over.*

16 **parricidio** = *treason.*

18 **nisi . . . agris**, i.e. Sulla's confiscations of estates, especially of those Italians who had fought against him.

24-25 **ad p. R. circumveniundum** = *for oppressing*(enslaving) *the people of Rome.*

M. Aemillus Lepidus, Consul 78 B.C., a disappointed Optimate, jealous of Sulla's power, but without Sulla's ability. He posed as leader of the democratic party, took up arms against the State, but was defeated by Q. Catulus at the Milvian Bridge, 77 B.C.

WAR WITH SERTORIUS IN SPAIN, 78-72 B.C. (1)

Sertorius and his Fawn.

Huic Sertorio cerva alba eximiae pulchritudinis et vivacissimae celeritatis a Lusitano quodam dono data est. Hanc sibi oblatam divinitus, et instinctam Dianae numine colloqui secum, monereque, et docere, quae utilia factu essent, persuadere omnibus instituit: 5ac, si quid durius videbatur, quod imperandum militibus foret, a cerva sese monitum tum praedicabat. Id cum dixerat, universi, tamquam si deo, libentes parebant. Ea cerva quodam die, cum incursio esset hostium nuntiata, festinatione ac tumultu consternata 10in fugam se proripuit, atque in palude proxima delituit; et postea requisita perisse credita est. Neque multis diebus post inventam esse cervam Sertorio nuntiatur. Tum, qui nuntiaverat, iussit tacere: ac, ne cui palam diceret, interminatusest: 15praecepitque, ut eam postero die repente in eum locum, in quo ipse cum amicis esset, immitteret: admissis deinde amicis postridie, visum sibi esse ait in quiete cervam, quae perisset, ad se reverti, et, ut prius consueverat, quod opus esset facto praedicare.20Tum servo, quod imperaverat, significat. Cerva emissa in cubiculum Sertorii introrupit; clamor factus et orta admiratio est: eaque hominum barbarorum credulitas Sertorio in magnis rebus magno usui fuit.25

GELLIUS, Noctes Atticae, xv. 22.

1 **alba** = a *dull* white as opp. to **ater** = *dull* black. Cf.**candidus** = *shining* white as opp. to **niger** = *shining*black.

3 **instinctam** = *fired, animated.*

15 **interminatus** = *he forbade with threats.* **inter** + **minor**, freq. in Plautus and Terence.

23-25 'Sertorius did not disdain to turn to account the superstition of the ruder Spanish tribes, and to have his plans of war brought to him as commands of Diana by the white fawn of the goddess.'—M.

Character of Sertorius. 'He was the only democratic (Marian) officer who knew how to prepare and to conduct war, and the only democratic statesman who opposed the furious doings of his party with statesmanlike energy. His Spanish soldiers called him the new Hannibal, and not merely because he had, like that hero, lost an eye in war. He in reality reminds us of the great Phoenician by his equally cunning and courageous strategy, and by the quickness of his ingenuity in turning to good account his victories and averting the consequences of his defeats.'—M.

180

B₂₁

WAR WITH SERTORIUS IN SPAIN (2)

A. A New Hannibal.

Sertorius, exsul et profugus feralis illius tabulae, vir summae quidem sed calamitosae virtutis, malis suis maria terrasque permiscuit; et iam Africae, iam Balearibus insulis fortunam expertus usque in Oceanum Fortunatasque insulas penetravit consiliis, 5tandem Hispaniam armavit. Viro cum viris facile convenit. Nec alias magis apparuit Hispani militis vigor quam Romano duce. Quamquam ille non contentus Hispania ad Mithridatem quoque Ponticosque respexit regemque classe iuvit. Et quid futurum 10fuit satis tanto hosti, cui uno imperatore resistere res Romana non potuit? Additus Metello Gnaeus Pompeius. Hi copias attrivere viri prope tota Hispania persecuti. Diu et ancipiti; semper acie pugnatum est nec tamen prius bello quam suorum scelere 15et insidiis extinctus est.

FLORUS, III. xxii. 2-6. A.

1 **feralis illius tabulae** = *from that fatal list*, i.e. Sulla's list of proscribed Marians 82 B.C.

9-10 **ad Mithridatem . . . iuvit.** In 75 B.C. he concluded a formal treaty of alliance with Mithridates, and sent him the propraetor M. Marius to lead his troops. Cf. alliance between Hannibal and Philip.

14-15 **Diu et ancipiti semper acie pugnatum est**, e.g. the defeat of Pompey near Lauro. (For a graphic account of the strategy by which the battle was won see Frontinus, *Strat.* ii. 5.)

B. The Death of Sertorius.

M. Perpenna praetorius e proscriptis, gentis clarioris quam animi, Sertorium inter cenam Oscae interemit Romanisque certam victoriam, partibus suis excidium, sibi turpissimam mortem pessimo 20auctoravit facinore. Metellus et Pompeius ex Hispaniis triumphaverunt.

VELL. PATERC. ii. 30.

17 **M. Perpenna praetorius** (= *ex-praetor*), with the remnant of the army of Lepidus (defeated by Pompey in 77 B.C.) joined Sertorius in Spain. After serving under Sertorius for some years, through jealousy, he brought about his leader's assassination.

21 **auctoravit** = *he brought about.* More usu. as **auctorari**= *to hire oneself out for some service*, e.g. of gladiators.

The Death of Sertorius. 'So ended one of the greatest men that Rome had hitherto produced—a man who under more fortunate circumstances would perhaps have become the regenerator of his country.'—M.

181

B₂₂

Character and Early Career of Lucullus.

Magnum ingenium L. Luculli, magnumque optimarum artiumstudium, tum omnis liberalis et digna homine nobili ab eo perceptadoctrina, quibus temporibus florere in foro maxime potuit, caruitomnino rebus urbanis. Ut enim admodum adolescens, 5cum fratre pari pietate et industria praedito, paternas inimicitias magna cum gloria est persecutus, in Asiam quaestor profectus, ibi permultos annos admirabili quadam laude provinciae praefuit: deinde absens factus aedilis, continuo praetor: licebat 10enim celerius legis praemio: post in Africam: inde ad consulatum: quem ita gessit ut diligentiam admirarentur omnes, ingenium cognoscerent. Post ad Mithridaticum bellum missus a senatu non modo opinionem vicit omnium quae de virtute eius erat, sed 15etiam gloriam superiorum. Idque eo fuit mirabilius, quod ab eo laus imperatoria non admodum exspectabatur, qui adolescentiam in forensi opera, quaesturae diuturnum tempus, Murena bellum in Ponto gerente, in Asiae pace consumpserat. . . . 20In eodem tanta prudentia fuit in constituendis temperandisque civitatibus, tanta aequitas, ut hodiestet Asia Luculli institutis servandis et quasi vestigiis persequendis.

CICERO, *Academica*, ii. 1.

1-3 **ingenium, studium, doctrina**, subjects of **caruit**.

3-5 **quibus temporibus . . . urbanis** = *all this was divorced*(**caruit**, lit. *was cut off from*) *from the business of the capital, at the season when he might have had a specially brilliant career in the forum.*—J. S. Reid.

6 **paternas inimicitias** = *his father's quarrel.* The first appearance of Lucullus in public life was as the accuser of the Augur Servilius who had procured the banishment of his father.

7-9 **in Asiam . . . praefuit**, i.e. as Sulla's quaestor in the first Mithridatic War, 88-84 B.C. and then till 80 B.C. in charge of the province of Asia (= orig. Kingdom of Pergamus, N.W. part of Asia Minor).

11 **legis praemio** = *owing to a privilege conveyed by statute.* J. S. R.

13-14 **ad Mithridaticum bellum**, i.e. the 3rd M. War, which he carried on for eight years (74-66 B.C.) with great success, until superseded by Pompeius in 66 B.C.

19-20 **Murena . . . gerente.** Lic. Murena, anxious for distinction, provoked the disastrous 2nd Mithridatic War, 83-81 B.C., when by the peremptory orders of Sulla the peace was renewed.

23 **stet . . . servandis** = *persists in maintaining* (lit. *stands by*) *the ordinances of L.*—J. S. R.

Reference. For *Character of Lucullus*, see Mommsen, vol. iv. pp. 337-8. Cf. also Vell. Paterc. ii. 32.

182

B_{23}

A. A Soldier of Lucullus.

Luculli miles collecta viatica multis
Aerumnis, lassus dum noctu stertit, ad assem
Perdiderat; post hoc vehemens lupus, et sibi et hosti
Iratus pariter, ieiunis dentibus acer,
30
Praesidium regale loco deiecit, ut aiunt,
Summe munito et multarum divite rerum.
Clarus ob id factum donis ornatur honestis,
Accipit et bis dena super sestertia nummum.
Forte sub hoc tempus castellum evertere praetor
35
Nescio quod cupiens hortari coepit eundem
Verbis, quae timido quoque possent addere mentem:
'I, bone, quo virtus tua te vocat, i pede fausto,
Grandia laturus meritorum praemia. Quid stas?'
Post haec ille catus, quantumvis rusticus, 'Ibit,
40
Ibit eo quo vis qui zonam perdidit,' inquit.

HORACE, *Ep.* II. ii. 26-40.

26 **viatica** = *savings* (cf. *prize-money*). **viaticum** = originally *travelling-money.*

28 **vehemens lupus** = *a very wolf in his fury.* Cf. Vergil's simile for a forlorn hope—'lupi ceu | Raptores.'—Wickham.

32 **donis honestis** = *gifts of honour*—i.e. the *corona muralis*, the *mural crown*, such as is worn by the goddess Cybele.

33 **nummum** (= *nummorum*) = *in hard cash.*

39 **catus** = *shrewd, witty*, a Sabine word, = *acutus.*

39-40 **Ibit . . . quo vis**, the original of Juvenal's *ad caelum, iusseris, ibit.*

40 **zonam** = *purse.* The **zona** here was a broad belt made double or hollow to carry money in.

B. The Wealth of Lucullus.

20
   Chlamydes Lucullus, ut aiunt,
Si posset centum scaenae praebere rogatus,
'Qui possum tot?' ait; 'tamen et quaeram, et quot habebo
Mittam': post paulo scribit sibi milia quinque
Esse domi chlamydum; partem vel tolleret omnes.

HORACE, *Ep.* I. vi. 40-44.

Subject. Horace says 'I am like Lucullus' soldier—when his pocket was empty he would volunteer for forlorn hopes; when it was full again he would do so no more. It was poverty that made me write verses.'—W.

40 **Chlamydes.** The Chlamys was the light short mantle of the Greeks, here wanted for a pageant on the stage.

44 **tolleret.** The subj. is the praetor or person giving the show.—W.

Reference. For *the magnificence of his Villas* at Tusculum and near Neapolis, see Cicero *De Fin.* ii. § 107, *De Leg.* iii. § 30, Pliny, *N. H.* ix. 170.

183

B_{24}

WAR WITH SPARTACUS, 73-71 B.C.

Spartacus and his Gladiators.

Spartacus, Crixus, Oenomaus effracto Lentuli ludo cum triginta aut amplius eiusdem fortunae viris erupere Capua; servisque ad vexillum vocatis cum statim decem amplius milia coissent, homines modo effugisse contenti iam et vindicari volebant. 5Prima sedes velut rabidis beluis mons Vesuvius placuit. Ibi cum obsiderentur a Clodio Glabro, per fauces cavi montis vitineis delapsi vinculis ad imas eius descendere radices et exitu invisonihil tale opinantis ducis subito impetu castra rapuerunt. Adfluentibus 10in diem copiis cum iam esset iustus exercitus, e viminibus pecudumque tegumentis inconditos sibi clipeos et ferro ergastulorum recocto gladios ac tela fecerunt, Indo iam consulares quoque aggressus in Appennino Lentuli exercitum percecidit, apud 15Mutinam Gai Cassi castra delevit. Tandem enim totis imperii viribus contra mirmillonem consurgunt, pudoremque Romanum Marcus Crassus asseruit: a quo pulsi fugatique hostes in extrema Italiae refugerunt. Ibi circa Bruttium angulum clusi cum 20fugam in Siciliam pararent neque navigia suppeterent ratesque ex trabibus et dolia connexa virgultis rapidissimo freto frustra experirentur, tandem eruptione facta dignam viris obiere mortem, et quod sub gladiatore duce oportuit, sine missione25pugnatum est. Spartacus ipse in primo agmine fortissime dimicans quasi imperator occisus est.

FLORUS, III. xx. 3-14 (sel.).

1 **Spartacus**, by birth a Thracian, who had served among the Thracian auxiliaries in the Roman army, had deserted and become a chief of banditti. He was taken prisoner and sold to a trainer of gladiators.

Crixus, Oenomaus, the slave-names of two Celts.

1-2 **effracto ludo** = *broke out of the gladiators' school.*

8 **vitineis vinculis** = *by means of ropes made of vine-branches.*

9 **inviso** = *unknown,* lit. *unseen.*

13 **ergastulorum** = *from the slaves' work-houses.*

17 **mirmillonem.** The Mirmillones were a class of gladiators usually matched with the Thraces or the *retiarii* (*net-fighters*).

18 **Marcus Crassus**, the Triumvir of 60 B.C.

asseruit = *maintained.* Cf. our *assert.*

21 **in Siciliam**, where the slaves had risen in 133 and 104B.C., and only waited an impulse to break out a third time.

25 **sine missione** = *without quarter.* Cf. *missio* = *the discharge* from service of soldiers and gladiators.

184

B25

THE THIRD MITHRIDATIC WAR, 74-63 B.C. (1)

Lucullus Ponticus.

Quoniam de genere belli dixi, nunc de magnitudine pauca dicam. Atque ut omnes intellegant me L. Lucullo tantum impertire laudis, quantum forti viro et sapienti homini et magno imperatori debeatur, dico eius adventu maximas Mithridatis 5copias omnibus rebus ornatas atque instructas fuisse urbemque Asiae clarissimam nobisque amicissimam, Cyzicenorum, obsessam esse ab ipso rege maxima multitudine et oppugnatam vehementissime, quam L. Lucullus virtute, assiduitate, consilio summis 10obsidionis periculis liberavit: ab eodem imperatore classem magnam et ornatam, quae ducibus Sertorianis ad Italiam studio inflammata raperetur, superatam esse atque depressam; magnas hostium praeterea copias multis proeliis esse deletas patefactumque 15nostris legionibus esse Pontum, qui antea populo Romano ex omni aditu clausus fuisset; Sinopen atque Amisum, quibus in oppidis erant domicilia regis, omnibus rebus ornatas atque refertas, ceterasque urbes Ponti et Cappadociae permultas uno 20aditu adventuque esse captas; regem spoliatum regno patrio atque avito ad alios se regesatque ad alias gentes supplicem contulisse: atque haec omniasalvis populi Romani sociis atque integris vectigalibus esse gesta.25

CICERO, *pro Lege Manilia,* 20, 21.

5-6 **maximas . . . fuisse.** M. had 140,000 well-trained men, Roman officers sent by Sertorius, 16,000 cavalry, a war-fleet of 400 ships, and abundance of stores.

7-11 **urbemque . . . liberavit.** The city of Cyzicus stood on the S. side of the island of the same name in the Propontis (Sea of Marmora), close to the shore of Mȳsia, to which it was joined by two bridges.

12-14 **classem . . . depressam,** i.e. probably the Battle of Tenedos 73 B.C., in which Marcus Marius and the ablest of the Roman emigrants met their death, and the whole Aegean fleet of Mithridates was annihilated.

123

15 **multis proeliis**, e.g. of Cabira, 72 B.C.; Tigranocerta, 69B.C.

18 **Sinopen. Sinope**, on the W. headland of the great bay of which the delta of the R. Halys forms the E. headland, was the birthplace and residence (**domicilia**) of M.

22 **ad alios reges**, e.g. to his son-in-law, Tigranes of Armenia.

23-24 **salvis . . . vectigalibus**, i.e. without ruining the provincial by forced contributions and requisitions.

Reference. For *Siege of Cyzicus*, see Mommsen, vol. iv. pp. 326-328; Frontinus, *Strat.* ii. 13. 6.

185

B₂₆

CN. POMPEIUS MAGNUS, 106-48 B.C.

His Character, and Career to *66 B.C.*

Iam vero virtuti Cn. Pompei quae potest oratio par inveniri? Quid est quod quisquam aut illo dignum, aut vobis novum aut cuiquam inauditum possit adferre? Neque enim illae sunt solae virtutes imperatoriae, quae vulgo esistimantur, labor in 5negotiis, fortitudo in periculis, industria in agendo, celeritas in conficiendo, consilium in providendo, quae tanta sunt in hoc uno, quanta in omnibus reliquis imperatoribus, quos aut vidimus aut audivimus, non fuerunt. Testis est Italia, quam ille ipse 10victor L. Sulla huius virtute et subsidio confessus est liberatam: testis est Sicilia, quam multis undique cinctam periculis non terrore belli, sed consilii celeritate explicavit: testis est Africa, quae magnis oppressa hostium copiis eorum ipsorum sanguine 15redundavit: testis est Gallia, per quam legionibus nostris iter in Hispaniam Gallorum internecione patefactum est: testis est Hispania, quae saepissime plurimos hostes ab hoc superatos prostratosque conspexit: testis est iterum et saepius Italia, quae 20cum servili bello taetro periculosoque premeretur, ab hoc auxilium absente expetivit, quod bellum exspectatione eius attenuatum atque imminutum est, adventu sublatum ac sepultum: testes nunc vero iam omnes orae atque omnes exterae gentes ac nationes.25

CICERO, *pro Lege Manilia*, 29-31.

10-12 **Testis est Italia . . . liberatam.** In 83 B.C. Pompeius, aged twenty-four, raised three legions in Picenum, gained several advantages over the Marian generals, and was saluted by Sulla as Imperator.

12-14 **testis est Sicilia . . . explicavit.** In 82 B.C. Pompeius, sent as propraetor to Sicily, quickly took possession of the island for Sulla.

14-16 **testis est Africa . . . redundavit.** In 81 B.C. Pompeius defeated at Utica the Marian Ahenobarbus (allied with Hiarbas of Numidia), and was, though *a simple Roman eques*, granted a triumph by Sulla and saluted as**Magnus**.

16-18 **testis est Gallia . . . patefactum est.** In 77 B.C., on his way to Spain as proconsul against Sertorius, he had to cut his way through the Transalpine Gauls, and laid out a new and shorter road over the Cottian Alps.

21 **servili bello.** On his return from Spain he cut to pieces the scattered remnants of the army of Spartacus.

21-23 **ab hoc . . . imminutum est.** Cic. assumes that the enemy was crippled even by the mere notion of sending for Pompeius.

References. Plutarch, *Pompeius*; Vell. Paterc. ii. 29.

186

B₂₇

GAIUS IULIUS CAESAR (1)

The Man Caesar.

Fuisse traditur excelsa statura, colore candido, teretibus membris, ore paulo pleniore, nigris vegetisque oculis, valetudine prospera; nisi quod tempore extremo repente animo linqui atque etiam per somnum exterreri solebat. Armorum et equitandi 5peritissimus, laboris ultra fidem patiens erat. In agmine nonnunquam equo, saepius pedibus anteibat, capite detecto, seu sol seu imber esset; longissimas vias incredibili celeritate confecit. In obeundis expeditionibus dubium cautior an audentior, 10exercitum neque per insidiosa itinera duxit umquam nisi perspeculatus locorum situs. A Brundisio Dyrrachium inter oppositas classes hieme transmisitcessantibusque copiis, quas subsequi iusserat, cum ad accersendas frustra saepe misisset, 15novissime ipse clam noctu parvulum navigium solus obvoluto capite conscendit, neque aut quis esset ante detexit aut gubernatorem cedere adversae tempestati passus est, quam paene obrutus fluctibus. Ne religione quidem ulla a quoquam incepto absterritus 20umquam vel retardatus est. Cum immolanti aufugisset hostia, profectionem adversus Scipionem et Iubam non distulit. Prolapsus etiam in egressu navis, verso ad melius omine Teneo te, inquit, Africa.

SUETONIUS, *Divus Iulius*, 45, 57-59 (sel.)

124

4 **animo linqui** = *he was subject to fainting-fits.*

8 **capite detecto**, so Cyrus the Younger and Hannibal.

9 **incredibili celeritate**, cf. Cic. *Ep. ad Att.* viii. 9 *hoc* τέρας(= prodigy) *horribili vigilantia, celeritate, diligentia est.* Cf. also Napoleon the Great.

14 **cessantibusque copiis** = *and when the troops delayed their coming.* Caesar did not then know that Antonius had himself been attacked at Brundisium by a Pompeian fleet, and had shown great skill in baffling it, and forcing it to put to sea again. Once more Antonius set sail with 4 legions and 800 horsemen, and fortunately a strong S. wind carried him safely to the port of Lissus (N. of Dyrrachium).

18-19 **gubernatorem . . . passus est.** '*Quid times? Caesarem vehis!*' was Caesar's famous exhortation to the pilot. (Florus.)

21-22 **Cum . . . hostia**: if the victim even tugged at the rope when being led to sacrifice, it was considered unfortunate, and hence a long slack rope was used. Cf. Juv. xii. 5 *Sed procul extensum petulans* (butting)*quatit hostia funem.*

24 According to Frontinus his words were '*Teneo te, terra mater.*'

The man Caesar. 'We may picture him as a man the dignity of whose bodily presence was in due proportion to the greatness of his mental powers.'—Warde Fowler.

187

B₂₈

GAIUS IULIUS CAESAR (2)

Captured by Pirates.

Studies Oratory at Rhodes, 76-75 B.C.

Composita seditione civili Cornelium Dolabellam consularem et triumphalem repetundarum postulavit; absolutoque Rhodum secedere statuit, et ad declinandam invidiam et ut per otium ac requiem Apollonio Moloni clarissimo tunc dicendi magistro5operam daret. Huc dum hibernis iam mensibus traicit, circa Pharmacussam insulam a praedonibus captus est, mansitque apud eos, non sine summa indignatione, prope quadraginta dies cum uno medico et cubicularis duobus. Nam comites servosque 10ceteros initio statim ad expediendas pecunias, quibus redimeretur, dimiserat. Numeratis deinde quinquaginta talentis, expositus in litore non distulit quin e vestigio classe deducta persequeretur abeuntis, ac redactos in potestatem supplicio, quod saepe illis15minatus inter iocum fuerat, adficeret. Vastante regiones proximas Mithridate ne desidere in discrimine sociorum videretur, ab Rhodio quo pertenderat, transiit in Asiam, auxiliisque contractis et praefecto regis provincia expulso, nutantes ac dubias civitates20retinuit in fide.

SUETONIUS, *Divus Iulius*, 4.

1 **Composita seditione civili**, i.e. after the abortive attempt of Lepidus to make himself master of the state 77 B.C.

C. Dolabellam, impeached for illegal extortion during his government of Macedonia.

Repetundarum (sc. *pecuniarum*), post-Aug. for *de repetundis* (*pecuniis*), used i. of money extorted by an official and to be returned, ii. of money extorted as a bribe. Caesar lost his case, but succeeded in showing that Sulla's senatorial judges were corrupt.

4 **Apollonio Moloni,** the famous rhetorician, whose pupil Cicero was both at Rome and at Rhodes. Very possibly Caesar took this step by the advice of Cicero.

7 **circa Pharmacussam insulam:** S.W. of Miletus (= mod.*Farmako*).

8-9 **non sine summa indignatione:** Plutarch, *Caes.* gives a picturesque account of his adventures as their prisoner.

10 **cubicularis** (*cubiculum*) = lit. *chamber-servants.*

11 **pecunias . . .** Velleius says that Caesar's ransom was paid out of public funds.

14 **e vestigio** (= *statim*) = *immediately.*

Caesar at Rhodes. 'Caesar, from what we know of his taste and character, could hardly have found the same delight as Cicero in his studies at Rhodes. He nevertheless became one of the greatest orators of his day, and according to some accounts, second only to Cicero. It is characteristic of Caesar, but unfortunate for us, that he never took any pains to collect and preserve his speeches.'—Warde Fowler.

188

B₂₉

CICERO PROSECUTES VERRES, 70 B.C.

A Roman Citizen maltreated.

Quid ego de P. Gavio, Consano municipe, dicam, indices? Aut qua vi vocis, qua gravitate verborum, quo dolore animi dicam? Quod crimen eius modi est ut, cum primum ad me delatum est, usurum me illo non putarem; tametsi enim verissimum esse 5 intellegebam, tamen credibile fore non arbitrabar. Quid nunc agam? Rem in medio ponam: quae tantum habet ipsa gravitatis ut neque mea, quae nulla est, neque cuiusquam ad inflammandos vestros animos eloquentia requiratur. 10

Caedebatur virgis in medio foro Messanae civis Romanus, iudices; cum interea nullus gemitus, nulla vox alia illius miseri inter dolorem crepitumque plagarum audiebatur, nisi haec, *Civis Romanus sum*. Hac se commemoratione civitatis omnia verbera 15 depulsurum, cruciatum a corpore deiecturum arbitrabatur. Is non modo hoc non perfecit ut virgarum vim deprecaretur, sed cum imploraret saepius usurparetque nomen civitatis, crux, crux, inquam, infelici et aerumnoso comparabatur. 20

O nomen dulce libertatis! O ius eximium nostrae civitatis! O lex Porcia legesque Semproniae! O graviter desiderata et aliquando reddita plebi Romanae tribunicia potestas! Hucine tandem omnia reciderunt ut civis Romanus in provincia populi Romani, 25 in oppido foederatorum, ab eo qui beneficio populi Romani fasces et secures haberet deligatus in foro virgis caederetur?

CICERO, in Verrem, ii. 5. 62.

1 **Consano municipe** = *a burgess of Consa*, on the borders of Lucania.

22 **Lex Porcia.** Passed by M. Porcius Cato, 197 B.C., forbade the execution or scourging of a Roman citizen.

Leges Semproniae, a code of laws passed by C. Sempronius Gracchus, 123 B.C. One of these declared it to be the sole right of the people to decide capital cases.

22-24 **O graviter desiderata . . . potestas!** Sulla (Dictator 82-79 B.C.) took from the tribunes *the right of proposing laws*, and left them only their original right of Intercessio or veto. In 70 B.C. Pompeius, who had formally accepted the democratic programme, gave back to the tribunes the power to initiate legislation.

The Orationes In Verrem. Cicero, as patronus of the Sicilians, undertook the prosecution of the Senator C. Verres for his gross misconduct as governor of Sicily, 73-71 B.C.

189

B₃₀

CN. POMPEIUS MAGNUS, 106-48 B.C.

The Lex Gabinia, *67 B.C.*

Converterat Cn. Pompei persona totum in se terrarum orbem et per omnia maior cive habebatur. Qui cum consul perquam laudabiliter iurasset se in nullam provinciam ex eo magistratu iturum idque servasset, post biennium A. Gabinius tribunus 5 legem tulit, ut cum belli more, non latrociniorum, orbem classibus iam, non furtivis expeditionibus, piratae terrerent, quasdamque etiam Italiae urbis diripuissent, Cn. Pompeius ad eos opprimendos mitteretur essetque ei imperium aequum in omnibus 10 provinciis cum proconsulibus usque ad quinquagesimum miliarium a mari. Quo decreto paene totius terrarum orbis imperium uni viro deferebatur; sed tamen idem hoc ante biennium in M. Antoni praetura decretum erat. Sed interdum persona ut exemplo 15 nocet, ita invidiam auget aut levat: in Antonio homines aequo animo passi erant; raro enim invidetur eorum honoribus, quorum vis non timetur: contra in iis homines extraordinaria reformidant, qui ea suo arbitrio aut deposituri aut retenturi videntur 20 et modum in voluntate habent. Dissuadebant optimates, sed consilia impetu victa sunt.

VELLEIUS PATERCULUS, ii. 31.

3-5 **Qui cum consul . . . servasset.** Pompeius, consul with Crassus in 71-70 B.C., thought it beneath his dignity to accept a consular province, and waited in Rome as a simple citizen until an opportunity should be offered him to play an extraordinary part.

5 **A. Gabinius**, a client of Pompeius, a man ruined in finances and character, but a dexterous negotiator, a bold orator, and a brave soldier. In 57 B.C. did excellent service as proconsul of Syria.

6-9 **ut cum belli more . . . diripuissent.** 'For twenty years the sea had been rendered unsafe by these curses of human society.' The commerce of the whole Mediterranean was in their power.

13-15 **sed tamen . . . decretum erat.** In 74 B.C.M. Antonius, son of the orator and father of the triumvir, was entrusted by the Senate with the task of clearing the seas from the corsairs. In spite of his extensive powers, the utter incapacity of Antonius, and the mismanagement of the Senate, caused the expedition to end in failure and disgrace.

Result. 'The Gabinio-Manilian proposals terminated the struggle between the senate and the popular party, which the Sempronian laws (133-123 B.C.) had begun. As the Sempronian laws first constituted the revolutionary party into a *political opposition*, the Gabinio-Manilian first converted it from an *opposition* into a *government*.'—M.

126

CN. POMPEIUS MAGNUS, 106-48 B.C.

Pompeius clears the Seas of Pirates, *67 B.C.*

Quis enim umquam aut obeundi negoti aut consequendi quaestus studio tam brevi tempore tot loca adire, tantos cursus conficere potuit, quam celeriter Cn. Pompeio duce tanti belli impetusnavigavit? Qui nondum tempestivo ad navigandum mari Siciliam5adiit, Africam exploravit, in Sardiniam cum classe venit, atque haec tria frumentaria subsidia rei publicae firmissimis praesidiis classibusque munivit. Inde cum se in Italiam recepisset, duabus Hispaniis et Gallia transalpina praesidiis ac navibus confirmata,10missis item in oram Illyrici maris et in Achaiam omnemque Graeciam navibus Italiae duo maria maximis classibus firmissimisque praesidiis adornavit, ipse autem, ut Brundisio profectus est, undequinquagesimo die totam ad imperium populi Romani 15Ciliciam adiunxit: omnes, qui ubique praedones fuerant, partim capti interfectique sunt, partim unius huius se imperio ac potestati dediderunt. Ita tantum bellum, tam diuturnum, tam longe lateque dispersum, quo bello omnes gentes ac nationes20premebantur, Cn. Pompeius extrema hieme adparavit, ineunte vere suscepit, media aestate confecit.

CICERO, pro Lege Manilia, 34, 35.

4 **tanti belli impetus,** fig. for *an attacking fleet of such force*, which from its size would ordinarily sail slowly.—Wilkins.

5-8 **Qui . . . munivit.** Early in the year (**nondum tempestivo ad navigandum**) Pompeius cleared of pirates the Sicilian, African, and Sardinian waters, so re-establish the supply of grain from these provinces to Italy.

14-18 **undequagesimo . . . dediderunt.** The bold Cilician seakings alone ventured to face the Roman fleet in the offing of Coracesium (at the W. frontier of Cilicia), but were completely defeated. Forty-nine days (**undequinquagesimo**) after Pompeius had appeared in the Eastern seas, Cilicia was subdued, and the war at an end. 'In all about 1300 piratical vessels are said to have been destroyed: besides which the richly filled arsenals and magazines of the buccaneers were burnt. Of the pirates, about 10,000 perished (**interfecti**); upwards of 20,000 fell alive (**partim capti—partim se dediderunt**) into the hands of the victor.'—M.

22 **ineunte vere . . . confecit.** 'In the summer of 67 B.C., three months after the beginning of the campaign, commerce resumed its wonted course, and instead of the former famine abundance prevailed in Italy.'—M.

This was the first trial of rule centralised in a single hand,and Pompeius fully justified the confidence that was placed in him.

THE THIRD MITHRIDATIC WAR, 74-63 B.C. (2)

Pompeius subdues Mithridates and Tigranes.

Pompeius interea memorabile adversus Mithridaten, qui post Luculli profectionem magnas novi exercitus vires reparaverat, bellum gessit. At rex fusus fugatusque et omnibus exutus copiis Armeniam Tigranenque generum petit, regem eius temporis, 5nisi qua Luculli armis erat infractus, potentissimum. Simul itaque duos persecutus Pompeius intravit Armeniam. Prior filius Tigranis, sed discors patri, pervenit ad Pompeium: mox ipse supplex et praesens se regnumque dicioni eius permisit, 10praefatus neminem alium neque Romanum neque ullius gentis virum futurum fuisse, cuius se societate commissurus foret, quam Pompeium; non esse turpe ab eo vinci, quem vincere esset nefas, neque inhoneste aliquem summitti huic, quem fortuna super 15omnes extulisset. Servatus regi honos imperi, sed multato ingenti pecunia, quae omnis, sicuti Pompeio moris erat, redacta in quaestoris potestatem ac publicis descripta litteris. Syria aliaeque, quas occupaverat, provinciae ereptae, et aliae restitutae populo 20Romano, aliae tum primum in eius potestatem redactae, ut Syria, quae tum primum facta est stipendiaria. Finis imperi regi terminatus Armenia.

VELLEIUS PATERCULUS, ii. 37.

Context. In 66 B.C. Lucullus, of whom Mommsen says 'hardly any other Roman general accomplished so much with so trifling means,' was superseded by Pompeius. By the Lex Manilia Pompeius obtained, in addition to the extensive powers conferred upon him by the Lex Gabinia 67 B.C., the military administration of Asia as far as Armenia. 'Never since Rome stood had such power been united in the hands of a single man.'—M.

3-4 **rex fusus . . . copiis,** i.e. in Lesser Armenia, on S. bank of R. Lycus, where Pompeius afterwards founded Nicopolis.

5 **Tigranenque generum petit.** Tigranes had married Cleopatra, the daughter of Mithridates.

17-19 **quae omnis . . . litteris,** i.e. paid into the Roman treasury. Cf. Lucan ix. 197 *Immodicas possedit opes, sed plura retentis | Intulit* sc. *in aerarium.*

The End of Mithridates. After his defeat at Nicopolis the aged king took refuge in his Northern capital of Panticapaeum (on the Cimmerian Bosporus). Here, when all turned against him, he took poison, 63 B.C. 'In him a great enemy was borne to the tomb, a greater than had ever yet withstood the Romans in the indolent East.'—M.

Syria made a Roman Province, 65 B.C.

192
B₃₃

GAIUS IULIUS CAESAR (3)

A. **Curule Aedile,** *65 B.C.*

Aedilis praeter comitium ac forum basilicasque etiam Capitolium ornavit porticibus ad tempus exstructis, in quibus abundante rerum copia pars apparatus exponeretur. Venationes autem ludosque et cum collega et separatim edidit, quo factum est, 5ut communium quoque impensarum solus gratiam caperet, nec dissimularet collega eius Marcus Bibulus evenisse sibi quod Polluci: ut enim geminis fratribus aedes in foro constituta tantum Castoris vocaretur, ita suam Caesarisque munificentiam unius Caesaris10dici.

SUETONIUS, *Divus Iulius,* 10.

1 **Aedilis.** As curule-aedile Caesar exceeded all previous expenditure. This was meant to secure the favour of the democracy, and gain the position of its leader, which was in fact vacant; for Crassus was never popular, and Pompeius was absent in the East.

basilicas (βασιλική sc. οἰκία and στοά: *regia*) = *halls.*

2 **porticibus:** these acted as booths, in a grand fair, as we should say.

4 **Venationes,** here of the combats with wild beasts.

7 **M. Bibulus,** also Caesar's colleague in his first consulship, 59 B.C.

B. **Propraetor in Further Spain,** *61 B.C.*

Ex praetura ulteriorem sortitus Hispaniam, retinentes creditores interventu sponsorum removit, ac neque more neque iure, ante quam provinciae ornarentur, profectus est; pacataque provincia, pari 15festinatione, non expectato successore, ad triumphum simul consulatumque decessit. Sed cum, edictis iam comitiis, ratio eius haberi non posset nisi privatus introisset urbem, et ambienti ut legibus solveretur multi contradicerent, coactus est triumphum, 20ne consulatu excluderetur, dimittere.

SUETONIUS, *Divus Iulius,* 18.

Context. In 69 B.C. Caesar was elected to a Quaestorship (the lowest step in the ladder of official life) and discharged his judicial duties in Further Spain with tact and industry.

13 **retinentes . . . removit** = *freed himself from his creditors, who were for detaining him,* by the help of sureties. Caesar is said to have borrowed from Crassus 830 talents.

14-15 **ante quam provinciae ornarentur:** a regular phrase used of supplying the newly chosen magistrate with money, arms, attendants, etc.

18 **ratio . . . posset** = *his candidature could not be considered.*

Propraetor in F. Spain. 'His governorship enabled him partly to rid himself of his debts partly to lay the foundation for his military repute.'—M.

193
B₃₄

THE CONSPIRACY OF CATILINE, 63 B.C. (1)

Cicero declaims against the Audacity of Catiline.

Quo usque tandem abutere, Catilina, patientia nostra? Quam diu etiam furor iste tuus nos eludet? Quem ad finem sese effrenata iactabit audacia? Nihilne te nocturnum praesidium Palati, nihil urbis vigiliae, nihil timor populi, nihil concursus bonorum5omnium, nihil hic munitissimus habendi senatus locus, nihil horum ora voltusque moverunt? Patere tua consilia non sentis? Constrictam iam horum omnium scientia teneri coniurationem tuam non vides? Quid proxima, quid superiore nocte egeris, 10ubi fueris, quos convocaveris, quid consilii ceperis, quem nostrum ignorare arbitraris? O tempora! O mores! Senatus haec intellegit; consul videt: hic tamen vivit. Vivit? immo vero etiam in senatum venit: fit publici consilii particeps; notat at designat 15oculis ad caedem unum quemque nostrum. . . . Castra sunt in Italia contra rem publicam in Etruriae faucibus collocata: crescit in dies singulos hostium numerus; eorum autem castrorum imperatoremducemque hostium intra moenia atque 20adeo in senatu videmus intestinam aliquam cotidie perniciem rei publicae molientem. Si te iam, Catilina, comprehendi, si interfici iussero, credo, erit verendum mihi ne non hoc potius omnes boni serius a me quam quisquam crudelius factum esse dicat.25

128

1 **Quo usque tandem abutere** = *how long, pray, will you presume upon?* Catiline had been declared *hostis patriae*, and yet dared to appear in the Senate.

4 **praesidium Palati**: in the case of any threatening danger the **Mons Palatinus** was occupied as one of the most important military points in the city.

6-7 **senatus locus**, i.e. the temple of **Jupiter Stator**, on the N. slope of the Palatine, chosen as the safest meeting-place, and near Cicero's house.

17-18 **castra . . . collocata**, the camp of Manlius (one of the veteran centurions of Sulla) was planted at Faesulae (Fiesole), a rocky fastness three miles N.E. of Florence.

19 **imperatorem**: ironical, as though Catiline were the legally appointed general of the Republic.

In L. Catilinam Oratio i. 'This splendid oration, in its fiery vigour and mastery of invective, is unsurpassed except by the Second Philippic.'—Cruttwell.

Its effect on Catiline. *Tum ille furibundus 'quoniam quidem circumventus' inquit 'ab inimicis praeceps agor, incendium meum ruina restinguam.'* Sall. *Catil.* 31. That night Catiline left Rome for the camp of Manlius.

194
B₃₅

THE CONSPIRACY OF CATILINE, 63 B.C. (2)

The End of Catiline.

Sed confecto proelio tum vero cerneres, quanta audacia quantaque vis animi fuisset in exercitu Catilinae. Nam fere, quem quisque vivus pugnando locum ceperat, eum, amissa anima, corpore tegebat. Pauci autem, quos medios cohors praetoria disiecerat,5paulo divorsius, sed omnes tamen advorsis volneribus conciderant. Catilina vero longe a suis inter hostium cadavera repertus est, paululum etiam spirans ferociamque animi, quam habuerat vivus, in voltu retinens. Postremo ex omni copia neque in 10proelio neque in fuga quisquam civis ingenuus captus est. Ita cuncti suae hostiumque vitae iuxta pepercerant. Neque tamen exercitus populi Romani laetam aut incruentam victoriam adeptus erat; nam strenuissumus quisque aut occiderat in proelio, aut15graviter volneratus discesserat. Multi autem, qui de castris visundi aut spoliandi gratia processerant, volventes hostilia cadavera, amicum alii, pars hospitem aut cognatum reperiebant; fuere item, qui inimicos suos cognoscerent. Ita varie per omnem 20exercitumlaetitia, maeror, luctus atque gaudia agitabantur.

SALLUST, Bellum Catilinae, 61.

5 **cohors praetoria**: a *corps d'élite*, specially organised as a bodyguard of the general (*praetor* = *praeitor*, *prae* + *eo*), dating from the time when the praetores was the older name of the consuls (= *colleagues*).

8 **etiam** (= *adhuc*) = *still*. Cf. Verg. *Aen.* vi. 485 *etiam currus etiam arma tenentem.*

11 **civis ingenuus**, i.e. a free citizen born of free citizens.

12 **Ita cuncti . . . pepercerant** = *so unsparing had they all been alike of their own and their opponents' lives.*—Pollard.

21 **laetitia** = joy manifested, **gaudia** = joy felt.

luctus = grief shown by outward signs, e.g. by dress.

maeror = grief shown by inward signs, e.g. by tears, or a sad face.

The Battle of Pistoria (Pistoia, N.W. of Faesulae). 'Catiline showed on this day that nature had destined him for no ordinary things, and that he knew at once how to command and how to fight as a soldier. At length Petreius, with his bodyguard, broke the centre of the enemy, and then attacked the two wings from within. This decided the day.'—M.

The character of Catiline. 'He was one of the most wicked men in that wicked age. He possessed in a high degree the qualities which are required in the leader of a band of ruined and desperate men—the faculty of enjoying all pleasures and of bearing all privations, courage, military talent, knowledge of men, indomitable energy.'—M. Cf. Sall. *Catil.* 5.

195
B₃₆

GAIUS IULIUS CAESAR (4).

Forms the First Triumvirate: Consul, *60-59 B.C.*

Hoc igitur consule inter eum et Cn. Pompeium et M. Crassum inita potentiae societas, quae urbi orbique terrarum nec minus diverso quoque tempore ipsis exitiabilis fuit. Hoc consilium sequendi Pompeius causam habuerat, ut tandem acta in5transmarinis provinciis, quibus, ut praediximus, multi obtrectabant, per Caesarem confirmarentur consulem, Caesar autem, quod animadvertebat se cedendo Pompei gloriae aucturum suam et invidia communis potentiae in illum relegataconfirmaturum 10vires suas, Crassus, ut quem principatum solus adsequi non poterat, auctoritate Pompei, viribus teneret Caesaris. Adfinitas etiam inter Caesarem Pompeiumque contracta nuptiis, quippe Iuliam, filiam C. Caesaris, Cn. Magnus duxit uxorem. In15hoc consulatu Caesar legem tulit, ut ager Campanus plebei divideretur, suasore legis Pompeio: ita circiter XX milia civium eo deducta et ius urbis restitutum post annos circiter CLII quam bello Punico ab Romanis Capua in formam praefecturae 20redacta erat.Bibulus, collega Caesaris, cum actiones eius magis vellet impedire quam posset, maiore parte anni domi se tenuit: quo facto dum augere vult invidiam collegae, auxit potentiam. Tum Caesari decretae in quinquennium Galliae.25

VELL. PAT. ii. 44.

1-2 **inter eum . . . societas**, the famous First Triumvirate. 'It was at first an expedient to secure, as we should say, a working majority for a vigorous democratic policy, but the bitterness of its enemies transformed the coalition itself from an honourable union into the semblance of a three-headed tyranny.'—Warde Fowler.

4-7 The ultra-senatorial party (after Pompeius' great act of renunciation, when he dismissed his victorious veterans in 62 B.C.) had checked and worried Pompeius by refusing to ratify his arrangements in the East, and by criticising and opposing his plans for rewarding his veterans. Thus they deliberately drove him once more into the arms of Caesar and the democracy.

10 **relegata** = *attributed, imputed*, lit. *removed* (*re* + *lēgo*).

21 **Bibulus, collega Caesaris:** cf. Suet. *Divus Iulius* 20:
Non Bibulo quicquam, nuper sed Caesare factum est:
Nam Bibulo fieri consule nil memini.

Caesar's First Consulship. Among his other acts was the famous *Lex Iulia de pecuniis repetundis* (against official extortion in the provinces), which won strong praise even from Cicero himself.

196

B37

THE GALLIC WAR, 58-50 B.C. (1)

'That day he overcame the Nervii,' 57 B.C.

Caesar ab decimae legionis cohortatione ad dextrum cornu profectus, ubi suos urgeri signisque in unum locum collatis duodecimae legionis confertos milites sibi ipsos ad pugnam esse impedimento vidit—quartae cohortis omnibus centurionibus occisis, 5signifero interfecto, signo amisso, reliquarum cohortium omnibus fere centurionibus aut vulneratis aut occisis, in his primipilo P. Sextio Baculo, fortissimo viro, multis gravibusque volneribus confecto, ut iam se sustinere non posset; reliquos esse tardiores et nonnullos 10ab novissimis deserto proelio excedere ac tela vitare, hostes neque a fronte ex inferiore loco subeuntes intermittere et ab utroque latere instare, et rem esse in angusto vidit neque ullum esse subsidium quod submitti posset, scuto ab novissimis 15militi detracto, quod ipse eo sine scuto venerat, in primam aciem processit; centurionibusque nominatim appellatis reliquos cohortatus milites signa inferre et manipulos laxare iussit, quo facilius gladiis uti possent. Cuius adventu spe illata militibus ac 20redintegrato animo, cum pro se quisque in conspectu imperatoris etiam in extremis suis rebus operam navare cuperet, paulum hostium impetus tardatus est.

CAESAR, *de B. G.* ii. 25.

Context. The Nervii, the bravest of the Belgae, surprised Caesar's men while at work on their camp. There was no time to think: they took station where they could. The 9th and 10th legions on the left broke and pursued the enemy in front of them, and the two legions in the centre stood firm. But on the right there was a gap, and the Nervii were rapidly surrounding the two legions huddled together here, and the fight threatened every moment to become a second Cannae, **when Caesar restored the fight.** Labienus sent back the victorious 10th, who took the enemy in their rear, and the cavalry completed the victory.

14-15 **neque ullum . . . posset**: the rear guard, the 13th and 14th legions, had not yet come up.

18-19 **signa . . . laxare** = *to charge and* (thus) *open out the ranks.*

22-23 **operam navare** = *to do their very best.* **navo** (orig.*gnavo*; cf. γνώσκω) = lit. *to make known, to exhibit.*

The Battle of the Sambre. One of the most desperate that Caesar ever fought. The memory of it lived in Caesar's mind so vividly that he seems to fight the battle over again as he describes it, in language for him unusually strong and intense.—W. F.

Result of the Battle, the submission of North West Gaul.

197

B38

THE GALLIC WAR, 58-50 B.C. (2)

Naval Battle with the Veneti, 56 B.C.

Una erat magno usui res praeparata a nostris,—falces praecutae insertae affixaeque longuriis non absimili forma muralium falcium. His cum funes qui antemnas ad malos destinabant comprehensi adductique essent, navigio remis incitato praerumpebantur. 5Quibus abscisis antemnae necessario concidebant; ut, cum omnis Gallicis spes in velis armamentisque consisteret, his ereptis omnis usus navium uno tempore eriperetur. Reliquum erat certamen positum in virtute, qua nostri milites facile10superabant atque eo magis, quod in conspectu Caesaris atque omnis exercitus res gerebatur, ut nullum paulo fortius factum latere posset; omnes enim colles ac loca superiora, unde erat propinquus despectus in mare, ab exercitu tenebantur. Disiectis, ut diximus, 15antemnis, cum singulas binae ac ternae naves circumsteterant, milites summa vi transcendere in hostium naves contendebant. Quod postquam barbari fieri animadverterunt, expugnatis compluribus navibus, cum ei rei nullum reperiretur auxilium, fuga 20salutem petere contenderunt. Ac iam conversis in eam partem navibus quo ventus ferebat, tanta subito malacia ac tranquillitas exstitit ut se ex loco movere non possent. Quae quidem res ad negotium conficiendum maxime fuit opportuna; nam singulas 25nostri consectati expugnaverunt, ut perpaucae ex omni numero noctis interventu ad terram pervenerint, cum ab hora fere quarta usque ad solis occasum pugnaretur.

CAESAR, de B. G. iii. 14, 15.

Context. In the winter of 57-6 Roman officers, who came to levy requisitions of grain, were detained by the Veneti. Caesar's attack on their coast-towns failed to reduce them to submission: so he determined to wait for his fleet. This he entrusted to Decimus Brutus, an able and devoted officer. At first the Roman galleys were powerless against the high-decked strong sailing-vessels of the Veneti, but **the use of the murales falces, and the opportune calm, enabled Brutus to annihilate their fleet.**

11-12 **quod . . . gerebatur.** Napoleon (*Caesar*, vol. ii. p. 6) thinks that Caesar was encamped on the heights of Saint Gildas overlooking Quiberon Bay.

23 **malacia** = *a calm*, but μαλακία = *softness*, L. *mollities*.

Result of the Victory—the surrender of the Veneti and of all Brittany. **The earliest historical naval battle fought on the Atlantic Ocean.—M.**

198

B₃₉

THE GALLIC WAR, 58-50 B.C. (3)

Caesar's Bridge across the Rhine, 55 B.C.

Rationem pontis hanc instituit. Tigna bina sesquipedalia paulum ab imo praeacuta, dimensa ad altitudinem fluminis, intervallo pedum duorum inter se iungebat. Haec cum machinationibus immissa in flumen defixerat fistucisque adegerat—non sublicae5modo derecte ad perpendiculum, sed prone ac fastigate, ut secundum naturam fluminis procumberent—eis item contraria duo ad eundem modum iuncta intervallo pedum quadragenum ab inferiore parte contra vim atque impetum fluminis conversa statuebat. 10Haec utraque insuper bipedalibus trabibus immissis, quantum eorum tignorum iunctura distabat, binis utrimque fibulis ab extrema parte distinebantur; quibus disclusis atque in contrariam partem revinctis, tanta erat operis firmitudo atque 15ea rerum natura ut, quo maior vis aquae se incitavisset, hoc artius illigata tenerentur. Haec derecta materia iniecta contexebantur aclonguriis cratibusque consternebantur; ac nihilo setius sublicae et ad inferiorem partem fluminis oblique agebantur, quae 20pro ariete subiectae et cum omni opere coniunctae vim fluminis exciperent; et aliae item supra pontem mediocri spatio, ut, si arborum trunci sive naves deiciendi operis essent a barbaris immissae, his defensoribus earum rerum vis minueretur, neu ponti 25nocerent.

CAESAR, de B. G. iv. 17.

Context. The year 55 B.C. appears to have been marked by a general movement in the migration of the German tribes. An advance, consisting of two tribes, the Usipetes and Tenctri, crowded forward by the more powerful Suevi, crossed the Lower Rhine into N. Gaul. Caesar drove them back across the Rhine, **bridged the river**, followed them up into their own territories, and fully established the supremacy of the Roman arms.—Allen and Greenough.

5 **fistucisque adegerat** = *and had driven them home* (**ad-**)*with rammers.* For Plan of Bridge see Allen's *Caesar*, p. 103.

11-14 **Haec . . . distinebantur** = *these two sets were held apart by two-feet timbers laid on above, equal* (in thickness) *to the interval left by the fastening of the piles* (**quantum . . . distabat**), *with a pair of ties*(**fibulis**) *at each end.*—A. & G.

17-18 **Haec . . . contexebantur** = *these* (i.e. the framework of timber) *were covered over by boards* (**materia**) *laid lengthwise.*

131

longuriis = *with long poles.*

The Bridge (prob. near Bonn). 'With extraordinary speed (in ten days) the bridge was completed. It was a triumph of engineering and industry.'—W. F.

199

B₄₀

THE GALLIC WAR, 58-50 B.C. (4)

Cassivellaunus.

Second Invasion of Britain, *54 B.C.*

Cassivellaunus, omni deposita spe contentionis, dimissis amplioribus copiis, milibus circiter quattuor essedariorum relictis itinera nostra servabat: paulumque ex via excedebat locisque impeditis ac silvestribus sese occultabat, atque eis regionibus quibus 5nos iter facturos cognoverat pecora atque homines ex agris in silvas compellebat; et cum equitatus noster liberius praedandi vastandique causa se in agros eiecerat, omnibus viis semitisque essedarios ex silvis emittebat; et magno cum periculo nostrorum10equitum cum eis confligebat atque hoc metu latius vagari prohibebat. Relinquebatur ut neque longius ab agmine legionum discedi Caesar pateretur, et tantum in agris vastandis incendiisque faciendis hostibus noceretur quantum in labore atque itinere15legionarii milites efficere poterant. . . . Cassivellaunus hoc proelionuntiato, tot detrimentis acceptis, vastatis finibus, maxime etiam permotus defectione civitatum, legatos per Atrebatem Commiumde deditione ad Caesarem mittit.20

CAESAR, *de B. G.* v. 19, 22.

Context. The First Invasion of Britain (55 B.C.) was only a visit of exploration; but in the Second Invasion (54 B.C.) Caesar aimed at a partial conquest. He had been hearing of Britain ever since he came to Gaul, and knew it to be a refuge for his Celtic enemies and a secret source of their strength. He set sail from the Portus Ittius (mod. Wissant, some twelve miles W. of Calais) and after drifting some way to the N.E., made his way to his former landing-place, probably near Romney. Some severe fighting followed, till at length Caesar crossed the Thames (apparently between Kingston and Brentford) and **entered the country of Cassivellaunus, who gave Caesar much trouble by his guerilla tactics. Deserted by his allies, Cassivellaunus offered his submission, which Caesar gladly accepted.**

1 **Contentionis,** i.e. of a general engagement with Caesar.

12 **Relinquebatur ut** = *the consequence was that . . .*

17 **hoc proelio,** i.e. the storming by Caesar of his fortified camp, perh. St. Albans.

18-19 **defectione civitatum,** espec. of the Trinobantes (chief place *Camulodunum,* later *Colonia castrum =Colchester*).

19 **Commium,** Caesar had made him King of the Atrebates (N.W. Gaul).

Caesar In Britain. 'What he tells us of the geography and inhabitants of the Island comprises almost all we know, except from coins, down to the time of its final conquest by Clodius 51 A.D.'—W. F.

200

B₄₁

THE GALLIC WAR, 58-50 B.C. (5)

The Gallic uprising.

Fabian tactics of Vercingetorix, *52 B.C.*

Vercingetorix tot continuis incommodis acceptis suos ad concilium convocat. Docet 'longe alia ratione esse bellum gerendum atque antea gestum sit; omnibus modis huic rei studendum ut pabulatione et commeatu Romani prohibeantur: id esse 5facile, quod equitatu ipsi abundent et quod anni temporesubleventur; pabulum secari non posse; necessario dispersos hostes ex aedificiis petere; hos omnes cotidie ab equitibus deleri posse. Praeterea, salutis causa rei familiaris commoda neglegenda;10vicos atque aedificia incendi oportere hoc spatio quoqueversus, quo pabulandi causa adire posse videantur. Harum ipsis rerum copiam suppetere, quod quorum in finibus bellum geratur eorum opibus subleventur: Romanos aut inopiam non laturos aut 15magno cum periculo longius a castris processuros; neque interesse ipsosne interficiant an impedimentis exuant, quibus amissis bellum geri non possit. Praeterea, oppida incendi oportere quae non munitione et loci natura ab omni sint periculo tuta; ne 20suis sint ad detrectandam militiam receptacula, neu Romanis proposita ad copiam commeatus praedamque tollendam. Haec si gravia aut acerba videantur, multo illa gravius aestimari debere, liberos, coniuges in servitutem abstrahi, ipsos interfici; 25quae sit necesse accidere victis.'

CAESAR, *de B. G.* vii. 14.

Context. On his return from Britain, Caesar found the N. Gauls in open revolt. The division of Sabinus (at Aduatuca, near Liège) was annihilated by Ambiorix, and Caesar was only

132

just in time to relieve Q. Cicero at Charleroi. To prevent all further support to the Gauls from the Germans across the Rhine, Caesar again made a military demonstration across the river, and put an end to all the hopes of the Germans of breaking through this boundary. In the winter of 53-2 B.C., during his absence in Cisalpine Gaul, **a general uprising of the S. and Central Gauls took place under the Arvernian Vercingetorix, the hero of the whole Gallic race.**

6-7 **anni tempore**, i.e. scarcely yet spring, when no crops could be got off the land.

11-12 **hoc spatio quoqueversus, quo** = *so far in every direction as.*

19 **oppida incendi:** only Avaricum (Bourges) was to be spared.

22 **proposita** = *offered* to be captured by the Romans.

The tactics of Vercingetorix. 'He adopted a system of warfare similar to that by which Cassivellaunus had saved the Celts of Britain.'—M.

201

B₄₂

THE GALLIC WAR, 58-50 B.C. (6)

Siege of Gergovia.

Petronius dies to save his men, *52 B.C.*

Cum acerrime comminus pugnaretur, hostes loco et numero, nostri virtute confiderent, subito sunt Aedui visi ab latere nostris aperto, quos Caesar ab dextra parte alio ascensu manus distinendae causa miserat. Hi similitudine armorum vehementer5nostros perterruerunt. Eodem tempore L. Fabius centurio quique una murum ascenderant circumventi atque interfecti de muro praecipitabantur. M. Petronius, eiusdem legionis centurio, cum portas excidere conatus esset, a multitudine oppressus ac sibi desperans, 10multis iam volneribus acceptis, manipularibus suis qui illum secuti erant, 'Quoniam,' inquit, 'me una vobiscum servare non possum, vestrae quidem certe vitae prospiciam, quos cupiditate gloriae adductus in periculum deduxi. Vos data facultate vobis consulite.' 15Simul in medios hostes irrupit, duobusque interfectis reliquos a porta paulum submovit. Conantibus auxiliari suis, 'Frustra,' inquit, 'meae vitae subvenire conamini, quem iam sanguis viresque deficiunt. Proinde abite dum est facultas vosque ad 20legionem recipite.' Ita pugnans post paulum concidit ac suis saluti fuit.

CAESAR, *de B. G.* vii. 50.

Context. With a half-starved army Caesar stormed Avaricum after a most obstinate defence, and then laid siege to the Arvernian capital of Gergovia, in hope of destroying Vercingetorix and ending the war. As the town was too strong to be taken by storm, he resolved to try a blockade, but he failed, as at Dyrrachium in 49 B.C., from want of sufficient troops.

A last desperate attack on the town was repulsed, and Caesar, defeated for the first time, was forced to raise the siege.

3 **ab latere nostris aperto:** as a soldier carries his shield on the left arm, leaving the sword hand free, this (right) side is called **latus apertum.**—Compton.

4 **manus distinendae causa** = *for the purpose of diverting*(**distinendae**, lit. *hold off*) *the enemy's force.*

6 **perterruerunt:** this was all the more natural, as the Aeduan contingent was only awaiting the result of the blockade, to openly join the insurgents.

9 **excidere** = *to cut away, hew down,* i.e. from within.

Gergovia, 4 miles S. of Clermont. This famous stronghold consists of a rectangular plateau nearly a mile in length, and some 1300 feet above the plain through which the Allier flows, and descending steeply on all sides but one to the ground.

Caesar's failure. 'The fact was that chiefly owing to the nature of the ground and their own ardour, Caesar's men were not well in hand.'—W. F.

202

B₄₃

THE GALLIC WAR, 58-50 B.C. (7)

Siege of Alesia.

The Last Fight of Vercingetorix, *52 B.C.*

Vercingetorix ex arce Alesiae suos conspicatus ex oppido egreditur: crates, longurios, musculos, fasces, reliquaque quae eruptionis causa paraverat profert. Pugnatur uno tempore omnibus locis atque omnia temptantur; quae minime visa pars firma est huc5concurritur. Romanorum manus tantis munitionibus distinetur nec facile pluribus locis occurrit. . . . Labienus, postquam neque aggeres neque fossae vim hostium sustinere poterant, coactis XI cohortibus, quas ex proximis praesidiis deductas fors obtulit,10Caesarem per nuntios facit certiorem quid faciendum existimet. Accelerat Caesar ut proelio intersit. Eius adventu ex colore vestitus cognito (quo insigni in proeliis uti consuerat), turmisque equitum et cohortibus visis quas se sequi iusserat, ut de locis15superioribus haec declivia et devexa cernebantur, hostes proelium committunt. Utrimque clamore sublato excipit rursus ex vallo atque omnibus munitionibus clamor. Nostri omissis pilis gladiis rem gerunt. Repente post tergum equitatus cernitur: 20cohortes aliae appropinquant. Hostes terga vertunt; fugientibus equites occurrunt: fit magna caedes: pauci ex tanto numero se incolumes in castra recipiunt.

CAESAR, de B. G. vii. 84, 87, 88.

Context. After his successful defence of Gergovia, Vercingetorix allowed his judgment to be overruled, and attacked Caesar's army (now united to the division of Labienus) on the march. Caesar shook off the enemy with the help of his German cavalry, and turned their retreat into a rout. V. then threw himself with all his forces into Alesia. Caesar constructed an inner line of investment and an outer line of defence, and was thus able to wear out the besieged and **beat back the relieving host of the Gauls**.

1 **suos**, i.e. the host (some 250,000) of the relieving army of Gauls.

2 **musculos** (dimin. of *mus*) = *pent-houses* or *sheds*.

4 **omnibus locis**, i.e. along the whole length of Caesar's outer line of defence, *where it ran along the slope of Mont Réa*, to the N.W. of Alesia. This, as the relieving Gauls were quick to see, was the weakest point of the whole line.

13 **ex colore vestitus**, i.e. the purple or scarlet paludamentum.

Vercingetorix. The Celtic officers delivered up V. to Caesar, to be led in triumph five years later, and beheaded as a traitor. In 1865 a statue was erected on the summit of Alesia, in honour of the heroic Gaul.

The fall of Alesia decided the fate of Gaul.

203

B₄₄

CICERO IN EXILE, March 58 B.C.-August 57 B.C. (1)

His Banishment.

Per idem tempus P. Clodius, homo nobilis, disertus, audax, quique dicendi neque faciendi ullum nisi quem vellet nosset modum, malorum propositorum exsecutor acerrimus, cum graves inimicitias cum M. Cicerone exerceret (quid enim inter tam5dissimilis amicum esse poterat?) et a patribus ad plebem transisset, legem in tribunatu tulit, qui civem Romanum non damnatum interemisset, ei aqua et igni interdiceretur: cuius verbis etsi non nominabatur Cicero, tamen solus petebatur. Ita vir optime 10meritus de re publica conservatae patriae pretium calamitatem exili tulit.Non caruerunt suspicione oppressi Ciceronis Caesar et Pompeius. Hoc sibi contraxisse videbatur Cicero, quod inter xx virosdividendo agro Campano esse noluisset. Idem intra 15biennium sera Cn. Pompei cura, verum ut coepit intenta, votisque Italiae ac decretis senatus, virtute atque actione Anni Milonis tribuni pl. dignitati patriaeque restitutus est. Neque post Numidici exilium ac reditum quisquam aut expulsus invidiosius 20aut receptus est laetius: cuius domus quam infeste a Clodio disiecta erat, tam speciose a senatu restituta est.

VELLEIUS PATERCULUS, ii. 45.

6-7 **a patribus . . . transisset.** When Cicero refused to throw in his lot with the Triumvirs, Publius Clodius was (by the aid of Caesar as Pontifex Maximus) hurriedly transferred from a patrician to a plebeian gens, and then chosen a tribune of the people for the year 58 B.C. Clodius was thus enabled to satisfy his private hatred of Cicero, and Caesar was enabled to get rid of the man who persisted in opposing him.

7-8 **qui . . . interemisset:** aimed at Cicero for his share in the summary execution of the Catilinarians 63 B.C.Mommsen calls it a judicial murder. Undoubtedly the Senate had not the power of sentencing *citizens* to death. But Cicero argues that the legal effect of the*Senatus consultum ultimum* was to *disenfranchise*Lentulus and his associates, and to place them in the position of *outlaws*.

12-13 **Non caruerunt . . . Pompeius:** Caesar having in vain tried to win him over abandoned him to his fate, and Pompeius basely deserted him.

15 **dividendo agro Campano**, i.e. by Caesar's Agrarian Law of 59 B.C., to provide for Pompey's veterans.

18 **Anni Milonis:** the bravoes of Milo protected from disturbance the voters engaged in sanctioning the decree for the recall of Cicero.

19 **Numidici**, i.e. Q. Caecilius Metellus, general against Jugurtha, superseded by Marius and forced to retire to Rhodes.

204

B₄₅

CICERO IN EXILE, March 58 B.C.-August 57 B.C. (2)

His Return.

Pr. Nonas Sextiles Dyrrachio sum profectus, ipso illo die, quo lex est lata de nobis; Brundisium veni Nonis Sextilibus: ibi mihiTulliola mea fuit praesto natali suo ipso die, qui casu idem natalis erat et Brundisinae coloniae et tuae vicinae Salutis; quae 5res animadversa a multitudine summa Brundisinorum gratulatione celebrata est. Ante diem vi Idus Sextiles cognovi, cum Brundisii essem, litteris Quinti, mirifico studio omnium aetatum atque ordinum, incredibili concursu Italiae legem comitiis 10centuriatis esse perlatam: inde a Brundisinis honestissimis ornatus iter ita feci, ut undique ad me cum gratulatione legati convenerint. Ad urbem ita veni, ut nemo ullius ordinis homo nomenclatori notus fuerit, qui mihi obviam non venerit, praeter eos 15inimicos, quibus id ipsum, se inimicos esse, non liceret aut dissimulare aut negare. Cum venissem ad portam Capenam, gradus templorum ab infima plebe completi erant, a qua plausu maximo cum esset mihi gratulatio significata, similis et frequentia 20et plausus me usque ad Capitolium celebravit, in foroque et in ipso Capitolio miranda multitudo fuit. Postridie in senatu, qui fuit dies Nonarum Septembr., senatui gratias egimus.

CICERO, *Ep. ad Att.* iv. 1.

1 **Dyrrachio** (formerly *Epidamnus*, mod. *Durazzo*), a town in Illyria, on a peninsula in the Adriatic. It was the usual port of landing and departure from and for Brundisium (distant about 100 miles).

3 **Tulliola**, Cicero's dearly-loved daughter Tullia, the only one of his family of whose conduct he never complains, and his tender and sympathising companion in all his pursuits.

4-5 **qui casu . . . coloniae.** Brundisium was founded 244B.C. The Via Appia terminated here.

5 **tuae vicinae Salutis**, the Temple of Salus on the Quirinal was near the house of Atticus.

9 **Quinti** (sc. *Ciceronis*): Cicero's only brother, a gallant soldier (e.g. as legatus to Caesar in Gaul), but a man of violent temper. Proscribed by the Triumvirs, and put to death in 43 B.C.

11-12 **a Brundisinis . . . ornatus** = *having received attentions from the most respectable men of Brundisium.*

13 **legati** = *deputations*, i.e. from the various towns en route.

14 **nomenclatori** (= lit. *one who calls by name*, cf. καλ-έω,*Cal-endae*): a confidential slave who attended his master in canvassing, and on similar occasions, and told him the names of the people he met.

18 **ad portam Capenam** (*Porta S. Sebastiano*), by which the Via Appia led to Capua. 'Cicero, perhaps for effect, followed the line of triumphal procession.'—Impey.

205

B46

CICERO'S RECANTATION, 56 B.C.

In praise of Caesar.

Itaque cum acerrimis nationibus et maximis Germanorum et Helvetiorum proeliis felicissime decertavit: ceteras conterruit,compulit, domuit, imperio populi Romani parere assuefecit, et quas regiones, quasque gentes nullae nobis antea litterae, 5nulla vox, nulla fama notas fecerat, has noster imperator nosterque exercitus et populi Romani arma peragrarunt. Semitam tantum Galliae tenebamus antea, patres conscripti; ceterae partes a gentibus aut inimicis huic imperio, aut infidis, aut 10incognitis, aut certe immanibus et barbaris et bellicosis tenebantur; quas nationes, nemo umquam fuit, quin frangi domarique cuperet; nemosapienter de republica nostra cogitavit iam inde a principio huius imperi, quin Galliam maxime timendam huic 15imperio putaret; sed propter vim ac multitudinem gentium illarum numquam est anteacum omnibus dimicatum. Restitimus semper lacessiti. Nunc denique est perfectum, ut imperii nostri terrarumque illarum idem esset extremum.20

CICERO, *de Provinciis Consularibus*, § 33.

3 **compulit** = *checked*, usu. = *to constrain.*
5 **nullae litterae** = *no book.*
8 **Semitam tantum Galliae** = *it was but a strip of Gaul.*—W. F. **Semita** (*se* + *mi* = *go aside*, cf. *meo, trames*) = lit. *a narrow way, path.*
13-14 **nemo . . . cogitavit** = *there never has been a prudent statesman.*—W. F.
17 **cum omnibus**, i.e. with the Gauls as a nation.
19-20 **ut imperi . . . extremum**, i.e. that our Empire extends to the utmost limits of that land.

Cicero's Recantation (παλινῳδία). The time for the struggle between the Senatorial party (the Optimates) and the Triumvirs, weakened by their mutual jealousy, seemed to have

135

come. Accordingly Cicero proposed in a full house to reconsider Caesar's Agrarian Law (of 59 B.C.) for the allotment of lands in Campania; while Domitius Ahenobarbus (candidate for next year's Consulship) openly declared his intention to propose Caesar's recall. Caesar acted with his usual promptness, and the Conference at Luca restored an understanding between the three regents. Pompeius then crossed to Sardinia, and informed Q. Cicero that he would be held responsible for any act of hostility on the part of his brother. Cicero had no choice but to submit, and delivered in the Senate his oration *de Provinciis Consularibus*, a political manifesto on behalf of Caesar and Pompeius—the *Recantation* alluded to in *Ep. ad Att.* iv. 5, and elaborately explained in *Ep. ad Fam.* i. 9 (to Lentulus Spinther).

206

B₄₇

CARRHAE, 53 B.C. (1)

'Quem deus vult perdere, prius dementat.'

Dum Gallos per Caesarem in septentrione debellat, ipse interim ad orientem grave volnus a Parthis populus Romanus accepit. Nec de fortuna queri possumus; caret solacio clades. Adversis et dis et hominibus cupiditas consulis Crassi, dum Parthico 5inhiat auro, undecim strage legionum et ipsius capite multata est. Primum enim, qui solus et subvehere commeatus et munire poterat a tergo, relictus Euphrates, dum simulato transfugae cuidam Mazzarae Syro creditur. Tum in mediam camporum 10vastitatem eodem duce ductus exercitus, ut undique hosti exponeretur. Itaque vixdum venerat Carrhas cum undique praefecti regis Silaces et Surenas ostendere signa auro sericisque vexillis vibrantia. Tunc sine moracircumfusi undique equitatus in 15modum grandinis atque nimborum densa pariter tela fuderunt. Sic miserabili strage deletus exercitus. Ipse in colloquio sollicitatus signo dato vivus in hostium manus incidisset, nisi tribunis reluctantibus fugam ducis barbari ferro occupassent. Filium 20ducis paene in conspectu patris eisdem telis operuerunt. Reliquiae infelicis exercitus, quo quemque rapuit fuga, in Armeniam Ciliciam Syriamque distractae vix nuntium cladis rettulerunt.

FLORUS, III. xi. 1-10 (sel.)

Context. By the conference of the Triumvirs at Luca, it was arranged to secure the succession of Crassus to the government of Syria, in order to make war on the growing strength of the Parthian Empire beyond the Euphrates. Consul with Pompeius in 55 B.C. he set out for his province even before the expiration of his consulship 'eager to gather in the treasures of the East in addition to those of the West.'

7-14 **Primum enim . . . vibrantia.** The Arab prince Abgarus induced Crassus to leave the Euphrates, and cross the great Mesopotamian desert to the Tigris. When at length the enemy offered battle some 30 miles to the S. of Carrhae (Harran, not far from Edessa), by the side of the Parthian vizier stood prince Abgarus with his Bedouins.

15-17 **Tunc sine mora . . . exercitus.** The Roman weapons of close combat, and the Roman system of concentration yielded for the first time to cavalry and distant warfare (the bow).

20-21 **Filium ducis:** his young and brave son Publius, who had served with the greatest distinction under Caesar in Gaul.

22 **Reliquiae:** out of 40,000 Roman legionaries, who had crossed the Euphrates, not a fourth part returned: 20,000 fell, and 10,000 were taken prisoners.

Carrhae. 'The day of Carrhae takes its place side by side with the days of the Allia, and of Cannae.'—M.

207

B₄₈

CARRHAE, 53 B.C. (2)

After the Battle.

A.

Temporis angusti mansit concordia discors,
Paxque fuit non sponte ducum; nam sola futuri
100
Crassus erat belli medius mora. Qualiter undas
Qui secat et geminum gracilis mare separat Isthmos
Nec patitur conferre fretum: si terra recedat,
Ionium Aegaeo frangat mare: sic, ubi saeva
Arma ducum dirimens miserando funere Crassus
105
Assyrias Latio maculavit sanguine Carrhas,
Parthica Romanos solverunt damna furores.

Plus illa vobis acie quam creditis actum est,
Arsacidae: bellum victis civile dedistis.

LUCAN, *Pharsalia*, i. 98-108.

98 **Temporis . . . discors** = *the short-lived concord endured, but it was a*
jarring (**discors**) *concord.*—Haskins.

101 **Isthmos**, sc. *of Corinth*: Caesar planned to cut it, and thus to secure a direct route by
sea, connecting Italy and the East.

102 **Nec patitur . . . fretum** = *and suffers it* (**mare**, l. 101)*not to join its waters*, i.e. the
Corinthian and Saronic gulfs.

B.

Milesne Crassi coniuge barbara
Turpis maritus vixit, et hostium
(Pro curia inversique mores!)
8
Consenuit socerorum in armis
Sub rege Medo Marsus et Apulus,
Anciliorum et nominis et togae
Oblitus aeternaeque Vestae,
12
Incolumi Iove et urbe Roma?

HORACE, *Odes* III. v. 5-12.

Nearly 10,000 Roman prisoners were settled by the victors in the oasis of Merv, as
bondsmen compelled after the Parthian fashion to render military service (**in armis**, l. 8).

8 **Consenuit:** Carrhae (53 B.C.) was fought 26 years before this Ode was written
(27 B.C.).

10-11 **Anciliorum, aeternae Vestae**, pledges of the immortality of Rome.

10 **togae**, i.e. the Roman people, the *gens togata.*

12 **Iove**, Jove's temple on the Capitol.

C.

Crassus ad Euphraten aquilas natumque suosque
Perdidit, et leto est ultimus ipse datus.
"Parthe, quid exsultas?" dixit dea, "signa remittes,
468
Quique necem Crassi vindicet, ultor erit."

OVID, *Fasti*, vi. 465-468.

467-468 During the last few months of his life, Caesar was occupied with the preparations
for his expedition against the Parthians. In 36 B.C. Antonius carried on a disastrous campaign
against Phraates, King of Parthia, but in 20 B.C. Augustus received from the King the Eagles
(**signa**, l. 467) and prisoners captured at Carrhae.

208
B49

CICERO, GOVERNOR OF CILICIA, 51-50 B.C.

His humane Administration.

Ipse in Asiam profectus sum Tarso Nonis Ianuariis, non mehercule dici potest, qua
admiratione Ciliciae civitatum maximeque Tarsensium; postea vero quam Taurum transgressus
sum, mirifica exspectatio Asiae nostrarum dioecesium, quae sex5mensibus imperii mei nullas
meas acceperat litteras, numquam hospitem viderat. Illud autem tempus quotannis ante me fuerat
in hoc quaestu; civitates locupletes, ne in hiberna milites reciperent, magnas pecunias dabant,
Cyprii talenta Attica CC, qua ex 10insula—non ὑπερβολικῶς, sed verissime loquor—nummus
nullus me obtinente erogabatur. Ob haec beneficia, quibus illi obstupescunt, nullos honores mihi
nisi verborum decerni sino; statuas, fana,τέθριππα prohibeo, nec sum in ulla re alia
molestus 15civitatibus, sed fortasse tibi, qui haec praedicem de me. Perifer, si me amas; tu enim
me haec facere voluisti. Iter igitur ita per Asiam feci, ut etiam fames, qua nihil miserius est, quae
tum erat in hac mea Asia—messis enim nulla fuerat—, mihi optanda 20fuerit: quacumque iter
feci, nulla vi, nullo iudicio, nulla contumelia auctoritate et cohortatione perfeci, ut et Graeci et
cives Romani, qui frumentumcompresserant, magnum numerum populis pollicerentur.

CICERO, *Ep. ad Atticum*, v. 21.

1 **in Asiam**, i.e. to the districts N. of the Taurus range, which belonged geographically to
Asia in the Roman sense, but were politically attached to Cilicia.—Watson.

Tarso = on the R. Cydnus, about twelve miles above its mouth. Pompeius made Tarsus
the capital of the new province of Cilicia, 66 B.C.

6-7 **nullas meas . . . viderat** = *had never received demands*(**litteras**) *from me, never seen a man billeted on them.* The **hospites** = *soldiers or public officials.*

8 **fuerat in hoc quaestu** = *had been devoted to gain in the following fashion.*—Tyrrell.

9 **ne in hiberna milites reciperent:** Mommsen says 'A town suffered nearly to the same extent when a Roman army took up winter quarters in it as when an enemy took it by storm.'

15 τέθριππα = *statues in chariots drawn by four horses.*

20-21 **mihi optanda fuerit:** i.e. because it gave him the opportunity of showing the effect of his personal influence.—T.

23 **compresserant** = *had stowed away;* lit. *kept back,* rare.

Cicero as Governor. His administration seems to have been just, considerate and popular.

For **Cicero's Ideal of a Roman Governor,** see *Ep. ad Q. F.*i. 1 (Q. Cicero governed Asia as Propraetor 62-58 B.C.)

209

CAUSES OF THE CIVIL WAR.

Nec quemquam iam ferre potest Caesarve priorem

Pompeiusve parem.   —*LUCAN.*

56 B.C. By the Conference at Luca it was arranged:—

(i) to give Caesar a new term of five years' government in which to complete his work in Gaul (until March 1, 49);

(ii) to give Pompeius the government of the two Spains, and Crassus that of Syria, for five years also.

It was further agreed that Pompeius and Crassus should have the consulship for 55 B.C.

52 B.C. Pompeius Sole Consul. So things continued until 52 B.C., when the constant rioting (Clodius v. Milo), and utter lawlessness prevailing in Rome **gave Pompeius his opportunity.** The Senate in their distress caused Pompeius to be nominated sole Consul, with supreme power to meet the crisis. The death of Julia in 54 and of Crassus in 53 had removed the two strongest influences for peace, and from 52 onwards the breach between Pompeius and Caesar began to widen.

During Caesar's long absence from Rome his opponents, with Cato at their head, were waiting their chance to impeach him for numerous acts in his province, as soon as he appeared in Rome for the consular elections. He would then be merely a private citizen, and as such amenable to prosecution. Now Caesar's proconsulship of Gaul was to terminate on March 1, 49, and the consular elections would take place at the earliest in the following summer. **There would therefore be an interval between the two offices,** and Caesar would be exposed to the utmost peril, if he gave up province and army on March 1, 49. Caesar had long foreseen this. When the law was passed in 55, which added a fresh term of five years to his government, **Pompeius seems to have inserted in it** (doubtless in accordance with a previous promise to Caesar) **a clause prohibiting the discussion of a successor before March 1, 50.** Caesar therefore could not be superseded except by the consuls of 49, and these would not be able to succeed him (as proconsuls) till Jan. 1, 48. He would thus be able to retain his army and government throughout the year 49.

210

Caesar's canvass for the Consulship. As the law stood, he would have to come in person to Rome. But early in 52 **a decree was promulgated, with the support of Pompeius, which relieved him from the necessity of canvassing in person.** Caesar might now feel himself safe: he would retain both army and provinces throughout 49, and would not be forced to return to Rome until he was safe from prosecution as Consul.

Lex Pompeia de iure magistratuum. But this did not suit Caesar's enemies. Pompeius and the Senate combined to alter the whole legal machinery for appointing provincial governors. **There was to be an interval of five years between a consulship and a proconsulship,** which would prevent Caesar, even if he were duly elected Consul in 49, from obtaining a fresh provincial governorship until five years from the end of 48. When the bill became law (as it did in 51) there would be an interval of some years before any consuls would be qualified under it for provinces: and to fill up the governorships during the interval, the Senate was authorised to appoint any person of consular rank who had not as yet proceeded to a proconsulship. **Thus Caesar's resignation both of his army and his province could be demanded on March 1, 49.**

50 B.C. Caesar's overtures for peace. Caesar let it be known to the Senate through Curio that **he was willing to resign his army and provinces if Pompeius would simultaneously do the same:** and the Senate voted a resolution in this sense by a majority of

138

370 to 22. The presiding Consul, Gaius Marcellus, broke up the meeting in anger, and with the two Consuls elected for 49 (Claudius Marcellus and Lentulus Crus) requested Pompeius to put himself at the head of the two legions stationed at Capua and to call the Italian militia to arms. **Caesar had completely attained the object of devolving the initiative of Civil War on his opponents.** He had, while himself keeping on legal ground, compelled Pompeius to declare war, and to declare it not as the representative of the legitimate authority, but as general of a revolutionary minority of the Senate, which overawed the majority.—*Adapted from Long, Mommsen, and Warde Fowler.*

211

B₅₀

CIVIL WAR, 49-45 B.C. (1)

Caesar crosses the Rubicon, *49 B.C.*

Fonte cadit modico parvisque impellitur undis
Puniceus Rubicon cum fervida canduit aestas,
215
Perque imas serpit valles et Gallica certus
Limes ab Ausoniis disterminat arva colonis.
Tunc vires praebebat hiemps atque auxerat undas
Tertia iam gravido pluvialis Cynthia cornu
Et madidis Euri resolutae flatibus Alpes.
220
Primus in obliquum sonipes opponitur amnem
Excepturus aquas; molli tum cetera rumpit
Turba vado faciles iam fracti fluminis undas.
Caesar, ut adversam superato gurgite ripam
Attigit Hesperiae vetitis et constitit arvis,
225
'Hic' ait 'hic pacem temerataque iura relinquo;
Te, Fortuna, sequor; procul hinc iam foedera sunto,
Credidimus fatis, utendum est iudice bello.'
Sic fatus noctis tenebris rapit agmina ductor
Impiger; it torto Balearis verbere fundae
230
Ocior et missa Parthi post terga sagitta
Vicinumque minax invadit Ariminum, et ignes
Solis lucifero fugiebant astra relicto.
Iamque dies primos belli visura tumultus
Exoritur; seu sponte deum, seu turbidus Auster
235
Impulerat, maestam tenuerunt nubila lucem.

LUCAN, *Pharsalia*, i. 213-235.

Context. On Lentulus Crus and Claudius Marcellus, the Consuls for 49 B.C., must rest the immediate blame of the Civil War. On Jan. 1st Caesar's tribune Curio once more presented proposals from Caesar, which startle us by their marvellous moderation (cf. Suet. *Caesar*, 29, 30), but Lentulus would not allow them to be considered. On Jan. 7th the *Senatus consultum ultimum* was decreed, and a state of war declared. Caesar crossed the Rubicon, the narrow brook which separated his province from Italy, to pass which at the head of an army was high treason to the State.—W. F.

214 **puniceus** = *dark red*: **Rubicon**, as if from *ruber*.

216 **limes**, i.e. until the time of Augustus, by whom Italy was extended to the R. Varus, the boundary between Gallia Narbonensis and Italy.

218 I.e. prob. the third night after the change of moon; **gravido** = *surcharged with rain.*—Haskins.

219 **Alpes** = *mountains*, not *the* Alps.

225 **temerata**, i.e. by Pompeius and the senatorial party.

229 **verbere** = the *thong*, i.e. of the sling (**fundae**).

231 **Ariminum** (Rimini), at this period the frontier town of Italy.

The Passage of the Rubicon. 'When after nine years' absence he trod once more the soil of his native land, he trod at the same time the path of revolution. Alea iacta est.'—M.

212

B₅₁

139

CIVIL WAR, 49-45 B.C. (2)

Caesar defends himself before the Senate, *April 49 B.C.*

His rebus confectis Caesar, ut reliquum tempus a labore intermitteretur, milites in proxima municipia deducit; ipse ad urbem proficiscitur. Coacto senatu iniurias inimicorum commemorat. Docet se nullum extraordinarium honorem appetisse, sed exspectato 5legitimo tempore consulatus eo fuisse contentum, quod omnibus civibus pateret. Latum ab x tribunis plebis contradicentibus inimicis, Catone vero acerrime repugnante et pristina consuetudine dicendi mora dies extrahente, ut sui ratio absentis haberetur, ipso 10consule Pompeio; qui si improbasset, cur ferri passus esset? qui si improbasset△, cur se uti populi beneficio prohibuisset? Patientiam proponit suam, cum de exercitibus dimittendis ultro postulavisset; in quo iacturam dignitatis atque honoris ipse facturus 15esset. Acerbitatem inimicorum docet, qui, quod ab altero postularent, in se recusarent atque omnia permisceri mallent, quam imperium exercitusque dimittere. Iniuriam in eripiendis legionibus praedicat, crudelitatem et insolentiam in circumscribendis 20tribunis plebis; condiciones a se latas, expetita colloquia et denegata commemorat. Pro quibus rebus hortatur ac postulat, ut rem publicam suscipiant atque una secum administrent.

CAESAR, *de B. C.* i. 32.

Context. After his passage of the Rubicon, Caesar quickly made himself master of Italy. Town after town opened its gates to him. Corfinium (held in force by Domitius for Pompeius) surrendered, and the captured troops enlisted in his ranks. An attempt to blockade Pompeius in Brundisium was skilfully foiled. On the last day of March Caesar arrived at Rome. The Senate was legally summoned by the tribunes Antonius and Cassius, and **was invited to unite with him in carrying on the government**.

2 **municipia**, i.e. Brundisium, Tarentum, Hydruntum (Otranto).

10 **ut sui . . . haberetur**, i.e. allowing him to stand for the consulship in his absence.

15 **iacturam dignitatis** = sacrifice of prestige.—Long.

19 **eripiendis legionibus**, i.e. in 50 B.C. Caesar was required to send home a legion he had borrowed of Pompeius, and contribute another himself, ostensibly for the Parthian War; but the legions were detained by Pompeius in Italy, and the Parthian War was quietly dropped.

Caesar in Rome. All Caesar's acts after the crossing of the Rubicon were entirely unconstitutional. But when he told the senators that he was prepared to take the government on himself, he was justified to himself by the past, and to posterity by the result.—W. F.

213

B₅₂

CIVIL WAR, 49-45 B.C. (3)

The Campaign round Lerida: the Soldiers fraternise, *49 B.C.*

Dixit et ad montes tendentem praevenit hostem.
Illic exiguo paulum distantia vallo
Castra locant. Postquam spatio languentia nullo
170
Mutua conspicuos habuerunt lumina voltus,
Et fratres natosque sues videre, patresque;
Deprensum est civile nefas. Tenuere parumper
Ora metu, tantum nutu motoque salutant
Ense suos; mox ut stimulis maioribus ardens
175
Rupit amor leges, audet transcendere vallum
Miles, in amplexus effusas tendere palmas.
Hospitis ille ciet nomen, vocat ille propinquum,
Admonet hunc studiis consors puerilibus aetas;
179
Nec Romanus erat, qui non agnoverat hostem.
196
Pax erat, et miles castris permixtus utrisque
Errabat; duro concordes caespite mensas
Instituunt et permixto libamina Baccho;
Graminei luxere foci, iunctoque cubili
200
Extrahit insomnes bellorum fabula noctes,
Quo primum steterint campo, qua lancea dextrum
Exierit. Dum quae gesserunt fortia iactant,

140

Et dum multa negant, quod solum fata petebant,
Est miseris renovata fides, atque omne futurum
205
Crevit amore nefas.

LUCAN, iv. 167-179, 196-205.

Context. On leaving Rome Caesar set out for Spain to encounter the veteran army of
Pompeius under his legati Afranius and Petreius. If this were crushed, he felt he would be free to
take the offensive against Pompeius in the East. Round Lerida (*Ilerda*) on the R. Segres
(a tributary of the Ebro) he fought the most brilliant campaign of all his military life. After severe
losses and hardships, Caesar outmanœuvred the Pompeians, cut them off from their base on the
Ebro, and forced a surrender on most generous terms.

167 **Dixit**, sc. Caesar.

ad montes, i.e. the rocky hills through which the retreating Pompeians had to pass
before they could reach the Ebro valley. Caesar, by a wonderful march, outstrips (**praevenit**)
them and blocks the way.

169 **spatio** (sc. *interposito*) **languentia nullo** = *not failing*(**languentia**) *owing to the distance*, i.e.
they were so near they could not fail to recognise one another.—Haskins.

173 **metu**, i.e. of their leaders.

175 **Rupit leges** = *burst the bonds of discipline.*—H.

178 **Admonet . . . aetas** = *one is reminded of his friend by the time passed together in boyhood's
pursuits.*—H.

200 **Extrahit** = *whiles away.*

Result of the Campaign. The whole of the western half of the Empire was now in
Caesar's power, with the single exception of Massilia.

214

B₅₃

<h1 align="center">CIVIL WAR, 49-45 B.C. (4)</h1>

<h3 align="center">Siege of Massilia.</h3>

<h3 align="center">A Treacherous Sortie, 49 B.C.</h3>

A.
Iam satis hoc Graiae memorandum contigit urbi
Aeternumque decus, quod non impulsa nec ipso
390
Strata metu tenuit flagrantis in omnia belli
Praecipitem cursum, raptisque a Caesare cunctis
Vincitur una mora. Quantum est quod fata tenentur,
Quodque virum toti properans imponere mundo
Hos perdit fortuna, dies!

LUCAN, iii. 388-394.

Context. Caesar's appeal to the leading citizens to espouse his cause was at first
successful, but the arrival of Domitius (whom he had treated so generously at Corfinium) with a
fleet caused the Massiliots to change their mind. Unable to remain himself, Caesar entrusted the
siege to Trebonius, supported by Dec. Brutus with the fleet. He has, however, left us a detailed
account of their skill and energy, and of the heroic defence of the citizens, **marred by a
treacherous sortie under a truce**. He returned to receive its final submission, and left the city
unharmed, as a tribute 'rather to its ancient renown than to any claim it had on himself.'

389 **non impulsa** = *not urged by others*, i.e. by Pompeius and his adherents. But cf.
Caesar, *de B. C.* i. 34.

391 **raptis** = *speedily won.*—H.

B.At hostes sine fide tempus atque occasionem fraudis ac doli quaerunt; interiectisque
aliquot diebus, nostris languentibus atque animo remissis, 10subito meridiano tempore, cum alius
discessisset, alius ex diutino labore in ipsis operibus quieti se dedisset, arma vero omnia
reposita contectaque essent, portis se foras erumpunt, secundo magnoque vento ignem operibus
inferunt. Hunc sic distulit 15ventus, uti uno tempore agger, plutei, testudo,
turris,tormenta flammam conciperent, et prius haec omnia consumerentur, quam quem ad
modum accidisset animadverti posset. Nostri repentina fortuna permoti arma, quae possunt,
arripiunt; alii ex castris 20sese incitant. Fit in hostes impetus eorum, sed muro sagittis
tormentisque fugientes persequi prohibentur. Illi sub murum se recipiunt, et
ibique musculum turrimque latericiamlibere incendunt. Ita multorum mensium labor hostium
perfidia et vi 25tempestatis puncto temporis interiit.

CAESAR, de Bello Civili, ii. 14.

141

13 **contecta:** i.e. the shield kept in a leather casing.

16 **plutei** = *screens* or *mantlets* of hurdles covered with raw hides.

17 **tormenta** (*torqu* + *mentum*) = *artillery*, engines for throwing missiles by *twisted* ropes; e.g. the *ballista,catapulta.*

24 **musculum** = *sapping-shed.*

  turrim latericiam = *brick tower.*

25 **multorum mensium**, i.e. from May to August 49 B.C.

215

B₅₄

CIVIL WAR, 49-45 B.C. (5)

'Nothing in his life

Became him like the leaving it.'

Quid nunc rostra tibi prosunt turbata forumque
800
Unde tribunicia plebeius signifer arce
Arma dabas populis? Quid prodita iura senatus
Et gener atque socer bello concurrere iussi?
Ante iaces quam dira duces Pharsalia confert,
804
Spectandumque tibi bellum civile negatum est.
                              Libycas en nobile corpus
810
Pascit aves nullo contectus Curio busto.
At tibi nos, quando non proderit ista silere
A quibus omne aevi senium sua fama repellit,
Digna damus, iuvenis, meritae praeconia vitae.
Haud alium tanta civem tulit indole Roma,
815
Aut cui plus leges deberent recta sequenti.
Perdita nunc urbi nocuerunt saecula, postquam
Ambitus et luxus et opum metuenda facultas
Transverso mentem dubiam torrente tulerunt;
Momentumque fuit mutatus Curio rerum
820
Gallorum captus spoliis et Caesaris auro.
Ius licet in iugulos nostros sibi fecerit ense
Sulla potens Mariusque ferox et Cinna cruentus
Caesareaeque domus series; cui tanta potestas
Concessa est? Emere omnes, hic vendidit urbem.

LUCAN, *Pharsalia*, iv. 799-804, 809-end.

Context. In 49 B.C. Curio was sent by Caesar to wrest the corn-province of Africa from the Pompeians. He won a signal success over Varus (allied with Juba) at Utica, but allowed himself to be surprised on the plain of the Bagradas, and, when all was lost, died sword in hand.

800 **tribunicia arce** = *from the citadel of the tribune*, i.e. the inviolability of the office and the right of veto. As tribune Curio played an all-important part in the crisis of 50 B.C.

801 **prodita iura senatus**, i.e. of the right of the senators to appoint governors of the provinces.—Haskins.

802 **gener atque socer:** by the early death of Julia (54 B.C.)—a beloved wife and daughter—the personal relation between Pompeius and Caesar was broken up.

812 **senium** (*senex*) = *decay* (of lapse of time).

813 **digna . . . vitae** = *such a panegyric* (**praeconia**) *as thy life deserves.*—H.

815-818 As tribune Curio for a time played the part of an independent republican, till his talent induced Caesar to buy him up.

819 **momentum** (= *movi* + *mentum*) **rerum** = *that which turned the scale of history.*—H.

824 **vendidit:** perh. referred to by Verg. *Aen.* vi. 621-2:

Vendidit hic auro patriam dominumque potentem
Imposuit; fixit leges pretio atque refixit.

216

B₅₅

Dyrrachium.

Caesar's line of circumvallation, *48 B.C.*

Erat nova et inusitata belli ratio cum tot castellorum numerotantoque spatio et tantis munitionibus et toto obsidionis genere, tum etiam reliquis rebus. Nam quicumque alterum obsidere conati sunt, perculsos atque infirmos hostes adorti aut proelio superatos5aut aliqua offensione permotos continuerunt, cum ipsi numero equitum militumque praestarent; causa autem obsidionis haec fere esse consuevit, ut frumento hostes prohiberent. At tum integras atque incolumes copias Caesar inferiore militum 10numero continebat, cum illi omnium rerum copia abundarent; cotidie enim magnus undique navium numerus conveniebat, quae commeatum supportarent, neque ullus flare ventus poterat, quin aliqua ex parte secundum cursum haberent. Ipse autem consumptis 15omnibus longe lateque frumentis summis erat in angustiis. Sed tamen haec singulari patientia milites ferebant. Recordabantur enim eadem se superiore anno in Hispania perpessos labore et patientia maximum bellum confecisse, meminerant ad 20Alesiam magnam se inopiam perpessos, multo etiam maiorem ad Avaricum maximarum se gentium victores discessisse.

CAESAR, de B. C. iii. 47.

Context. In Jan. (48 B.C.) Caesar set sail from Brundisium and landed safely in Epirus. After a junction with Antonius, who followed him from Brundisium with reinforcements, Caesar established himself close to Dyrrachium (Durazzo), the key of the whole military situation. Pompeius refused to fight, and encamped on a hill close to the sea at Petra, a short distance S. of Dyrrachium, where his fleets could bring him supplies. Caesar now determined to hem him in by a line of circumvallation.

2 **tanto spatio**: eventually the whole circuit of circumvallation covered at the least 16 miles: to this was afterwards added, just as before Alesia, an outer line of defence.

6 **aut aliqua offensione permotos** = *or demoralised by some other mishap* (**offensione**, lit. *stumbling*, and so*failure*).

12-15 Pompeius still had undisputed command of the sea.

Caesar's lines broken. Pompeius was informed by Celtic deserters that Caesar had not yet secured by a cross wall the beach between his two chains of entrenchment on his left (200 yards apart), leaving it possible to land troops from the sea into the unprotected space. Troops were landed by night: Caesar's outer line of defence was carried, and his lines broken through. 'Like Wellington at Burgos in 1812, Caesar failed from want of a sufficient force. In each case the only safe course was a retreat: in each case the retreat was conducted with admirable skill.'— W. F.

DYRRACHIUM. [To face p. 216.

CIVIL WAR, 49-45 B.C. (7)

The Eve of Pharsalus.

Dream of Pompeius.

At nox, felicis Magno pars ultima vitae,
Sollicitos vana decepit imagine somnos.
Nam Pompeiani visus sibi sede theatri
10
Innumeram effigiem Romanae cernere plebis,
Attollique suum laetis ad sidera nomen
Vocibus, et plausu cuneos certare sonantes.
Qualis erat populi facies clamorque faventis,
Olim cum iuvenis primique aetata triumphi
15
Post domitas gentes quas torrens ambit Hiberus,
Et quaecumque fugax Sertorius impulit arma,
Vespere pacato, pura venerabilis aeque
Quam currus ornante toga, plaudente senatu,
Sedit adhuc Romanus eques: seu fine bonorum
20
Anxia venturis ad tempora laeta refugit,
Sive per ambages solitas contraria visis

143

Vaticinata quies magni tulit omina planctus,
Seu vetito patrias ultra tibi cernere sedes
Sic Romam fortuna dedit. Ne rumpite somnos.
25
Castrorum vigiles, nullas tuba verberet aures.
Crastina dira quies et imagine maesta diurna
Undique funestas acies feret undique bellum.
Unde pares somnos populi noctemque beatam?
O felix, si te vel sic tua Roma videret.

LUCAN, Pharsalia, vii. 7-29.

9 **Pompeiani theatri.** Pompeius built the first stone theatre at Rome, near the Campus
Martius, capable of holding 40,000 people.

10 **Innumeram . . . plebis** = *the image of the countless Roman people.* **innumeram** which
belongs to **plebis** is transferred to **effigiem.**—Haskins.

14 **Olim . . . triumphi**, i.e. over Africa 79 B.C. when only 24, and **adhuc Romanus
eques** (l. 19). It was not until 71 B.C. that he triumphed over Spain, after the murder of
Sertorius. Lucan confuses the two triumphs.

16 **impulit** = *set in motion* (lit. *drive forward*).

17-18 **pura venerabilis . . . toga** = *no less worshipful in pure white gown than* (he would have
been) *in that which usually adorns the car of triumph*, i.e. the **toga picta.**—H.

20 **anxia** (sc. *quies*) = *his repose full of anxiety for the future.*—H.

21-22 **solitas . . . vaticinata** = *foretelling the opposite of his visions* i.e. by the **plausus** of which
he dreamed, the **planctus** which was in store for him was foreshadowed.—H.

25 **nullas** = *at all.* Cf. Cic. *Ep.: nullus venit* = *he never came.*

26 **Crastina . . . diurna** = *to-morrow's night of horror haunted by the sad image of the day's
events.*—H.

29 **sic**, i.e. in dreams.

The Dream of Pompeius. Macaulay says 'I hardly know an instance of so great an effect
produced by means so simple.'
218
B57

CIVIL WAR, 49-45 B.C. (8)

Pompeius ill-advised at Pharsalus, *48 B.C.*

Inter duas acies tantum erat relictum spatii, ut satis esset ad concursum utriusque
exercitus. Sed Pompeius suis praedixerat, ut Caesaris impetum exciperent neve se loco
moverent aciemque eius distrahi paterentur; idque admonitu C. Triarii 5fecisse dicebatur, ut
primus excursus visque militum infringeretur aciesque distenderetur atque in suis ordinibus
dispositi dispersos adorirentur; leviusque casura pila sperabat in loco retentis militibus, quam si
ipsi immissis telis occucurrissent, simul fore, ut10duplicato cursu Caesaris milites exanimarentur
et lassitudine conficerentur. Quod nobis quidem nulla ratione factum a Pompeio videtur,
propterea quod est quaedam animi incitatio atque alacritas naturaliter innata omnibus, quae studio
pugnae incenditur. 15Hanc non reprimere, sed augere imperatores debent; neque frustra
antiquitus institutum est, ut signa undique concinerent clamoremque universi tollerent: quibus
rebus et hostes terreri et suos incitari existimaverunt.20

CAESAR, de Bello Civili, iii. 92.

Context. Caesar made for Apollonia, where he left his wounded, and then marched S.E.
into Thessaly, where he joined Domitius Calvinus. (He had been sent with two legions E. into
Macedonia, to stop reinforcements for Pompeius under Scipio, Pompeius' father-in-law.)
Pompeius followed Caesar, and encamped on the slope of a hill facing Caesar's position near
Pharsalus. Here he offered battle, his better judgment overruled by the clamorous Senators in his
camp.

4-5 **aciem . . . paterentur** = *so as to allow their* (advancing) *line to become
disorganised* (**distrahi**), by the force of its onset.

7 **in suis . . . dispositi** = *by maintaining their proper distances.*

Scene of the Fight. The battle was fought near the town of *Pharsalus*, while the territory of
the town was named *Pharsalia.* Cf. Catull. lxiv. 37:

Pharsalum *coeunt*, **Pharsalia** *late frequentant.*

The Battle. Pompeius had 47,000 infantry and 7000 cavalry against Caesar's 22,000
infantry and 1000 cavalry. Pompeius stationed his cavalry and archers on his left, and confidently
expected to outflank his enemy's right. But Caesar, foreseeing the defeat of his cavalry, had
stationed behind it in reserve 2000 of his best legionaries. When Caesar's cavalry fell back

144

outnumbered, this reserve ran forward at the charge, not discharging their *pila*, but using them as spears, and driving them against man and horse. Taken aback by so unusual an infantry attack, the Pompeian cavalry wavered and fled. Caesar's third line (forming a rear-guard) was now sent forward to support the two front lines, and this decided the battle.—**Result.**Submission of the East to Caesar.

219
B₅₈

CIVIL WAR, 49-45 B.C. (9)

A. **Pharsalus and Cannae compared.**

Non aetas haec carpsit edax monimentaque rerum
Putria destituit: crimen civile videmus
Tot vacuas urbes. Generis quo turba redacta est
400
Humani? Toto populi qui nascimur orbe
Nec muros implere viris nec possumus agros;
Urbs nos una capit. Vincto fossore coluntur
Hesperiae segetes, stat tectis putris avitis
In nullos ruitura domus, nulloque frequentem
405
Cive suo Romam, sed mundi faece repletam
Cladis eo dedimus, ne tanto in tempore bellum
Iam posset civile geri. Pharsalia tanti
Causa mali. Cedant feralia nomina Cannae
Et damnata diu Romanis Allia fastis.
410
Tempora signavit leviorum Roma malorum:
Hunc voluit nescire diem.

LUCAN, *Pharsalia*, vii. 397-411.

397-398 **monimentaque . . . destituit** = *and has abandoned to decay the monuments of the past.*—Haskins.

402 **vincto fossore** = *by a chained digger* (delver), in consequence of the dearth of free labour. Cf. Juv. xi. 80 *squalidus in magna . . . compede fossor.*

404 **in nullos ruitura** = *ready to fall, but on the heads of none.*—H.

405 **faece** = *dregs.* Cf. Juv. iii. 60, 61 *Non possum ferre Quirites | Graecam urbem* (a Greek Rome); *quamvis*(and yet) *quota portio* (how small a fraction) *faecis Achaei?*

406-407 **ne tanto . . . geri** = lit. *so that during the long time since, it is impossible to wage* **civil** *war,* i.e. from the dearth of genuine Roman soldiers.

409 **Allia**: 390 B.C. Cf. Vergil. *Aeneid*, vii. 717 *quosque secans infaustum interluit Allia nomen.*

411 **nescire** = *to ignore.*

B. **The Battlefields of Pharsalus and Philippi.**

Ergo inter sese paribus concurrere telis
490
Romanas acies iterum videre Philippi;
Nec fuit indignum superis, bis sanguine nostro
Emathiam et latos Haemi pinguescere campos.
Scilicet et tempus veniet, cum finibus illis
Agricola, incurvo terram molitus aratro,
495
Exesa inveniet scabra robigine pila,
Aut gravibus rastris galeas pulsabit inanes,
Grandiaque effossis mirabitur ossa sepulchris.

VERGIL, *Georg.* i. 489-497.

489 **Ergo** = *therefore*, in fulfilment of the terrible warnings at the death of Caesar.

490 **iterum**, i.e. at Philippi 42 B.C.; the first time at Pharsalus.

220
B₅₉

How Pompeius died, *48 B.C.*

Pompeius, deposito adeundae Syriae consilio, et aeris magno pondere ad militarem usum in naves imposito, duobusque milibus hominum armatis, Pelusium pervenit. Ibi casu rex erat Ptolemaeus, puer aetate, magnis copiis cum sorore Cleopatra5bellum gerens, quam paucis ante mensibus per suos propinquos atque amicos regno expulerat; castraque Cleopatrae non longo spatio ab eius castris distabant. Ad cum Pompeius misit, ut pro hospitio atque amicitia patris Alexandria reciperetur atque illius opibus in 10calamitate tegeretur. Sed, qui ab eo missi erant, confecto legationis officio, liberius cum militibus regis colloqui coeperant eosque hortari, ut suum officium Pompeio praestarent, neve eius fortunam despicerent. His tunc cognitis rebus amici regis, 15qui propter aetatem eius in procuratione erant regni, sive timore adducti, ne Pompeius Alexandriam Aegyptunique occuparet, sive despecta eius fortuna, iis, qui erant ab eo missi, palam liberaliter responderunt eumque ad regem venire iusserunt: ipsi, 20clam consilio inito, Achillan, praefectum regium, singulari hominem audacia, et L. Septimium, tribunum militum, ad interficiendum Pompeium miserunt. Ab his liberaliter ipse appellatus naviculam parvulam conscendit cum paucis suis, et ibi 25ab Achilla et Septimio interficitur.

CAESAR, de Bello Civili, iii. 103, 104 (sel.)

Context. After the battle of Pharsalus, Pompeius, closely pursued by Caesar, had thoughts of going to Parthia and trying to form alliances there. While in Cyprus he heard that Antioch (in Syria) had declared for Caesar and that the route to the Parthians was no longer open. So he altered his plan and sailed to Egypt, where a number of his old soldiers served in the Egyptian army.

4 **Pelusium**, on the E. side of the easternmost mouth of the Nile.

5 **cum sorore Cleopatra.** By his father's will, Ptolemy ruled jointly with his sister for three years, 51-48 B.C., when he expelled her. Cleopatra raised an army in Syria and invaded Egypt. The two armies were encamped opposite each other when Pompeius landed to seek the help of Ptolemy.

15 **amici regis**, e.g. Achillas, l. 21, and espec. Ptolemy's guardian Pothinus, the *de facto* ruler of Egypt.

'On the same day (28 Sept.) on which he had triumphed over Mithridates (61 B.C.) Pompeius died on the desert sands of the inhospitable Casian shore by the hands of one of his old soldiers (Septimius).'—M.

221

B₆₀

Cato's Eulogy on Pompeius.

190

'Civis obit,' inquit, 'multum maioribus impar
Nosse modum iuris sed in hoc tamen utilis aevo,
Cui non ulla fuit iusti reverentia; salva
Libertate potens, et solus plebe parata
Privatus servire sibi, rectorque senatus,
195
Sed regnantis, erat. Nil belli iure poposcit,
Quaeque dari voluit, voluit sibi posse negari.
Immodicas possedit opes, sed plura retentis
Intulit: invasit ferrum, sed ponere norat;
Praetulit arma togae, sed pacem armatus amavit;
200
Iuvit sumpta ducem, iuvit dimissa potestas.
Casta domus luxuque carens corruptaque numquam
Fortuna domini. Clarum et venerabile nomen
Gentibus, et multum nostrae quod proderat urbi.

.   .   .   .

208
O felix, cui summa dies fuit obvia victo,
Et cui quaerendos Pharium scelus obtulit enses!
Forsitan in soceri potuisses vivere regno.
211
Scire mori sors prima viris sed proxima cogi.'
215

Vocibus his maior, quam si Romana sonarent
Rostra ducis laudes, generosam venit ad umbram
Mortis honos.

LUCAN, *Pharsalia*, ix. 190-217.

190-191 **multum . . . iuris** = *far inferior to our ancestors in recognising the due bounds of power.*—Haskins.

193 **solus** (sc. *ex proceribus*) . . . **servire sibi** = *alone (of the chief men of the State) acting the private citizen when the populace were ready to be his slaves*, i.e. acting unlike Sulla or Caesar.—H.

195 **sed regnantis.** 'Pompeius came forward as the duly installed general of the Senate against the Imperator of the street, once more to save his country.'—M.

198 **Intulit**, sc. *in aerarium*. Cf. Shaksp. *Jul. C.* III. ii. (Mark Antony of Caesar) 'He hath brought many captives home to Rome | Whose ransoms did the general coffers fill.' 'Caesar devoted the proceeds of the confiscations (the property of defeated opponents) entirely to the benefit of the State.'—M.

208 **cui summa dies . . . victo** = *whom the day of death met when he was vanquished*, i.e. without his having to seek it himself.—H.

209 **Pharium** = *Egyptian*, lit. of *Pharos* (= Faro), an island near Alexandria, famous for its lighthouse.

211 One of Lucan's famous *sententiae* (γνῶμαι, *maxims*).

Pompeius. 'Even in his own age he would have had a clearly defined and respectable position, *had he contented himself with being the general of the Senate*, for which he was from the outset destined.'—M.

222

B_{61}

CIVIL WAR, 49-45 B.C. (12)

The Grave of Pompeius.

His Roll of Fame.

Tunc ne levis aura retectos
790
Auferret cineres, saxo compressit harenam:
Nautaque ne bustum religato fune moveret,
Inscripsit sacrum semiusto stipite nomen:
HIC SITUS EST MAGNUS. . . .
806
Quod si tam sacro dignaris nomine saxum,
Adde actus tantos monimentaque maxima rerum,
Adde truces Lepidi motus Alpinaque bella
Armaque Sertori revocato consule victa,
810
Et currus quos egit eques, commercia tuta
Gentibus et pavidos Cilicas maris: adde subactam
Barbariem gentesque vagas et quidquid in Euro
Regnorum Boreaque iacet. Die semper ab armis
Civilem repetisse togam, ter curribus actis
815
Contentum patriae multos donasse triumphos.
Quis capit haec tumulus? Surgit miserabile bustum
Non ullis plenum titulis, non ordine tanto
Fastorum, solitumque legi super alta deorum
Culmina et exstructos spoliis hostilibus arcus
820
Haud procul est ima Pompei nomen harena,
Depressum tumulo, quod non legat advena rectus,
Quod nisi monstratum Romanus transeat hospes.

LUCAN, *Pharsalia*, viii. 789-793, 806-822.

Subject. Cordus, whom Lucan calls *infaustus Magni comes* (or according to Plutarch Philippus the faithful freedman of Pompeius), finds the cast-up body of Pompeius and gives it honourable burial.

793 **HIC SITUS EST** = ἔνθαδε κεῖται, the regular inscription on a tombstone.

808 **truces Lepidi motus.** Cf. page 178, last note on page.

809 **revocato consule**, i.e. Metellus. Cf. page 180, A., l. 12.

811 **pavidos Cilicas maris** = *the Cilicians scared from the sea.*—Jebb. *Pompeius effecit ut piratae timerent maria quibus ipsi ante grassabantur* (= they sailed at will).—Schol.

813-814 **dic semper . . . togam**, e.g. after his triumph over Spain 71 B.C., and over Mithridates and the East in 61B.C.

814-815 **ter curribus . . . triumphos** = (tell how) *content with thrice driving the* (triumphal) *car he made a present to his fatherland of many triumphs*, i.e. he did not claim them when he might have done so.

817-818 **Non ordine tanto Fastorum** = *storied with no majestic annals.*—Jebb.

819 **arcus** = *triumphal arches*, orig. temporary structures of wood, but under the Empire built of marble, e.g. of Septimius Severus.

821 **Depressum . . . rectus** = *sunk low upon a tomb, which the stranger cannot read without stooping* (**rectus**).—Haskins.

223

B₆₂

CIVIL WAR, 49-45 B.C. (13)

Atrox Animus Catonis, *46 B.C.*

Complures interim ex fuga Uticam perveniunt. Quos omnes Cato convocatos una cum trecentis, qui pecuniam Scipioni ad bellum faciendum contulerant, hortatur, ut servitia manumitterent, oppidumque defenderent. Quorum cum partem assentire, partem5animum mentemque perterritam atque in fugam destinatam habere intellexisset, amplius de ea re agere destitit, navesque eis attribuit, ut in quas quisque partes vellet proficisceretur. Ipse, omnibus rebus diligentissime constitutis, liberis suis L. Caesari, 10qui tum ei pro quaestore fuerat, commendatis et sine suspicione, vultu atque sermone, quo superiore tempore usus fuerat, cum dormitum isset, ferrum intro clam in cubiculum tulit, atque ita se traiecit. Qui cum anima nondum exspirata concidisset, et, 15impetu facto in cubiculum ex suspicione, medicus familiaresque continere atque vulnus obligare coepissent, ipse suis manibus vulnus crudelissime divellit, atque animo praesenti se interemit.

ASINIUS POLLIO, *de B. Africo*, 88.

Context. After Pharsalus and the flight of Pompeius, we finally part company with Caesar as an author. The *Bellum Alexandrinum* (Caesar's perils in Egypt and his settlement of the East 48-47 B.C.), the *B. Africum* (Thapsus 46 B.C.), the *B. Hispaniense* (Munda 45 B.C.), are the work of eyewitnesses and officers of his army. After a delay of fifteen precious months Caesar landed in Africa (Jan. 46), and by investing Thapsus tempted Scipio (Pompeius' father-in-law) to try to save the city by a battle. His troops were quickly arranged as at Pharsalus, and by a single impetuous charge won a complete victory. The slaughter was terrible: the survivors fled to Utica, where Cato in vain tried to organise a defence and to restore order, and then in despair died by his own sword.

1 **Uticam:** second in importance to Carthage.

19 **animo praesenti** = *deliberately.*

After Thapsus. 'Caesar left Africa in June 46 B.C., and celebrated a magnificent triumph, not over Roman citizens, but over Gauls and Egyptians, Pharnaces and Juba. As Dictator he remained in Rome several months, in which more permanently valuable work was done than was ever achieved in the same space of time, unless it were by Cromwell in 1653-4. The senseless outbreak of the Pompeian party in Spain under Labienus and the two sons of Pompeius took him away from Rome: but the victory of Munda (45 B.C.) closed the civil strife. Caesar returned to Rome in September, and six months more of life was all that was left to him.'—W. F.

224

B₆₃

CIVIL WAR, 49-45 B.C. (14)

Cato Uticensis, *46 B.C.*

A.Hic genitus proavo M. Catone, principe illo familiae Porciae, homo Virtuti simillimus et per omnia ingenio diis quam hominibus propior, qui nunquam recte fecit, ut facere videretur, sed quia aliter facere non potuerat, cuique id solum visum 5est rationem habere, quod haberet iustitiae, omnibus humanis vitiis immunis semper fortunam in sua potestate habuit.

VELL. PATERC. ii. 35.

1 **M. Catone**, the famous Censor of 184 B.C.

principe = *founder.*

B.

Ut primum tolli feralia viderat arma,

375

Intonsos rigidam in frontem descendere canos

148

Passus erat maestamque genis increscere barbam:
Uni quippe vacat studiis odiisque carenti
Humanum lugere genus . . .
380
       Hi mores, haec duri immota Catonis
Secta fuit, servare modum finemque tenere
Naturamque sequi patriaeque impendere vitam
Nec sibi sed toti genitum se credere mundo.
Huic epulae, vicisse famem; magnique penates,
385
Summovisse hiemem tecto; pretiosaque vestis,
Hirtam membra super Romani more Quiritis
Induxisse togam . . .
389
Iustitiae cultor, rigidi servator honesti,
In commune bonus: nullosque Catonis in actus
Subrepsit partemque tulit sibi nata voluptas.

                         LUCAN, *Pharsalia*, ii. 374-391 (sel.)

    377 uni (sc. *Catoni*), as the only true representative of the wise man of the Stoics.—Haskins.

    381 secta (sc. *via*, lit. *a beaten way*) here = *disciplina* =*principles*.

    381-383 servare modum . . . mundo. These expressions are Stoic maxims. Lucan (the nephew of Seneca) depicts the Stoic idea of virtue in the character of Cato.

    382-383 patriaeque . . . mundo. Cato's aim is **patriae impendere vitam**. His devotion to the service of humanity is complete; it is his part **toti genitum se credere mundo**. But this humanity includes Rome in the first place, the rest of the world in a quite secondary sense.—H.

    386-387 hirtam togam = *a coarse* (lit. *hairy*) *toga*.

    389 honesti = τοῦ καλοῦ. Cicero defines **honestum** as *aut ipsa virtus, aut res gesta virtute*.

    Cato Uticensis. 'He was like Caesar alone in this, that he had clear political convictions and acted on them not only with consistency but with justice and humanity. It is "his vain faith and courage" that alone lights up the dark hours of the falling Commonwealth:—

    'Victrix causa deis placuit, sed victa Catoni.'—W. F.
225
B₆₄

GAIUS IULIUS CAESAR. (5)

Caesar dines with Cicero, *Dec. 19, 45 B.C.*

O hospitem mihi tam gravem ἀμεταμέλητον! fuit enim periucunde. Sed cum secundis Saturnalibus ad Philippum vesperi venisset, villa ita completa militibus est, ut vix triclinium, ubi cenaturus ipse Caesar esset, vacaret; quippe hominum ↄ ↄↄ.5Sane sum commotus, quid futurum esset postridie; at mihi Barba Cassius subvenit: custodes dedit. Castra in agro, villa defensa est. Ille tertiis Saturnalibus apud Philippum ad h. VII, nec quemquam admisit: rationes opinor cum Balbo. Inde ambulavit 10in litore; post h. viii in balneum; unctus est, accubuit. Et edit et bibit ἀδεῶς et iucunde, opipare sane et apparate, nec id solum, sed
            bene cocto,
15
condito, sermone bono et, si quaeri', libenter.

    Praeterea tribus tricliniis accepti οἱ περὶ αὐτὸν valde copiose. Libertis minus lautis servisque nihil defuit: nam lautiores eleganter accepti. Quid multa? homines visi sumus. Hospes tamen non is, cui diceres: 'amabo te, eodem ad me, cum revertere': semel 20satis est. Σπουδαῖον οὐδὲν in sermone, φιλόλογα multa. Quid quaeris? delectatus est et libenter fuit. Puteolis se aiebat unum diem fore, alterum ad Baias. Habes hospitium sive ἐπισταθμείαν,odiosam mihi, dixi, non molestam.25

                         CICERO, *Ep. ad Att.* xiii. 52.

    Subject. We here catch a glimpse of Caesar as he really was. He had spent a night near Puteoli (where Cicero also had a villa) with Philippus, the step-father of Octavianus. The Dictator proposed a visit, and Cicero in this memorable letter describes to Atticus what happened.

    1 O hospitem . . . ἀμεταμέλητον! = *Oh, what a formidable guest to have had, and yet I have had no reason to repent of it* (ἀμεταμέλητον).

    10 rationes (sc. *conferebat*) . . . **Balbo** = *he was settling accounts with Balbus, I suppose*.

L. Cornelius Balbus, a native of Gades (Cadiz), was Caesar's confidential secretary and faithful friend. He was the first enfranchised foreigner who attained to the highest magistracy (Consul 40 B.C.).

14-15

'Though the cook was good,
'Twas Attic salt (**sermone bono**) that flavoured most the food.'—Jeans.

18-19 **homines visi sumus** = *I showed myself a man of taste*, i.e. as host.

21 Σπουδαῖον οὐδέν = lit. *nothing serious*, i.e. *nothing political*. φιλόλογα = *literary chat*.

24-25 ἐπισταθμείαν = *billeting*, as Caesar's offer to dine with Cicero was equivalent to a command.

odiosam . . . molestam = *unwelcome, though not disagreeable.*

226

B₆₅

GAIUS IULIUS CAESAR. (6)

The Death of Caesar, *44 B.C.*

Assidentem conspirati specie officii circumsteterunt; ilicoque Cimber Tillius, qui primas partes susceperat, quasi aliquid rogaturus propius accessit, renuentique et gestu in aliud tempus differenti ab utroque umero togam apprehendit; deinde clamantem: 5*Ista quidem vis est*, alter e Cascis aversum vulnerat, paulum infra iugulum. Caesar Cascae brachium arreptum graphiotraiecit, conatusque prosilire alio vulnere tardatus est; utque animadvertit undique se strictis pugionibus peti, toga caput10obvolvit, simul sinistra manu sinum ad ima crura deduxit, quo honestius caderet etiam inferiore corporis parte velata. Atque ita tribus et viginti plagis confossus est, uno modo ad primum ictum gemitu sine voce edito; etsi tradiderunt quidam 15Marco Bruto irruenti dixisse: Καὶ σὺ τέκνον; Exanimis, diffugientibus cunctis, aliquamdiu iacuit, donec lecticae impositum, dependente brachio, tres servoli domum rettulerunt. Nec in tot vulneribus, ut Antistius medicus existimabat, letale ullum 20repertum est, nisi quod secundo loco in pectore acceperat.

SUETONIUS, *Divus Iulius*, 82.

Context. After his return from Spain (Sept. 45 B.C.), Caesar was busy with the reconstruction of the Senate, the completion of his vast buildings in Rome, and with other far-reaching projects. But during these months the clouds of ill-will were gathering and threatening him on every side. A conspiracy was formed, of which C. Cassius, 'a lean and hungry man,' of a bitter and jealous disposition, seems to have been the real instigator. He persuaded Brutus, a student of life chiefly in books, that liberty could only be gained by murder, and at last it was resolved that the deed should be done on the Ides (15th) of March.

8 **graphio** (γραφίον = *scriptorium*) = *a writing-style.*

12 **quo honestius caderet**, cf. Ovid, *Fasti* ii. 833 (of Lucretia):

Tunc quoque iam moriens ne non procumbat honeste
Respicit, haec etiam cura cadentis erat.

16 Καὶ σὺ τέκνον; there seems to be no authority for attributing the words *Et tu Brute?* to Caesar. Shakespeare found them in an earlier play.

The Murder of Caesar. 'It is the most brutal and the most pathetic scene that profane history has to record; it was, as Goethe has said, the most senseless deed that ever was done. It was wholly useless, for it did not and could not save Rome from monarchy. The deed was done by a handful of men, who, pursuing a phantom liberty and following the lead of a personal hatred, slew **the one man who saw the truth of things**.'—W. F.

227

B₆₆

GAIUS IULIUS CAESAR. (7)

'There may be many Caesars

Ere such another Julius.'—*Cymbeline.*

A.Fuit in illo ingenium, ratio, memoria, litterae, cura, cogitatio, diligentia; res bello gesserat quamvis rei publicae calamitosas, at tamen magnas; multos annos regnare meditatus magno labore multis periculis quod cogitarat effecerat; muneribus, monumentis,5congiariis, epulis multitudinem imperitam delenierat: suos praemiis, adversarios clementiae specie devinxerat.

CICERO, *Philippica*, ii. 45.

4 **regnare meditatus.** For Caesar monarchy meant the liberation of the Empire.

5-6 **muneribus** (sc. **gladiatoriis**) = *gladiatorial shows.*

monumentis = *public buildings*, e.g. his forum, amphitheatre, Temple of Venus Genetrix, and other public works begun (e.g. the *Curia Iulia*) and planned.

6 **congiariis** (sc. *donis*), orig. a *gift of wine* (a *congius* = about 6 pints), then = *wine-money* (Ger. *Trinkgeld*), and so of any largess.

7-8 **clementiae specie.** Cic. himself refutes this ungrateful taunt in his *pro Marcello*: *Recte igitur unus invictus est, a quo etiam ipsius victoriae condicio visque devicta est.*

B.

Sed non in Caesare tantum

Nomen erat nec fama ducis, sed nescia virtus
145
Stare loco, solusque pudor non vincere bello.
Acer et indomitus, quo spes quoque ira vocasset,
Ferre manum et numquam temerando parcere ferro.
Successus urguere suos, instare favori
Numinis, impellens quidquid sibi summa petenti
150
Obstaret, gaudensque viam fecisse ruina.

LUCAN, Pharsalia, i. 143-150.

143-144 **tantum nomen** = *not a mere name alone*, in contrast to Pompeius:—*Stat magni nominis umbra.*— Haskins.

147 **temerando parcere ferro** = *shrink from dyeing his sword* (in blood).—H.

Apotheosis of Caesar.

C. Periit sexto et quinquagesimo aetatis anno atque in deorum numerum relatus est, non ore modo decernentium sed et persuasione volgi. Si quidem ludis, quos primos consecrato ei heres Augustus edebat, 20stella crinita per septem continuos dies fulsit, exoriens circa undecimam horam, creditumque est animam esse Caesaris in caelum recepti; et hac de causa simulacro eius in vertice additur stella.

SUET. Div. Iul. 88.

21 **stella crinita** (= κομήτης); cf. Verg. *Georg.* iv. 466-8:

Ille (= the sun) *etiam exstincto miseratus Caesare Romam*
Cum caput obscura nitidum ferrugine (= gloom)*texit,*
Impiaque aeternam timuerunt saecula noctem.
228

'FACTA DUCIS VIVENT, OPEROSAQUE GLORIA RERUM.'—OVID.
'THE HERO'S DEEDS AND HARD-WON FAME SHALL LIVE.'

Caesar was the sole creative genius produced by Rome, and the last produced by the ancient world, which accordingly moved on in the path that he marked out for it until its sun went down.

Whatever he undertook and achieved was pervaded and guided by the cool sobriety which constitutes the most marked peculiarity of his genius. To this he owed the power of living energetically in the present, undisturbed either by recollection or by expectation: to this he owed the capacity of acting at any moment with collected vigour, and of applying his whole genius even to the smallest and most incidental enterprise. Gifts such as these could not fail to produce a statesman.

Caesar as a statesman.—From early youth Caesar was a statesman in the deepest sense of the term, and his aim was the **political, military, intellectual, and moral regeneration of his own deeply decayed nation, and of the still more deeply decayed Hellenic nation intimately akin to his own**. According to his original plan, he had proposed to reach his object, like Pericles and Gaius Gracchus, without force of arms, until, reluctantly convinced of the necessity for a military support, he, when already forty years of age, put himself at the head of an army.

His talent for organisation was marvellous.—No statesman has ever compelled alliances, no general has ever collected an army out of unyielding and refractory elements with such decision, and kept them together with such firmness, as Caesar displayed in constraining and upholding his coalitions and his legions; never did regent judge his instruments and assign each to the place appropriate for him with so accurate an eye.

He was monarch; but he never played the king.—'I am no king, but Caesar.' Even when absolute lord of Rome, he retained the deportment of the party-leader; perfectly pliant and smooth, easy and charming in conversation, complaisant towards 229everyone, it seemed as if he wished to be nothing but the first among his peers.

Caesar ruled as king of Rome for five years and a half, not half as long as Alexander: in the intervals of seven great campaigns, which allowed him to stay not more than fifteen months altogether in the capital of his empire, **he regulated the destinies of the world for the present**

151

and the future. The outlines were laid down, and thereby the new State was defined for all coming time: the boundless future alone could complete the structure. But precisely because the building was an endless one, the master so long as he lived restlessly added stone to stone, with always the same dexterity and always the same elasticity busy at work. Thus he worked and created as never did any man before or after him: and as a worker and creator he still, after well-nigh two thousand years, lives in the memory of the nations—the first and withal unique Imperator Caesar.

MOMMSEN.

230
B₆₇

CICERO AND ANTONIUS.

A. Peroration of the Second Philippic, *44 B.C.*

Respice, quaeso, aliquando rem publicam, M. Antoni: quibus ortus sis, non quibuscum vivas considera: mecum, uti voles: redi cum re publica in gratiam. Sed de te tu videris: ego de me ipso profitebor. Defendi rem publicam adulescens, non 5deseram senex: contempsi Catilinae gladios, non pertimescam tuos. Quin etiam corpus libenter obtulerim, si repraesentari morte mea libertas civitatis potest: ut aliquando dolor populi Romani pariat, quod iam diu parturit. Etenim si abhinc 10annos prope viginti hoc ipso intemplo negavi posse mortem immaturam esse consulari, quanto verius nunc negabo seni? Mihi vero, patres conscripti, iam etiam optanda mors est, perfuncto rebus eis quas adeptus sum quasque gessi. Duo modo haec 15opto: unum, ut moriens populum Romanum liberum relinquam—hoc mihi maius ab dis immortalibus dari nihil potest,—alterum, ut ita cuique eveniat ut de re publica quisque mereatur.

CICERO, *Phil.* ii. 46.

2 **quibus ortus sis**: espec. his grandfather M. Antonius, the famous orator, whom Cicero held in great esteem.

5 **adulescens**, i.e. in 63 B.C., when he was in his 44th year.

8 **repraesentari** = *be realised, won now and here.*—Jebb.

11 **templo**, i.e. *Concordiae*. Cic. refers to *In Catil.* iv.

The Peroration. 'Such a passage speaks to us with a living impression of unity and directness which we acknowledge without question. We admire and ask for nothing more.'—Nettleship.

B. On the Murder of Cicero, by order of Antonius.

Par scelus admisit Phariis Antonius armis:
Abscidit voltus ensis uterque sacros.
Illud, laurigeros ageres cum laeta triumphos,
4
Hoc tibi, Roma, caput, cum loquereris, erat.
Antoni tamen est peior quam causa Pothini:
Hic facinus domino praestitit, ille sibi.

MARTIAL, *Epig.* III. lxvi.

1 **Par Phariis armis** = *which matches (that committed by)the armed hand of an Egyptian*, i.e. Pothinus (the guardian of the young king) who planned the murder of Pompeius, when he fled to Egypt 48 B.C.

   sacros: *consecrated* to Rome from their public services.

3-4 **Illud caput** = Pompeius. **hoc caput** = Cicero. Cf. *Epig.*v. lxix: *Quid gladium demens* **Romana** *stringis* **in ora**?

6 **domino**, sc. Ptolemaeus, King of Egypt, jointly with Cleopatra.

231
B₆₈

CICERO.

A. Cicero as Orator and Poet.

Eloquium ac famam Demosthenis aut Ciceronis
115
Incipit optare et totis Quinquatribus optat
Quisquis adhuc uno parcam colit asse Minervam,
Quem sequitur custos angustae vernula capsae.
Eloquio sed uterque perit orator, utrumque
Largus et exundans leto dedit ingenii fons.
120
Ingenio manus est et cervix caesa, nec umquam

152

Sanguine causidici maduerunt rostra pusilli.
'O fortunatam natam me consule Romam':
Antoni gladios potuit contemnere, si sic
Omnia dixisset. Ridenda poemata malo
125
Quam te, conspicuae divina Philippica famae,
Volveris a prima quae proxima.

JUVENAL, Satires, x. 114-126.

114-118 Boys at school long to be a Demosthenes or a Cicero.

115 **totis Quinquatribus**, i.e. during all the five days of the Quinquatria, an annual feast of Minerva, March 19-23: it was always a holiday time at schools, and the school year began at the close of it.

116 **parcam Minervam** = *a cheap kind of learning*, and **uno asse** = *an entrance fee of one* **as**. But Duff says **ashere** = **stips**, i.e. the boy's contribution to the goddess of wisdom, who can make him wise, and **parcam** (=*economical*), transferred from **asse** to **Minervam**.

117 **vernula** = *a little home-born slave*, **capsa** a circular box of beech-wood, used for the transport of books.

121 **causidici pusilli** = *of a petty pleader*, as opposed to orator.

122 From Cicero's poem *de suo consulatu*. Another line quoted in the 2nd Philippic is *Cedant arma togae, concedat laurea laudi.*

124 **Ridenda poemata malo**, i.e. they are better as being safer. Juvenal himself refutes this argument:
> *Summum crede nefas animam praeferre pudori*
> *Et propter vitam vivendi perdere causas.*

B. Cicero as Advocate.

Disertissime Romuli nepotum,
Quot sunt quotque fuere, Marce Tulli,
Quotque post aliis erunt in annis,
Gratias tibi maximas Catullus
5
Agit pessimus omnium poeta,
Tanto pessimus omnium poeta
Quanto tu optimus omnium patronus.

CATULLUS, xlix.

2 **Marce Tulli**: the formal address suits the formal expression of thanks to a *patronus* (= *advocate*).

5 **pessimus omnium poeta:** the self-depreciation heightens the praise of the last line.—Merrill.

232

B₆₉

CICERO.

His Death, by order of Antonius, *43 B.C.*

M. Cicero sub adventum triumvirorum urbe cesserat pro certo habens id quod erat, non magis se Antonio eripi quam Caesari Cassium et Brutum posse: primo in Tusculanum fugerat, inde transversis itineribus in Formianum ut ab Caieta navem5conscensurus proficiscitur. Unde aliquoties in altum provectum cum modo venti adversi retulissent, modo ipse iactationem navis caeco volvente fluctu pati non posset, taedium tandem eum et fugae et vitae cepit, regressusque ad superiorem villam, quae paulo 10plus mille passibus a mari abest, 'moriar,' inquit, 'in patria saepe servata.' Satis constat servos fortiter fideliterque paratos fuisse ad dimicandum; ipsum deponi lecticam et quietos pati quod sors iniqua cogeret iussisse. Prominenti ex lectica praebentique15immotam cervicem caput praecisum est. Nec satis stolidae crudelitati militum fuit: manus quoque scripsisse aliquid in Antonium exprobrantes praeciderunt. Ita relatum caput ad Antonium iussuque eius inter duas manus in rostris positum, ubi20ille consul, ubi saepe consularis, ubi eo ipso anno adversus Antonium quanta nulla umquam humana vox cum admiratione eloquentiae auditus fuerat: vix attollentes prae lacrimis oculos homines intueri trucidati membra civis poterant. Vixit tres et sexaginta 25annos, ut si vis afuisset, ne immatura quidem mors videri possit.

LIVY, Fr. ap. Sen. Rh. Suas. vii.

1 **triumvirorum**, sc. Antonius, Octavianus, and Lepidus. These three allies (about the end of Oct. 43 B.C.) held their famous meeting on an island in the R. Rhenus (a tributary of the Padus) near Bononia (Bologna), at which they constituted themselves a commission of three with

absolute powers for five years. This was followed by a proscription of their principal opponents, of whom seventeen, including Cicero (sacrificed to Antonius), were at once put to death.

4 **in Tusculanum**, i.e. to his villa at Tusculum, richly adorned with pictures and statues.

5 **in Formianum**, i.e. to his villa at Formiae, on the Appian Way, in the innermost corner of the beautiful Gulf of Caieta (Gaëta). Near this villa Cicero was murdered.

The Death of Cicero. Cicero's work was over, and the tragedy of his death was the natural outcome of his splendid failure. The restoration of the Commonwealth of the Scipios was but a dream; still it was a beautiful dream, and Cicero gave his life for it.—Tyrrell.

233

B$_{70}$

In Praise of Cicero.

A.Nihil tamen egisti, M. Antoni, nihil, inquam, egisti mercedem caelestissimi oris et clarissimi capitis abscisi numerando,auctoramentoque funebri ad conservatoris quondam rei publicae tantique consulis irritando necem. Rapuisti tum Ciceroni lucem5sollicitam et aetatem senilem et vitam miseriorem te principe quam sub te triumviro mortem, famam vero gloriamque factorum atque dictorum adeo non abstulisti, ut auxeris. Vivit vivetque per omnem saeculorum memoriam, dumque hoc vel forte vel10providentia vel utcumque constitutum rerum naturae corpus, quod ille paene solus Romanorum animo vidit, ingenio complexus est, eloquentia illuminavit, manebit incolume, comitem aevi sui laudem Ciceronis trahet omnisque posteritas illius in te scripta mirabitur, 15tuum in eum factum exsecrabitur citiusque e mundo genus hominum quam Ciceronis memoria cedet.

VELLEIUS PATERCULUS, ii. 66.

3-4 **auctoramentoque funebri irritando** = lit. *and by stimulating* (*provoking*) *by a fatal reward*(**auctoramento**) *the death.* . . .

10-15 **dumque . . . trahet**, in reference to Cicero's philosophical works, in which Cicero propounds no original scheme of philosophy, claiming only that he renders the conclusions of Greek thinkers accessible to his own countrymen.

B.Ingenium et operibus et praemiis operum felix; ipse fortunae diu prosperae et in longo tenore felicitatis 20magnis interim ictus vulneribus, exilio, ruina partium pro quibus steterat, filiae exitu tam tristi tamque acerbo, omnium adversorum nihil ut viro dignum erat tulit praeter mortem, quae vere aestimanti minus indigna videri potuit, quod a victore 25inimico nil crudelius passurus erat quam quod eiusdem fortunae compos victo fecisset. Si quis tamen virtutibus vitia pensaret, vir magnus ac memorabilis fuit, et in cuius laudes exsequendas Cicerone laudatore opus fuerit.30

LIVY, *Fr. ap. Sen.*

21-22 **ruina . . . steterat**, i.e. the restoration of the Commonwealth of the Scipios.

Cicero. 'It happened many years after that Augustus once found one of his grandsons with a work of Cicero's in his hands. The boy was frightened, and hid the book under his gown; but Caesar took it from him, and, standing there motionless, he read through a great part of the book; then he gave it back to the boy, and said "This was a great orator, my child; a great orator, and a man who loved his country well."'—Plutarch, *Cicero*, 49.

234

B$_{71}$

LAUS ITALIAE.

Si te forte iuvant Helles Athamantidos urbes,
Nec desiderio, Tulle, movere meo,
Tu licet aspicias caelum omne Atlanta gerentem,
8
Sectaque Persea Phorcidos ora manu,
Geryonis stabula et luctantum in pulvere signa
Herculis Antaeique Hesperidumque choros,
Tuque tuo Colchum propellas remige Phasim,
12
Peliacaeque trabis totum iter ipse legas,
Qua rudis Argoa natat inter saxa columba
In faciem prorae pinus adacta novae,
Et siqua Ortygii visenda est ora Caystri,
16
Et quae septenas temperat unda vias;
Omnia Romanae cedent miracula terrae;
Natura his posuit, quicquid ubique fuit.

Armis apta magis tellus, quam commoda noxae:
20
Famam, Roma, tuae non pudet historiae.
Nam quantum ferro, tantum pietate potentes
Stamus: victrices temperat illa manus.
Hic Anio Tiburne fluis, Clitumnus ab Umbro
24
Tramite, et aeternum Marcius umor opus,
Albanus lacus et foliis Nemorensis abundans,
26
Potaque Pollucis lympha salubris equo.
39
Haec tibi, Tulle, parens, haec est pulcherrima sedes;
Hic tibi pro digna gente petendus honos;
Hic tibi ad eloquium cives, hic ampla nepotum
42
Spes et venturae coniugis aptus amor.

PROPERTIUS, III. (IV.) xxii. 5-26, 39-42.

Subject. Go where thou wilt, my Tullus, know that all the sights and marvels of all lands, from West to East, are outdone by those of thine own Italy. A truly famous land! A land ever victorious, ever merciful; full of fair lakes and streams. Here, Tullus, is thy true abode: here seek a life of honour and a home.

8 **Phorcidos ora** = *the head of Medusa*, the daughter of Phorcus.

15 **Ortygii Caystri.** Ortygia, an old name for Ephesus, near the mouth of the R. Cayster: the haunt of *quails(Ortygia,* ὄρτυξ).

16 **temperat septenas vias** = *moderates its seven channels*, of the delta of the Nile.—Ramsay.

19-22 Cf. Verg. *Aen.* vi. 853 *Parcere subiectis et debellare superbos.*

19 **commoda noxae** = *disposed to harm.*—North Pinder.

24 **Marcius umor**, i.e. the aqueduct of Q. Marcius Rex; built 145 B.C.

25 The Alban and Arician Lakes (**Nemorensis** = mod.*Nemi*) are close together.

26 i.e. the well Iuturna in the Forum ('the well that springs by Vesta's fane') at which the Dioscuri washed their horses after their hot ride from Lake Regillus.

41 **ad eloquium cives** = *citizens to hear and profit by your eloquence.*—N. P.

235
B₇₂

LAUS ROMAE.

150
Haec est in gremium victos quae sola recepit
Humanumque genus communi nomine fovit
Matris, non dominae ritu: civesque vocavit
Quos domuit, nexuque pio longinqua revinxit.
Huius pacificis debemus moribus omnes
155
Quod veluti patriis regionibus utitur hospes:
Quod sedem mutare licet: quod cernere Thulen
Lusus, et horrendos quondam penetrare recessus:
Quod bibimus passim Rhodanum, potamus Orontem;
Quod cuncti gens una sumus. Nec terminus unquam
160
Romanae dicionis erit. Nam cetera regna
Luxuries vitiis odiisque superbia vertit.
Sic male sublimes fregit Spartanus Athenas
Atque idem Thebas cecidit. Sic Medus ademit
Assyrio, Medoque tulit moderamina Perses:
165
Subiecit Macedo Persen, cessurus et ipse
Romanis. Haec auguriis firmata Sibyllae,
Haec sacris animata Numae: huic fulmina vibrat
Iuppiter: hanc tota Tritonia Gorgone velat.
Arcanas huc Vesta faces, huc orgia Bacchus
170
Transtulit, et Phrygios genetrix turrita leones.

155

Huc defensurus morbos Epidaurius hospes
Reptavit placido tractu, vectumque per undas
Insula Paeonium texit Tiberina draconem.

CLAUDIAN, de Consulatu Stilichonis, iii. 150-173.

153 **nexuque . . . revinxit** = *and has linked far places in a bond of love.*—Jebb.

156 **Thulen:** cf. Vergil's *ultima Thule*, of the northernmost island known, variously identified with the Shetlands, Iceland, or Norway.

158 **Orontem:** the largest river of Syria, whence Juvenal, iii. 62, uses it of the Syrian people—

Iam pridem Syrus in Tiberim defluxit Orontes.

159 **Quod cuncti . . . sumus** = *that the whole earth is one people.*

164 **moderamina** = *the reins of power;* lit. *a means of managing.*

168 **hanc tota . . . velat** = *she it is above whom Pallas spreads the whole shadow of the aegis* (**tota Gorgone**). Cf. Verg. *Aen.* viii. 435-8:

Aegidaque horriferam, turbatae Palladis arma,
Certatim squamis serpentum auroque polibant,
Connexosque angues ipsamque in pectore divae
Gorgona, desecto vertentem lumina collo.

170 **genetrix turrita,** i.e. Cybele, the goddess of settled life.

171 **Epidaurius hospes,** i.e. Asclepius (Aesculapius), who had a famous temple at Epidaurus (in Argolis), whence his worship was introduced into Rome to avert a pestilence 293 B.C.

172 **reptavit placido tractu** = *came gently gliding on his voyage.* Jebb.— For **reptavit** cf. *repo*, ἕρπω, and our *creep*.

173 **Paeonium draconem** = *the serpent of the healer.* Cf.Παιών.

236

B₇₃

'QUOD CUNCTI GENS UNA SUMUS.' —CLAUDIAN.

Vis dicam, quae causa tuos, Romane, labores
In tantum extulerit, quis gloria fotibus aucta
585
Sic cluat, impositis ut mundum frenet habenis?
Discordes linguis populos et dissona cultu
Regna volens sociare Deus, subiungier uni
Imperio, quidquid tractabile moribus esset,
Concordique iugo retinacula mollia ferre
590
Constituit, quo corda hominum coniuncta teneret
Relligionis amor: nec enim fit copula Christo
592
Digna, nisi implicitas societ mens unica gentes.
608
Ius fecit commune pares et nomine eodem
Nexuit et domitos fraterna in vincla redegit.
Vivitur omnigenis in partibus, haud secus ac si
Cives congenitos concludat moenibus unis
612
Urbs patria atque omnes lare conciliemur avito.
634
En ades omnipotens, concordibus influe terris:
Iam mundus te, Christe, capit, quem congrege nexu
Pax et Roma tenent: capita haec et culmina rerum
Esse iubes, nec Roma tibi sine pace probatur:
Et pax ut placeat, facit excellentia Romae,
Quae motus varios simul et dicione coercet
640
Et terrore premit.

PRUDENTIUS, contra Symmachum, ii. 583-640 (scl.).

Subject. In a remarkable passage, Prudentius (circ. 400A.D.) views the victorious empire of Rome as preparing the way for the coming of Christ. The triumphs of the Romans were not, he says, the gifts of false gods, grateful for sacrifices, but were designed by Providence to break down the barriers between the jarring nationalities of the world, and familiarise them with a

156

common yoke, by way of disciplining them for a common Christianity. An "universal peace is struck through sea and land," and Law, Art, Commerce, and Marriage constitute the world one city and one family. Thus the way was paved for the coming of Christ by the unity of the empire and the civilisation of the individual subject.—North Pinder.

584 **fotibus** (cf. *fotum, foveo*) = *cherishings, supports*, post-classical.

585 **sic cluat** = *is so famed*, for *cluo* (ante and post-class.) cf. κλέος.

590-591 **quo** (sc. *iugo*) . . . **amor**, i.e. hearts once knit together by a common yoke would best be held together by a common faith.—N. P.

609 **fraterna in vincla** = *in the bonds of brotherhood, not those of slavery, as* **domitos** *would naturally suggest.*

634 **concordibus** = *now they are in harmony and peace*, emphatic.

635 **capit** = *is fit to receive thee.*

237

238

PROPEMPTICON VERGILIO.*

The Perils of the Deep.

A.

Sic te diva potens Cypri,
Sic fratres Helenae, lucida sidera,
Ventorumque regat pater
4
Obstrictis aliis praeter Iapyga,
Navis, quae tibi creditum
Debes Vergilium, finibus Atticis
Reddas incolumem precor
8
Et serves animae dimidium meae.
Illi robur et aes triplex
Circa pectus erat, qui fragilem truci
Commisit pelago ratem
12
Primus, nec timuit praecipitem Africum
Decertantem Aquilonibus
Nec tristes Hyadas nec rabiem Noti,
Quo non arbiter Hadriae
16
Maior, tollere seu ponere vult freta.
Quem mortis timuit gradum,
Qui siccis oculis monstra natantia,
Qui vidit mare turbidum et
20
Infames scopulos Acroceraunia?
Nequiquam deus abscidit
Prudens Oceano dissociabili
Terras, si tamen impiae
24
Non tangenda rates transiliunt vada.
* A 'God-speed' to Vergil's ship.

'Nought is there for man too high.'

B.

Audax omnia perpeti
Gens humana ruit per vetitum nefas:
Audax Iapeti genus
28
Ignem fraude mala gentibus intulit;
Post ignem aetheria domo
Subductum macies et nova febrium
Terris incubuit cohors
32
Semotique prius tarda necessitas

157

Leti corripuit gradum.
Expertus vacuum Daedalus aera.
Pinnis non homini datis;
36
Perrupit Acheronta Herculeus labor.
Nil mortalibus arduist;
Caelum ipsum petimus stultitia neque
Per nostrum patimur scelus
40
Iracunda Iovem ponere fulmina.

HORACE, *Od.* I. iii.

239

PROPEMPTICON MAECIO CELERI.

A Prayer for his friend's safety.

A.

Di, quibus audaces amor est servare carinas
Saevaque ventosi mulcere pericula ponti,
Sternite molle fretum placidumque advertite votis
Concilium, et lenis non obstrepat unda precanti:
5
Grande tuo rarumque damus, Neptune, profundo
Depositum. Iuvenis dubio committitur alto
Maecius atque animae partem super aequora nostrae
Maiorem transferre parat. Proferte benigna
Sidera et antemnae gemino considite cornu,
10
Oebalii fratres; vobis pontusque polusque
Luceat; Iliacae longe nimbosa sororis
Astra fugate, precor, totoque excludite caelo.
Vos quoque caeruleum ponti, Nereides, agmen
Quis honor ei regni cessit fortuna secundi,
15
Dicere quae magni fas sit mihi sidera ponti,
Surgite de vitreis spumosae Doridos antris
Baianosque sinus et feta tepentibus undis
Litora tranquillo certatim ambite natatu,
Quaerentes ubi celsa ratis, quam scandere gaudet
20
Nobilis Ausoniae Celer armipotentis alumnus. . . .

His Prayer is heard.

Man's audacity.

B.

Et pater, Aeolio frangit qui carcere ventos
Cui varii flatus omnisque per aequora mundi
Spiritus atque hiemes nimbosaque nubila parent,
45
Artius obiecto Borean Eurumque Notumque
Monte premat: soli Zephyro sit copia caeli,
Solus agat puppes summasque supernatet undas
Assiduus pelago; donec tua turbine nullo
Laeta Paraetoniis assignet carbasa ripis. . . .
50
Audimur. Vocat ipse ratem nautasque morantes
Increpat. Ecce meum timido iam frigore pectus
Labitur et nequeo, quamvis movet ominis horror,
Claudere suspensos oculorum in margine fletus. . . .
61
Quis rude et abscissum miseris animantibus aequor
Fecit iter solidaeque pios telluris alumnos
Expulit in fluctus pelagoque immisit hianti

158

Audax ingenii? nec enim temeraria virtus
65
Illa magis, summae gelidum quae Pelion Ossae
Iunxit anhelantemque iugis bis pressit Olympum.

STATIUS, Silvae, III. ii. 1-20, 42-53, 61-66.

240

SENECA.

For those 'qui corporis cura mentem obruerunt.'

A.Stulta est enim, mi Lucili, et minime conveniens litterato viro occupatio exercendi lacertos et dilatandi cervicem, ac latera firmandi. Cum tibi feliciter sagina cesserit, et tori creverint: nec vires unquam opimi bovis, nec pondus aequabis. Adice nunc, quod maiore corporis sarcina animus eliditur, et minus agilis est. Itaque, quantum potes circumscribe corpus tuum, et animo locum laxa. Multa sequuntur incommoda huic deditos curae. Primum exercitationes, quarum labor spiritum exhaurit, et inhabilem intentioni ac studiis acrioribus reddit; deinde copia ciborum subtilitas animi impeditur. Accedunt pessimae notae, mancipia in magisterium recepta, homines inter oleum et vinum occupati: quibus ad votum dies est actus, si bene desudaverunt, si in locum eius quod effluxit, multum potionis altius ieiuno gutture regesserunt. Bibere et sudare, vita cardiaci est. Sunt exercitationes et faciles et breves, quae corpus et sine mora laxent, et tempori parcant: cuius praecipua ratio habenda est. Cursus, et cum aliquo pondere manus motae, et saltus, vel ille qui corpus in altum levat, vel ille qui in longum mittit, vel ille (ut ita dicam) saliaris, aut (ut contumeliosius dicam) fullonius. Quodlibet ex his elige, usu fit facile. Neque ego te iubeo semper imminere libro, aut pugillaribus. Dandum et aliquod intervallum animo: ita tamen ut non resolvatur, sed remittatur.

SENECA, Ep. xv. 8.

'They needs must die.'

B.

Incognitum istud facinus, ac dirum nefas
A me quoque absit. Quod scelus miseri luent?
Scelus est Iason genitor, et maius scelus
Medea mater. Occidant: non sunt mei.
Pereant? mei sunt. Crimine et culpa carent.
Sunt innocentes, fateor: et frater fuit.
Quid, anime, titubas? ora quid lacrimae rigant?
Variamque nunc huc ira nunc illuc amor
Diducit? anceps aestus incertam rapit.

SENECA, Medea, 920.

241

CRITICISM OF POETS.

An Estimate of early Roman Dramatists.

A.

Ennius, et sapiens et fortis et alter Homerus,
51
Ut critici dicunt, leviter curare videtur,
Quo promissa cadant et somnia Pythagorea.
Naevius in manibus non est et mentibus haeret
Paene recens? Adeo sanctum est vetus omne poema.
55
Ambigitur quotiens uter utro sit prior, aufert
Pacuvius docti famam senis, Accius alti,
Dicitur Afrani toga convenisse Menandro,
Plautus ad exemplar Siculi properare Epicharmi,
Vincere Caecilius gravitate, Terentius arte.
60
Hos ediscit et hos arto stipata theatro
Spectat Roma potens, habet hos numeratque poetas
Ad nostrum tempus Livi scriptoris ab aevo.

HOR. Ep. II. i. 50-62.

'Teréntio non símilem dices quémpiam.'

B.

Tu quoque tu in summis, o dimidiate Menander,

159

Poneris, et merito, puri sermonis amator.
Lenibus atque utinam scriptis adiuncta foret vis,
Comica ut aequato virtus polleret honore
Cum Graecis neve hac despectus parte iaceres!
Unum hoc maceror ac doleo tibi deesse, Terenti.

CAESAR, ap. SUETON. vit. Ter.

Ovid on his Contemporaries.

C.

Temporis illius colui fovique poetas,
Quotque aderant vates, rebar adesse deos.
Saepe suas volucres legit mihi grandior aevo,
44
Quaeque nocet serpens, quae iuvat herba, Macer.
Saepe suos solitus recitare Propertius ignes,
Iure sodalicio qui mihi iunctus erat.
Ponticus heroo, Bassus quoque clarus iambis
48
Dulcia convictus membra fuere mei;
Et tenuit nostras numerosus Horatius aures,
Dum ferit Ausonia carmina culta lyra.
Vergilium vidi tantum: nec amara Tibullo
52
Tempus amicitiae fata dedere meae.
Successor fuit hic tibi, Galle, Propertius illi;
Quartus ab his serie temporis ipse fui:
Utque ego maiores, sic me coluere minores,
56
Notaque non tarde facta Thalia mea est.

OVID, Tr. IV. x. 41-56.

Cf. OVID, Am. I. xv. 9-30; Am. III. ix. 38-68; Rem. Am. 65-388; QUINT. X. i. 85-90.
242

STORMS BY SEA AND LAND.

Ovid describes a Storm at Sea.

A.

Me miserum, quanti montes volvuntur aquarum!
20
Iam iam tacturos sidera summa putes.
Quantae diducto subsidunt aequore valles!
Iam iam tacturas Tartara nigra putes.
Quocumque aspicio, nihil est nisi pontus et aer,
24
Fluctibus hic tumidus, nubibus ille minax.
Inter utrumque fremunt inmani murmure venti:
Nescit, cui domino pareat, unda maris.
Nam modo purpureo vires capit Eurus ab ortu,
28
Nunc Zephyrus sero vespere missus adest,
Nunc sicca gelidus Boreas bacchatur ab Arcto,
Nunc Notus adversa proelia fronte gerit.
Rector in incerto est nec quid fugiatve petatve
32
Invenit: ambiguis ars stupet ipsa malis.

OVID, Tr. I. ii. 19-32.

The passing of Romulus.

B.

Sol fugit, et removent subeuntia nubila caelum,
Et gravis effusis decidet imber aquis.
Hinc tonat, hinc missis abrumpitur ignibus aether,
Fit fuga, rex patriis astra petebat equis.

OVID, Fast. ii. 493-496.

Thunder and Hail.

C.

Ínterea prope iam óccidente sóle inhorrescít mare,
Ténebrae conduplicántur, noctisque ét nimbum occaecát nigror,
Flámma inter nubés coruscat, caélum tonitru cóntremit,
Grándo mixta imbri largifico súbita praecipitáns cadit,
Úndique omnes vénti erumpunt, saévi exístunt túrbines,
Férvit aestu pélagus.

PACUVIUS ap. CIC. De Div. I. xiv. 24.

The Argo in a Gale.

D.

Tollitur atque intra Minyas Argoaque vela
Styrus adest: vasto rursus desidit hiatu
Abrupta revolutus aqua. Iamque omnis in astra
Itque reditque ratis, lapsoque reciproca fluctu
Descendit. Vorat hos vertex, hos agmine toto
30
Gurges agit. Simul in voltus micat undique terror;
Crebra ruina poli caelestia limina laxat.

VAL. FL. Argon. viii. 328-334.

Cf. VERG. Aen. i. 81-123, Aen. iv, 160-168; STAT. Theb. i. 336-363.
243

PETS RENOWNED IN SONG.

Lesbia's Sparrow.

A.

Lugete, o Veneres Cupidinesque,
Et quantumst hominum venustiorum.
Passer mortuus est meae puellae,
Passer, deliciae meae puellae,
5
Quem plus illa oculis suis amabat.
Nam mellitus erat suamque norat
Ipsam tam bene quam puella matrem;
Nec sese a gremio illius movebat,
Sed circumsiliens modo huc modo illuc
10
Ad solam dominam usque pipiabat.
Qui nunc it per iter tenebricosum
Illuc, unde negant redire quemquam.
At vobis male sit, malae tenebrae
Orci, quae omnia bella devoratis:
15
Tam bellum mihi passerem abstulistis.
Vae factum male! vae miselle passer!
Tua nunc opera meae puellae
Flendo turgiduli rubent ocelli.

CATULLUS, iii.

'My Parrot an obtrusive bird.'

B.

Psittace, dux volucrum, domini facunda voluptas,
Humanae sollers imitator, psittace, linguae,
Quis tua tam subito praeclusit murmura fato?

STATIUS, Silv. ii. 4

The Lap-dog and its Portrait.

C.

Issa est passere nequior Catulli,
Issa est purior osculo columbae,
Issa est blandior omnibus puellis,
Issa est carior Indicis lapillis,

161

5
Issa est deliciae catella Publi.
Hanc tu, si queritur, loqui putabis;
Sentit tristitiamque gaudiumque.
Collo nixa cubat capitque somnos,
Ut suspiria nulla sentiantur.
10
Hanc ne lux rapiat suprema totam,
Picta Publius exprimit tabella,
In qua tam similem videbis Issam,
Ut sit tam similis sibi nec ipsa.
Issam denique pone cum tabella:
15
Aut utramque putabis esse veram,
Aut utramque putabis esse pictam.

MARTIAL, I. cix.

Cf. CATULL. ii.; OVID, *Am.* ii. 6.
244

THE ROMAN SATIRISTS. (1)

A. Satura quidem tota nostra est, in qua primus insignem laudem adeptus Lucilius quosdam
ita deditos sibi adhuc habet amatores, ut eum non eiusdem modo operis auctoribus, sed omnibus
poetis praeferre non dubitent. Ego quantum ab illis tantum ab Horatio dissentio, qui
Lucilium *fluere lutulentum et esse aliquid, quod tollere possis*, putat. Nam et eruditio in eo mira et libertas
atque inde acerbitas, et abunde salis. Multum eo est tersior ac purus magis Horatius, et, nisi labor
eius amore, praecipuus. Multum et verae gloriae, quamvis uno libro, Persius meruit.

QUINT. X. i. 93.

A Criticism of Lucilius.

B.
Eupolis atque Cratinus Aristophanesque poetae
Atque alii, quorum comoedia prisca virorum est,
Siquis erat dignus describi, quod malus ac fur,
Quod moechus foret aut sicarius aut alioqui
5
Famosus, multa cum libertate notabant.
Hinc omnis pendet Lucilius, hosce secutus
Mutatis tantum pedibus numerisque, facetus,
Emunctae naris, durus componere versus.
Nam fuit hoc vitiosus: in hora saepe ducentos,
10
Ut magnum, versus dictabat stans pede in uno;
Cum flueret lutulentus, erat quod tollere velles;
Garrulus atque piger scribendi ferre laborem.

HORACE, *Sat.* I. iv. 1-12.

Juvenal's Reasons for Writing Satire.

C.
Cur tamen hoc potius libeat decurrere campo,
Per quem magnus equos Auruncae flexit alumnus,
21
Si vacat ac placidi rationem admittitis, edam.
26
Cum pars Niliacae plebis, cum verna Canopi
Crispinus Tyrias umero revocante lacernas
Ventilet aestivum digitis sudantibus aurum
Nec sufferre queat maioris pondera gemmae,
30
Difficile est saturam non scribere.

JUVENAL, *Sat.* i. 19-21, 26-30.

His Subject.

D.
Ex quo Deucalion, nimbis tollentibus aequor,

Navigio montem ascendit sortesque poposcit,
Paulatimque anima caluerunt mollia saxa,
85
Quidquid agunt homines, votum, timor, ira, voluptas,
Gaudia, discursus, nostri farrago libelli est.

JUVENAL, Sat. i. 81-86.

245

THE ROMAN SATIRISTS. (2)

Virtue defined.

A.

Virtus, Albine, est pretium persolvere verum
Quis in versamur, quis vivimus rebus potesse:
Virtus est homini scire id quo quaeque habeat res.
Virtus scire homini rectum, utile, quid sit honestum;
5
Quae bona, quae mala item, quid inutile, turpe, inhonestum;
Virtus quaerendae finem rei scire modumque:
Virtus divitiis pretium persolvere posse:
Virtus, id dare, quod re ipsa debetur, honori;
Hostem esse atque inimicum hominum morumque malorum,
10
Contra defensorem hominum morumque bonorum;
Hos magni facere, his bene velle, his vivere amicum;
Commoda praeterea patriai prima putare,
Deinde parentum, tertia iam postremaque nostra.

LUCILIUS, Sat. Frag.

'The names of men so poor

Who could do mighty deeds.'

B.

Cum tremerent autem Fabios durumque Catonem
91
Et Scauros et Fabricium rigidique severos
Censoris mores etiam collega timeret,
Nemo inter curas et seria duxit habendum
Qualis in Oceani fluctu testudo nataret
95
Clarum Troiugenis factura et nobile fulcrum,
Sed nudo latere et parvis frons aerea lectis
Vile coronati caput ostendebat aselli,
Ad quod lascivi ludebant ruris alumni.
Tales ergo cibi qualis domus atque supellex.

JUVENAL, Sat. xi. 90-99.

Persius in Praise of his Tutor, Cornutus.

C.

Cum primum pavido custos mihi purpura cessit
31
Bullaque succinctis Laribus donata pependit;
Cum blandi comites totaque inpune Subura
Permisit sparsisse oculos iam candidus umbo,
Cumque iter ambiguum est et vitae nescius error
35
Deducit trepidas ramosa in compita mentes,
Me tibi supposui. Teneros tu suscipis annos
Socratico, Cornute, sinu; tum fallere sollers
Apposita intortos extendit regula mores,
Et premitur ratione animus vincique laborat
40
Artificemque tuo ducit sub pollice vultum.

PERSIUS, Sat. v. 19-25, 30-40.

246

163

THE THEATRE.

Objections to a Permanent Theatre, *151 B.C.*

A.Cum locatum a censoribus theatrum exstrueretur, P. Cornelio Nasica auctore tamquam inutile et nociturum publicis moribus ex senatus consulto destructum est, populusque aliquamdiu stans ludos spectavit.

LIVY, Epit. 48.

Scenic Arrangements.

B.Apud maiores theatri gradus tantum fuerunt. Nam scena de lignotantum ad tempus fiebat, unde hodieque permansit consuetudo, ut componantur pegmata a ludorum theatralium editoribus. Scena autem, quae fiebat, aut versilis erat aut ductilis. Versilis tunc erat, cum subito tota machinis quibusdam convertebantur, et aliam picturae faciem ostendebat. Ductilis tunc, cum tractis tabulatis hac atque illac species picturae nudabatur interior. Unde perite utrumque tetigit, dicens, 'Versis discedat frontibus': singula singulis complectens sermonibus. Quod Varro et Suetonius commemorant.

SUET. ap. Serv. Georg. iii. 24.

The Awnings.

C.

Et vulgo faciunt id lutea russaque vela
76
Et ferrugina, cum magnis intenta theatris
Per malos volgata trabesque trementia flutant;
Namque ibi consessam caveai subter et omnem
Scaenai speciem, patrum coetumque decorum
80
Inficiunt coguntque suo fluitare colore.

LUCRETIUS, iv. 75-80.

The Law of Otho, *67 B.C.*

D.L. Roscius Otho tribunus plebis legem tulit, ut equitibus Romanis in theatro quattuordecim gradus proximi adsignarentur.

LIVY, Epit. 99.

Usurpers of Equestrian Privileges.

E.

'Sectus flagellis hic triumviralibus
12
Praeconis ad fastidium
Arat Falerni mille fundi iugera
Et Appiam mannis terit
Sedilibusque magnus in primis eques
16
Othone contempto sedet.'

HORACE, Epod. iv. 11-16.

247

SPINNING.

The Parcae spin the Web of Fate.

A.

Laeva colum molli lana retinebat amictum,
Dextera tum leviter deducens fila supinis
Formabat digitis, tum prono in pollice torquens
Libratum tereti versabat turbine fusum,
315
Atque ita decerpens aequabat semper opus dens,
Laneaque aridulis haerebant morsa labellis,
Quae prius in levi fuerant extantia filo:
Ante pedes autem candentis mollia lanae
Vellera virgati custodibant calathisci.
320
Haec tum clarisona pellentes vellera voce
Talia divino fuderunt carmine fata,

Carmine perfidiae quod post nulla arguet aetas.
'O decus eximium magnis virtutibus augens,
Emathiae tutamen opis, clarissime nato,
325
Accipe, quod laeta tibi pandunt luce sorores,
Veridicum oraclum—sed vos quae fata secuntur
Currite ducentes subtemina, currite fusi.'

CATULLUS, lxiv. 311-327.

The Skill of Arachne.

Her Contest with Pallas.

B.

Sive rudem primos lanam glomerabat in orbes,
20
Seu digitis subigebat opus repetitaque longo
Vellera mollibat nebulas aequantia tractu
Sive levi teretem versabat pollice fusum,
Seu pingebat acu scires a Pallade doctam.

.   .   .   .

53
Haud mora constituunt diversis partibus ambae
Et gracili geminas intendunt stamine telas.
55
Tela iugo vincta est, stamen secernit harundo,
Inseritur medium radiis subtemen acutis
Quod digiti expediunt, atque inter stamina ductum
Percusso paviunt insecti pectine dentes.
Utraque festinant cinctaeque ad pectora vestes
60
Bracchia docta movent, studio fallente laborem.

OVID, Met. vi. 19-23, 53-60.

The Pastime of Circe.

C.

Proxima Circaeae raduntur litora terrae
Dives inaccessos ubi Solis filia lucos
Assiduo resonat cantu, tectisque superbis
Urit odoratam nocturna in lumina cedrum,
Arguto tenues percurrens pectine telas.

VERG. Aen. vii. 10-14.

Cf. OVID, *Met.* iv. 220-229; *Fasti*, iii. 815-20.
248

ANDROMEDA. (1)

The Approach of the Monster.

A.

Andromedan poenas immitis iusserat Ammon.
Quam simul ad duras religatam bracchia cautes
Vidit Abantiades, nisi quod levis aura capillos
Moverat et tepido manabant lumina fletu,
675
Marmoreum ratus esset opus. Trahit inscius ignes
Et stupet et visae correptus imagine formae
Paene suas quatere est oblitus in aere pennas. . . .
706
Ecce velut navis praefixo concita rostro
Sulcat aquas, iuvenum sudantibus acta lacertis,
Sic fera dimotis inpulsu pectoris undis
Tantum aberat scopulis, quantum Balearica torto
710
Funda potest plumbo medii transmittere caeli;
Cum subito iuvenis pedibus tellure repulsa
Arduus in nubes abiit. Ut in aequore summo

165

Umbra viri visa est, visam fera saevit in umbram.
Utque Iovis praepes, vacuo cum vidit in arvo
715
Praebentem Phoebo liventia terga draconem,
Occupat aversum, neu saeva retorqueat ora,
Squamigeris avidos figit cervicibus ungues,
Sic celeri missus praeceps per inane volatu
Terga ferae pressit dextroque frementis in armo
720
Inachides ferrum curvo tenus abdidit hamo.

How Perseus won his Bride.

B.

Vulnere laesa gravi modo se sublimis in auras
Attollit, modo subdit aquis, modo more ferocis
Versat apri, quem turba canum circumsona terret.
Ille avidos morsus velocibus effugit alis;
725
Quaque patet, nunc terga cavis super obsita conchis,
Nunc laterum costas, nunc qua tenuissima cauda
Desinit in piscem, falcato vulnerat ense.
Belua puniceo mixtos cum sanguine fluctus
Ore vomit; maduere graves adspergine pennae.
730
Nec bibulis ultra Perseus talaribus ausus
Credere, conspexit scopulum, qui vertice summo
Stantibus extat aquis, operitur ab aequore moto.
Nixus eo rupisque tenens iuga prima sinistra
Ter quater exegit repetita per ilia ferrum.
735
Litora cum plausu clamor superasque deorum
Inplevere domos; gaudent generumque salutant
Auxiliumque domus servatoremque fatentur
Cassiope Cepheusque pater, resoluta catenis
Incedit virgo, pretiumque et causa laboris.

OVID, *Met.* iv. 671-677, 706-720, 721-739.

ANDROMEDA. (2)

'From afar, unknowing, I marked thee,

Shining, a snow-white cross on the dark-green walls of the sea-cliff.'—*KINGSLEY.*

A.

Tandem Gorgonei victorem Persea monstri
Felix illa dies redeuntem ad litora duxit.
Isque ubi pendentem vidit de rupe puellam,
570
Deriguit facie, quam non stupefecerat hostis;
Vixque manu spolium tenuit; victorque Medusae
Victus in Andromeda est. Iam cautibus invidet ipsis
Felicesque vocat, teneant quae membra, catenas.
Et postquam poenae causam cognovit ab ipsa,
575
Destinat in thalamos per bellum vadere ponti,
Altera si Gorgo veniat, non territus ira.
Concitat aerios cursus flentesque parentes
Promissu vitae recreat pactusque maritam
Ad litus remeat. Gravidus nam surgere pontus
580
Coeperat, et longo fugiebant agmine fluctus
Impellentis onus monstri. Caput eminet undis
Scindentis pelagusque movet. Circumsonat aequor
Dentibus, inque ipso rapidum mare navigat ore.

The Death of the Monster.

B.

Illa* subit contra versoque a gurgite frontem
596
Erigit et tortis innitens orbibus alte
Emicat ac toto sublimis corpore fertur.
Sed quantum illa subit semet iaculata profundo,
In tantum revolat laxumque per aethera ludit
600
Perseus et ceti subeuntis verberat ora.
Nec cedit tamen illa viro, sed saevit in auras
Morsibus, et vani crepitant sine vulnere dentes;
Efflat et in caelum pelagus mergitque volantem
Sanguineis undis pontumque extollit in astra.
605
Spectabat pugnam pugnandi causa puella;
Iamque oblita sui, metuit pro vindice tali
Suspirans, animoque magis quam corpore pendet.
Tandem confossis subsedit belua membris
Plena maris summasque iterum remeavit ad undas
610
Et magnum vasto contexit corpore pontum,
Tunc quoque terribilis nec virginis ore videnda.
Perfundit liquido Perseus in marmore corpus
Maior et ex undis ad cautes pervolat alto
Solvitque haerentem vinclis de rupe puellam
615
Desponsam pugna, nupturam dote mariti.

MANILIUS, *Astronomica*, v. 667-583, 595-615.

* *illa* = *belua*.
250

SCHOOLS.

The School of Flavius, at Venusia.

A.

Causa fuit pater his, qui macro pauper agello
Noluit in Flavi ludum me mittere, magni
Quo pueri magnis e centurionibus orti,
Laevo suspensi loculos tabulamque lacerto,
75
Ibant octonos refererentes Idibus aeris.

HOR. *Sat.* I. vi. 71-75.

Ovid and his Brother educated at Rome.

B.

Protinus excolimur teneri, curaque parentis
Imus ad insignes Urbis ab arte viros.
Frater ad eloquium viridi tendebat ab aevo,
Fortia verbosi natus ad arma fori.
At mihi iam puero caelestia sacra placebant,
20
Inque suum furtim Musa trahebat opus.

OVID, *Tristia*, IV. x. 15-20.

The Schoolmaster's life a hard one.

C.

Dummodo non pereat, mediae quod noctis ab hora
Sedisti, qua nemo faber, qua nemo sederet,
Qui docet obliquo lanam deducere ferro;
225
Dummodo non pereat, totidem olfecisse lucernas,
Quot stabant pueri, cum totus decolor esset
Flaccus, et haereret nigro fuligo Maroni.

Early School.

D.

Surgite: iam vendit pueris ientacula pistor,
Cristataeque sonant undique lucis aves.

MARTIAL, XIV. ccxxiii.

Homogeneous Divisions.

E. Non inutilem scio servatum esse a praeceptoribus meis morem, qui, cum pueros in classes distribuerent, ordinem discendi secundum vires ingeni dabant.

QUINTIL. I. ii. 23.

Plagosus Orbilius.

F.

Quid tibi nobiscum est, ludi scelerate magister,
Invisum pueris virginibusque caput?
Nondum cristati rupere silentia galli:
Murmure iam saevo verberibusque tonas.

MARTIAL, IX. lxviii. 1-4.

Cf. JUV. x. 114-7; MARTIAL, X. lxii.; HOR. *Ep.* II. i. 69-71.
251

BOOKS.

A.

Parve (nec invideo) sine me, liber, ibis in urbem:
Ei mihi, quod domino non licet ire tuo.
Vade, sed incultus, qualem decet exsulis esse:
4
Infelix habitum temporis huius habe.
Nec te purpureo velent vaccinia fuco:
Non est conveniens luctibus ille color:
Nec titulus minio nec cedro charta notetur,
8
Candida nec nigra cornua fronte geras.
Felices ornent haec instrumenta libellos:
Fortunae memorem te decet esse meae.
Nec fragili geminae poliantur pumice frontes,
12
Hirsutus sparsis ut videare comis.
Neve liturarum pudeat. Qui viderit illas
De lacrimis factas sentiat esse meis.
Vade, liber, verbisque meis loca grata saluta:
16
Contingam certe quo licet illa pede.

OVID, Trist. I. i. 1-16.

B.

Lutea sed niveum involvat membrana libellum,
Pumex et canas tondeat ante comas
Summaque praetexat tenuis fastigia chartae
12
Indicet ut nomen littera facta meum,
Atque inter geminas pingantur cornua frontes:
Sic etenim comptum mittere oportet opus.

TIBULLUS, III. i. 9-14.

C.

Qui tecum cupis esse meos ubicumque libellos
Et comites longae quaeris habere viae,
Hos eme, quos artat brevibus membrana tabellis:
4
Scrinia da magnis, me manus una capit.
Ne tamen ignores ubi sim venalis et erres
Urbe vagus tota, me duce certus eris:
Libertum docti Lucensis quaere Secundum

8
Limina post Pacis Palladiumque forum.

MARTIAL, I. ii.

Cf. HOR. *Epist.* I. xx.; CATULL. xxii, 4-8; STATIUS, *Silvae*, IV. ix.
252

ARETHUSA.

'As an eagle pursuing

A dove to its ruin

Down the streams of the cloudy wind.' —*SHELLEY.*

A.
Lassa revertebar (memini) Stymphalide silva;
586
Aestus erat, magnumque labor geminaverat aestum.
Invenio sine vertice aquas, sine murmure euntes,
Perspicuas ad humum, per quas numerabilis alte
589
Calculus omnis erat, quas tu vix ire putares. . . .
597
Nescioquod medio sensi sub gurgite murmur
Territaque insisto propioris margine fontis.
'Quo properas Arethusa?' suis Alpheos ab undis,
600
'Quo properas?' iterum rauco mihi dixerat ore. . . .
604
Sic ego currebam, sic me ferus ille premebat,
Ut fugere accipitrem penna trepidante columbae,
Ut solet accipiter trepidas urguere columbas.
Usque sub Orchomenon Psophidaque Cyllenenque
Maenaliosque sinus gelidumque Erymanthon et Elin
Currere sustinui; nec me velocior ille.
610
Sed tolerare diu cursus ego, viribus inpar,
Non poteram; longi patiens erat ille laboris.
Per tamen et campos, per opertos arbore montes,
Saxa quoque et rupes et qua via nulla, cucurri.

'Alpheum fama est huc Elidis amnem

Occultas egisse vias subter mare, qui nunc

Ore, Arethusa, tuo Siculis confunditur undis.' —*VERGIL.*

B.
Sol erat a tergo: vidi praecedere longam
615
Ante pedes umbram, nisi si timor illa videbat,
Sed certe sonitusque pedum terrebat et ingens
Crinales vittas afflabat anhelitus oris.
Fessa labore fugae 'fer opem, deprendimur,' inquam,
'Armigerae, Diana, tuae, cui saepe dedisti
620
Ferre tuos arcus inclusaque tela pharetra.'
Mota dea est spississque ferens e nubibus unam
Me super iniecit. lustrat caligine tectam
Amnis et ignarus circum cava nubila quaerit.
Bisque locum, quo me dea texerat, inscius ambit
625
Et bis 'io Arethusa, io Arethusa' vocavit. . . .
636
In latices mutor, sed enim cognoscit amatas
Amnis aquas, positoque viri, quod sumpserat, ore
Vertitur in proprias, ut se mihi misceat, undas.

Delia rupit humum, caecisque ego mersa cavernis
640
Advehor Ortygiam, quae me cognomine divae
Grata meae superas eduxit prima sub auras.

OVID, *Met.* v. 586-641 (sel.).

253

HYLAS

Οὕτω μὲν κάλλιστος Ὕλας μακάρων ἀριθμεῖται.

A.

Namque ferunt olim Pagasae navalibus Argon
Egressam longe Phasidis isse viam,
Et iam praeteritis labentem Athamantidos undis
20
Mysorum scopulis applicuisse ratem.
Hic manus heroum, placidis ut constitit oris,
Mollia composita litora fronde tegit.
At comes invicti iuvenis processerat ultra,
24
Sacram sepositi quaerere fontis aquam.
25
Hanc circum irriguo surgebant lilia prato
Candida purpureis mixta papaveribus.
Quae modo decerpens tenero pueriliter ungui
40
Proposito florem praetulit officio,
Ex modo formosis incumbens nescius undis
Errorem blandis tardat imaginibus.
Tandem haurire parat demissis flumina palmis
44
Innixus dextro plena trahens umero.
Cuius ut accensae Hydriades candore puellae
Miratae solitos destituere choros.
Prolapsum leviter facili traxere liquore:
48
Tum sonitum rapto corpore fecit Hylas.

PROPERTIUS, I. xx. 17-24, 37-48.

Litus 'Hyla Hyla' omne sonabat.

B.

Continuo, volucri ceu pectora tactus asilo
Emicuit Calabria taurus per confraga saeptis
Obvia quaque ruens, tali se concitat ardens
In iuga senta fuga: pavet omnis conscia late
585
Silva, pavent montes, luctu succensus acerbo
Quid struat Alcides tantaque quid apparet ira.
Ille, velut refugi quem contigit improba Mauri
Lancea sanguineus vasto leo murmure fertur,
Frangit et absentem vacuis sub dentibus hostem,
590
Sic furiis accensa gerens Tirynthius ora
Fertur et intento decurrit montibus arcu.
Heu miserae quibus ille ferae, quibus incidit usquam
Immeritis per lustra viris! volat ordine nullo
Cuncta petens; nunc ad ripas deiectaque saxis
595
Flumina, nunc notas nemorum procurrit ad umbras.
Rursus Hylan et rursus Hylan per longa reclamat
Avia: responsant silvae et vaga certat imago.

VALERIUS FLACCUS, *Argonautica*, iii. 581-597.

Cf. APOLLONIUS RHODIUS, *Argonautica*, i. 1224-1239.

254

170

PLAUTUS.

The Portmanteau Fish.

(TRACHALIO—GRIPUS.)

TR.

                        Quid ais, impudens?
Ausu's etiam comparare vidulum cum piscibus?
Eadem tandem res videtur? GR. In manu non est mea:
Ubi demisi rete atque hamum, quidquid haesit extraho
5
Meum quod rete atque bami nancti sunt, meum potissimumst.
TR.
Immo hercle haud est, siquidem quod vas excepisti.
GR.

                                   Philosophe!
TR.
Sed tu, enunquam piscatorem vidisti, venefice,
Vidulum piscem cepisse aut protulisse ullum in forum?
Non enim tu hic quidem occupabis omnes quaestus quos voles:
10
Et vitorem et piscatorem te esse, impure, postulas.
Vel te mihi monstrare oportet piscis qui sit vidulus:
Vel quod in mari non natumst neque habet squamas ne feras.
GR.
Quid tu? nunquam audisti antehac vidulum esse piscem?TR. Scelus,
Nullus est. GR. Immost profecto: ego qui sum piscator scio.
15
Verum rare capitur: nullus minus saepe ad terram venit.
TR.
Nil agis: dare verba speras mihi te posse, furcifer.
Quo colorest? GR. Hoc colore capiuntur pauxilluli:
Sunt alii puniceo corio, magni autem, atque atri.
TR.

                                     Scio:
Tu hercle, opino, in vidulum piscem te convortes, nisi caves:
20
Fiet tibi puniceum corium, postea atrum denuo.

                                     Rudens, IV. iii. 58-77.

255

TERENCE.

'Humani nil a me alienum puto.'

(CHREMES—MENEDEMUS.)

A.

CH.
Numquam tam mane egredior neque tam vesperi
Domum revortor, quin te in fundo conspicer
Fodere aut arare aut aliquid ferre. Denique
Nullum remittis tempus neque te respicis.
5
Haec non voluptati tibi esse satis certo scio.
'Enim,' dices, 'quantum hic operis fiat poenitet.'
Quod in opere faciundo operae consumis tuae,
Si sumas in illis exercendis, plus agas.
ME.
Chremes, tantumne ab re tuast oti tibi,
10
Aliena ut cures ea quae nil ad te attinent?
CH.
Homo sum: humani nil a me alienum puto.
Vel me monere hoc vel percontari puta:
Rectumst, ego ut faciam; non est, te ut deterream.
ME.

171

Mihi sic est usus: tibi ut opus factost, face.
CH.
An quoiquamst usus homini, se ut cruciet?
ME.

                                 Mihi.

CH.
Siquid laborist, nollem: sed quid istuc malist?
Quaeso, quid de te tantum commeruisti?
ME.

                                 Eheu.

CH.
Ne lacruma, atque istuc, quidquid est, fac me ut sciam;
Ne retice, ne verere, crede inquam mihi:
20
Aut consolando aut consilio aut re iuvero.

Hautont. I. i. 15-34.

Cicero on Terence.
B.
'Tu quoque, qui solus lecto sermone, Terenti,
Conversum expressumque Latina voce Menandrum
In medium nobis sedatis vocibus effers,
Quiddam come loquens, atque omnia dulcia miscens.'

SUETON. *Vit. Ter.* p. 34.

Terence defends his use of 'Contaminatio.'*
C.
Nam quod rumores distulerunt malivoli
Multas contaminasse Graecas, dum facit
Paucas Latinas: factum id esse hic non negat,
Neque se pigere et deinde facturum autumat.
20
Habet bonorum exemplum, quo exemplo sibi
Licere id facere quod illi fecerunt putat.

Hautont. Prol. 16-21.

    * *Contaminatio* = the *blending* of the parts of different comedies into one whole—e.g.
the *Andria* of Terence, an adaptation of Menander's *Andria* and *Perinthia.*
256

PLINY THE ELDER.
The Song of the Nightingale.
    A.Lusciniis diebus ac noctibus continuis xv garrulus sine intermissu cantus densante se
frondium germine, non in novissimum digna miratu ave. Primum tanta vox tam parvo in
corpusculo, tam pertinax spiritus; deinde in una perfecta musica scientia: modulatus editur sonus,
et nunc continuo spiritu trahitur in longum, nunc variatur inflexo, nunc distinguitur conciso,
copulatur intorto, promittitur revocato, infuscatur ex inopinato interdum et secum ipse
murmurat, plenus, gravis, acutus, creber, extentus, ubi visum est, vibrans, summus, medius, imus;
breviterque omnia tam parvulis in faucibus quae tot exquisitis tibiarum tormentis ars hominum
excogitavit, ut non sit dubium hanc suavitatem praemonstratam efficaci auspicio, cum in ore
Stesichori cecinit infantis. Ac ne quis dubitet artis esse, plures singulis sunt cantus, nec iidem
omnibus, sed sui cuique. Certant inter se, palamque animosa contentio est: victa morte finit saepe
vitam, spiritu prius deficiente quam captu. Meditantur iuveniores versusque quos imitentur
accipiunt: audit discipula intentione magna et reddit vicibusque reticent; intelligitur emendatae
correptio et in docente quaedam reprehensio.

Hist. Nat. x. 81.

PLINY THE YOUNGER.
A Corinthian Statuette.
    B.Ex hereditate, quae mihi obvenit, emi proxime Corinthium signum, modicum quidem,
sed festivum et expressum, quantum ego sapio, qui fortasse in omni re, in hac certe perquam
exiguum sapio: hoc tamen signum ego quoque intellego. Est enim nudum, nec aut vitia, si qua
sunt, celat, aut laudes parum ostentat. Effingit senem stantem: ossa, musculi, nervi, venae, rugae
etiam ut spirantis apparent: rari et cedentes capilli, lata frons, contracta facies, exile collum. Aes
ipsum, quantum verus color indicat, vetus et antiquum. Talia denique omnia, ut possint artificum

oculos tenere, delectare imperitorum. Quod me, quamquam tirunculum, solicitavit ad emendum. Emi autem, non at haberem domi, verum ut in patria nostri celebri loco ponerem; ac potissimum in Iovis templo. Videtur enim dignum templo, dignum deo donum.

Ep. iii. 6.

METHODS OF WORK.

Helps to Style.

A.Quaeris, quemadmodum in secessu, quo iam diu frueris, putem te studere oportere. Utile in primis, et multi praecipiunt, vel ex Graeco in Latinum, vel ex Latino vertere in Graecum: quo genere exercitationis proprietas splendorque verborum, copia figurarum, vis explicandi, praeterea imitatione optimorum similia inveniendi facultas paratur; simul quae legentem fefellissent transferentem fugere non possunt. Intelligentia ex hoc et iudicium adquiritur. Nihil obfuerit, quae legeris hactenus, ut rem argumentumque teneas, quasi aemulum scribere lectisque conferre, ac sedulo pensitare quid tu, quid ille commodius. Magna gratulatio, si non nulla tu; magnus pudor, si cuncta ille melius. Licebit interdum et notissima eligere, et certare cum electis. Poteris et, quae dixeris, post oblivionem retractare, multa retinere, plura transire, alia interscribere, alia rescribere. Laboriosum istud et taedio plenum sed difficultate ipsa fructuosum, recalescere ex integro, et resumere impetum fractum omissumque, postremo nova velut membra peracto corpori intexere, nec tamen priora turbare. Fas est et carmine remitti, non dico continuo et longo (id enim perfici nisi in otio non potest), sed hoc arguto et brevi, quod apte quantaslibet occupationes curasque distinguit.

PLINY THE YOUNGER, Ep. vii. 9 (sel.)

Importance of Concentration.

B.Sed silentium et secessus et undique liber animus ut sunt maxime optanda, ita non semper possunt contingere, ideoque non statim, si quid obstrepet, abiciendi codices erunt et deplorandus dies, verum incommodis repugnandum et hic faciendus usus, ut omnia quae impedient vincat intentio: quam si tota mente in opus ipsum direxeris, nihil eorum, quae oculis vel auribus incursant, ad animum perveniet. An vero frequenter etiam fortuita hoc cogitatio praestat, ut obvios non videamus et itinere deerremus; non consequemur, si et voluerimus? Non est indulgendum causis desidiae. Nam si nonnisi refecti, nonnisi hilares, nonnisi omnibus aliis curis vacantes studendum existimaverimus, semper erit propter quod nobis ignoscamus.

QUINTILIAN, Inst. Or. X. iii. 28.

258

PHAEDRUS.

De Simonide.

A.
Homo doctus in se semper divitias habet.
Simonides, qui scripsit egregium melos,
Quo paupertatem sustineret facilius,
Circum ire coepit urbes Asiae nobiles,
5
Mercede accepta laudem victorum canens.
Hoc genere quaestus postquam locuples factus est,
Revenire in patriam voluit cursu pelagio;
Erat autem, ut aiunt, natus in Chia insula.
Ascendit navem, quam tempestas horrida
10
Simul et vetustas medio dissolvit mari.
Hi zonas, illi res pretiosas colligunt,
Subsidium vitae. Quidam curiosior:
'Simonide, tu ex opibus nil sumis tuis?'
'Mecum,' inquit, 'mea sunt cuncta.'* Tunc pauci enatant,
15
Quia plures onere degravati perierant.
Praedones adsunt, rapiunt quod quisque extulit,
Nudos relinquunt. Forte Clazomenae prope
Antiqua fuit urbs; quam petierunt naufragi.
Hic litterarum quidam studio deditus,
20
Simondis qui saepe versus legerat

173

Eratque absentis admirator maximus,
Sermone ab ipso cognitum cupidissime
Ad se recepit; veste, nummis, familia
Hominem exornavit. Ceteri tabulam suam
25
Portant rogantes victum. Quos casu obvios
Simonides ut vidit, 'Dixi' inquit 'mea
Mecum esse cuncta: vos quod habuistis, perit.'

iv. 23.

* Cf. 'Omnia bona mea mecum sunt.'—SENECA, *Ep.* 9.

Mons Parturiens.
B.
Mons parturibat, gemitus immanes ciens,
Eratque in terris maxima expectatio.
At ille murem peperit. Hoc scriptum est tibi,
Qui, magna cum minaris, extricas nihil.

iv. 24.

Nihil ita occultum esse quod non reveletur.
C.
Pastor capellae cornu baculo fregerat:
Rogare coepit, ne se domino proderet . . .
'Quamvis indigne laesa, reticebo tamen;
Sed res clamabit ipsa quid deliqueris.'

Appendix, 22.

259

TIBULLUS.

The Golden Age.
A.
Quam bene Saturno vivebant rege, priusquam
36
Tellus in longas est patefacta vias!
Nondum caeruleas pinus contempserat undas,
Effusum ventis praebueratque sinum,
Nec vagus ignotis repetens compendia terris
40
Presserat externa navita merce ratem.
Illo non validus subiit iuga tempore taurus,
Non domito frenos ore momordit equus,
Non domus ulla fores habuit, non fixus in agris
44
Qui regeret certis finibus arva, lapis.
Ipsae mella dabant quercus, ultroque ferebant
Obvia securis ubera lactis oves.
Non acies, non ira fuit, non bella, nec ensem
48
Immiti saevus duxerat arte faber.
Nunc Iove sub domino caedes et vulnera semper,
Nunc mare, nunc leti mille repente viae.

I. iii. 35-50.

Cf. CATULLUS, lxiv.; VERGIL, *Ecl.* iv.

Birthday Wishes.
B.
Dicamus bona verba: venit natalis ad aras:
Quisquis ades, lingua, vir mulierque fave.
Urantur pia tura focis, urantur odores,
4
Quos tener e terra divite mittit Arabs.
Ipse suos Genius adsit visurus honores,
Cui decorent sanctas mollia serta comas.
Illius puro destillent tempora nardo,

174

8
Atque satur libo sit madeatque mero,
Adnuat et, Cornute, tibi quodcumque rogabis.
En age, quid cessas? adnuit ille: roga.
Auguror, uxoris fidos optabis amores;
12
Iam reor hoc ipsos edidicisse deos.
Nec tibi malueris, totum quaecumque per orbem
Fortis arat valido rusticus arva bove,
Nec tibi, gemmarum quidquid felicibus Indis
16
Nascitur, Eoi qua maris unda rubet.
Vota cadunt: utinam strepitantibus advolet alis
Flavaque coniugio vincula portet Amor,
Vincula, quae maneant semper, dum tarda senectus
20
Inducat rugas inficiatque comas.
Hic veniat natalis avis prolemque ministret,
Ludat et ante tuos turba novella pedes.

II. ii.

Cf. TIBULL. I. vii. 49-54; PERSIUS, ii. 1-4.
260

HUNTING.

On the delights of hunting with a note-book.

A.Ridebis, et licet rideas. Ego ille, quem nosti apros tres, et quidem pulcherrimos, cepi. Ipse? inquis. Ipse; non tamen ut omnino ab inertia mea et quiete discederem. Ad retia sedebam: erat in proximo, non venabulum aut lancea, sed stilus et pugillares. Meditabar aliquid enotabamque, ut, si manus vacuas, plenas tamen ceras reportarem. Non est, quod contemnas hoc studendi genus. Mirum est ut animus agitatione motuque corporis excitetur. Iam undique silvae et solitudo, ipsumque illud silentium, quod venationi datur, magna cogitationis incitamenta sunt. Proinde cum venabere, licebit auctore me ut panarium et lagunculam sic etiam pugillares feras. Experieris non Dianam magis montibus, quam Minervam inerrare. Vale.

PLINY, Ep. i. 6.

Oenone Paridi.

B.
Quis tibi monstrabat saltus venatibus aptos
Et tegeret catulos qua fera rupe suos?
Retia saepe comes maculis distincta tetendi;
Saepi cites egi per iuga longa canes.

OVID, Her. v. 17-20.

The Hunting Party.

C.
Oceanum interea surgens Aurora reliquit.
130
It portis iubare exorto delecta iuventus;
Retia rara, plagae, lato venabula ferro,
Massylique ruunt equites et odora canum vis.
Reginam thalamo cunctantem ad limina primi
Poenorum exspectant, ostroque insignis et auro
135
Stat sonipes ac frena ferox spumantia mandit.
.   .   .   .
151
Postquam altos ventum in montes atque invia lustra
Ecce ferae, saxi deiectae vertice, caprae
Decurrere iugis; alia de parte patentes
Transmittunt cursu campos atque agmina cervi
155
Pulverulenta fuga glomerant montisque relinquunt.
At puer Ascanius mediis in vallibus acri

175

Gaudet equo, iamque hos cursu, iam praeterit illos
Spumantemque dari pecora inter inertia votis
Optat aprum aut fulvum descendere monte leonem.

VERG. Aen. iv. 129-135, 151-159.

261

ROMAN DAY.

Its Duties and Amusements.

A.

Prima salutantes atque altera conterit hora;
Exercet raucos tertia causidicos;
In quintam varies extendit Roma labores;
4
Sexta quies lassis; septima finis erit;
Sufficit in nonam nitidis octava palaestris;
Imperat exstructos frangere nona toros;
Hora libellorum decima est, Eupheme, meorum,
8
Temperat ambrosias cum tua cura dapes
Et bonus aetherio laxatur nectare Caesar
Ingentique tenet pocula parca manu.
Tunc admitte iocos: gressu timet ire licenti
12
Ad matutinum nostra Thalia Iovem.

MARTIAL, IV. viii.

The Simple Life.

How Horace spent his day.

B.110

Hoc ego commodius quam tu praeclare senator,
Milibus atque aliis vivo. Quacunque libido est
Incedo solus, percontor quanti holus ac far,
Fallacem circum vespertinumque pererro
Saepe forum, adsisto divinis. Inde domum me
115
Ad porri et ciceris refero laganique catinum;
Cena ministratur pueris tribus, et lapis albus
Pocula cum cyatho duo sustinet, astat echinus
Vilis, cum patera guttus, Campana supellex.
Deinde eo dormitum, non sollicitus, mihi quod cras
120
Surgendum sit mane, obeundus Marsya, qui se
Voltum ferre negat Noviorum posse minoris.
Ad quartam iaceo; post hanc vagor, aut ego, lecto
Aut scripto quod me tacitum iuvet, unguor olivo,
Non quo fraudatis immundus Natta lucernis.
125
Ast ubi me fessum sol acrior ire lavatum
Admonuit, fugio campum lusumque trigonem.
Pransus non avide quantum interpellet inani
Ventre diem durare, domesticus otior. Haec est
Vita solutorum misera ambitione gravique.
130
His me consolor victurum suavius, ac si
Quaestor avus pater atque meus patruusque fuisset.

HORACE, Sat. I. vi. 110-131.

Cf. Cic. <i>ad Fam.</i> ix. 20; Lucr. ii. 14-33; Verg. <i>Georg.</i> ii. 458-474; Hor. <i>Od.</i> III, i.
262

TACITUS.

'Lives of great men all remind us,

We can make our lives sublime.'

A.Si quis piorum manibus locus, si, ut sapientibus placet, non cum corpore extinguuntur magnae animae, placide quiescas, nosque domum tuam ab inferno desiderio et muliebribus lamentis ad contemplationem virtutum tuarum voces, quas neque lugeri neque plangi fas est. Admiratione te potius et immortalibus laudibus et, si natura suppeditet, similitudine colamus: is verus honos, ea coniunctissimi cuiusque pietas. Id filiae quoque uxorique praeceperim, sic patris, sic mariti memoriam venerari, ut omnia facta dictaque eius secum revolvant, formamque ac figuram animi magis quam corporis complectantur, non quia intercedendum putem imaginibus quae marmore aut aere finguntur, sed, ut vultus hominum, ita simulacra vultus imbecilla ac mortalia sunt, forma mentis aeterna, quam tenere et exprimere non per alienam materiam et artem, sed tuis ipse moribus possis. Quidquid ex Agricola amavimus, quidquid mirati sumus, manet mansurumque est in animis hominum, in aeternitate temporum, in fama rerum; nam multos veterum velut inglorios et ignobilis oblivio obruet: Agricola posteritati narratus et traditus superstes erit.

Agricola 46.

The Climate and Products of Britain.

B.Caelum crebris imbribus ac nebulis foedum; asperitas frigorum abest. Dierum spatia ultra nostri orbis mensuram; nox clara et extrema Britanniae parte brevis, ut finem atque initium lucis exiguo discrimine internoscas. Quod si nubes non officiunt, aspici per noctem solis fulgorem, nec occidere et exsurgere, sed transire affirmant. Scilicet extrema et plana terrarum humili umbra non erigunt tenebras, infraque caelum et sidera nox cadit. Solum praeter oleam vitemque et cetera calidioribus terris oriri sueta patiens frugum, fecundum: tarde mitescunt, cito proveniunt; eademque utriusque rei causa, multus umor terrarum caelique. Fert Britannia aurum et argentum et alia metalla, pretium victoriae. Gignit et oceanus margarita, sed subfusca ac liventia.

Agricola 12.

263

TRIMALCHIO'S SUPPER.

Le Bourgeois Gentilhomme.

An Ignorant Connoisseur.

A.Plausum post hoc automatum familia dedit, et 'Gaio feliciter!' conclamavit: nec non cocus potione oneratus est, et argentea corona poculumque in lance accepit Corinthia. Quam cum Agamemnon propius consideraret, ait Trimalchio: 'Solus sum, qui vera Corinthea habeam.' Exspectabam, ut pro reliqua insolentia diceret sibi vasa Corintho afferri. Sed ille melius: 'Et forsitan,' inquit, 'quaeris, quare solus Corinthea vera possideam? Quia scilicet aerarius, a quo emo, Corinthus vocatur; quid est autem Corintheum, nisi quis Corinthum habeat? Et ne me putetis nesapium esse, valde bene scio, unde primum Corinthea nata sint. Cum Ilium captum est, Hannibal, homo vafer, et magnus stelio, omnes statuas aeneas, et aureas, et argenteas in unum rogum congessit, et eas incendit; factae sunt in unum aera miscellanea. Ita ex hac massa fabri sustulerunt, et fecerunt catilla et paropsides et statuncula. Sic Corinthea nata sunt, ex omnibus in unum, nec hoc, nec illud.'

PETRONIUS ARBITER, 50.

The Glass Bowl, and its Maker.

B.'Ignoscetis mihi,' inquit Trimalchio, 'quod dixero: ego malo mihi vitrea; certe non olunt. Quod si non frangerentur, mallem mihi, quam aurum; nunc autem vilia sunt. Fuit tamen faber, qui fecit phialam vitream, quae non frangebatur. Admissus ergo Caesarem est cum suo munere; deinde fecit se porrigere Caesari, et illam in pavimentum proiecit. Caesar non pote validius, quam expavit. At ille sustulit phialam de terra: collisa erat, tanquam vasum aeneum. Deinde marceolum de sinu protulit, et phialam otio belle correxit. Hoc facto putabat se solium Iovis tenere, utique, postquam illi dixit: "Numquid alius scit hanc condituram vitreorum?" Vide modo. Postquam negavit, iussit illum Caesar decollari; quia enim, si scitum esset, aurum pro luto haberemus.'

PETRONIUS ARBITER, 51.

264

177

PRONUNCIATION.*

H.

I. Diu deinde servatum ne consonantibus (veteres) adspirarent, ut in *Graecis* et in *triumpis.* Erupit brevi tempore nimius usus, ut *choronae, chenturiones, praechones* adhuc quibusdam in inscriptionibus maneant, qua de re Catulli nobile epigramma est.

QUINT. i. 5. 20.

> Chommoda dicebat, si quando commoda vellet
> Dicere, et insidias Arrius *h*insidias,
> Et tum mirifice sperabat se esse locutum,
> Cum quantum poterat dixerat *h*insidias.
> Credo, sic mater, sic liber avonculus eius,
> Sic maternus avos dixerat atque avia.
> Hoc misso in Syriam requierant omnibus aures:
> Audibant eadem haec leviter et leviter,
> Nec sibi postilla metuebant talia verba,
> Cum subito adfertur nuntius horribilis,
> Ionios fluctus, postquam illuc Arrius isset,
> Iam non Ionios esse, sed *H*ionios.

CATULLUS, lxxxiv.

* For further information see Dr. Postgate's *How to pronounce Latin* (Bell & Sons).

A Street Cry.

II. Cum M. Crassus exercitum Brundisii imponeret, quidam in portu, caricas Cauno advectas vendens, *Cauneas!* clamitabat. Dicamus, si placet, monitum ab eo Crassum, caveret, ne iret (*cau[e] n[e] eas = do not go*): non fuisse periturum, si omini paruisset. Quae si suscipiamus, pedis offensio nobis et abruptio corrigiae et sternutamenta erunt observanda.

CICERO, *Div.* ii. 40. 84.

K. Q. C.

III.

> **K** perspicuum est littera quod vacare possit;
> Et **Q**, similis, namque eadem vis in utraque est;
> Quia qui locus est primitus unde exoritur **C**,
> Quascunque deinceps libeat iugare voces,
> Mutare necesse est sonitum quidem supremum,
> Refert nihilum, **K** prior an **Q** siet an **C**.

TERENTIANUS MAURUS (*circ.* 300 A.D.).

U.

IV.

ME. Egon' dedi?

PE.   Tu tu, istic, inquam! Vin' adferri noctuam

Quae *tu tu* usque dicat tibi? Nam nos iam defessi sumus.

PLAUTUS, *Men.* 553-6.

265

PROVERBIAL EXPRESSIONS.

I. Nam quae volumus et credimus libenter.

CAES. *B. Civ.* ii. 27.

II. Cuiusvis hominis est errare; nullius nisi insipientis in errore perseverare. Posteriores enim cogitationes, ut aiunt, sapientiores solent esse.

CIC. *Phil.* xii. 5.

III. Dimidium facti qui coepit habet.

HOR. *Ep.* I. ii. 40.

IV. Nemo repente fuit turpissimus.

JUV. *Sat.* ii. 83.

V. Velut materiam igni praebentes.

LIVY, xxi. 10.

VI. Et quasi cursores vitai lampada tradunt.

LUCR. ii. 79.

VII.

Non amo te, Sabidi, nec possum dicere quare:
Hoc tantum possum dicere, non amo te.

MARTIAL, *Ep.* I. xxxii.

VIII.

quem di diligunt
Adulescens moritur.

PLAUT. *Bacch.* I. ii. 36.

IX. Nullumst iam dictum, quod non sit dictum prius.

TERENCE, *Eun. Prol.* 41.

X.Quot homines tot sententiae: suus cuique mos.

TER. *Phormio*, II. iv. 14.

XI. Stultum facit fortuna, quem vult pedere.

PUB. SYRUS.

XII.

Vita brevis est, longa ars.
Vita, si scias uti, longa est.

SEN. *de Brevit. vitae*, i. 2.

XIII. Omne ignotum pro magnifico.

TAC. *Agric.* 30.

XIV. Divina natura dedit agros, ars humana aedificavit urbes.

VARRO, *de Re Rust.* iii. 1.

XV.

Tu ne cede malis, sed contra audentior ito
Quam tua te Fortuna sinet.

VERG. *Aen.* vi. 95.

XVI.

. . . . Sunt hic etiam sua praemia laudi;
Sunt lacrimae rerum, et mentem mortalia tangunt.

VERG. *Aen.* i. 461-2.

266

CONSOLATIO.

'Whom the gods love die young.'

A.Una post haec Quintiliani mei spe ac voluptate nitebar: at poterat sufficere solatio. Non enim flosculos, sicut prior, sed iam decimum aetatis ingressus annum, certos ac deformatos fructus ostenderat. Iuro per mala mea, per infelicem conscientiam, per illos manes, numina mei doloris, has me in illo vidisse virtutes ingeni, non modo ad percipiendas disciplinas, quo nihil praestantius cognovi plurima expertus studiique iam tum non coacti (sciunt praeceptores), sed probitatis, pietatis, humanitatis, liberalitatis, ut prorsus posset hinc esse tanti fulminis metus, quod observatum fere est, celerius occidere festinatam maturitatem: et esse nescio quam quae spes tantas decerpat invidiam, ne videlicet ultra, quam homini datum est, nostra provehantur. Etiam illa fortuita aderant omnia, vocis iucunditas claritasque, oris suavitas, et in utracumque lingua, tanquam ad eam demum natus esset, expressa proprietas omnium litterarum. Sed haec spes adhuc: illa maiora, constantia, gravitas, contra dolores etiam ac metus robur. Nam quo ille animo, qua medicorum admiratione, mensium octo valetudinem tulit! ut me in supremis consolatus est! quam etiam deficiens, iamque *non *noster*, ipsum illum alienatae mentis errorem circa solas literas habuit!

QUINTILIAN, *Inst. Or.* VI. i. 9.

* Cf. 'Invalidasque tibi tendens, heu *non tua*, palmas.'—VERG. *G.* iv. 498.

Servius Sulpicius to Cicero.

B.Quae res mihi non mediocrem consolationem attulerit, volo tibi commemorare, si forte eadem res tibi dolorem minuere possit. *Ex Asia rediens, cum ab Aegina Megaram versus navigarem, coepi regiones circumcirca prospicere. Post me erat Aegina, ante me Megara, dextra Piraeeus, sinistra Corinthus: quae oppida quodam tempore florentissima fuerunt, nunc prostrata et diruta ante oculos iacent. Coepi egomet mecum sic cogitare: 'Hem! nos homunculi indignamur, si quis nostrum interiit aut occisus est, quorum vita brevior esse debet, cum uno loco tot oppidum cadavera proiecta iacent? Visne tu te, Servi, cohibere et meminisse hominem te esse natum?'

CICERO, *Ep. ad Fam.* iv. 5.

* Cf. Byron, *Childe Harold*, iv. 44-5.

267

ELEGIES.

Catullus at the Grave of his Brother.

A.

Multas per gentes et multa per aequora vectus
Advenio has miseras, frater, ad inferias,
Ut te postremo donarem munere mortis
4
Et mutam nequiquam alloquerer cinerem,
Quandoquidem fortuna mihi tete abstulit ipsum,
Heu miser indigne frater adempte mihi.
Nunc tamen interea haec prisco quae more parentum
8
Tradita sunt tristes munera ad inferias,
Accipe fraterno multum manantia fletu,
Atque in perpetuum, frater, ave atque vale.

CATULLUS, ci.

To Calvus on the Death of his Wife.
B.
Si quicquam muteis gratum acceptumve sepulcris
Accidere a nostro, Calve, dolore potest,
Cum desiderio veteres renovamus amores
Atque olim amissas flemus amicitias,
Certe non tanto mors immatura dolori est
Quintiliae, quantum gaudet amore tuo.

CATULLUS, xcvi.

The Plea of Cornelia to her Husband.
C.
Desine, Paule, meum lacrimis urgere sepulcrum:
Panditur ad nullas ianua nigra preces.
Cum semel infernas intrarunt funera leges,
4
Obserat umbrosos lurida porta locos. . . .
73
Nunc tibi commendo communia pignora natos:
Haec cura et cineri spirat inusta meo.
Te Lepide, et te, Paule, meum post fata levamen;
76
Condita sunt vestro lumina nostra sinu.
Fungere maternis vicibus, pater: illa meorum
Omnis erit collo turba ferenda tuo.
Oscula cum dederis tua flentibus, adice matris:
80
Tota domus coepit nunc onus esse tuum.

PROPERTIUS, IV. (V.) xi. 1-4, 73-80.

Mors Tibulli.
D.
Memnona si mater, mater ploravit Achillem,
Et tangunt magnas tristia fata deas,
Flebilis indignos, Elegia, solve capillos:
A nimis ex vero nunc tibi nomen erit!
Ille tui vates operis, tua fama, Tibullus
Ardet in exstructo corpus inane rogo.

OVID, *Am.* III. ix. (sel.)

268

MARTIALIS APOPHORETA* (1).

Lectori.
Quo vis cumque loco potes hunc finire libellum:
Versibus explicitumst omne duobus opus.
Lemmata si quaeris cur sint adscripta, docebo,
Ut, si malueris, lemmata sola legas.

Chartae Epistulares.
I.

Seu leviter noto seu caro missa sodali
Omnes ista solet charta vocare suos.

Theca Libraria.

II.

Sortitus thecam calamis armare memento:
Cetera nos dedimus, tu leviora para.

Umbella.

III.

Accipe quae nimios vincant umbracula soles:
Sit licet et ventus, te tua vela tegent.

Parazonium.

IV.

Militiae decus hoc gratique erit omen honoris,
Arma tribunicium cingere digna latus.

Falx.

V.

Pax me certa ducis placidos curvavit in usus.
Agricolae nunc sum, militis ante fui.

Scrinium.

VI.

Selectos nisi das mihi libellos,
Admittam tineas trucesque blattas.

Candelabrum Corinthium.

VII.

Nomina candelae nobis antiqua dederunt.
Non norat parcos uncta lucerna patres.

Pila Paganica.

VIII.

Haec quae difficili turget paganica pluma,
Folle minus laxast et minus arta pila.

Pila Trigonalis.

IX.

Si me mobilibus scis expulsare sinistris,
Sum tua. Tu nescis? rustice, redde pilam.

Follis.

X.

Ite procul, iuvenes: mitis mihi convenit aetas:
Folle decet pueros ludere, folle senes.

* Apophoreta (ἀποφόρητα = to be carried away), Christmas presents which were
interchanged at the Saturnalia.

269

MARTIALIS APOPHORETA (2).

Vergilius in membranis.

I.

Quam brevis immensum cepit membrana Maronem!
Ipsius vultus prima tabella gerit.

Cicero in membranis.

II.

Si comes ista tibi fuerit membrana, putato
Carpere te longas cum Cicerone vias.

Monobyblos Properti.

III.

Cynthia, facundi carmen iuvenale Properti,
Accepit famam; non minus ipsa dedit.

181

Titus Livius in membranis.

IV.

Pellibus exiguis artatur Livius ingens,
Quem mea non totum bybliotheca capit.

Sallustius.

V.

Hic erit, ut perhibent doctorum corda virorum,
Primus Romana Crispus in historia.

Lucanus.

VI.

Sunt quidam qui me dicunt non esse poetam:
Sed qui me vendit bybliopola putat.

Catullus.

VII.

Tantum magna suo debet Verona Catullo,
Quantum parva suo Mantua Vergilio.

Fistula.

VIII.

Quid me corapactam ceris et harundine rides?
Quae primum structa est fistula talis erat.

Catella Gallicana.

IX.

Delicias parvae si vis audire catellae
Narranti brevis est pagina tota mihi.

Minerva argentea.

X.

Dic mihi, virgo ferox, cum sit tibi cassis et hasta
Quare non habeas aegida. 'Caesar habet.'

Hercules fictilis.

XI.

Sum fragilis: sed tu, moneo, ne sperne sigillum:
Non pudet Alciden nomen habere meum.

Toga.

XII.

'Romanos rerum dominos gentemque togatam'
Ille facit, magno qui dedit astra patri.
270

EPITAPHS AND INSCRIPTIONS.

On Naevius (by himself).

I.

'Immortales mortales si foret fas flere
Flerent divae Camenae Naevium poetam;
Itaque postquam est Orci traditus thesauro
Obliti sunt Romai loquier lingua Latina.'

On Ennius (by himself).

II.

'Aspicite, o cives, senis Enni imaginis formam:
Hic vestrum panxit maxima facta patrum.
Nemo me lacrumis decoret nec funera fletu
Faxit. Cur? Volito vivas per ora virum.'

On Pacuvius (by himself).

III.

'Adulescens, tametsi properas, te hoc saxum rogat,
Ut sese aspicias, deinde quod scriptum est, legas.
Hic sunt poetae Pacuvi Marci sita

Ossa. Hoc volebam nescius ne esses. Vale.'

On Plautus *(by himself)*.

IV.

'Postquam est mortem aptus Plautus, Comoedia luget,
Scena est deserta, ac dein Risus, Ludus, Iocusque,
Et Numeri innumeri simul omnes collacrumarunt.'

On Tibullus.

V.

'Te quoque Vergilio comitem non aequa, Tibulle,
Mors iuvenem campos misit ad Elysios,
Ne foret aut elegis molles qui fleret amores
Aut caneret forti regia bella pede.'

DOMITIUS MARSUS.

In tumulo hominis felicis.

VI.

'Sparge mero cineres, bene olentis et unguine nardi,
Hospes, et adde rosis balsama puniceis.
Perpetuum mihi ver agit illacrimabilis urna
Et commutavi saecula, non obii.
Nulla mihi veteris perierunt gaudia vitae,
Seu meminisse putes omnia, sive nihil.'

AUSONIUS, Epit. 36.

Thermopylae.

VII.

'Ὦ ξεῖν᾽, ἀγγέλλειν Λακεδαιμονίοις, ὅτι τῇδε
Κείμεθα, τοῖς κείνων ῥήμασι πειθόμενοι.'

SIMONIDES of Ceos.

'Dic, hospes, Spartae, nos te vidisse iacentes,
Dum sanctis patriae legibus obsequimur.'

Transl. by CICERO, Tusc. i. 42. 101.

271

EPILOGUE.

Horace.

A.

Exegi monumentum aere perennius
Regalique situ pyramidum altius,
Quod non imber edax, non Aquilo impotens
Possit diruere aut innumerabilis
5
Annorum series et fuga temporum.
Non omnis moriar, multaque pars mei
Vitabit Libitinam: usque ego postera
Crescam laude recens, dum Capitolium
Scandet cum tacita virgine pontifex.
10
Dicar, qua violens obstrepit Aufidus
Et qua pauper aquae Daunus agrestium
Regnavit populorum, ex humili potens
Princeps Aeolium carmen ad Italos
Deduxisse modos. Sume superbiam
15
Quaesitam meritis et mihi Delphica
Lauro cinge volens, Melpomene, comam.

HORACE, Od. III. xxx.

Ovid.

B.

Iamque opus exegi, quod nec Iovis ira nec ignis
Nec poterit ferrum nec edax abolere vetustas.

183

Cum volet, illa dies, quae nil nisi corporis huius
Ius habet, incerti spatium mihi finiat aevi;
875
Parte tamen meliore mei super alta perennis
Astra ferar nomenque erit indelebile nostrum.
Quaque patet domitis Romana potentia terris,
Ore legar populi perque omnia saecula fama,
Siquid habent veri vatum praesagia, vivam.

OVID, Met. xv. 871-9.

Martial.

C.

Ohe, iam satis est, ohe, libelle,
Iam pervenimus usque ad umbilicos:
Tu procedere adhuc et ire quaeris,
Nec summa potes in schida teneri,
5
Sic tamquam tibi res peracta non sit,
Quae prima quoque pagina peracta est.
Iam lector queriturque deficitque;
Iam librarius hoc et ipse dicit
'Ohe, iam satis est, ohe, libelle.'

MARTIAL, Epig. IV. lxxxix.

273

APPENDICES

274

APPENDIX I
LIST OF IMPORTANT CONJUNCTIONS

I. CO-ORDINATE.—These conjunctions join sentences of equal
grammatical *rank* (**ordo**), that is, each sentence is grammatically independent of the other.

They are generally divided into FIVE classes:—

(1) COPULATIVE (*link*) conjunctions are those which connect both the sentences and the meaning.

et, -quĕ, ac, atque ... *and.*
et ... et, -que ... -que (poet.) ... *both ... and.*
ĕtĭam, quŏque ... *also.*

Divide **et** *impera.*
Divide **and** control.

184

(2) DISJUNCTIVE conjunctions join together the sentence but they *disjoin* or separate from each other the thoughts conveyed.

aut ... aut, vĕl ... vĕl (vĕ) ... *either ... or.*

sĭve (seu) ... seu ... *whether ... or.*

nĕc (nĕque) ... nec (neque) ... *neither ... nor.*

aut *vincemus* **aut** *moriemur.*

We will **either** conquer **or** die.

(3) ADVERSATIVE conjunctions *oppose* two statements to each other.

sĕd, vērum, vērō, cētĕrum ... *but.*

autem, tămen ... *however.*

ăt ... *but, on the other hand.*

Ille quidem tardior: tu **autem** *ingeniosus,* **sed** *in omni vita inconstans.*

He is a little dull: **while** you are clever, **but** unstable in all your actions.

275

(4) INFERENTIAL.—The statement of one sentence *brings in* (**infert**) or proves the other.

Ergo, īgĭtur, ĭtăque ... *therefore, accordingly.*

'*Unus homo nobis cunctando restituit rem.*

Ergo *postque magisque viri nunc gloria claret.*'

ENNIUS.

(5) CAUSAL.

nam, namque, ĕnim, ĕtĕnim ... *for.*

quāpropter, quārē, quămobrem ... *wherefore.*

Ex.: '**quamobrem,** *Quirites, celebratote illos dies cum coniugibus ac liberis vestris.* **nam** *multi saepe honores dis immortalibus iusti habiti sunt, sed profecto iustiores nunquam.*'

II. SUBORDINATE.—These conjunctions attach to a sentence or clause another clause which holds (grammatically) a lower or *subordinate* position, qualifying the principal clause just as an adverb qualifies a verb.

Thus in 'I will do this, *if* you do,' the *if* clause is equivalent to the adverb *conditionally.*

They are generally divided into EIGHT classes:—

(1) FINAL introduce a clause expressing a *purpose.*

ŭt, quō ... *that, in order to.*

nē, quōmĭnus ... *that not, lest.*

qui ... *who* (= **ut is** ...).

Edo **ut** *vivam.*

Ne *ignavum te putemus, fortiter pugna.*

Pauci mihi sunt **quos** *mittam.*

(2) CONSECUTIVE introduce a clause expressing a *consequence* or *result.*

ŭt ... *so that, so as to.*

ŭt nōn, quīn ... *so as not to.*

qui ... *who (of such a kind as to...).*

Ex.: *Tam fortis adest nemo* **ut** *solus muros ascendat.*

Tam fortis est **ut** *hostes* **non** *timeat.*

Dignus erat **qui** *rex fieret.*

(3) TEMPORAL.

cum, quandō ... *when.*

ŭbĭ, ŭt ... *when, as.*

sĭmŭl, sĭmŭl atque (ac) ... *as soon as.*

postquam ... *after that.*

276**dum, dōnec, quŏad** ... *until, as long as, while.*

prĭus ... quam, antĕ ... quam ... *before that.*

Discedere **prius** *noluit* **quam** *ducem vidisset.*

Pompeius **ut** *equitatum suum pulsum vidit, acie excessit.*

(4) CONDITIONAL.

sī, nĭsī (nī), si non, quod sī ... *if, unless, if not, but if.*

mŏdŏ, dummŏdo, si mŏdo ... *if only, provided that.*

dummŏdo nē (dum nē, mŏdo nē) ... *provided only not.*

Ne *promiseris unquam* **nisi** *fidem praestare potes.*

Never promise **if** *you cannot keep your word.*

(5) COMPARATIVE AND PROPORTIONAL.

ut, utī, sīcut, vĕlut ... *just as, as.*

tanquam, quăsī ... *as if.*

quo ... ĕo ... *the more ... the more.*

> *Poenas dedit* **sicut** *meritus est.*

> *E corpore velut e carcere, evolat animus.*

The soul flies forth from the prison-house of the body.

> **quo** *difficilius* **eo** *praeclarius.*

(6) CONCESSIVE.

etsī, ĕtĭamsi, tămetsi ... *even if.*

quamquam ... *although.*

quamvīs, quamlĭbet ... *however much.*

līcet, ut, cum ... *though, although.*

> **Cum** *liber esse posset, servire maluit.*

(7) CAUSAL.

quĭă, quŏd, quŏnĭam, quandō ... *because.*

cum ... *since.*

proptĕrĕā ... quod ... *for this reason ... that.*

quandōquĭdem, quippe ... *since indeed, inasmuch as.*

> *Quae* **cum** *ita sint, ab urbe discedam.*

> *Socrates accusatus est* **quod** *iuventutem corrumperet.*

(8) INTERROGATIVE (with dependent clauses).

cūr, ūtrum ... ăn, num ... *why, whether ... or, if.*

quemadmŏdum, ut ... *how.*

ŭbī, quandō ... *when.*

> *Caesar* **utrum** *iure caesus fuerit,* **an** *nefarie necatus, dubitari potest.*

Whether Caesar was rightfully put to death, **or** foully murdered, is open to question.

APPENDIX II
LIST OF IMPORTANT PREFIXES

I. PREPOSITIONS.—In these compounds the Prepositions retain their original adverbial force.

A-, AB-, ABS-, = **away, from** (of the starting-place)

(i) = *separation.*

abire = *go away.*

abscēdere = *go away.*

āvŏcare = *call away.*

(ii) = *consumption.*

absūmere = *take away, consume.*

ăbūti = *use up.*

AD-, AC-, A-, = **to** (of a person, place, or thing, as the goal of motion).

(i) = *to, at* (local).

accēdere = *approach.*

adfāri = *speak to.*

(ii) = *in addition.*

acquīrere = *get in addition.*

ANTE = **before** (of place and time).

antecēdere = *come before.*

anteferre = *prefer.*

CIRCUM = **around.**

circumdăre = *surround.*

circumdūcere literally, and with secondary meaning, =*cheat.*

circumscrībere

circumvĕnire

COM-, CON- (CUM), CO-, COL-, COR-, = together.

(i) = *collectively.*

conclāmare = *shout together.*

commiscēre = *mix together.*

(ii) = *completely* (often apparently only pleonastic).

consectari = *follow persistently.*

confirmare = *strengthen.*

278

DE-, = down, from.

(i) = *down, down off, down to.*

decĭdere = *fall down,* or *off.*

devĕnire = *come to.*

(ii) = *off, away, aside.*

dēcēdere = *depart.*

deflectere = *turn aside.*

deterrēre = *frighten.*

(iii) = *completely.*

depŏpŭlari = *lay waste.*

debellare = *bring a war to an end.*

(iv) = *un-* (negative).

despērare = *despair.*

deesse = *be wanting.*

E-, EX-, EC-, EF-, = out of.

(i) = *out, forth.*

excēdere = *go out.*

effundere = *pour forth.*

(ii) = *throughout, to the end, thoroughly.*

explēre = *fill to the brim.*

exposcere = *earnestly ask.*

IN-, IM-, IR-, I-, = in, on, against.

(i) = *in, into, on.*

inclūdere = *shut in.*

incĭdere = *fall on.*

invĭdere = *look at* (with ill intent),*envy.*

(ii) = *intensive,* almost *pleonastic.*

incĭpere = *take up, begin.*

implēre = *fill.*

INTER = between.

(i) = *between, among.*

intercēdere = *come between.*

intellĕgere = *pick among, perceive.*

(ii) = *breaking a continuity.*

interclūdere = *shut off, blockade.*

interfĭcere = *destroy* (lit. *put between*).

OB-, OBS-, OC-, OF-, OP-, O-, = against, on account of.

(i) = *over against, before* (as an obstruction).

offendere = *strike against.*

oblŏqui = *speak against.*

279

(ii) = *towards,* with the idea of *favour* or *compliance.*

oboedire = *hearken to.*

obsĕqui = *follow compliantly.*

PER-, = through, along.

(i) = *through, all over.*

perrumpere = *break through.*

perspĭcēre = *look through.*

(ii) = *thoroughly, to completion.*

187

perdiscere = *learn thoroughly.*

perfungi = *go through a duty, discharge.*

permagnus = *very large.*

PRAE = **in front.**

  (i) = (of place) *before, in front.*

praefīcere = *put at the head of.*

praeses (sĕdeo) = *guardian.*

  (ii) = (of time) *before, too soon.*

praediscere = *learn beforehand.*

praevĕnire = *outstrip.*

  (iii) = *before others, in comparison, greatly.*

praecellens = *surpassing.*

PRO-, PROD-, = **before, in front of, forth.**

prod-ire = *come forth.*

provĭdēre = *look onwards or ahead.*

SUB-, SUF-, SUM-, SUP-, SUR-, SU-, SUS-, = **beneath, under.**

  (i) = *under.*

subĭcere = *throw under, subject.*

supprĭmere = *press under, suppress.*

  (ii) = *up.*

succingere = *gird up.*

sustĭnēre = *hold up, check.*

  (iii) = *to the help of, close to.*

subvĕnire = *come up to aid of.*

  (iv) = *secretly.*

subdūcere = *withdraw secretly.*

  (v) = *slightly.*

subrīdere = *laugh somewhat, smile.*

sublustris = *giving some light.*

280

SUPER = **over, upon.**

  (i) = *over, upon* (of place).

superpōnere = *place upon or over.*

  (ii) = *metaphorically.*

sŭperesse = *remain, survive, abound.*

TRANS-, TRA-, = **across.**

  (i) = *across.*

transgrĕdi = *step across.*

  (ii) = *a change or transference.*

trādere = *hand over, surrender.*

  (iii) = *through to the end.*

transĭgere = *complete* a business.

II. SEPARABLE PARTICLES, which do not appear as Prepositions in Latin.

AMB-, AM-, AN-, = **around, on both sides.**

ambīre = *go around, canvass.*

amplecti = *fold oneself round, embrace.*

DIS-, DI-, DIF-, DIR-, = **in twain.**

  (i) = *asunder, apart.*

discēdere = *part asunder, depart.*

discernere = *separate, distinguish.*

dīmittere = *send in different directions.*

  (ii) = *un-* (negative).

displĭcēre = *displease.*

diffīdere = *distrust.*

  (iii) = *exceedingly.*

differtus = *crammed to bursting.*

  (iv) = *individually, separately.*

dīnŭmĕrare = *count up (singly).*

IN- (cf. ἀν-, ἀ-) = **UN-**, usually with adjectives.

ignoscere = *not to know, forget, pardon.*

innŏcens = *not guilty, harmless.*

PER- (cf. παρά) = in a sense of **wrong** or **injury**.

perdere = *destroy.*

perfĭdus = *faithless.*

281

RED-, RE-, = **back**.

(i) = *back, backwards.*

rĕcumbere = *lie down.*

rĕflectere = *bend back.*

(ii) = *in response*, or *return*.

reddere = *give in return.*

(iii) = *against, behind.*

rĕpugnare = *fight against.*

rĕlinquere = *leave behind.*

(iv) = *again.*

rĕfĭcere = *make again, repair.*

rĕpĕrire = *find again, discover.*

(v) = *intensive action.*

rĕvellere = *pluck by the roots.*

(vi) = *un-* (negative).

rĕfīgere = *unfix.*

SED-, SE-, = **apart**.

sēcernere = *sift away, separate.*

sēcēdere = *go aside, withdraw.*

sēd-ĭtio = *a going apart, secession.*

282

APPENDIX III
LIST OF IMPORTANT SUFFIXES

I. DERIVATION OF NOUNS.

(i.) **TOR (-SOR)**, M. **Agent** or **doer** of an action

-TRIX, F.

ac-tor = *doer,*	formed fr om	√**ag** = *do.*
auc-tor = *maker*	,,	√**aug** = *increase.*
vic-tor = *conqueror*	,,	√**vic** = *conquer.*
petī-tor = *candidate*	,,	√**pet** = *seek.*
ton-sor = *barber*	,,	√**tem** = *cut.*

(ii.) **Abstract** Nouns and **Names** of **Actions**.

-OR, -SUS (= -TUS), M.

-ĒS, -IA (-IES), -TIA (-TIES), -IŌ, -TIŌ,

-TĀS, -TŪS, -TŪDŌ, -DŌ, -GŌ, -NIA,

-US, -IUM, -ITIUM, -NIUM, -LIUM, -CINIUM, N.

tĭm-or = *fear*	formed fr om	**tĭm-ere** = *to fear.*
sen-sus = *feeling*	,,	**sent-ire** = *to feel.*
sēd-ēs = *seat*	,,	**sĕd-ēre** = *to sit.*

189

audāc- ia	= *boldne* *ss* ,,	**audax** = *bold.*
segnĭt- ies	= *lazines* *s* ,,	**segnis** = *lazy.*
tristĭ-tia *s*	= *sadnes* ,,	**tristis** = *sad.*
lĕg-io	= *a* *collecting* ,, *a legion*	**lĕg-ere** = *to* *collect.*
sălūtā- tio	= *a* *greeting* ,,	**salutare** = *to* *greet.*
bŏnĭ-tas	= *goodne* *ss* ,,	**bonus** = *good.*
sĕnec- tūs	= *age* ,,	**senex** = *old.*
magni- tudo	= *greatne* *ss* ,,	**magnus** = *great.*
cupī-dō	= *desire* ,,	**cupere** = *to* *desire.*
vertī-go	= *a* *turning* ,, *giddiness*	**vertere** = *to* *turn.*
pĕcū- nia	= *money* (*chattels*) ,,	**pecus** = *cattle.*
gĕn-us	= *race,* *birth* ,,	**√gen** = *to be* *born.*
283**ausp** **īc-ium**	= an *omen* ,,	**auspex** = *a* *soothsayer.* **avis + spicio**
gaud- ium	= *joy* ,,	**gaudēre** = *to* *rejoice.*
lātro- cinium	= *robber* *y* ,,	**latro** = *robber.*
auxĭ- lium	= *help* ,,	**augēre** = *to* *increase.*

(iii.) **Nouns** denoting **acts**, or **means** and **results of acts**.
-MŌNIA, F.; **-MEN, -MENTUM, -MŌNIUM**, N.
quĕri-monia = *complaint*, formed from **quĕri** = *to complain.*

-men= **ag**
line
of march formed
from **agere √ag** = *to lead.*
band

mŏnŭ-mentum = a *memorial*, formed from **mon-ēre** = *to remind.*
nō-men = a *name* formed from **√gno** = *to know.*
(iv.) **Nouns** denoting **means** or **instrument**.
-BŬLUM, -CŬLUM, -BRUM, -CRUM, -TRUM, N.

stă-
bulum = *stall* formed fr
om **stare** = *to*
stand.

vĕhĭ-
cŭlum = *wagon* ,, **vehere** = *t*
o carry.

sĕpu	=		sepelīre =
l-crum	*tomb*	„	*to bury.*
ărā-	=		arāre = *to*
trum	*plough*	„	*plough.*

II. DERIVATION OF ADJECTIVES.

(i.) **Adjectives** expressing **diminution**, and used as **Diminutive Nouns.**

-ŬLUS, -ŎLUS, -CŬLUS, -ELLUS, -ILLUS.

rīv-ulus	=	formed fr	rīvus = a *brook.*
	a *streamlet*	om	
fīlĭ-olus	=		filius = a *son.*
	a *little son*	„	
mūnus	=		munus = a *gift.*
-culum	a *little gift*	„	
cōdic-	= *writi*		codex = a *block*
illi	*ng tablets*	„	*of wood.*
līb-	=		līber = a *book.*
ellus	a *little book*	„	

(ii.) **Patronymics**, indicating **descent** or **relationship.**

-ADES, -ĬDES, -ĪDES, -EUS, M.

-AS, -IS, -EIS, F.

Atlanti-		formed	A
adēs = *Mercury*		from	tlas.

Atlant-idĕs = the *Pleiads*

Tȳd-			T
īdēs = *Diomedes*		„	ydeus.

Cissē-is = *Hecuba*			C
		„	isseus.

284

(iii.) **Adjectives** meaning **full of, prone to.**

-ŌSUS, -LENS, -LENTUS.

for	=	formed fr	forma
m-ōsus	*beautiful*	om	= *beauty.*
pes	=		pestis
ti-lens	*pestilent*	„	= *plague.*
vĭŏ	=		vis = *for*
-lentus	*violent*	„	*ce.*

(iv.) **Adjectives** meaning **provided with.**

-TUS, -ĀTUS, -ĬTUS, -ŪTUS.

fū	=	formed fr	funus (funer-
nes-tus	*deadly*	om	) =*death.*
ba	=		barba =
rb-ātus	*bearded*	„	a *beard.*
tur	=		turris = a *tower.*
r-ītus	*turreted*	„	
cor	=		cornu = a *horn.*
n-ūtus	*horned*	„	

(v.) **Adjectives** meaning **made of** or **belonging to,** or **pertaining to.**

-EUS, -ĬUS, -ĀNEUS, -TĬCUS,

-ĀLIS, -ĀRIS, -ĪLIS, -ŪLIS,

-ĀNUS, -ĒNUS, -ĪNUS, -ENSIS,

-TER (-TRIS), -ESTER (-ESTRIS), -TĬMUS,

-ERNUS, -URNUS, -TURNUS (-TERNUS).

aur-	= *golden*	formed fr	aurum =*gold.*
eus		om	

patr-ius	= *paternal* "	pater = a*father.*
subterr-aneus	= *subterranean* "	sub terrā =*underground.*
dŏmes-ticus	= *domestic* "	domus = a*house.*
nātūr-ālis	= *natural* "	natura =*nature.*
pŏpŭl-aris	= *fellow-countryman* "	populus = a*people.*
vĕtĕr-ānus	= *veteran* "	vetus (veter-) = *old.*
sĕr-ēnus	= *calm, of evening stillness* "	serus = *late.*
dīv-īnus	= *divine* "	divus = *god.*
fŏr-ensis	= *of the forum* "	forum = *a market-place.*
lac-teus	= *milky* "	lac (lacti-) =*milk.*
subl-icius	= *resting on piles* "	sublica = a*pile.*
pălus-ter	= *marshy* "	palūs = a*marsh.*
silv-ester	= *woody* "	silva = a*wood.*
fīnĭ-timus	= *neighbouring* "	finis = a*boundary.*
ver-nus	= *vernal* "	vēr = *spring.*
dĭ-urnus	= *daily* "	dies = *day.*
diū-turnus	= *lasting* "	diū = *long*(time) .

285

(vi.) **Adjectives** expressing the action of the Verb as **a quality** or**tendency.**
-AX, -ĬDUS, -ŪLUS, -VUS (-UUS, -ĪVUS, -TĪVUS).

pugn-ax	= *pugnacious*	formed from	pugnare = *to fight.*
cŭp-idus	= *eager* "		cupere = *to desire.*
bĭb-ulus	= *thirsty* (of sand etc.) "		bibere = *to drink.*
nŏc-uus	= *hurtful* "		nocēre = *to hurt.*
cap-tivus	= *captive* "		capere = *to take.*

(vii.) **Adjectives** expressing **passive qualities** but **occasionally active.**
-ILIS, -BĬLIS, -ĬUS, -TĪLIS.

ăg-ilis	= *fra*il	formed from	frange re√frag = *to break.*
ō-bilis	= *wel*l known "		noscer e√gno = *to know.*
ex	= *cho*		eximer = *to*

192

| **ĭm-ius** | *ice, rare* | „ | | e | | *ake out.* |

| **te** | = *wo* | | **texere** | = *t* |
| **x-tilis** | *ven* | „ | | *o weave.* |

(viii.) **Adjectives originally gerundives.**
-NDUS, -BUNDUS, -CUNDUS.

sĕcu-					
ndus	= *second* (the*f*		formed fr	**sequi** = *t*
	ollowing)	om		*o follow.*

favourable

| **mŏrĭ-** | = *dying* | | | **mori** = *t* |
| **bundus** | | „ | | *o die.* |

| **fā-** | = *eloquent* | | | **fa-ri** = *to* |
| **cundus** | | „ | | *speak.* |

III. NOUNS WITH ADJECTIVE SUFFIXES.

-ĀRIUS, denotes **person employed about** anything.
argent-ārius = *silversmith, banker* formed from **argentum**= *silver.*

-ĀRIUM, denotes **place of** a thing.
aer-arium = *treasury* formed from **aes** = *copper.*

-ĪLE denotes **stall of an animal.**

| **b** | = *c* | | formed fr | **bōs** |
| **ŏv-īle** | *attle-stall* | om | | **(bŏv-)** = *ox.* |

| **ŏ** | = *s* | | | **ovis** = *sh* |
| **v-īle** | *heep-fold* | „ | | *eep.* |

-ĒTUM denotes **place where a tree or plant grows.**
querc-ētum = *oak-grove* formed from **quercus** = *an oak.*

IV. DERIVATION OF VERBS.

(i.) **From Nouns and Adjectives.**

| **stĭmŭlo** | = *to* | | formed fr | **stimulus** = *a goad.* |
| **, -āre** | *goad,incite* | om | | |

| **nŏvo, -** | = *to* | | | **novus** = *new.* |
| **āre** | *renew* | „ | | |

| **286vĭgĭ** | = *to* | | | **vigil** = *awake.* |
| **lo, -āre** | *watch* | „ | | |

| **albeo, -** | = *to be* | | | **albus** = *white.* |
| **ēre** | *white* | „ | | |

| **mĕtuo,** | = *to* | | | **metus** = *fear.* |
| **-ere** | *fear* | „ | | |

| **ăcuo, -** | = *to* | | | **acus** = *needle.* |
| **ere** | *sharpen* | „ | | |

| **mōlior,** | = *to* | | | **moles** = *mass.* |
| **-īri** | *toil* | „ | | |

| **custōdi** | = *to* | | | **custos (custod-** |
| **o, -īre** | *guard* | „ | |) =*guardian.* |

(ii.) **Verbs from other Verbs.**

-SCO denotes the **beginning** of an action. (Third Conjugation.)

| **lă** | = *begin* | | formed fr | **labo** |
| **bā-sco** | *to totter* | om | | = *totter.* |

| **m** | = *grow* | | | **mītis** |
| **ītē-sco** | *mild* | „ | | = *mild.* |

-TO, -ĬTO, (rarely **-SŌ**), **-ESSO**, denote **forcible or repeated action.**

| **iac-to,** | = *hurl* | | formed fr | **iacio** = |
| **-āre** | | om | | *throw.* |

| **quas-** | = *shatter* | | | **quatio** |
| **so, āre** | | „ | | =*shake.* |

făc-esso, -ĕre	= *do* (with energy) „	**facio** = *do*.

-TŬRIO (-SŬRIO) denotes **longing or wishing**.

par-turio, -īre	= *produce* formed fr om *to bring forth*	**pario** = *bri ng forth*.
ĕ-surio (= *ed-turio*) = *to be hungry* „		**edo** = *to eat*.

287

APPENDIX IV
GROUPS OF RELATED (COGNATE) WORDS

		English derivative.
√AC = sharp.		
ăc-er	= *sharp*.	eager (F. aigre).
ăc-erbus	= *harsh, cruel*.	acerbity (= harshness).
ăc-ervus	= *a heap*.	
ăc-ies	= *edge, keen look. army in battle array.*	Fr. acier (= steel).
ăc-idus	= *sour*.	acid.
ăc-uo	= *to sharpen*.	
ăc-utus	= *sharpened, sharp*.	acute (Fr. aigu).
ăc-umen	= *a point, acuteness*.	acumen.
ăc-us	= *a needle*.	Fr. aiguille.

√AUG = be active, strong.		
aug-eo	= *increase*.	
aug-mentum	= *an increase*.	augment.
auc-tio	= *a sale by increase of bids, an auction*	auction.
auc-tor	= *a maker, producer*.	author.
auc-toritas	= *a producing, authority*.	authority.
aug-ustus	= *majestic, august*.	august.
aux-ilium	= *aid, help*.	auxiliary.

√CAP = take hold of, seize.		
căp-io	= *take hold of*.	captive.
căp-ax	= *capacious*.	capacious.
căp-ulus	= *handle, hilt of a sword*.	
ac-cĭp-io (*ad + capio*)	= *take to, receive*.	accept.
ex-cĭp-io	= *take up*.	exception.

194

(*ex + capio*)

man-cĭp- **ium**	= *property, a slave.*	emancipate.

(*manus + capio*)

288**muni-** **cĭp-ium**	= *a free town.*	municipal.

(*munia + capio*)

prin-ceps	= *first, chief.*	principal.

(*primus + capio*)

prince.

√GEN-, GNA- = beget, become, produce.

gi-gn-o	= *to beget.*	indigenous.

(= *gi-gĕn-o*)

gĕn-i-tor	= *a father.*	(pro)genitor.
gen-s	= *clan, house, race.*	gentile.
in-gens	= *vast.*	
gĕn-us	= *birth, race.*	genus (Fr. genre).
in-gĕn- **ium**	= *innate quality,* *character.*	
in-gĕn-uus	= *native, free-born,* *frank.*	ingenuous.
in-gĕn- **iosus**	= *of good natural* *abilities.*	ingenious.
pro-gĕn- **ies**	= *descent,* *descendants.*	progenitor.
gĕn-er	= *son-in-law.*	
gĕn-ius	= *the innate superior* *nature,* *tutelary* (*protecting*)*deity.*	genius.
indi-gĕn-a	= *nature.*	indigenous.
gĕn-erōsus	= *of noble birth,* *noble-minded*	generous.
gĕn-ĕro	= *to beget, produce.*	generate.
gĕn-ĕtivus	= *of or belonging to* *birth,* *genitive.*	genitive.
na-scor	= *to be born.*	native.

= *gna-scor*

nā-tūra	= *nature.*	nature.
nā-tio	= *birth, a race.*	nation.

289

APPENDIX V
HOW TO THINK IN LATIN

Numbers in the left margin (Ia, Ib...) were added by the transcriber for use with the notes.

*Flaminius atones for his rashness.*44

|| Ia, IbTres ferme horas pugnatum est et ubique atrociter; circa consulem tamen acrior infestiorque pugna est. || IIaEum et robora virorum sequebantur, et ipse, quacunque in parte premi ac laborare senserat suos, impigre ferebat opem; || IIbinsignemque armis et hostes summa vi petebant et tuebantur cives, donec Insuber eques (Ducario nomen erat) facie quoque noscitans consulem, ||IIc'En' inquit 'hic est' popularibus suis, 'qui legiones nostras cecidit agrosque et urbem est depopulatus. || IIIIam ego hanc victimam manibus peremptorum foede civium dabo.' || IVaSubditisque calcaribus equo per confertissimam hostium turbam impetum facit,

obtruncatoque prius armigero, qui se infesto venienti obviam obiecerat, consulem lancea transfixit; | | IVbspoliare cupientem triarii obiectis scutis arcuere.

LIVY, xxii. 6.

The heading and the author will at once suggest the stirring incident in the Battle of Lake Trasimene, when Flaminius atoned for his rashness by his gallant example and death.

You have seen how Analysis helps you to arrive at the main thought of the sentence, and you are familiar with the principles that govern the order of words in Latin, and the important part played by the emphatic position of words. So you may now try to **think in Latin**; that is, to take the thought in the Latin order, without reference to analysis or the English order. You will do well to follow closely this advice of experienced teachers:—'Read every word as if it were the last on the page, and you had to turn over without being able 290to turn back. If, however, you are obliged to turn back, begin again at the beginning of the sentence and proceed as before. Let each word of the Latin suggest some conception gradually adding to and completing the meaning of the writer. If the form of the word gives several possibilities, hold them all in your mind, so far as may be, till something occurs in the progress of the sentence to settle the doubt.'

Ia1. **Tres ferme horas** = *for nearly three hours.* This construction (Acc. of extent of time) will be familiar to you. Notice the emphatic position of the phrase.

pugnatum est = *the battle was fought.* This use of the so-called impersonal passive is very frequent, and is generally best translated by taking the root-idea of the verb as a subject.

et ubique atrociter = *and everywhere fiercely.*

Ib2. **circa consulem tamen** = *around the consul however.*

acrior infestiorque pugna est = *the battle is more keen and more vehement.* This presents no difficulty; **acrior** and **infestior** must qualify**pugna**, which follows immediately.

IIa3. **eum** = *him*, plainly *consulem* (i.e. Flaminius), for no one else has been mentioned. Notice the emphatic position of **eum**.

et robora virorum sequebantur = *both the strongest of his troops followed.* You may know that **robur** (lit. *hard wood*) is often used of*the toughest troops, the flower of an army.*

et ipse = *and himself,* i.e. the consul (Flaminius).

3-4. **quacunque in parte** = *in whatever part.*

4. **premi ac laborare senserat suos** = *he had seen his men hard pressed and in distress.* No other meaning is possible, nor does the order present any difficulty, but notice the emphatic position of **suos**.

4-5. **impigre ferebat opem** = *actively he bore help.*

IIb5. **insignemque armis** = *and distinguished by his arms,* clearly referring to **consulem** (l. 2). Cf. **eum** (l. 3).

et hostes summa vi petebant = *both the enemy with all their might attacked.* **et** might, of course, = *also* (cf. **et**, l. 2), but the second **et**which immediately follows determines the meaning *both*.

6. **et tuebantur cives** = *and his fellow-citizens* (Romans) *defended*(him).

291

donec Insuber eques = *until an Insubrian trooper.* **donec** may mean*while*, but the context shows that *until* or *at last* is the right meaning here.

6-7. **Ducario nomen erat** = (his) *name was Ducarius,* i.e. *ei nomen erat Ducario,* where **Ducario** is possess. dat. in appos. to *ei*understood. It is, however, possible that the trooper's name was Ducarius, but cf. page 126, l. 2.

7. **facie quoque noscitans consulem** = *by his face also* (i.e. as well as by his armour) *recognising the consul.*

IIc7-8. **'En' inquit 'his est' popularibus suis** = *See, said he, to his fellow-countrymen* (comrades), *this is the man.*

8. **qui legiones nostras cecīdit** = *who slaughtered our legions.* There is a slight difficulty here, but a moment's thought will remove it. It must be **cecīdit**, perf. of *caedo*, and not *cecĭdit*, perf. of *cado*, which is intransitive.

8-9. **agrosque et urbem est depopulatus** = *and laid waste our fields and our city.*

III9-10. **Iam ego hanc victimam mānibus peremptorum foede civium dabo** = *now I will give this victim to the shades of our countrymen foully slain.* **Mānibus** cannot = *hands* (*mănibus*), for **peremptorum civium**, which immediately follows, fixes the right meaning.

IVa10-11. **subditisque calcaribus equo** = *and putting spurs to his horse.* You will not attempt to translate this Abl. Absol. literally.

11-12. **per confertissimam hostium turbam impetum facit** =*through the closely packed crowd of the enemy he makes his charge.*

12. **obtruncatoque prius armigero** = *and first cut down the armour-bearer* (i.e. of Flaminius).

196

12-13. qui se infesto venienti obviam obiecerat = *who had thrown himself in the way of him advancing at the charge.*

infesto venienti is clearly dative with **obviam**.

13. consulem lancea transfixit = *ran the Consul through with his lance.*

IVb13-14. **spoliare cupientem** = (him, i.e. Ducarius) *wishing to spoil* (the consul).

14. triarii obiectis scutis arcuere = *the triarii* (veterans) *thrusting their shields in the way kept off.*

292

This passage is quite simple, but it will serve to show you how you may with practice learn to **take the thought in the Latin order**, and to grasp the writer's meaning. All that now remains for you to do is to write out a translation in good English, using short coordinate sentences, each complete in itself, in place of the more involved structure of the original. The following version by the late Professor Jebb will serve as a model:—

They fought for about three hours, and everywhere with desperation. Around the consul, however, the fight was peculiarly keen and vehement. He had the toughest troops with him; and he himself, whenever he saw that his men were hard pressed, was indefatigable in coming to the rescue. Distinguished by his equipment, he was a target for the enemy and a rallying-point for the Romans. At last a Lombard trooper, named Ducario, recognising the person as well as the guise of the consul, cried out to his people, 'Here is the man who cut our legions to pieces and sacked our city—now I will give this victim to the shades of our murdered countrymen.' Putting spurs to his horse, he dashed through the thick of the foe. First he cut down the armour-bearer, who had thrown himself in the way of the onset. Then he drove his lance through the consul. He was trying to despoil the corpse, when some veterans screened it with their shields.

44. Cf. p. 126.

293

APPENDIX VI

SHORT LIVES OF ROMAN AUTHORS

DECIMUS MAGNUS AUSONIUS, 309-392 A.D.

1. Life.

AUSONIUS.

Born at Burdigala (*Bordeaux*), and carefully educated. At the age of thirty appointed professor of rhetoric in his native University, where he became so famous that he was appointed tutor to Gratian, son of the Emperor Valentinian (364-375 A.D.), and was afterwards raised to the highest honours of the State (Consul, 379A.D.). Theodosius (Emperor of the East, 378-395 A.D.) gave him leave to retire from court to his native country, where he closed his days in an honoured literary retirement.

2. Works.

A very voluminous writer both in prose and verse.

1. Prose: The only extant specimen is his *Gratiarum Actio* to Gratianus for the Consulship.

2. Verse: Of this we have much: it has little value as poetry, but in point of contents and diction it is interesting and valuable. Some of his*Epigrammata* and *Epitaphia* are worth preserving, but his claim to rank as a poet rests on his *Mosella*, a beautiful description of the R. Moselle, which is worthy to be compared with Pliny's description of the R. Clitumnus (*Ep.* viii. 8).

'In virtue of this poem Ausonius ranks not merely as the last, or all but the last, of Latin, but as the first of French poets.'—Mackail.

GAIUS JULIUS CAESAR, 102 (or 100?)-44 B.C.

1. Important Events in Caesar's Life.

CAESAR.

B.C. 102. Gaius Julius Caesar, nephew of Marius, born July 12th.

„ 83. Marries Cornelia, daughter of Cinna, the friend of Marius.

294

B.C. 81-78. Served with distinction in Asia.

„ 76. Studies oratory at Rhodes.

„ 68. Begins his political career as Quaestor, partly at Rome, partly in Spain.

„ 65. Curule Aedile. Incurs enormous debts by his splendid shows.

„ 61. Propraetor in Spain: conquers Lusitanians: amasses wealth.

„ 60. Coalition of Pompeius, Caesar, and Crassus: First Triumvirate.

„ 59. Consul. The Leges Iuliae.

„ 58-50. Subjugation of Gaul and two invasions of Britain (55 and 54).

„ 56. Meeting of Triumvirate at Luca.

„ 50. The trouble with Pompeius begins.

„ 49. Crosses the Rubicon. Civil war with Pompeius. Dictator a first time.

197

„ 48. Pharsalus. Defeats Pompeius. Dictator a second time.
„ 46. Thapsus. Defeats Scipio, Sulla, and Afranius. Declared Dictator for ten years.
„ 45. Munda. Defeats Gn. Pompeius and Labienus. Dictator and Imperator for life.
„ 44. Assassinated in the Senate House on the Ides of March.

2. Works.

(1) **THE DE BELLO GALLICO.**—This work describes Caesar's operations in Gaul, Germany, and Britain during the years 58-52 B.C., the events of each year occupying a separate Book.

Book	B.C.	
BOOK I.	B.C. 58.	The Helvetii and Ariovistus the German defeated.
„ II.	„ 57.	The Nervii, the bravest Belgian tribe, almost exterminated.
„ III.	„ 56.	Conquest of the coast tribes of Brittany (Veneti, &c.) and of the South-West (Aquitani).
„ IV.	„ 55.	Inroad of Germans into Northern Gaul repulsed. Caesar crosses the Rhine a first time. First invasion of Britain.
„ V.	„ 54.	Second invasion of Britain. Fresh risings of the Gauls put down by Labienus and Q. Cicero.
„ VI.	„ 53.	Caesar crosses the Rhine a second time. Northern Gaul reduced to peace.
„ VII.	„ 52.	Uprising of the Gauls under Vercingetorix. Siege and capture of Alesia. Surrender of Vercingetorix. He is taken in chains to Rome, to adorn Caesar's triumph.
„ VIII.	„ 51	(added by HIRTIUS). Final subjugation of Gaul.

Caesar's object was threefold:—

(i) To provide materials for professed historians.

(ii) To justify the conquest he describes.

(iii) To vindicate in the eyes of the world his opposition to the Senate and the Government.

(2) **DE BELLO CIVILI.**—This work, in three Books, is similar in plan to the *De Bello Gallico*. It describes the events of the Civil War during the years 49-48 B.C. Book III. ends abruptly with the words:

Haec initia belli Alexandrini fuerunt.

Book	B.C.	
BOOK I.	B.C. 49.	Caesar crosses the Rubicon. Follows Pompeius to Brundusium and conquers Afranius in Spain.
„ II.	„ 49.	Caesar takes Massilia. Submission of Varro in Further Spain. Defeat and death of Curio before Utica.
„ III.	„ 48.	Caesar follows Pompeius into Illyria. The lines of Dyrrachium and the Battle of Pharsalus. The beginning of the Alexandrine War.

(3) **OTHER WORKS.**—All Caesar's other writings (Speeches, Poems, &c.) have been lost, with the exception of a few brief Letters to Cicero.

3. Style.

Remarkable for brevity, directness, and simplicity. The simplest facts told in the simplest way. *Ars est celare artem.*

296

'Caesar's Commentaries are worthy of all praise; they are unadorned, straightforward, and elegant, every ornament being stripped off as if it were a garment.'—CICERO.

MARCUS PORCIUS CATO, 234-149 B.C.

1. Life.

CATO.

For his military and political career, his Consulship (195B.C.), his famous Censorship (184 B.C.), and his social reforms, see some good history, e.g. Mommsen, vol, iii.

2. Works.

His chief works are:—

(1) His treatise **De Re Rustica** or **De Agri Cultura** (his only extant work).—A series of terse and pointed directions following one on another, somewhat in the manner of Hesiod, and interesting 'as showing the practical Latin style, and as giving the prose groundwork of Vergil's stately and beautiful embroidery in the *Georgics*.'—Mackail.

(2) **The Origines.**—'The oldest historical work written in Latin, and the first important prose work in Roman literature.'—Mommsen. Nepos, *Cato*, 3, summarises the contents of the seven books.

Cato struggled all his life against Greek influence in literature and in manners, which he felt would be fatal to his ideal of a Roman citizen. In a letter to his son Marcus he says *Quandoque ista gens suas litteras dabit, omnia corrumpet.* He was famous for his homely wisdom, which gained him the title of *Sapiens*, e.g. *Rem tene: verba sequentur*—'Take care of the sense: the words will take care of themselves.'

GAIUS VALERIUS CATULLUS, circ. 84-54 B.C.

1. Life.

CATULLUS.

Born at Verona, of a family of wealth and position, as is seen from his having estates at Sirmio:—

Salve, O venusta Sirmio, atque ero gaude (C. 31)

and near Tibur: *O funde noster seu Sabine seu Tiburs* (C. 44). His father was an intimate friend of Caesar. He went to Rome early, where he spent the greater part of his short life,
297

Romae vivimus: illa domus,

Illa mihi sedes, illic mea carpitur aetas (C. 68),

with the exception of an official journey to Bithynia, 57 B.C. to better his fortunes: cf. *Iam ver egelidos refert tepores ... Linquantur Phrygii, Catulle, campi* (C. 46). After a life of poetic culture and free social enjoyment he died at the early age of thirty, 'the young Catullus,'*hedera iuvenilia tempora cinctus* (Ovid, *Am.* III. ix. 61).

2. Works.

116 poems written in various metres and on various subjects, Lyric, Elegiac, Epic.

'The event which first revealed the full power of his genius, and which made both the supreme happiness and supreme misery of his life, was his love for Lesbia (Clodia).'—Sellar.

'Catullus is one of the great poets of the world, not so much through vividness of imagination as through his singleness of nature, his vivid impressibility, and his keen perception. He received the gifts of the passing hour so happily that to produce pure and lasting poetry it was enough for him to utter in natural words something of the fulness of his heart. He says on every occasion exactly what he wanted to say, in clear, forcible, spontaneous language.'—Sellar.

'The most attractive feature in the character of Catullus is the warmth of his affection. If to love warmly, constantly, and unselfishly be the best title to the love of others, few poets in any age or country deserve a kindlier place in the hearts of men than "the young Catullus."'—Sellar.

MARCUS TULLIUS CICERO, 106-43 B.C.

1. Important Events in Cicero's Life, and chief Works.

CICERO.

B.C. 106. Born at Arpinum. Birth of Pompeius.

„ 102. Birth of Quintus Cicero, and of Caesar.

B.C. 91. Assumes the *toga virilis*. Q. Mucius Scaevola the augur becomes his tutor in civil law. Writes an heroic poem in praise of Marius.

„ 89. Serves his first and only campaign under Pompeius Strabo.

„ 87. Studies Rhetoric at Rome under Apollonius Molo of Rhodes.
298

„ 81. Delivers his first speech (*causa privata*) **Pro P. Quinctio.**

„ 80. Delivers his first speech (*causa publica*) **Pro S. Roscio Amerino.**

„ 79-7. Studies at Athens and Rhodes. Marries Terentia.

„ 75-4. Quaestor at Lilybaeum in Sicily.

„ 70. The six speeches **In C. Verrem.**

„ 69. Curule Aedile. The **Pro Caecina.**

„ 68. Date of the earliest extant letter.

„ 67. Praetor. The Lex Gabinia.

„ 66. The De Imperio Cn. Pompeii (**Pro Lege Manilia**).

„ 64. Birth of his son Marcus. Marriage of Tullia to C. Piso Frugi.

„ 63. Consul. The four speeches **In Catilinam.** The **Pro Murena.**

„ 62. Cicero hailed 'pater patriae.' The **Pro Sulla** and **Pro Archia.**

„ 60. Poem 'De consulatu meo.'

„ 59. The First Triumvirate (Caesar, Pompeius, and Crassus). The**Pro Valerio Flacco.**

„ 58-7. Cicero in Exile. The four speeches **Post Reditum.**

„ 56. The **Pro Sestio** and **De Provinciis Consularibus** (his recantation).

„ 55. The **De Oratore** and **De temporibus meis.**

199

„ 52. The **Pro Milone**. The **De Legibus**: the **De Republica**.

„ 51-50. Proconsul of Cilicia. Is granted a *supplicatio*.

„ 49. Joins Pompeius at Dyrrachium.

„ 47. Becomes reconciled to Caesar.

„ 46. The **Brutus** and **Orator**.

„ 45. Death of Tullia. The **De Finibus** and **Academics**.

„ 44. The **Tusculanae Disputationes**: the **De Natura Deorum**: **De Divinatione**: **De Amicitia**: **De Senectute**: **De Officiis**.

      Philippics i-iv.

„ 43. **Philippics v-xiv.** The Second Triumvirate (Antonius, Octavianus, and Lepidus). Murder of Cicero.

2. Works.

(1) **Speeches.**—We possess 57 speeches, and fragments of about 20 more, and we know of 33 others delivered by Cicero.

'As a speaker and orator Cicero succeeded in gaining a place 299beside Demosthenes. His strongest point is his style; there he is clear, concise and apt, perspicuous, elegant and brilliant. He commands all moods, from playful jest to tragic pathos, but is most successful in the imitation of conviction and feeling, to which he gave increased impression by his fiery delivery.'—Teuffel. Quintilian says of him that his eloquence combined the power of Demosthenes, the copiousness of Plato, and the sweetness of Isocrates.

(2) **Philosophical Works.**—The chief are the *De Republica* (closed by the *Sommium Sciponis*): the *De Legibus*: the *De Finibus Bonorum et Malorum*: the *Academics*: *Tusculan Disputations* with the *De Divinatione*: the *De Senectute* and *De Amicitia*: *De natura Deorum*, and the *De Officiis*.

As a philosopher Cicero had no pretensions to originality. He found the materials for most of these works in the writings of the Greek philosophers. 'I have to supply little but the words,' he writes, 'and for these I am never at a loss.' It was however no small achievement to mould the Latin tongue to be a vehicle for Greek philosophic thought, and thus to render the conclusions of Greek thinkers accessible to his own countrymen.

(3) **Rhetorical treatises.**—The chief are the *De Oratore* (in 3 Books), perhaps the most finished example of the Ciceronian style: the *Brutus* or *De Claris Oratoribus*, and the *Orator* (or *De optime Genere Dicendi*).

(4) **Letters.**—Besides 774 letters written by Cicero, we have 90 addressed to him by friends. The two largest collections of his Letters are the *Epistulae ad Atticum* (68-43 B.C.) and the *Epistulae ad Familiares* (62-43 B.C.).

These letters are of supreme importance for the history of Cicero's time. 'The quality which makes them most valuable is that they were not (like the letters of Pliny, and Seneca, and Madame de Sévigné) written to be published. We see in them Cicero as he was. We behold him in his strength and in his weakness—the bold advocate, and yet timid and vacillating statesman, the fond husband, the affectionate father, the kind master, the warm-hearted friend.'—Tyrrell.

The style of the Letters is colloquial but thoroughly accurate. 'The art of letter-writing suddenly rose in Cicero's hands to its full perfection.'—Mackail.

(5) **Poems.**—The fragments we possess show that verse-writing came easily to him, but he never could have been a great 300poet, for he had not the *divinus afflatus*, so finely expressed by Ovid in the line *Est Deus in nobis, agitante calescimus illo*.

'Cicero stands in prose like Vergil in poetry, as the bridge between the ancient and the modern world. Before his time Latin prose was, from a wide point of view, but one among many local ancient dialects. As it left his hands it had become a universal language, one which had definitely superseded all others, Greek included, as the type of civilised expression.'—Mackail.

CLAUDIUS CLAUDIANUS, flor. 400 A.D.

1. Life.

CLAUDIAN.

Born probably at Alexandria, where he lived until, in the year of the death of Theodosius 395 A.D., he acquired the patronage of Stilicho, the great Vandal general, who, as guardian of the young Emperor Honorius, was practically ruler of the Western Empire. He remained attached to the Court at Milan, Rome and Ravenna, and died soon after the downfall of his patron Stilicho, 408 A.D.

2. Works.

In his historical epics he derived his subjects from his own age, praising his patrons Stilicho (*On the Consulate of Stilicho*) and Honorius (*on the Consulate of Honorius*), and inveighing against Rufinus and Eutropius, the rivals of Stilicho. Of poems on other subjects, 'his three books of the unfinished Rape of Proserpine are among the finest examples of the purely literary epic.'—Mackail.

'Claudian is the last of the Latin poets, forming the transitional link between the Classic and the Gothic mode of thought.'—Coleridge.

3. Style.

'His faults belong almost as much to the age as to the writer. In description he is too copious and detailed: his poems abound with long speeches: his parade of varied learning, his partiality for abstruse mythology, are just the natural defects of a lettered but uninspired epoch.'—North Pinder.

301

QUINTUS ENNIUS, 239-169 B.C.

1. Life.

ENNIUS.

He was born at Rudiae in Calabria (about 19 miles S. of Brundisium), a meeting-place of three different languages, that of common life (Oscan, cf. *Opici*), that of culture and education (Greek), that of military service (Latin). Here he lived for some twenty years, availing himself of those means of education which at this time were denied to Rome or Latium. We next hear of him serving as centurion in Sardinia, where he attracted the attention of Cato, then quaestor, and accompanied him to Rome, 204 B.C. Here for some fifteen years he lived plainly, supporting himself by teaching Greek, and making translations of Greek plays for the Roman stage, and so won the friendship of the elder Scipio. In 189 B.C. M. Fulvius Nobilior took Ennius with him in his campaign against the Aetolians, as a witness and herald of his deeds. His son obtained for Ennius the Roman citizenship (184 B.C.) by giving him a grant of land at Potentia in Picenum. *Nos sumus Romani, qui fuimus ante Rudini.* The rest of his life was spent mainly at Rome in cheerful simplicity and active literary work.

2. Works.

The chief are:—

(1) **Tragedies.**—Mainly translations, especially from Euripides. A few fragments only remain. 'It was certainly due to Ennius that Roman Tragedy was first raised to that pitch of popular favour which it enjoyed till the age of Cicero.'—Sellar.

(2) **Annales.**—An Epic Hexameter poem, in 18 books, which dealt with the History of Rome from the landing of Aeneas in Italy down to the Third Macedonian War (Pydna, 168 B.C.). About 600 lines are extant.

'In his Annals he unfolds a long gallery of national portraits. His heroes are men of one common aim—the advancement of Rome; animated with one sentiment, devotion to the State. All that was purely personal in them seems merged in the traditional pictures which express only the fortitude, dignity and sagacity of the Republic.'—Sellar.

302

3. Style.

For the first time Ennius succeeded in moulding the Latin language to the movement of the Greek hexameter. In spite of imperfections and roughness, his *Annals* remained the foremost and representative Roman poem till Vergil wrote the *Aeneid.* Lucretius, whom he influenced, and to whom Vergil owes so much, says of him:

Ennius ut noster cecinit, qui primus amoeno
Detulit ex Helicone perenni fronde coronam,
Per gentes Italas hominum quae clara clueret;

'As sang our Ennius, the first who brought down from pleasant Helicon a chaplet of unfading leaf, the fame of which should ring out clear through the nations of Italy.'

And later, Quintilian, X. i. 88: 'Ennium sicut sacros vetustate lucos adoremus, in quibus grandia et antiqua robora iam non tantam habent speciem quantam religionem: Let us venerate Ennius like the groves, sacred from their antiquity, in which the great and ancient oak-trees are invested, not so much with beauty, as with sacred associations.'—Sellar.

FLAVIUS EUTROPIUS, fl. 375 A.D.

1. Life.

EUTROPIUS.

Very little is known of his life. He is said to have held the office of a secretary under Contanstine the Great (*ob.* 337 A.D.), and to have served under the Emperor Julian in his ill-fated expedition against the Persians, 363 A.D.

2. Works.

His only extant work is his

Breviarium Historiae Romanae.—A brief compendium of Roman History in ten books from the foundation of the city to the accession of Valens, 364 A.D., to whom it is inscribed.

201

3. Style.

His work is a compilation made from the best authorities, with good judgment and impartiality, and in a simple style. Its brevity and practical arrangement made it very popular.

303

1. Life.

FLORUS.

L. Julius (or Annaeus) Florus lived at Rome in the time of Trajan or Hadrian. Little else is known of his life.

2. Works.

An Epitome of the Wars of Livy, in two Books:—

Book I. treats of the good time of Rome, 753-133 B.C. (the Gracchi).

„ II. treats of the decline of Rome, 133-29 B.C. (Temple of Janus closed).

3. Style.

A pretentious and smartly written work abounding in mistakes, contradictions, and misrepresentations of historical truth. It was, however, popular in the Middle Ages on account of its brevity and its rhetorical style. Florus is useful in giving us a short account of events in periods where we have no books of Livy to guide us.

S. JULIUS FRONTINUS, circ. 41-103 A.D.

1. Life.

FRONTINUS.

He was *praetor urbanus* 70 A.D., and in 75 succeeded Cerealis as governor oi Britain, where, as Tacitus tells us, he distinguished himself by the conquest of the Silures: *sustinuit molem Iulius Frontinus, vir magnus, quantum licebat, validamque et pugnacem Silurum gentem armis subegit.* 'Julius Frontinus was equal to the burden, a great man as far as greatness was then possible (i.e. under the jealous rule of Domitian), who subdued by his arms the powerful and warlike tribe of the Silures.'

In 97 he was nominated *curator aquarum*, administrator of the aqueducts of Rome: the closing years of his life were passed in studious retirement at his villa on the Bay of Naples. Cf. Mart. X. lviii.

2. Works.

Two works of his are extant:—

(1) **De Aquis Urbis Romae.**—A treatise on the Roman water-supply, published under Trajan, soon after the death of Nerva, 97 A.D.; a complete and valuable account.

304

(2) **Strategemata.**—A manual of strategy, in three books, consisting of historical examples derived chiefly from Sallust, Caesar, and Livy.

3. Style.

Simple and concise: 'he shuns the conceits of the period and goes back to the republican authors, of whom (and especially of Caesar's Commentaries) his language strongly reminds us.'— Cruttwell.

As a mark of his unaffected modesty, Pliny (*Ep.* ix. 19) tells us: *vetuit exstrui monimentum: sed quibus verbis? 'impensa monimenta supervacua est: memoria nostri durabit, si vita meruimus.'*

AULUS GELLIUS, circ. 123-175 A.D.

1. Life.

GELLIUS.

All that is known about his life is gathered from occasional hints in his own writings. He seems to have spent his early years at Rome, studying under the most famous teachers, first at Rome and afterwards at Athens, and then to have returned to Rome, where he spent the remaining years of his life in literary pursuits and in the society of a large circle of friends.

2. Works.

The **Noctes Atticae** (so called because it was begun during the long nights of winter in a country house in Attica) in twenty books consists of numerous extracts from Greek and Roman writers on subjects connected with history, philosophy, philology, natural science and antiquities, illustrated by abundant criticisms and discussions. It is, in fact, a commonplace book, and the arrangement of the contents is merely casual, following the course of his reading of Greek and Latin authors. The work is, however, of special value to us from the very numerous quotations from ancient authors preserved by him alone.

3. Style.

His language is sober but full of archaisms, which he much affected (he gives, therefore, no quotations from post-Augustan writers). His style shows the defects of an age in which men had ceased to feel the full meaning of the words they used, and strove to hide the triviality of a subject under obscure phrases 305and florid expression. Yet, on the whole, he is a very interesting writer, and the last that can in any way be called classical.

'*Vir elegantissimi eloquii et multae ac facundae scientiae.*'—St. Augustine, 400 A.D.

QUINTUS HORATIUS FLACCUS, 65-8 B.C.

1. Important Events in the Life of Horace.

HORACE.

B.C. 65. Born at Venusia (*Venosa*) on the confines of Apulia and Lucania.

B.C. 53-46. Educated at Rome under the famous *plagosus* Orbilius.

„ 46-44. At the University of Athens.

„ 44-42. Served under Brutus as *tribunus militum*. fought at Philippi.

„ 42-39. Pardoned by Octavianus and allowed to return to Rome. His poverty compelled him to write verses, prob. *Sat.* I, ii. iii. iv., and some *Epodes*. Through these he obtained the notice of Varius and Vergil, who became his fast friends and

„ 38. introduced him to Maecenas, the trusted minister of Augustus.

„ 35. **Satires, Book I** published. (Journey to Brundisium described,*Sat.* I. v.)

„ 33. Maecenas bestowed upon him a Sabine farm (about 15 miles N.E. of Tivoli). For fullest description see *Epist.* I. xvi.

„ 31. **Satires, Book II, and Epodes** published.

„ 23. **Odes, Books I-III** published.

„ 20. **Epistles, Book I** published.

„ 17. **Carmen Saeculare** written at the request of Augustus for the*Ludi Saeculares.*

„ 13. **Odes, Book IV** published.

„ 12. **Epistles, Book II** published.

„ 8. Died in the same year as his friend and patron Maecenas.

3. Works.

(1) **Odes**, in four books, and **Epodes**.—The words of Cicero (*pro Archia* 16) best describe the abiding value of the four Books of the Odes—*Adolescentiam alunt* (strengthen), *senectutem oblectant, secundas res ornant, adversis perfugium ac* 306*solacium praebent, delectant domi, non impediunt foris, pernoctant nobiscum, peregrinantur, rusticantur.* In them we see a poet, as Quintilian says,*verbis felicissime audax*—most happily daring in his use of words and endowed, as Petronius says, with *curiosa felicitas*, a subtle happiness of expression—'what oft was thought but ne'er so well express'd.'

(2) **Satires (Sermones)** in two Books.—Horace's chief model is Lucilius, whom he wished to adapt to the Augustan age. To touch on political topics was impossible; Horace employed satire to display his own individuality and his own views on various subjects. Book I (his earliest effort) is marred by faults in execution and is often wanting in good taste; but in Book II 'he uses the hexameter to exhibit the semi-dramatic form of easy dialogue, with a perfection as complete as that of Vergil in the stately and serious manner. In reading these Satires we all read our own minds and hearts.'—Mackail.

(3) **The Epistles (Sermones)** in two Books, and **Ars Poetica** (*Ep. ad Pisones*).—These represent his most mature production. As a poet Horace now stood without a rival. Life was still full of vivid interest for him, but years (*fallentis semita vitae*) had brought the philosophic mind. 'To teach the true end and wise regulation of life, and to act on character from within, are the motives of the more formal and elaborate epistles.'—Sellar.

The **Ars Poetica** is a *résumé* of Greek criticism on the drama.

3. Style.

'With the principal lyric metres, the Sapphic and Alcaic, Horace had done what Vergil had accomplished with the dactylic hexameter, carried them to the highest point of which the foreign Latin tongue was capable.'—Mackail.

'As Vergil is the most idealising exponent of what was of permanent and universal significance in the time, Horace is the most complete exponent of its actual life and movement. He is at once the lyrical poet, with heart and imagination responsive to the deeper meaning and lighter amusements of life, and the satirist, the moralist, and the literary critic of the age.'—Sellar.

JUSTINUS, circ. 150 A.D. (*temp.* Antoninus Pius).

1. Life.

JUSTINUS.

We know nothing positively about him, though probably he lived in the age of the Antonines. Teuffel says 'Considering his correct mode of thinking and the 307style of his preface, we should not like to put him much later than Florus, who epitomised Livy.'

2. Works.

Epitoma Historiarum Philippicarum Pompei Trogi, in forty-four Books.—An abridgment of the Universal History of Pompeius Trogus (*temp.* Livy). The title *Historiae Philippicae* was given to it by Trogus because its main object was to give the history of the

Macedonian monarchy, with all its branches, but he allowed himself, like Herodotus, to indulge in such large digressions that it was regarded by many as a Universal History. It was arranged according to nations; it began with Ninus, the Nimrod of legend, and was brought down to about 9 A.D.

3. Style.

Justinus (as he tells us in his Preface) made it his business to form an attractive reading-book—*breve veluti florum corpusculum feci* (an anthology)—and his chief merit is that he seems to have been a faithful abbreviator.

DECIMUS JUNIUS JUVENALIS, 55-138 A.D.

1. Life.

JUVENAL.

Of Juvenal's life very little is certainly known. Thirteen lives of him exist, which are confused and contradictory in detail. From the evidences of the Satires we learn that he lived from early youth at Rome, but went for holidays to Aquinum, a town of the Volscians (where perhaps he was born in the reign of Nero); that he had a small farm at Tibur, and a house in Rome, where he entertained his friends in a modest way; that he had been in Egypt; that he wrote Satires late in life; that he reached his eightieth year, and lived into the reign of Antoninus Pius. He complains frequently and bitterly of his poverty and of the hardships of a dependent's life. In short, the circumstances of his life were very similar to those of Martial, who speaks of Juvenal as a very intimate friend.

The famous inscription at Aquinum—which Duff considers does not refer to the poet but to a wealthy kinsman of his—indicates that he had served in the army as commander of a Dalmatian cohort, and, as one of the chief men of the town, 308was superintendent of the civic worship paid to Vespasian after his deification.

All the Lives assert that Juvenal was banished to Egypt—Juvenal himself never alludes to this—for offence given to an actor who was high in favour with the reigning Emperor (Hadrian according to Prof. Hardy), and that he died in exile.

2. Works.

Saturae, sixteen, grouped in five Books.

Books I-III (Satires 1-9) are sharply divided both in form and substance from Books IV-V (Satires 10-16), which are not satires at all, but moral essays, in the form of letters. The first nine satires present a wonderfully vivid picture of the seamy side of life at Rome at the end of the first century. We must, however, read side by side with them the contemporary Letters of Pliny, in which we find ourselves in a different world from that scourged by the satirist.

'His chief literary qualities are his power of painting lifelike scenes, and his command of brilliant epigrammatic phrase.'—Duff. Nothing, for instance, could surpass his picture of the fall of Sejanus (Sat. x. 56-97). His power of coining phrases is seen in these *sententiæ: nemo repente fuit turpissimus—expende Hannibalem: quot libras in duce summo | invenies: maxima debetur puero reverentia: mens sana in corpora sano*—which are familiar proverbs among educated men.

Juvenal tells us that he takes all life, all the world, for his text:

Quidquid agunt homines, Votum, Timor, Ira, Voluptas,
Gaudia, Discursus, nostri est farrago libelli

(the motley subject of my page).—Sat. i. 85-6.

TITUS LIVIUS PATAVINUS, circ. 59 B.C.-17 A.D.

1. Life.

LIVY.

Livy was born at Patavium (*Padua*) between the years 59 and 57 B.C. Little is known of his life, but his aristocratic sympathies, as seen in his writings, seem to suggest that he was of good family. Padua was a populous and busy place, where opportunities for public speaking were abundant and the public life vigorous; thus Livy was early trained in eloquence, and lived amid scenes of 309human activity. About 30 B.C. he settled at Rome, where his literary talents secured the patronage and friendship of Augustus. But though a courtier he was no flatterer. 'Titus Livius,' says Tacitus (*Ann.*iv. 34), 'pre-eminently famous for eloquence and truthfulness, extolled Cn. Pompeius in such a panegyric that Augustus called him Pompeianus, and yet this was no obstacle to their friendship.' He returned to his native town before his death, 17 A.D., at the age of about 75.

2. Works.

History of Rome (*Ab urbe condita Libri*), a comprehensive account in 142 Books of the whole History of Rome from the foundation of the City to the death of Drusus, 9 A.D. It is probable that he intended to continue his work in 150 Books, down to the death of Augustus in 14A.D., the point from which Tacitus starts. The number of Books now extant is 35, about one fourth of the whole number, but we possess summaries (*Periochae* or *Argumenta*) of nearly the

204

whole work. The division of the History into decades (sets of ten Books), though merely conventional, is convenient. According to this arrangement the Books now extant are:

Books I-X, 754-293 B.C., to nearly the close of the Third Samnite War.

Books XXI-XXX, 219-201 B.C., the narrative of the Second Punic War.

Books XXXI-XLV, 201-167 B.C., describe the Wars in Greece and Macedonia, and end with the triumph of Aemilius Paulus after Pydna, 168 B.C.

3. Style.

His style is characterised by variety, liveliness, and picturesqueness. 'As a master of style Livy is in the first rank of historians. He marks the highest point which the enlarged and enriched prose of the Augustan age reached just before it began to fall into decadence. . . . The periodic structure of Latin prose, which had been developed by Cicero, is carried by him to an even greater complexity and used with a greater daring and freedom. . . . His imagination never fails to kindle at great actions; it is he, more than any other author, who has impressed the great soldiers and statesmen of the Republic on the imagination of the world.'—Mackail.

310

4. The Speeches.

'The spirit in which he writes History is well illustrated by the Speeches. These, in a way, set the tone of the whole work. He does not affect in them to reproduce the substance of words actually spoken, or even to imitate the colour of the time in which the speech is laid. He uses them rather as a vivid and dramatic method of portraying character and motive.'—Mackail. 'Everything,' says Quintilian (X. i. 101), 'is perfectly adapted both to the circumstances and personages introduced.'

5. The Purpose of his History.

The first ten books of Livy were being written about the same time as the *Aeneid*; both Vergil and Livy had the same patriotic purpose, 'to celebrate the growth, in accordance with a divine dispensation, of the Roman Empire and Roman civilisation.'—Nettleship. Livy, however, brought into greater prominence the moral causes which contributed to the growth of the Empire. In his preface to Book I, § 9, he asks his readers to consider *what have been the life and habits of the Romans, by aid of what men and by what talents at home and in the field their Empire has been gained and extended.* Only by virtue and manliness, justice and piety, was the dominion of the world achieved.

'In ancient Rome he sees his ideal realised, and *romanus* hence signifies in his language all that is noble. He thus involuntarily appears partial to Rome, and unjust to her enemies, notably to the Samnites and Hannibal.'—Teuffel.

'As the title of *Gesta Populi Romani* was given to the *Aeneid* on its appearance, so the *Historiae ab Urbe Condita* might be called, with no less truth, a funeral eulogy—*consummatio totius vitae et quasi funebris laudatio* (Sen. *Suas.* VI. 21)—delivered, by the most loving and most eloquent of her sons, over the grave of the great Republic.'—Mackail.

M. ANNAEUS LUCANUS, 39-65 A.D.

1. Life.

LUCAN.

Important Events in the Life of Lucan.

A.D. 39. Born at Corduba (*Cordova*) on the R. Baetis (*Guadalquivir*).

A.D. 40. His father migrates with his family to Rome.

,, 54-68. Nero Emperor.

311

,, 55. Lucan under Cornutus, the tutor also of Persius.

,, 57-9. At the University of Athens.

,, 60. Wins the favour of Nero, who begins to hate Seneca.

,, 61. Lucan quaestor: famous as a reciter and pleader.

,, 62. Disgrace of Seneca. **Pharsalia I.-III.** published. Death of Persius.

,, 63. Marries Polla Argentaria, a marriage of affection.

,, 64. Nero, from jealousy, forbids Lucan to publish poems or to recite them.

,, 65. Pisonian conspiracy discovered. Lucan compelled to die.

Lucan was a nephew of M. Annaeus Novatus (the Gallio of Acts xviii. 12-17), and of Seneca, the philosopher and tutor of Nero. 'Rhetoric and Stoic dogma were the staple of his mental training. For a much-petted, quick-witted youth, plunged into such a society as that of Rome in the first century A.D., hardly any training could be more mischievous. Puffed up with presumed merits and the applause of the lecture-room and the *salon*, he became a shallow rhetorician, devoted to phrase-making and tinsel ornament, and ready to write and declaim on any subject in verse or prose at the shortest notice.'—Heitland. Silenced by Nero, in an enforced retirement—probably in the stately gardens spoken of by Juvenal vii. 79-80 *contentus fama iaceat*

205

*Lucanus in hortis Marmoreis—Lucan may repose in his park adorned with statues and find fame enough—*he brooded over his wrongs, and despairing of any other way of restoration to public life, joined the ill-fated conspiracy of Piso.

2. Works.

The **Pharsalia** (or *De Bello Civili*), an epic poem in ten Books, from the beginning of the Civil War down to the point where Caesar is besieged in Alexandria, 49-48 B.C. His narrative thus runs parallel to Caesar's *De Bello Civili*, but it contains some valuable additional matter and gives a faithful picture of the feeling general among the nobility of the day.

3. Style.

'To Lucan's rhetorical instincts and training, and the influence of the recitations which Juvenal *Sat.* iii. tells us were 312so customary and such a nuisance in his day, are due the great defects of the *Pharsalia*. We see the sacrifice of the whole to the parts, neglect of the matter in an over-studious regard for the manner, a self-conscious tone appealing rather to an audience than to a reader, venting itself in apostrophes, digressions, hyperbole (over-drawn description), episodes and epigrams, an unhappy laboriousness that strains itself to be first-rate for a moment, but leaves the poem second-rate for ever.'—Heitland.

The general effect of Lucan's verse is one of steady monotony, due to a want of variety in the pauses and in the ending of lines, and a too sparing use of elision, by which Vergil was able to regulate the movement of lines and make sound and sense agree.

'In spite of its immaturity and bad taste the poem compels admiration by its elevation of thought and sustained brilliance of execution; it contains passages of lofty thought and real beauty, such as the dream of Pompeius, or the character which Cato gives of Pompeius, and is full of quotations which have become household words; such as, *In se magna ruunt—Stat magni nominis umbra—Nil actum reputans si quid superesset agendum* (a line which rivals Caesar's energy).'—Mackail.

The brief and balanced judgment of Quintilian (*Inst. Orat.* X. i. 90) sums up Lucan in words which suggest at once his chief merits and defects as a poet: *Lucanus ardens et concitatus et sententiis clarissimus et magis oratoribus quam poetis imitandus—Lucan has fire and point, is very famous for his maxims, and indeed is rather a model for orators than poets.*

GAIUS LUCILIUS, circ. 170-103 B.C.

1. Life.

LUCILIUS.

Lucilius was born in the Latin town of Suessa of the Aurunci, in Campania, of a well-to-do equestrian family. Velleius tells us that the sister of Lucilius was grandmother to Pompeius, and that Lucilius served in the cavalry under Scipio in the Numantine war, 134 B.C. Lucilius lived on very intimate terms with Scipio Africanus Minor and Laelius, and died at Naples (103 B.C.), where he was honoured with a public funeral.

2. Works.

Saturae in thirty Books, in various metres. Fragments only are extant.

313

'After Terence he is the most distinguished and the most important in his literary influence among the friends of Scipio. The form of literature which he invented and popularised, that of familiar poetry, was one which proved singularly suited to the Latin genius. He speaks of his own works under the name of *Sermones* (talks)—a name which was retained by his great successor and imitator Horace; but the peculiar combination of metrical form with wide range of subject and the pedestrian style of ordinary prose received in popular usage the name*Satura* (mixture).'—Mackail.

Satura quidem tota nostra est, in qua primus insignem laudem adeptus Lucilius.—Quint. X. i. 93.

'The chief social vices which Lucilius attacks are those which reappear in the pages of the later satirists. They are the two extremes to which the Roman temperament was most prone: rapacity and meanness in gaining money, vulgar ostentation and coarse sensuality in using it.'—Sellar.

Juvenal says of him (*Sat.* i. 165-7):

'When old Lucilius seems to draw his sword and growls in burning ire, the hearer blushes for shame, his conscience is chilled for his offences, and his heart faints for secret sins.'

T. LUCRETIUS CARUS, circ. 99-55 B.C.

1. Life.

LUCRETIUS.

Very little is known of his life. The subject of his poem prevented him from telling his own history as Catullus, Horace, and Ovid have done, and his contemporaries seldom refer to him. The name Lucretius suggests that he was descended from one of the most ancient patrician houses of Rome, famous in the early annals of the Republic. He was evidently a man of wealth and position, but he deliberately chose the life of contemplation, and lived apart from the ambitions and follies of his day. Donatus, in his life of Vergil, tells us that Lucretius died on the day on which Vergil assumed the *toga virilis*, Oct. 15, 55 B.C.

2. Works.

The **De Rerum Natura**, a didactic poem in hexameter verse in six Books. The poem was left unfinished at his death, and Munro supports the tradition that Cicero both corrected it and superintended its publication. The object of the poem is to 314deliver men from the fear of death and the terrors of superstition by the new knowledge of Nature:

Hunc igitur terrorem animi tenebrasque necessest
Non radii solis neque lucida tela diei
Discutiant, sed naturae species ratioque.

This terror of the soul, therefore, and this darkness must be dispelled, not by the rays of the sun or the bright shafts of day, but by the outward aspect and harmonious plan of nature.—S.

The source of these terrors is traced to the general ignorance of certain facts in Nature—ignorance, namely, of the constitution and condition of our minds and bodies, of the means by which the world came into existence and is still maintained, and, lastly, of the causes of many natural phenomena. Thus:

Books I and II uphold the principles of the Atomic Theory as held by Epicurus (*fl.* 300 B.C.).

Book I states that the world consists of atoms and void. At line 694 is stated the important doctrine that the evidence of the senses alone is to be believed—*sensus, unde omnia credita pendent, the senses on which rests all our belief.*

Book II treats of the *motions* of atoms, including the curious doctrine of the *swerve*, which enables them to combine and makes freedom of will possible: then of their *shapes* and *arrangement.*

Book III shows the nature of mind (*animus*) and life (*anima*) to be material and therefore mortal. Therefore death is nothing to us:

Nil igitur mors est ad nos neque pertinet hilum,
Quandoquidem natura animi mortalis habetur.
Death therefore to us is nothing, concerns us not a jot,
Since the nature of the mind is proved to be mortal.—(M.)

Book IV gives Lucretius' theory of vision and the nature of dreams and apparitions.

Book V explains the origin of the heavens, of the earth, of vegetable and animal life upon it, and the advance of human nature from a savage state to the arts and usages of civilisation.

Book VI describes and accounts for certain natural phenomena—thunderstorms, tempests, volcanoes, earthquakes, and the like. It concludes with a theory of disease, illustrated by a fine description of the plague at Athens.

Professor Tyrrell says: 'It is interesting to point to places 315in which Lucretius or his predecessors had really anticipated modern scientific research. Thus Lucretius recognises that in a vacuum every body, no matter what its weight, falls with equal swiftness; the circulation of the sap in the vegetable world is known to him, and he describes falling stars, aerolites, etc., as the unused material of the universe.' The great truth that matter is not destroyed but only changes its form is very clearly stated by Lucretius, and his account (Book V) of the beginnings of life upon the earth, the evolution of man, and the progress of human society is interesting and valuable.

3. Style.

'Notwithstanding the antique tinge (e.g. his use of archaism, assonance, and alliteration) which for poetical ends he has given to his poem, the best judges have always looked upon it as one of the purest models of the Latin idiom in the age of its greatest perfection.'—Munro.

'The language of Lucretius, so bold, so genial, so powerful, and in its way so perfect.'—Nettleship.

Carmina sublimis tunc sunt peritura Lucreti,
Exitio terras cum dabit una dies.

Ovid. Am. l. xv. 23.

'But till this cosmic order everywhere
Shattered into one earthquake in one day
Cracks all to pieces ... till that hour
My golden work shall stand.'

Tennyson, Lucretius.

MARCUS MANILIUS, fl. 12 A.D.

1. Life.

MANILIUS.

Nothing is known of his life. That he was not of Roman birth (perhaps a native of N. Africa) is probable from the foreign colouring of his language at the outset, which in the later books becomes more smooth and fluent from increased practice.

2. Works.

The **Astronomica** in five Books of hexameter verse. The poem should rather be called Astrology, as Astronomy is treated only in Book I. He is proud of being the first writer on this subject in Latin literature. A close study of Lucretius is obvious from several passages: he often imitates Vergil, and in the legends (e.g. of Perseus and Andromeda) Ovid.

316

3. Style.

He is not a great poet; but he is a writer of real power both in thought and style. In his introductions to each Book, and in his digressions, he shows sincere feeling and poetical ability.

M. VALERIUS MARTIALIS, circ. 40-102 A.D.

1. Life.

MARTIAL.

He was born at Bilbilis in Hispania Tarraconensis (E. Spain), a town situated on a rocky height overlooking the R. Salo:

Municipes, Augusta mihi quos Bilbilis acri
Monte creat, rapidis quem Salo cingit aquis.

X. ciii. 1-2.

His father gave him a good education, and at the age of twenty-three (63 A.D.) he went to Rome. After living there for thirty-five years, patronised by Titus and Vespasian, he returned to Bilbilis soon after the accession of Trajan (98 A.D.), where he died *circ.* 102 A.D.

At Rome he for a time found powerful friends in his great countrymen of the house of Seneca (Lucan and Seneca were then at the height of their fame), and from 79 to 96 (*temp.* Trajan and Domitian) he received the patronage of the Court, and numbered among his friends Pliny the Younger, Quintilian, Juvenal, Valerius Flaccus, and Silius Italicus. His complaints of his poverty are incessant. It is true that he lived throughout the life of a dependent, but it is probable that Martial was a poor man who contrived to get through a good deal of money, and who mistook for poverty a capacity for spending more than he could get.

2. Works.

Epigrammata in fourteen Books (Books XIII and XIV, *Xenia* and*Apophoreta*, are two collections of inscriptions for presents at the Saturnalia); also a **Liber Spectaculorum** on the opening of the grand Flavian amphitheatre (the Coliseum) begun by Vespasian and completed by Titus.

3. Style.

'Martial did not create the epigram. What he did was to differentiate the epigram and elaborate it. Adhering always to 317what he considered the true type of the literary epigram, consisting of i. the *preface*, or description of the occasion of the epigram, rousing the curiosity to know what the poet has to say about it; and, ii. the explanation or commentary of the poet, commonly called the *point*—he employed his vast resources of satire, wit, observation, fancy, and pathos to produce the greatest number of varieties of epigram that the type admits of. . . . What Martial really stands convicted of on his own showing is of laughing at that which ought to have roused in him shame and indignation, and of making literary capital out of other men's vices.'—Stephenson. Among his good points are his candour, his love of nature, and the loyalty of his friendships.

Pliny says of him: *Audio Valerium Martialem decessisse et moleste fero. Erat homo ingeniosus, acutus, acer, et qui plurimum in scribendo et sltis haberet et fellis, nec candoris minus—I hear with regret that V. Martial is dead. He was a man of talent, acuteness, and spirit: with plenty of wit and gall, and as sincere as he was witty.*—Pliny, *Ep.*iii. 21.

'The greatest epigrammatist of the world, and one of its most disagreeable literary characters.'—Merrill.

CORNELIUS NEPOS, circ. 100-24 B.C.

1. Life.

NEPOS.

Nepos was probably born at Ticinium on the R. Padus. He inherited an ample fortune, and was thereby enabled to keep aloof from public life and to devote himself to literature and to writing works of an historical nature. In earlier life he was one of the circle of Catullus, who dedicated a collection of poems to him (Catull.*C.* i.): 'To whom am I to give my dainty, new-born little volume? To you, Cornelius.' He was also a friend and contemporary of Cicero, and after Cicero's death (43 B.C.) was one of the chief friends of Atticus.

2. Works.

Of his numerous writings on history, chronology, and grammar we possess only a fragment of his **De Viris Illustribus** (originally in sixteen Books), a collection of Roman and foreign biographies. Of this work there is extant one complete section, **De Excellentibus Ducibus Exterarum Gentium**, and two lives, 318those of Atticus and Cato the Younger, from his **De Historicis Latinis**.

3. Style.

Nepos is a most untrustworthy historian, and his work possesses little independent value. But his style is clear, elegant, and lively, and he did much to make Greek learning popular among his fellow-citizens.

PUBLIUS OVIDIUS NASO, 43 B.C.-18 A.D.

1. Life.

OVID.

Ovid's own writings (espec. *Tr.* IV. x.) supply nearly all the information we possess regarding his life. He was born at Sulmo, a town in the cold, moist hills of the Peligni, one of the Sabine clans, situated near Corfinium, and about ninety miles E. of Rome. He was of an ancient equestrian family, and together with his elder brother received a careful education at Rome, and studied also at Athens. He was trained for the Bar, but in spite of his father's remonstrances preferred poetry to public life. 'An easy fortune, a brilliant wit, an inexhaustible memory, and an unfailing social tact soon made him a prominent figure in society; and his genuine love of literature and admiration for genius made him the friend of the whole contemporary world of letters.'—Mackail. Up to his fiftieth year fortune smiled steadily upon Ovid: his works were universally popular, and he enjoyed the favour and patronage of the Emperor himself. But towards the end of 8 A.D. an imperial edict ordered him to leave Rome on a named day and take up his residence at the small barbarous town of Tomi, on the Black Sea, at the extreme outposts of civilisation. Augustus proved deaf to all entreaties to recall him, Tiberius remained alike inexorable, and Ovid died of a broken heart at the age of sixty, in the tenth year of his banishment.

2. Works.

(1) **Amores**, in three Books, poems in elegiac verse, nearly all on Corinna, who was probably no real person, but only a name around which Ovid grouped his own fancies, and wrote as the poet of a fashionable, pleasure-loving society. The *Mors Psittaci* is pleasing and the *Mors Tibulli* is a noble tribute to a brother poet.

319

(2) **Heroides**, twenty letters in elegiac verse, feigned to have been written by ladies or chiefs of the heroic age to the absent objects of their love (15-20 are in pairs, e.g. Paris to Helen and Helen to Paris, and are probably spurious). 'The Letters 1-14 are thoroughly modern: they express the feelings and speak the language of refined women in a refined age, and all exhibit an artificiality both in the substance and the manner of their pleading.'—Sellar.

(3) **Ars Amatoria**, in elegiac verse in three Books. This is an ironical form of didactic poetry in which Ovid teaches the art of lying quite as much as the art of loving.

(4) **Remedia Amoris**, in elegiac verse, while professing to be a recantation of the *Ars Amatoria*, shows, if possible, a worse taste.

(5) **Metamorphoses**, in hexameter verse in fifteen Books, containing versions of legends on transformations (*mutatae formae*) from Chaos down to Caesar's transformation into a star. In some respects this is his greatest poem: Ovid himself makes for it as strong a claim to immortality as Horace does for his Odes:

> *Quaque patet domitis Romana potentia terris,*
> *Ore legar populi perque omnia saecula fama,*
> *Siquid habent veri vatum praesagia, vivam.*

Met. XV. 877-end.

'The attractiveness of this work lies in its descriptions; but the attempt to divest it of the character of a dictionary of mythology by interweaving stories, after the fashion of the *Arabian Nights*, is only partially successful.'—Tyrrell.

(6) **Fasti**, in elegiac verse in six Books, a poetical calendar of the Roman year. Each month has a Book allotted to it, and Ovid probably sketched out Books vii-xii, but his exile made it impossible for him to complete the work. It contains much valuable information on Roman customs and some exquisitely told stories (*e.g.* the Rape of Proserpine), but leaves the impression of being an effort to produce on the reader the effect of a patriotism which the writer did not feel.

(7) **Poems Written in Exile.**

(i) **Tristia**, in elegiac verse in five Books: letters to Augustus, to Ovid's wife (for whom he had a deep affection) and to friends, praying for pardon or for a place of exile nearer Rome. 320

(ii) **Epistulae ex Ponto**: similar to the *Tristia*.

'These poems are a melancholy record of flagging vitality and failing powers.'—Mackail.

3. Style.

The real importance of Ovid in literature and his gift to posterity lay in the new and vivid life which he imparted to the fables of Greek mythology. 'No other classical poet has furnished more ideas than Ovid to the Italian poets and painters of the Renaissance, and to our own poets—from Chaucer to Pope, who, like Ovid,

"'Lisped in numbers, for the numbers came.'"

AULUS PERSIUS FLACCUS, 34-62 A.D.

1. Life.

PERSIUS.

He was born at Volaterrae in Etruria, and was the son of a Roman knight of wealth and rank. At twelve years of age Persius was removed to Rome, where he placed himself under the guidance of the Stoic Cornutus, who remained his close friend to the end of his short life. Persius (*Sat.* v.) touchingly describes his residence with Cornutus, and the influence of this beloved teacher in moulding his character:

Pars tua sit, Cornute, animae, tibi, dulcis amice,
Ostendisse iuvat:
'My delight is to show you, Cornutus, how large a share of my inmost being is yours, my beloved friend.'—C.

He was nearly related to Arria, daughter of that 'true wife' who taught her husband Paetus how to die (Mart. I. xiii.; Pliny *Epist.* i. 16). In the consistent life of Thrasea (the husband of Arria), who was a Cato in justice and more than a Cato in goodness, Persius had a noble example to follow. So during the short span of his life the poet lived and worked, a man of maidenly modesty, an excellent son, brother, and nephew, of frugal and moderate habits.

2. Works.

Saturae, six Satires in hexameter verse. The first, devoted to an attack upon the literary style of the day, is the only real Satire: the other five are declamations or dogmas of the Stoic system (e.g. Sat. ii., on right and wrong prayers to the gods), interspersed with dramatic scenes. It was to Lucilius that 321Persius owed the impulse that made him a writer of Satire, but his obligations to Horace are paramount. 'He was what would be called a plagiarist, but probably no writer ever borrowed so much and yet left on the mind so decided an impression of originality. Where he draws from his own experience, his portraits have an imaginative truth, minutely accurate yet highly ideal, which would entitle them to a distinguished place in any portrait gallery.'—Nettleship.

3. Style.

'The involved and obscure style of much of his work is the style which his taste leads him to assume for satiric purposes. He feels that a clear, straightforward, everyday manner of speech would not suit a subject over which the gods themselves might hesitate whether to laugh or weep. As the poet of Stoicism, using the very words of Vergil, he calls upon a benighted race to acquaint itself with the *causes* of things: to an inquiry into the purpose of man's being, the art of skilful driving in the chariot-race of life, and the ordained position of each individual in the social system.'—Nettleship.

'Persius is the sole instance among Roman writers of a philosopher whose life was in accordance with the doctrines he professed.'—Cruttwell.

Multum et verae gloriae quamvis uno libro Persius meruit.—Quint.*Inst. Orat.* X. i. 94.

PETRONIUS ARBITER, obiit 66 A.D.

1. Life.

PETRONIUS.

He is probably the Petronius of whose life and character Tacitus has given us a brilliant sketch in the*Annals*, xvi. 18. 19. 'His days were passed,' says Tacitus, 'in sleep, his nights in the duties or pleasures of life: where others toiled for fame he had lounged into it. Yet, as governor of Bithynia, and afterwards as consul, he showed himself a vigorous and capable administrator; then relapsing into the habit or assuming the mask of vice, he was adopted as **Elegantiae Arbiter** (*the authority on taste*) into the small circle of Nero's intimate companions. No luxury was charming or refined till Petronius had given it his approval, and the jealousy of Tigellinus was roused against a rival and master in the science of pleasure.' Petronius anticipated his inevitable fate by committing suicide.

322

2. Works.

Satirae (or **Satiricon**), a character-novel, often called, from its central and most entertaining incident, *The Supper of Trimalchio.* 'This is the description of a Christmas dinner-party given by a sort of Golden Dustman and his wife, people of low birth and little education, who had come into an enormous fortune. The dinner itself, and the conversation on literature and art that goes on at the dinner-table, are conceived in a spirit of the wildest humour.'—Mackail.

The chief interest of the *Satiricon* for us is the glimpse which it affords of everyday manners and conversation under the Empire among all orders of society, from the highest to the lowest.

PHAEDRUS (*temp.* Augustus to Nero).

1. Life.

PHAEDRUS.

The Latin Fabulist, of whom we know nothing except what may be gathered or inferred from his fables. He was originally a slave, and was born in Thrace, possibly in the district of Pieria. He was brought to Rome at an early age, and there became acquainted with Roman literature. His patron appears to have been Augustus, who gave him his freedom. After publishing two books of fables he incurred the resentment of Augustus and was imprisoned. This was due probably to the bold outspokenness of many of his fables. He survived the attacks made on him, and Book V was written in his old age.

2. Works.

Fables, in five Books, written in *iambic senarii*, like those of Terence and Publius Syrus. The full title of his work is *Phaedri Augusti liberti fabularum Aesopiarum libri.* 'Phaedrus constantly plumes himself on his superiority to his model Aesop, but his animals have not the lifelike reality of those of the latter. With Phaedrus the animals are mere lay-figures: the moral comes first, and then he attaches an animal to it.'—Tyrrell.

'The chief interest of the Fables lies in the fact that they form the last survival of the *urbanus sermo* (the speech of Terence) in Latin poetry.'—Mackail.

'Phaedrus is the only important writer during the half-century 323of literary darkness between the Golden and the Silver Age.'—Tyrrell.

T. MACCIUS PLAUTUS, circ. 254-184 B.C.

1. Life.

PLAUTUS.

Plautus was born in the little Umbrian town of Sarsina, of free but poor parents. He came to Rome and made a small fortune as a stage-carpenter, but lost it by rash investment. He was then reduced to working for some years in a corn-mill, during which time he wrote plays, and continued to do so until his death.

2. Works.

Comedies. About 130 plays were current under the name of Plautus, but only 21 (*Fabulae Varronianae*) were, as Varro tells us, universally admitted to be genuine. Of these, all except one are extant.

Though his comedies are mainly free versions of Greek originals—of Philemon, Diphilus and Menander, the writers of the New Comedy 320-250 B.C.—the characters in them act, speak, and joke like genuine Romans, and he thereby secured the sympatliy of his audience more completely than Terence could ever have done.

'In point of language his plays form one of the most important documents for the history of the Latin language. In the freedom with which he uses, without vulgarising, popular modes of speech, he has no equal among Latin writers.'—Sellar.

For Horace's unfavourable judgment of Plautus see *Epist.* I. i. 170-176, and A. P. 270-272; Cicero's criticism is more just: *Duplex omnino est iocandi genus: unum illiberale petulans flagitiosum obscenum(vulgar, spiteful, shameful, coarse), alterum elegans urbanum ingeniosum facetum (in good taste, gracious, clever, witty). Quo genere non modo Plautus noster et Atticorum antiqua comoedia* (i.e. of Aristophanes), *sed etiam philosophorum Socraticorum libri referti sunt.—De Off.* I. civ.

GAIUS PLINIUS SECUNDUS, 23-79 A.D.

1. Life.

PLINY THE ELDER.

Born at Comum (*Como*) in the middle of the reign of Tiberius, Pliny passed his life in high public employments, both military and civil, which took him successively over nearly all the provinces 324of the Empire. He had always felt a strong interest in science, and he used his military position to secure information that otherwise might have been hard to obtain. Vespasian (70-78 A.D.), with whom he was on terms of close intimacy, made him admiral of the fleet stationed at Misenum. It was while here that news was brought him of the memorable eruption of Vesuvius in 79 A.D. 'In his zeal for scientific investigation he set sail for the spot in a man-of-war, and lingering too near the zone of the eruption was suffocated by the rain of hot ashes. The account of his death, given by his nephew, Pliny the Younger, in a letter to the historian Tacitus (*Ep*.vi. 16), is one of the best known passages in the classics.'—Mackail.

2. Works.

A **Natural History**, in thirty-seven Books, is Pliny's only extant work. (For his numerous other writings see Pliny the Younger, *Ep.* iii. 5.) 'It is a priceless storehouse of information on every branch of natural science as known to the ancient world.'—Mackail.

His work has been called the first popular encyclopedia of natural science.

Plinius Aetatis Suae Doctissimus.—Gellius.

C. PLINIUS CAECILIUS SECUNDUS, 62-113 A.D.

1. Life.

**PLINY
THE YOUNGER.**

Pliny the Younger was the son of C. Caecilius and of Plinia, the sister of the elder Pliny. He was born at Comum (*Como*), also the birthplace of his celebrated uncle. His father died when he was eight years old, and he was placed under the care of a guardian, Verginius Rufus, one of the most distinguished Romans of the day, since he had held the crown within his grasp and had declined to wear it, 68 A.D. Verginius was not much of a student, but Pliny learned from him high ideals of duty and noble thoughts about the Rome of earlier days, and never lost his unbounded admiration and respect for his guardian (*Ep.* ii. 1). Under his uncle's watchful care he received the best education Rome could give, and studied rhetoric under the great Quintilian. His bachelor uncle on his death in 79 left him his heir, adopting him in his will. Gifted with wealth, enthusiasm, taste for publicity, and a wide circle of influential friends, Pliny could not be content 325with the career of a simple *eques*. Accordingly he began the course of office that led to the Senate and the Consulship, and finally in 111 A.D. was appointed by Trajan governor of Bithynia, where he discharged his duties with skill and ability. His service seems to have been terminated only with his death.

2. Works.

Epistulae, Letters in nine Books, to which is added Pliny's correspondence with Trajan during his governorship of Bithynia. These and his **Panegyricus**, in praise of Trajan, are his only extant works.

It is on his Letters that Pliny's fame now rests, and both in tone and style they are a monument that does him honour. In many cases they were written for publication, and thus can never have the unique and surpassing interest that belongs to those of Cicero, but they give a varied and interesting picture of the time. 'In the Letters the character of the writer, its virtues and its weakness, is throughout unmistakeable. Pliny, the patriotic citizen,—Pliny, the munificent patron,—Pliny, the eminent man of letters,—Pliny, the affectionate husband and humane master,—Pliny, the man of principle, is in his various phases the real subject of the whole collection.'—Mackail.

'Pliny is an almost perfect type of a refined pagan gentleman.'—Cruttwell.

SEXTUS PROPERTIUS, circ. 50-15 B.C.

1. Life.

PROPERTIUS.

Of his life little or nothing is known, except what is recorded by himself. He was an Umbrian by birth, and probably a native of Asisium (*Assisi*), a town on the W. slope of the Apennines, not far from Perusia. Like Vergil and Tibullus, he lost his family property in the confiscation of lands by the Triumvirs in 42B.C.; but his mother's efforts secured for him a good education, to complete which she brought him to Rome. He entered on a course of training for the Bar, but abandoned it in favour of poetry (IV. i. 131-4).

Mox ubi bulla rudi dimissa est aurea collo,
Matris et ante deos libera sumpta toga,
Tum tibi pauca suo de carmine dictat Apollo
Et vetat insano verba tonare foro.

326

His earliest poems (Book I, *Cynthia*), published at the age of about twenty, brought him into notice and gained him admission to the literary circle of Maecenas. He lived in close intimacy with Vergil, Ovid, and most of his other literary contemporaries, with the remarkable exception of Horace, to whom the sensitive vanity and passionate manner of the young elegiac poet were alike distasteful. He died young, before he was thirty-five, about 15 B.C.

2. Works.

Elegies, in four Books. (Some editors divide Book II into two Books, El. 1-9 Book II, and El. 10-34 Book III, so that III and IV of the MSS. and of Postgate become IV and V.)

Books I and II are nearly all poems on Cynthia.

Book III contains, besides poems on Cynthia, themes dealing with friendship (El. 7. 12. 22) and events of national interest (El. 4. 11. 18). The poet struggles to emancipate himself from the thraldom of Cynthia and to accomplish work more worthy of his genius.

Book IV contains poems on Roman antiquities (El. 2. 4. 9. 10), written at the suggestion of Maecenas, the paean on the great victory at Actium (El. 6), and the noblest of his elegiacs, the Elegy on Cornelia (El. 11).

3. Style.

The aim of Propertius was to be the Roman Callimachus: **Umbria Romani patria Callimachi** (IV. i. 64).

The flexibility and elasticity of rhythm of the finest Greek elegiacs he made his own. The pentameter, instead of being a weaker echo of the hexameter, is the stronger line of the two, and has a weightier movement. In Book I he ends the pentameter freely with words of three, four, and five syllables, and we find long continuous passages in which there is scarcely any pause: e.g. in I. xx. 33-37:

> *Hic erat Arganthi Pege sub vertice montis*
> *Grata domus Nymphis umida Thyniasin,*
> *Quam supra nullae pendebant debita curae*
> *Roscida desertis poma sub arboribus,*
> *Et circum irriguo surgebant lilia prato*
> *Candida purpureis mixta papaveribus.*

'In some respects both Tibullus and Ovid may claim the advantage over Propertius: Tibullus for refined simplicity, for 327natural grace and exquisiteness of touch; Ovid for the technical merits of execution, for transparency of construction, for smoothness and polish of expression. But in all the higher qualities of a poet Propertius is as much their superior.'— Postgate.

AURELIUS PRUDENTIUS CLEMENS, 348-circ. 410 A.D.

1. Life.

PRUDENTIUS.

Prudentius (as he tells us in the brief metrical autobiography prefixed to his poems) was born in the N. of Spain, and, like so many of the Roman poets, began his public life as an advocate. He was afterwards appointed by Theodosius (379-395 A.D.) judge over a district in Spain. His active and successful discharge of this office induced Theodosius (or Honorius, 395-423A.D.) to promote him to some post of honour about the Emperor's person. His later years he devoted to the composition of sacred poetry, and published his collected works 405 A.D., after which date we know no more of his history.

2. Works.

His best known works are his **Cathemerina**, a series of poems on the Christian's day and life, of which the most graceful and pathetic is the*Funeral Hymn*, e.g.

> *Iam maesta quiesce querella,*
> *Lacrimas suspendite matres,*
> *Nullus sua pignora plangat,*
> *Mors haec reparatio vitae est,*

and his **Peristephanon** (περὶ στεφάνων *liber*) in praise of Christian martyrs. 'These represent the most substantial addition to Latin lyrical poetry since Horace.'—Mackail. We also have his **Contra Symmachum** in two Books of indifferent hexameter verse, in which he combats Symmachus (Consul 391 A.D.), the last champion of the old faith, and claims the victories of the Christian Stilicho as triumphs alike of Rome and of the Cross.

'Prudentius has his distinct place and office in the field of Latin literature, as the chief author who bridged the gulf between pagan poetry and Christian hymnology.'—North Pinder.

328

MARCUS FABIUS QUINTILIANUS, circ. 35-95 A.D.

1. Life.

QUINTILIAN.

Quintilian is the last and perhaps the most distinguished of that school of Spanish writers (Martial, the two Senecas, and Lucan) which played so important a part in the literary history of the first century. Born at Calagurris, a small town on the Upper Ebro, he was educated at Rome, and afterwards returned to his native town as a teacher of rhetoric. There he made the acquaintance of the proconsul Galba (68-9), and was brought back by him to Rome in 68 A.D., where for twenty years he enjoyed the highest reputation as a teacher of eloquence. Among his pupils were numbered Pliny the Younger and the two sons of Flavius Clemens, grand-nephews of Domitian, destined for his successors. In 79 A.D. he was appointed by Vespasian professor of rhetoric, the first teacher who received a regular salary from the imperial exchequer. Domitian (81-96A.D.) conferred upon him an honorary consulship, and the last ten years of his life were spent in an honoured retirement, which he devoted to recording for the benefit of posterity his unrivalled experience as a teacher of rhetoric.

2. *Works.*

Institutio Oratoria, the *Training of an Orator,* in twelve Books. This great work sums up the teaching and criticism of his life, and gives us the complete training of an orator, starting with him in childhood and leading him on to perfection.

Thus:—

Book I gives a sketch of the elementary training of the child from the time he leaves the nursery. Quintilian rightly attaches the greatest importance to early impressions.

Book II deals with the general principles and scope of the art of oratory, and continues the discussion of the aims and methods of education in its later stages.

Books III-VII are occupied with an exhaustive treatment of the *matter* of oratory, and are highly technical. 'Now that the formal study of the art of rhetoric has ceased to be a part of the higher education these Books have lost their general interest.'—Mackail.

Books VIII-XI treat of the *manner* (style) of oratory. In Book X, cap. i, in the course of an enumeration of the Greek 329and Latin authors likely to be most useful to an orator, Quintilian gives us a masterly sketch of Latin literature, 'in language so careful and so choice that many of his brief phrases have remained the final words on the authors, both in prose and verse, whom he mentions in his rapid survey.'—Mackail.

Book XII treats of the moral qualifications of a great speaker. The good orator must be a good man.

'Quintilian with admirable clearness insists on the great truth that bad education is responsible for bad life, and expresses with equal plainness the complementary truth that education, from the cradle upwards, is something which acts on the whole intellectual and moral nature, and that its object is the production of the *good man.*'—Mackail.

3. *Style.*

The style of Quintilian is modelled on that of Cicero, whom he is never tired of praising, and is intended to be a return to the usages of the best period. In spite of some faults characteristic of the Silver Age (e.g. his excessive use of antithesis) 'for ordinary use it would be difficult to name a manner that combines so well the Ciceronian dignity with the rich colour and high finish added to Latin prose by the writers of the earlier empire.'—Mackail.

For the death of his son, aged ten, a boy of great promise, for whose instruction he wrote the work, see Preface to Book VI.

Quintiliane, vagae moderator summe iuventae,
Gloria Romanae, Quintiliane, togae.

Mart. II. xc. 1-2.

Nihil in studiis parvum est.
Cito scribendo non fit ut bene scribatur, bene scribendo fit ut cito.

Quintilian.

GAIUS SALLUSTIUS CRISPUS, 86-35 B.C.

1. *Life.*

SALLUST.

A member of a plebeian family, Sallust was born 86 B.C.at Amiternum, in the country of the Sabines. As tribune of the people in 52 B.C. he took an active part in opposing Milo (Cicero's client) and the Pompeian party in general. In 48 B.C. he commanded a legion in Illyria without 330distinction, and next year Caesar sent him to treat with the mutinous legions in Campania, where he narrowly escaped assassination. He afterwards followed Caesar to Africa, and apparently did good service there, for he was appointed in 46 the first governor of the newly formed province of Numidia. In 45 he returned to Rome a very rich man, and built himself a magnificent palace, surrounded by pleasure grounds (the famous Gardens of Sallust, in the valley between the Quirinal and the Pincius), which in after years emperors preferred to the palace of the Caesars. After Caesar's death Sallust retired from public life, and it is to the leisure and study of these ten years that we owe the works that have made him famous.

2. *Works.*

(1) **De Catilinae Coniuratione** (or *Bellum Catilinae*), a monograph on the famous conspiracy, in which Sallust writes very largely from direct personal knowledge of men and events.

(2) **Bellum Iugurthinum** (111-106 B.C.) The writing of this monograph involved wide inquiry and much preparation.

(3) **Historiae**, in five books, dealing with the events from 78 B.C.(death of Sulla) to 67 B.C., of which only a few fragments are extant.

3. Style.

'Sallust aimed at making historical writing a branch of literature. He felt that nothing had yet been done by any Roman writer which would stand beside Thucydides. It was his ambition to supply the want. That could only be done by offering as complete a contrast to the tedious annalist as possible, and Sallust neglected no means of giving variety to his work. From Thucydides he probably borrowed the idea of his introductions, the imaginary speeches and the character portraits; from Cato the picturesque descriptions of the scenes of historical events and the ethnographical digressions.'—Cook.

'The style of Sallust is characterised by the use of old words and forms (especially in the speeches). He makes use of alliteration, extensively employs the Historic Infinitive, and shows a partiality for conversational expressions which from a literary point of view are archaic. His abrupt unperiodic style of writing (rough periods without particles of connexion) has won for Sallust his reputation for brevity.His style is, however, the expression of the writer's character, direct, 331incisive, emphatic, and outspoken; to have been a model for Tacitus is no slight merit.'—Cook.

Nec minus noto Sallustius epigrammate incessitur:
'Et verba antiqui multum furate Catonis,
Crispe, Iugurthinae conditor historiae.'

Quint. VIII. iii. 29.

'The last of the Ciceronians, Sallust is also in a sense the first of the imperial prose-writers.'—Mackail.

Primus Romana Crispus in Historia (Mart. XIV. cxci.)
L. ANNAEUS SENECA THE YOUNGER, circ. 4 B.C.-65 A.D.

1. Life.

SENECA.

The son of Seneca the Elder, the famous rhetorician, was born at Corduba (*Cordova*), in Spain, and brought to Rome by his parents at an early age. His life was one of singularly dramatic contrasts and vicissitudes. Under his mother Helvia's watchful care he received the best education Rome could give. Through the influence of his mother's family he passed into the Senate through the quaestorship, and his successes at the bar awakened the jealousy of Caligula (37-41 A.D.) By his father's advice he retired for a time and spent his days in philosophy. On the accession of Claudius (41-54 A.D.) he was banished to Corsica at the instance of the Empress Messalina, probably because he was suspected of belonging to the faction of Agrippina, the mother of Nero. After eight years he was recalled (49 A.D.) by the influence of Agrippina (now the wife of Claudius), and appointed tutor to her son Nero, then a boy of ten. When Nero became emperor, at the age of seventeen (54 A.D.), Seneca, in conjunction with his friend Burrus, the prefect of the praetorian guards, became practically the administrator of the Empire. 'The mild and enlightened administration of the earlier years of the new reign, the famous *quinquennium Neronis*, may indeed be largely ascribed to Seneca's influence; but this influence was based on an excessive indulgence of Nero's caprices, which soon worked out its own punishment.'—Mackail. His connivance at the murder of Agrippina (59 A.D.) was the death-blow to his influence for good, and the death of Burrus (63 A.D.) was, as Tacitus says (*Ann.* xiv. 52), 'a blow to Seneca's power, for virtue had not the same strength when one of its 332champions, so to speak, was removed, and Nero began to lean on worse advisers.' Seneca resolved to retire, and entreated Nero to receive back the wealth he had so lavishly bestowed. The Emperor, bent on vengeance, refused the proffered gift, and Seneca knew that his doom was sealed. In the year 65, on the pretext of complicity in the conspiracy of Piso, he was commanded to commit suicide, and Tacitus (*Ann.* xv. 61-63) has shown his love for Seneca, in spite of all his faults, by the tribute he pays to the constancy of his death.

2. Works.

His chief works are:—

(1) **Dialogorum Libri XII**, of which the most important are the **De Ira**and the **Consolatio** to his mother Helvia, whom he tenderly loved.

(2) **De Clementia**, in three Books, addressed to Nero, written in 55-6A.D., to show the public what sort of instruction Seneca had given his pupil, and what sort of Emperor they had to expect.

(3) **De Beneficiis**, in seven Books. Seneca proves that a tyrant's benefits are not kindnesses, and sets forth his views on the giving and receiving of benefits.

215

(4) **Epistulae morales ad Lucilium.** 124 letters are extant, and form the most important and most pleasing of his works.

(5) **Tragedies.** Nine are extant, derived from plays by Sophocles and Euripides. The only extant Latin tragedies.

'As a moral writer Seneca stands deservedly high. Though infected with the rhetorical vices of the age his treatises are full of striking and often gorgeous eloquence, and in their combination of high thought with deep feeling have rarely, if at all, been surpassed.'—Mackail.

'Seneca is a lamentable instance of variance between precept and example.'—Cruttwell.

SILIUS ITALICUS, circ. 25-100 A.D.

1. Life.

SILIUS.

A letter of Pliny (iii. 7) is the chief source of our knowledge of the life of Silius. Pliny tells us that Silius had risen by acting as a *delator* (informer) under Nero, who made him consul 68A.D. He goes on to say 'He had gained much credit by his proconsulship in Asia (under 333Vespasian, *circ.* 77 A.D.), and had since by an honourable leisure wiped out the blot which stained the activity of his former years.' Martial also, who has the effrontery to speak of him as a combined Vergil and Cicero, tells us of his luxurious and learned retirement in Campania, and of his reverence for his master Vergil, 'whose birthday he kept more religiously than his own.' According to Martial (xi. 49) the tomb of Vergil had been practically forgotten, and was in the possession of some poor man when Silius bought the plot of ground on which it stood:

Iam prope desertos cineres et sancta Maronis
Nomina qui coleret, pauper et unus erat.
Silius optatae succurrere censuit umbrae,
Silius et vatem, non minor ipse, colit.

2. Works.

The **Punica**, an Epic poem in seventeen Books, on the Second Punic War, closes with Scipio's triumph, after the Battle of Zama, 202 B.C.

Silius closely followed the history as told by Livy, and without any inventive or constructive power of his own copies, with tasteless pedantry, Homer and Vergil. 'He cannot perceive that the divine interventions which are admissible in the quarrel of Aeneas and Turnus are ludicrous when imported into the struggle between Scipio and Hannibal. Who can help resenting the unreality when at Saguntum Jupiter guides an arrow into Hannibal's body, which Juno immediately withdraws, or when, at Cannae, Aeolus yields to the prayer of Juno and blinds the Romans by a whirlwind of dust?'—Cruttwell.

The *Punica* is valuable for its historical accuracy, but it is one of the longest and one of the worst Epic poems ever written.

Scribebat carmina maiore cura quam ingenio.

Pliny, *Epist.* iii. 7.

P. PAPINIUS STATIUS, circ. 60-100 A.D.

1. Life.

STATIUS.

Statius was born at Naples, but early removed to Rome, where he was carefully educated and spent the greater part of his life. His father was a scholar, rhetorician, and poet of some distinction, and acted for a time as tutor to Domitian. Statius had thus access to the Court, 334and repaid the patronage of Domitian by incessant and shameless flattery. After the completion of his **Thebais** he retired to Naples, which was endeared to him by its associations with Vergil, and there satisfied his real love of nature.

2. Works.

(1) The **Thebais**, an Epic poem in twelve Books, on the strife between the brothers Eteocles and Polynices, and the subsequent history of Thebes to the death of Creon.

The Thebaid became very famous: Juvenal (*Sat.* vii. 82-4) tells us

Curritur ad vocem iucundam et carmen amicae
Thebaidos, laetam cum fecit Statius urbem
promisitque diem (i.e. for a public recitation of his poem).

'Its smooth versification, copious diction, and sustained elegance made it a sort of canon of poetical technique. Among much tedious rhetoric and cumbrous mythology there is enough imagination and pathos to make the poem interesting and even charming.'—Mackail.

(2) The **Silvae**, in five Books, are occasional poems, descriptive and lyrical, on miscellaneous subjects. These may well be considered his masterpiece. 'Genuine poetry,' says Niebuhr, 'imprinted with the character of the true poet, and constituting some of the most graceful productions of Roman literature.'

Among the best known are the touching poem to his wife Claudia (iii. 5), the marriage song to his brother-poet Arruntius Stella (i. 2), the *Propempticon Maecio Celeri* (iii. 2), the *Epicedion* (funeral song) on the death of his adopted son (v. 5), and the short poem (v. 4) on Sleep.

The greatest poet of the Decline.

GAIUS SUETONIUS TRANQUILLUS, circ. 75-160 A.D.

1. Life.

SUETONIUS.

The little we know of his life is chiefly gathered from the Letters of Pliny the Younger, and from scattered allusions in his own works. The son of an officer of the Thirteenth Legion, Suetonius in early life practised as an advocate, and subsequently became one of Hadrian's private secretaries (*magister epistularum*), but was dismissed from office in 121 A.D. After his retirement from the service 335of the Court he devoted the rest of his long life to literary research and compilation, and published a number of works on a great variety of subjects, so that he became famous as the Varro of the imperial period.

2. Works.

His extant works are:

(1) **De Vita Caesarum**, the Lives of the Twelve Caesars, in eight Books (I-VI Julius-Nero; VII Galba, Otho, and Vitellius; VIII Vespasian, Titus, and Domitian). This is his most interesting and most valuable work. His Lives are not works of art: he is simply a gatherer of facts, collected from good sources with considerable care and judgment. 'He follows out with absolute faithfulness his own theory, which makes it necessary to omit no possible detail that can throw light upon the personality of his subject.'—Peck.

(2) **De Viris Illustribus**, a history of Latin literature up to his day. The greater part of the section **De grammaticis et rhetoribus** is extant, as well as the Lives of Terence, Horace, and Lucan (partly), from the section **De poetis**, and fragments of the Life of Pliny the Elder from the section **De historicis**.

Extracts made from this work by Jerome (*circ.* 400 A.D.) in his Latin version of Eusebius' Chronicles are the source from which much of our information as to Latin authors is derived.

'Suetonius is terse, and in that respect he resembles Tacitus; he is deeply interesting, and there he shows some likeness to Livy; but his style is one of his own creation. His chief desire is to present the facts stripped of any comment whatever, grouped in such a way as to produce their own effect without the adventitious aid of rhetoric; and then to leave the reader to his own conclusions.'—Peck.

Probissimus, honestissimus, eruditissimus vir.

Pliny, *Epist. ad Trai.* 94.

PUBLILIUS SYRUS, circ. 45 B.C.

1. Life.

SYRUS.

All we know of him is that he was an enfranchised Syrian slave, a native of Antioch, and wrote for the stage *mimes*(farces) which were performed with great applause. Mime-writing was also practised at this time by the Knight Laberius, and Caesar is said to have patronised these writers in the hope of elevating their art.

336

2. Works.

Sententiae (*Maxims*). We possess 697 lines from his mimes (unconnected and alphabetically arranged), a collection made in the early Middle Ages, and much used in schools. As proverbs of worldly wisdom, and admirable examples of the terse vigour of Roman philosophy, they are widely known, e.g.

Cuivis potest accidere quod cuiquam potest.

CORNELIUS TACITUS, circ. 54-120 A.D.

1. Life.

TACITUS.

The personal history of Tacitus is known to us only from allusions in his own works, and from the letters of his friend the younger Pliny. He was born early in the reign of Nero, probably in Rome; his education, political career, and marriage into the distinguished family of Agricola prove that he was a man of wealth and position. He studied rhetoric under the best masters (possibly under Quintilian), and had, as Pliny tells us (*Epist.* II. i. 6), a great reputation as a speaker. He passed through the usual stages of an official career and was appointed *consul suffectus* under Trajan, 98 A.D., when he was a little over forty. From 89 to 93 A.D. he was absent from Rome, probably in some provincial command, and during these years he may have acquired some personal knowledge of the German peoples. In 100 A.D. he was associated with Pliny in the prosecution for extortion of Marius Priscus, proconsul of Africa, of whom Juvenal says (*Sat*.viii. 120):

Cum tenues nuper Marius discinxerit Afros.
Since Marius has so lately stripped to their girdles (i.e. thoroughly plundered) *the needy Africans.*
From this date Tacitus seems to have devoted himself entirely to literary pursuits and to have lived to or beyond the end of Trajan's reign, 116 A.D.

2. Works.

(1) **Dialogus de Oratoribus**, an inquiry into the causes of the decay of oratory, his earliest extant work. In the style of this work the influence of Quintilian and Cicero is strongly seen.

(2) **De Vita et Moribus Iulii Agricolae liber**, an account of the life of his father-in-law, particularly of his career in Britain, 337published shortly after the accession of Trajan, 98 A.D. 'The Sallustian epoch of Tacitus finds its expression in the *Agricola* and *Germania*.'—Teuffel.

The *Agricola* is perhaps the most beautiful biography in ancient literature.

(3) The **Germania**, or *Concerning the Geography, the Manners and Customs, and the Tribes of Germany*, published in 98 or 99. 'The motive for its publication was apparently the pressing importance, in Tacitus' opinion, of the "German question," and the necessity for vigorous action to secure the safety of the Roman Empire against the dangers with which. it was threatened from German strength.'—Stephenson.

'The **Germania** is an inestimable treasury of facts and generalisations, and of the general faithfulness of the outline we have no doubt.'—Stubbs.

(4) **Historiae**, consisting originally of fourteen Books, is a narrative of the events of the reigns of Galba, Otho, Vitellius, Vespasian, Titus, and Domitian, 69-96 A.D. Only Books I-IV and the first half of Book V are extant, and give the history of 69 and most of 70 A.D.

'The style of the *Historiae* still retains some traces of the influence of Cicero: it has not yet been pressed tight into the short *sententiae* which were its final and most characteristic development, but shows in a marked degree the influence of Vergil.'—Cruttwell.

In the *Historiae*, as Tacitus himself says, 'the secret of the imperial system was divulged—that an emperor could be made elsewhere than at Rome'; or, in other words, that the imperial system was a military and not a civil institution.

(5) The **Annales, ab excessu divi Augusti**, in sixteen Books, containing the history of the reigns of Tiberius, Caligula, Claudius, Nero, 14-68 A.D. There are extant only Books I-IV, parts of V and VI, and XI-XVI.

'The old criticism, tracing the characteristics of the style of Tacitus to poetic colouring (almost wholly Vergilian) and to the study of brevity and of variety, is well founded. They may be explained by the fact that he was the most finished pleader of an age which required above all that its orators should be terse, brilliant, and striking, and by his own painful consciousness of the dull monotony and repulsive sadness of great part of his subject, which needed the help of every sort of variety to stimulate the flagging interest of the reader.'—Furneaux.

338

His aim as an historian is best given in his own words: 'I hold it the chief office of history to rescue virtue from oblivion, and to hold out the reprobation of posterity as a terror to evil words and deeds' (*Ann*.iii. 65).

The greatest of Roman historians.

PUBLIUS TERENTIUS AFER, circ. 185-159 B.C.

1. Life

TERENCE.

Terence was born probably at Carthage, reached Rome as a slave-boy, and passed there into the possession of a rich and educated Senator, P. Terentius Lucanus, by whom he was educated and manumitted, taking from him the name of Publius Terentius the African. 'A small literary circle of the Roman aristocracy admitted young Terence to their intimate companionship; and soon he was widely known as making a third in the friendship of Gaius Laelius with the first citizen of the Republic, the younger Scipio Africanus. Six plays had been subjected to the criticism of this informal academy of letters and produced on the stage, when Terence undertook a prolonged visit to Greece for the purpose of further study. He died of fever in the next year, 159 B.C., at the early age of twenty-six.'—Mackail.

2. Works.

Comedies.—All the six plays written and exhibited at Rome by Terence are extant. They are the *Andria* (exhibited 166 B.C., when the poet was only eighteen years of age), the *Heauton Timoroumenos,Eunuchus, Phormio, Hecyra, Adelphoe.*

'With Terence Roman literature takes a new departure. The Scipionic circle believed that the best way to create a national Latin literature was to deviate as little as possible, in spirit, form, and substance, from the works of Greek genius. The task which awaited Terence was the complete Hellenising of Roman comedy: accordingly his aim was to give a true picture of Greek life and manners in the purest Latin style. He was not a popular poet, in the sense in which Plautus was popular: he has none of the purely Roman characteristics of Plautus in sentiment, allusion, or style; none of his extravagance, and none of his vigour and originality.'—Sellar. Terence is, accordingly, in substance and form, as Caesar styles him, a *dimidiatus Menander* (*halved Menander*):

Tu quoque, tu in summis, o dimidiate Menander,
Poneris, et merito, puri sermonis amator.
339

A Roman only in language, but as *puri sermonis amator* worthy to be ranked by the side of Caesar himself and the purest Latin authors.

ALBIUS TIBULLUS, circ. 54-19 B.C.

1. Life.

TIBULLUS.

Tibullus was a Roman *eques*, and was probably born at Pedum, a Latin town just at the foot of the Apennines, and a few miles north of Praeneste, where his father possessed an ample estate. Much of his inherited property was lost; and it is possible that, like Vergil, Horace, and Propertius, he was a victim to the confiscations of the Triumvirs in 42 B.C. He, however, retained or recovered enough to afford him a modest competence. In 31-30 B.C. he served on the staff of his life-long friend and patron M. Valerius Messalla, the eminent general and statesman, not less distinguished in literature than in politics. The rest of his short life the poet spent on his ancestral farm at Pedum, amid the country scenes and employments congenial to his nature and habits.

2. Works.

Elegies, in four Books (or three, Postgate). Tibullus published in his lifetime two Books of elegiac poems: after his death a third volume was published, containing a few of his own poems, together with poems by other members of the literary circle of Messalla. Books I and II consist mainly of poems addressed to Delia and to Nemesis (cf. Ov.*Am.* III. ix. 31-32):

Sic Nemesis longum, sic Delia nomen habebunt;
Altera cura recens, altera primus amor.
And to Messalla, e.g. *El.* I. vii. 55-6:
At tibi succrescat proles, quae facta parentis
Augeat et circa stet veneranda senem.
3. Style.

'Tibullus is pre-eminently Roman in his genius and poetry. He is the natural poet of warm, tender, and simple feeling. Neither Greek mythology nor Alexandrine learning had any attractions for his purely Italian genius. His language may be limited in range and variety, but it is terse, clear, simple, and popular. His constructions are plain and direct.'—North Pinder.
340
'To Tibullus belongs the distinction of having given artistic perfection to the Roman elegy.'—Sellar.

Elegia quoque Graecos provocamus, cuius mihi tersus atque elegans maxime videtur auctor Tibullus.
'*In elegy also we rival the Greeks, of which Tibullus appears to me the purest and finest representative.*'
Quint. *Inst. Or.* X. i. 93.

'Tibullus might be succinctly and perhaps not unjustly described as a Vergil without the genius.'—Mackail.

'Tibullus and Vergil are alike in their human affection and their piety, in their capacity of tender and self-forgetful love, in their delight in the labours of the field and their sympathy with the herdsman and the objects of his care.'—Sellar.

Quid voveat dulci nutricula maius alumno,
Qui sapere et fari possit quae sentiat, et cui
Gratia, fama valetudo contingat abunde,
Et mundus victus, non deficiente crumena!

Horace to Tibullus, *Epist.* I. iv. 8-11.

Si tamen e nobis aliquid nisi nomen et umbra
Restat, in Elysia valle Tibullus erit.

.   .   .   .   .

Ossa quieta, precor, tuta requiescite in urna,
Et sit humus cineri non onerosa tuo.

219

C. VALERIUS FLACCUS, fl. 70 A.D.

1. Life.

VALERIUS FLACCUS.

He lived in the reign of Vespasian (70-78 A.D.), to whom he dedicated his poem, in which he refers to Vespasian's exploits in Britain and to the capture of Jerusalem by Titus, 70 A.D. There are also references to the eruption of Vesuvius in 79 A.D. Quintilian is the only Roman writer who mentions him (X. i. 90): *Multum in Valerio Flacco nuper amisimus*, which shows that he must have died *circ.* 90 A.D.

2. Works.

The Argonautica, an Hexameter poem in eight Books, apparently unfinished. The poem is in part a translation, in part a free imitation of the Alexandrine epic of Apollonius Rhodius (222-181 B.C.) 'His descriptive power, particularly 341shown in touches of natural scenery, his pure diction and correct style have inclined some critics to set Valerius Flaccus above his Greek model.'—North Pinder. The rhetorical treatment of the subject, so characteristic of the period of the decline, is, however, too prominent throughout his work. Both his rhythm and language are closely modelled on Vergil.

VALERIUS MAXIMUS, fl. 26 A.D.

1. Life.

VALERIUS MAXIMUS.

All that we know of him is that he visited Asia in company with Sextus Pompeius (the friend of Ovid and of Germanicus), *circ.* 27-30 A.D.

2. Works.

Facta et Dicta Memorabilia, in nine Books. Each Book is divided into chapters on separate subjects (e.g. *De Severitate, De Verecundia,De Constantia*), under each of which he gives illustrations from Roman history and from the history of other nations, in order to show the native superiority (as he thinks) of Romans to foreigners, and especially to Greeks. As an historian he is most untrustworthy, but there are many gaps in Roman history (e.g. owing to the lost books of Livy) which he helps to supply. His style shows all the faults of his age and rhetorical training; his work was probably intended to be a commonplace-book for students and teachers of rhetoric.

M. TERENTIUS VARRO, 116-27 B.C.

1. Life.

VARRO.

Born at Reate, in the Sabine territory, which was the nurse of all manly virtues, Varro was brought up in the good old-fashioned way. 'For me when a boy,' he says, 'there sufficed a single rough coat and a single under-garment, shoes without stockings, a horse without a saddle.' Bold, frank, and sarcastic, he had all the qualities of the country gentleman of the best days of the Republic. On account of his personal valour he obtained in the war with the Pirates, 67 B.C., where he commanded a division of the fleet, the naval crown. In politics he belonged, as was natural, to the constitutional party, and bore an honourable and energetic part in its doings and sufferings. On the outbreak of the Civil 342War he served as the legatus of Pompeius in command of Further Spain, but was compelled to surrender his forces to Caesar, 69 B.C. When the cause of the Republic was lost Caesar, who knew Varro's worth, employed him in superintending the collection and arrangement of the great library at Rome designed for public use. After Caesar's death Varro was exposed to the persecution of Antonius, whose drunken revels and excesses at Varro's villa at Casinum are vividly described by Cicero (*Phil.* ii. 103 sqq.) Through the influence of his many friends Varro obtained the protection of Octavianus, and was enabled to live at Rome in peace until his death, 27 B.C., in his ninetieth year.

2. Works.

Of all the works of Varro, embracing almost all branches of knowledge and literature, only two have come down to us:

(1) The **De Re Rustica**, in three Books, in the form of a dialogue, written in his eightieth year. It was a subject of which he had a thorough practical knowledge, and is the most important of all the treatises upon ancient agriculture now extant. Book I treats of agriculture; Book II of stock-raising; Book III of poultry, game, and fish.

(2) **De Lingua Latina**, in twenty-five Books, of which only V-X have been preserved. These contain much valuable information not found elsewhere, but Varro's notions of etymology are extremely crude.

Of his other works, we have much cause to regret the loss of his **Antiquities of Things Human and Divine**, the standard work on the religious and secular antiquities of Rome down to the time of Augustus, and his **Imagines**, biographical sketches, with portraits, of seven hundred famous Greeks and Romans, the first instance in history of the publication of an illustrated book.

'Varro belongs to the genuine type of old Roman, improved but not altered by Greek learning, with his heart fixed in the past, deeply conservative of everything national, and even in his style of speech protesting against the innovations of the day.'—Cruttwell.

Omnium facile acutissimus, et sine ulla dubitatione doctissimus.—Cicero.

Studiosum rerum tantum docet, quantum studiosum verborum Cicero delectat.—St. Augustine.

343

1. Life.

VELLEIUS PATERCULUS.

All we know of him is derived from his own pages. He descended from a distinguished family in Campania, and his father was a Praefectus equitum. He accompanied C. Caesar, the grandson of Augustus, on his mission to the East, and was present at the interview with the Parthian king. Two years afterwards, 4 A.D., he served under Tiberius in Germany as Praefectus equitum. For the next eight years Paterculus served under Tiberius in Pannonia and Dalmatia. Tiberius' sterling qualities as a soldier gained him the friendship of many of his officers, and Velleius by his energy and ability secured that of Tiberius in return. The last circumstance of his life that he records is the election to the praetorship of his brother and himself as candidates of Caesar (Tiberius) in 14 A.D.

2. Works.

The **Historia Romana** in two Books. The beginning of Book I is lost; chapters 1-8 in our text are occupied with a rapid survey of universal history, especially of the East and of Greece. Chapter 8 breaks off at the rape of the Sabine women, and there is a great gap in the text before we reach in c. 9 the defeat of Perseus at Pydna in 168 B.C. Chapters 9-13 carry the narrative down to the destruction of Carthage and Corinth in 146 B.C. Book II continues the history and ends at the death of Livia 27 A.D.

'The pretentiousness of his style is partly due to the declining taste of the period, partly to an idea of his own that he could write in the manner of Sallust. It alternates between a sort of laboured sprightliness and a careless, conversational manner full of endless parentheses. Yet Velleius has two real merits: the eye of a trained soldier for character, and an unaffected, if not a very intelligent, interest in literature.'—Mackail.

P. VERGILIUS MARO, 70-19 B.C.

1. Important Events in Vergil's Life, and Chief Works.

VERGIL.

B.C. 70. Born at Andes, near Mantua.

„ 65. Birth of Horace.

B.C. 55. Assumes the *Toga Virilis* at Cremona. Death of Lucretius.

344

„ 53. Studies philosophy at Rome under the Epicurean Siron.

„ 42. **Eclogues II, III, V**, and perhaps **VI**, written.

„ 41. Suffers confiscation of his estate. Takes refuge in *Siron's* villa. Estates restored by Octavianus through Pollio. **Eclogue I.**

„ 40. Vergil evicted a second time. **Eclogues IV, VI, IX**. Becomes a member of the literary circle of Maecenas.

„ 39. **Eclogues VIII** and **X**.

„ 38. Introduces Horace to Maecenas.

„ 37. Begins the **Georgics** at the suggestion of Maecenas.

„ 29. **Completed Georgics** read to Octavianus. **Aeneid** begun.

„ 27. Augustus Emperor.

„ 26. Banishment and death of his friend Gallus.

„ 25. Marriage of Marcellus to Julia, daughter of Augustus.

„ 23. Death of Marcellus: **Aeneid, Book VI**, read to the Imperial family.

„ 19. Journey of Vergil to Greece: is taken ill, dies at Brundusium, and is buried at Naples:

Mantua me genuit, Calabri rapuere, tenet nunc
Parthenope: cecini pascua, rura, duces.

2. Works.

(1) **Bucolica** (Pastoral Poems), ten **Eclogues** (selected pieces), written 42-39 B.C. These are closely modelled on Theocritus, and have all the weaknesses of imitative poetry. 'The Eclogues of Vergil have less of consistency but more of purpose than the Idylls of Theocritus. They are an advocacy of the charm of scenery and the pleasures of the country addressed to a luxurious and artificial society of dwellers in a town.'—Myers.

(2) **Georgica**, in four Books, written 37-30 B.C., at the suggestion of Maecenas, 'the Home Minister of Augustus, and public patron of art and letters in the interest of the new government.'—Mackail. 'The details of his subject Vergil draws mainly from his Greek predecessors, Hesiod, Xenophon, Aratus, and Nicander, but it is to Lucretius he is chiefly indebted. The language of Lucretius, so bold, so genial, so powerful, and in its way so perfect, is echoed a thousand times in the Georgics.'—Nettleship.

Book I treats of agriculture, Book II of the cultivation of trees, Book III of domestic animals, Book IV of bees (including the Myth of Aristaeus, ll. 315-558).
345

The *purpose of the Georgics* is to ennoble the annual round of labour in which the rural life was passed and to help the policy of Augustus by inducing the people to go back to the land.

'The motto of the Georgics might well be said to be *Ora et labora*.'—Tyrrell.

'The Georgics represent the art of Vergil in its matured perfection, and in mere technical finish are the most perfect work of Latin literature.'—Mackail.

(3) The **Aeneid**, in twelve Books, written 29-19 B.C.

The *choice of the subject* was influenced by the wish of Augustus to establish the legendary tradition of the connection of the gens Iulia with Aeneas through his son Iulus, and by Vergil's own desire to write an epic on the greatness of Rome, in the manner of Homer. Thus 'the centre of the mythical background was naturally Aeneas, as Augustus was the centre of the present magnificence of the Roman Empire. *We surpass all other nations*, says Cicero (*De Nat. Deor.* ii. 8), *in holding fast the belief that all things are ordered by a Divine Providence*. The theme of the *Aeneid* is the building up of the Roman Empire under this Providence. Aeneas is the son of a goddess, and his life the working out of the divine decrees.'—Nettleship.

Tu regere imperio populos, Romane, memento;
Hae tibi erunt artes; pacisque imponere morem.

Aen. vi. 851-2.

'At a verse from the *Aeneid*, the sun goes back for us on the dial; our boyhood is recreated, and returns to us for a moment like a visitant from a happy dreamland.'—Tyrrell.

'In merely technical quality the supremacy of Vergil's art has never been disputed. The Latin Hexameter, *the stateliest measure ever moulded by the lips of man*, was brought by him to a perfection which made any further development impossible.'—Mackail.

'As Homer among the Greeks, so Vergil among our own authors will best head the list; he is beyond doubt the second epic poet of either nation.'—Quint. X. i. 85.

'The chastest poet and royalest, Vergilius Maro, that to the memory of man is known.'—Bacon.
347

APPENDIX VII.
NOTE

THE following Chronological Outlines of Roman History and Literature are intended to illustrate the passages selected for translation. Important events and writers in contemporary History and Literature are added, in order to emphasise the comparative method of treating History.

The names of those Latin authors from whose works passages have been selected are printed in capitals in the Literature Column.

A fuller outline of the Imperial Period will be given in a later volume.

PERIODS OF LATIN LITERATURE.

PERIOD I.	The Growth of Latin Literature	250-80 B.C.
PERIOD II.	The Golden Age of Latin Literature	80 B.C.-14 A.D.
PERIOD III.	The Silver Age of Latin Literature	14-117 A.D.
PERIOD IV.	The Later Empire	from 117 A.D.

B. C.	ROME.	OTHER NATIONS.	B. C.	LITERATURE.	B. C.
		PART I.—REGAL PERIOD, 753-509 B.C.			
		Foundation of Carthage	878	Amos	c. 760
753	**Foundation of Rome**	Rise of Corinth	745	Isaiah	c. 720
753-716	ROMULUS Roman Senate of 200 *Spolia opima*(1)	Captivity of Israel	721	Hesiod	c. 700
716-673	NUMA POMPILIUS Religious Institutions	Carentum founded	708		
673-640	TULLUS HOSTILIUS Destruction of *Alba*	Destruction of Sennacherib's host	701	Tyrtaeus (Sparta)	c. 680
	Legend of **Horatii** and**Curiatii**	Cyrene founded	641	Archilochus.	650
640-616	ANCUS MARTIUS. Conquest of Latin Towns	Josiah's reformation	625	Jeremiah	c. 625
	Ostia, first maritime colony	Periander, tyrant of Corinth	625-585		
616-578	TARQUINIUS PRISCUS. Public Works: the *Circus Maximus, Cloaca Maxima*, and Temple of Jupiter	Draco, the law-giver at Athens. **Massilia founded**	621 / 600	Alcaeus Sappho Solon	600 / 600
578-534	SERVIUS TULLIUS. The Census, basis of*ComitiaCenturiata* The Servian Wall includes theQuirinal, Viminal and Esquiline hills, i.e. Rome of Republican times	Captivity of Judah	606-536		
		Solon at Athens	594	Thales	590
		Peisistratus at Athens	560-527	Ezekiel	585
		Croesus in Lydia	560-546	Aesop	c. 570
534-509	TARQUINIUS SUPERBUS Conquest of*Gabii*	Cyrus enters Babylon	538	Theognis	540
	Tyrannyleading to expulsion of the Tarquins and abolitionof the monarchy	Return of Jews under Zerubbabel	536	Pythagoras	530
		Expulsion of	510	Anacreon	530

PART II.—EARLY REPUBLIC, 509-366 B.C.

Date	Rome	Greece & the East	Date	Literature & Art	Date
509	**Two Consuls (Praetors) first appointed** *Lex Valeria* establishes right of appeal	Darius Hystaspes	521-486	Aeschylus	525-456
		Pindar	518-c. 443		
507	Rome taken by Etruscans under Porsena	Ionian Revolt	501-493	Heracleitus	500
498	**Latin War** **Dictator first appointed** Battle of *Lake Regillus*	Miltiades at Athens	493-489	Simonides (Ceos)	490
		Ionians defeated at Lade	494		
494	First Session of the Plebs *Tribuni Plebis*	Battle of Marathon	490		
489	Volscian War (**Coriolanus**)	Aristides and Themistocles	490-470	Parmenides	490
486-5	Agrarian Law Spurius Cassius put to death	Xerxes	485-465	Bacchylides	470
477	Destruction of the **Fabii** at *Cremera*	Thermopylae. Salamis. Himera	480	Anaxagoras	460
458	War with Aequians—Battle of *Mt. Algidus* Cincinnatus Dictator	Plataea (Pausanians). Mycale	479	Sophocles	496-406
		Hiero I at Syracuse	478-467	Euripides	480-406
451	**First Decemvirate Ten Tables**	Pericles at Athens	469-429	Herodotus	c. 484-425
450	Second Decemvirate Two new Tables (**Appius Claudius**)	Cimon at Athens	466-449	*Phidias (Parthenon)*	448
448	Second Secession of the Plebs, resulting in the *Valerio-Horatian* Laws	Athenian defeat at Coronea	447	Empedocles	445
		Ezra and Nehemiah	c. 444		
350351445	Military tribunes with consular power appointed	Athenian colony to Thurii	444	Era of the Sophists (Gorgias, Protagoras)	440
443	Censors first appointed				

	Rome	Greece		Persons	
439	Spurius Maelius killed				
437	War with Etruscans **Cossus** wins *Spolia opima* (2)	War of Corinth and Corcyra	435	Antiphon	*c.* 480-411
424	Capua taken by the Samnites	Peloponnesian War	431-405	Thucydides	*c.* 471-402
		Sphacteria (Demosthenes, Cleon)	425	*Zeuxis Parrhasius*	*pa inters c.* 420
		Alcibiades at Athens	424-404		
		Syracusan Expedition	415-413	Lysias	*c.* 445-378
406-396	**War with Veii Camillus Dictator**	Battle of Aegospotami	405	Aristophanes	*c.* 450-385
406	Roman soldiers first receive pay	Lysander enters Athens	404	Cratinus	449
		Critias and Thirty Tyrants	404	Eupolis	429
		Democracy restored (Thrasybulus)	403		
390	**Invasion of the Gauls** Battle of the *Allia* Burning of Rome (**Brennus**) **Manlius Capitolinus Camillus** *Parens Patriae* *History based on documents begins*	Artaxerxes II	405-359		
		Expedition of Cyrus the Younger (The *Anabasis* of Xenophon)	401		
		Xenophon	*c.* 430-355		
		Socrates condemned	399	Socrates	468-399
389	Rome rebuilt	Dionysius I of Syracuse, Wars of Syracuse and Carthage	405-368	Plato	420-348
				Isocrates	436-338
376-366	**The Licinian Laws** **First Plebeian Consul** First Praetor (Judge) appointed	Pelopidas and Epaminondas (Thebes)	378-362	Isaeus	420-348
		Supremacy of Thebes (Leuctra)	371		
		Death	36		

| | | of Epaminondas (Mantinea) | 2 | | |

PART III.—THE CONQUEST OF ITALY, 366-266 B.C.

361	Second Invasion of the Gauls Legend of **Manlius Torquatus**	Dionysius II of Syracuse	368-343	Diogenes (Cynic)	*c.* 419-324
		Battle of Mantinea	362	**Ludi Scenici at Rome**	365
356	C. Marcius Rutilus, First Plebeian Dictator	Philip of Macedon	359-336		
349	War with Gauls Legend of **M. Valerius Corvus**	Dion at Syracuse	357-353	*Praxiteles (sculptor)*	*fl.* 360
348	*Treaty of Rome with Carthage*	Olynthus taken by Philip	348	Aeschines	389-314
343-341	**First Samnite War**			Demosthenes	384-322
	Battle of *Mt. Gaurus* (M. Valerius Corvus)			Aristotle	384-322
340-338	**The Latin War** Devotion of **Decius Mus I**	Battle of Chaeronea	338	*Apelles (inter)*	336
	Battle of *Mt. Vesuvius*				
339	*Leges Publiliae Supremacy of Comitia Tributa*	**Alexander the Great**	336-323		
326-304	**Second Samnite War (C. Pontius)**	Battle of Issus	333	Menander	344-292
321	**Caudine Forks**. The Yoke	Foundation of Alexandria	332		
311	Appius Claudius, Censor The *Via Appia*	Battle of Arbela	331		
311-309	Etruscan War First Battle at *Lake Vadimo*	Alexander's Successors Battle of Ipsus (301)	323-301		
305	Battle of *Bovianum*				
298-290	**Third Samnite War**	Ptolemy I (Soter)	323-285	Euclid	*fl.* 300
		Agathocles at Syracuse	317-289	Theophrastus	*c.* 384-277
295	Battle of *Sentinum* Devotion	Demetrius Poliorcetes	308-283	Zeno, the Stoic	*c.* 366-264

ofDecius Mus II

B.C.	ROME.	OTHER NATIONS. .C.		LITERATURE. B.C.	
287	Last Secession of the Plebs	Rhodes powerful	300-200	Epicurus	341-270
2353287	*Lex Hortensia.* Legislative power of Comitia Tributa finally established				
	Political distinction between the Patricians and Plebeians now at an end	Aetolian League	284-167 us	Theocritus	*fl.* 280
283	Renewed Etruscan and Gallic War Second Battle at *Lake Vadimo*	Achaean League	280-146	Bion and Moschus	*fl.* 270
281-275	**War with Tarentines and Pyrrhus**				
280	Battle of *Heraclea.* Victory of the phalanx	Gauls in Greece	280-278		
279	Battle of *Asculum* **Fabricius the Just**	Ptolemy II (Philadelphus)	285-247	*Septuagint*	*c.* 277
278	**Rome and Carthage allied**				
277	Pyrrhus masters nearly all Sicily				
275	Battle near *Beneventum* (**M'. Curius Dentatus**) Pyrrhus returns to Epirus				
273	Treaty of Rome with Egypt *Recognition of Rome as one of the great powers*			*Aratus (astronomer)*	*fl.* 270
272	Pyrrhus killed at Argos Surrender of Tarentum				
266	**All Italy (south of the Apennines) Roman**				

B. C.	ROME.	OTHER NATIONS. .C.		LITERATURE. B.C.	

PART IV.—THE CONTEST WITH CARTHAGE, 264-202 B.C.

264-241	**First Punic War**				
263	**Hiero of Syracuse** joins Rome	**Hiero of Syracuse**	269-219		
261	Romans build a fleet				

B.C.					Latin Literature
26 0	Naval victory of**Duilius** near*Mylae* *Columna Rostrata*	Aratus, General of Achaean League	45	Callimachus *fl.* 260	
25 6	Naval victory of**Regulus** at*Ecnomus*				
25 5	Regulus defeated by Xanthippus of Sparta				

				LATIN LITERATURE. B.C.	
				PROSE.	VERSE.
				PERIOD I.—THE GROWTH OF LATIN LITERATURE, 250-80 B.C.	

B.C.	Roman Events	Greek Events	date	Prose	Verse
25 0	Roman victory at *Panormus*(Metellus)				
24 9	Carthaginianvictory at*Drepana*(Claudius)				
24 8-241	**Hamilcar Barca** in Sicily	Ptolemy III (Euergetes)	247-222		
24 1	Victory of Lutatius off the*Aegates Insulae* *Peace with Carthage* **Sicily made a Roman Province** (1)				
24 1-238	War of Carthage with her Mercenaries **Corsica and Sardinia made a Roman Province** (2)				Livius Andronicus (*fl.* 240)
23 6-228	**Hamilcar in Spain. Hannibal's oath**				Naevius (*fl.* 235)
23 0-229	Illyrian War. (Queen Teuta)	Athens joins Achaean League	229		
22 8	Corinth admits the Romans to the Isthmian Games **Hasdrubal**succeeds Hamilcar in Spain *Founds New Carthage.* The*Iberus* (*Ebro*) fixed as the Carthaginian boundary	**Roman Embassy to Greece**	28		

Date	Rome / West	East	Date	Literature
225-223	Gallic rising (Boii and Insubres) Great victory near *Telamon*	Reforms of Cleomenes at Sparta	226-5	
222	Victory over the Insubres at *Clastidium* **M. Marcellus** wins the *spolia opima* (3) Subjugation of Gaul south of the Alps	Aratus and Antigonus take Sparta	221	
		Antiochus the Great (Syria)	224-187	
221	**Hannibal succeeds Hasdrubal in Spain**			
219	Hannibal takes *Saguntum* (ally of Rome)	Ptolemy IV (Philopator)	222-205	
218-202	**Second Punic War**	Philip V (Macedon)	221-179	PLAUTUS (254-184)
218	Hannibal crosses the Alps Battles of the *Ticinus* and *Trebia*			
217	Battle of *Lake Trasimene* Death of **Flaminius** **Q. Fabius Maximus, Dictator**			
216	Battle of *Cannae*. Death of **Paulus**	**Philip allied with Hannibal**	216	Fabius Pictor (*fl.* 216) ENNIUS (239-169)
216-211	**Revolt of Capua**			
215	Marcellus saves Nola	First Macedonian War	214-205	
214-212	**Siege and Capture of Syracuse by Marcellus**	**Death of Archimedes**	212	
212	P. & Cn. Scipio defeated by Hasdrubal Loss of Spain south of the Ebro Hannibal seizes Tarentum			
211-206	**P. Cornelius Scipio** (Africanus Maior) in Spain	Rome allied with Aetolians	211	
21	Scipio			

0	surprises New Carthage			
20 8	**Hasdrubal** (son of Hamilcar) eludes Scipio and crosses the Pyrenees to join Hannibal	Philopoemen, General of Achaean League	08-183	
20 7	**Defeat and Death of Hasdrubal at the Metaurus (Nero)**			
20 4	Scipio goes to Africa: blockades *Utica*	**Peace of Rome with Philip**	05	
20 3	**Hannibal recalled: leaves Italy**			
20 2	Battle of *Zama*. Peace made			

PART V.—FORMATION OF EMPIRE BEYOND ITALY, 200-183 B.C.

20 0-196	**Second Macedonian War**			
19 7	Battle of *Cynoscephalae* (**Flaminius**)			
19 6	*Proclamation of the Freedom of Greece*			
19 5	Hannibal takes refuge with Antiochus			Cato (234-149)
20 0-191	War with Insubrian and Boian Gauls **Gallia Cisalpina a Roman Province** (3)	Antiochus in Greece	92	
19 1-190	**War with Antiochus of Syria**			
19 1	Battle of *Thermopylae* (**Cato**)			
19 0	Battle of *Magnesia*. (L. Scipio and Domitius)	Hannibal with Prusias, King of Bithynia	90-183	PACUVIUS (220-132)
18 4	**Censorship of Cato**			
18 3	*Deaths of Hannibal, Scipio and Philopoemen*			
35 6357179	T. Sempronius Gracchus in Spain	War of Antiochus and Egypt	72-168	

17 1-168	Third Macedonian War (Perseus)			
16 8	Battle of *Pydna*(**Aemilius Paulus**) Egypt accepts the protectorate of Rome	Judas Maccabaeus (a treaty with Rome, 161)	66- 161	TERENCE (185-159)
14 9-146	**Third Punic War (Scipio Africanus Minor)** *Destruction of Carthage*B			
14 8-146	War with Andriscus (the pseudo-Philip) and the Achaeans.*Destruction of Corinth*(**Mummius**)			LUCILIUS (180-103)
14 8	**Macedonia made a Roman Province (4)**B **Illyricum made a Roman Province (5)**			
14 9-140	War with**Viriathus**, the Lusitanian Hero	Judaea free from Syrian control (Simon Maccabaeus)	42	
14 3-133	**Numantine War**			
13 3	*Destruction of Numantia*(Scipio Africanus Minor) **Roman Province in Spain (7)**B **Achaia made a Roman Province (8)**			Accius (*c.* 170-90)
13 3	Attalus III bequeaths the Kingdom of Pergamum to Rome. This becomes the**Roman Province of Asia (9)**			

PART VI.—PERIOD OF CIVIL STRIFE IN ITALY, ETC. 133-44 B.C.

---

13 3-121	Attempted reforms (*Leges Semproniae*) of the Gracchi			
13 3	Agrarian Law of**Tiberius**	John Hyrcanus	29	

Year	Event		Year	
	Gracchus / Murder of Tib. Gracchus (P. Scipio Nasica) / First civil bloodshed in Rome	subdues Idumea and Samaria		
131	*Two plebeian Consuls* (the first time)			
129	Death of Scipio Africanus Minor (Carbo suspected)			
123-2	**Tribunate of C. Gracchus**	*Roman Colony sent to Carthage*	23	
121	Death of C. Gracchus / Conquest of S. Gaul / **Province of Narbonensis**(10)	**Mithridates (Pontus)**	20-63	Afranius (*fl.* 100)
118	Death of Micipsa, King of Numidia			
111-106	**The Jugurthine War (Metellus, Marius, Sulla)**	Conquests of Mithridates on the Black Sea	12-110	
106	Jugurtha betrayed to Sulla			
105	The Cimbrians defeat the Romans at *Arausio*			
102	Marius defeats Teutones at *Aquae Sextiae*			
101	Marius (with Catulus) defeats Cimbri at *Vercellae*			
100	Marius Consul a sixth time	Sulla on the Euphrates	? 2	
91	**Tribunate of M. Livius Drusus**			
91-81	**The Social or Marsic War**	**Tigranes**(*Armenia*)	95-60	
90	*Lex Iulia*, granting the *civitas* to the Italian States not in rebellion			
89	Battle of *Asculum*			
35	**First Civil**			

| 835988-86 | War (between Marius and Sulla) | | |

PERIOD II.—THE GOLDEN AGE OF LATIN LITERATURE, 80 B.C.-14 A.D.

88	Sulla occupies Rome. *First invasion of Rome by a Roman army*		
87 -84	**Cinnan revolution.** Marius' reign of terror		
88 -84	**First Mithridatic War. (Sulla)**		
88	Massacre of Romans in Asia		
86	Victory at *Chaeronea.* Sulla takes Athens Death of Marius		
85	Victory at *Orchomenus*	Tigranes at war with Rome	6-85	LUCRETIUS (97-53)
84	*Peace of Dardanus with Mithridates*		
83 -82	**Second Civil War (between Marius and Sulla)**		
82	Death of the younger Marius *Sulla Felix*		
83 -81	*The Sullan Proscriptions* Second Mithridatic War (Murena)	Pompeius in Africa: triumphs as an Eques	1	
81 -79	Sulla Dictator *Leges Corneliae*		
80	**Cilicia made a Roman Province** (11)		
78	Death of Sulla		
78 -72	**War with Sertorius in Spain (Pompeius)**	Pharisees supreme in Judaea	8	Sisenna (*fl.* 78)
75	Mithridates in alliance with Sertorius		
74	**Bithynia made a Roman Province** (12)	*Nicomedes leaves Bithynia to Rome*	5	VARRO (116-27)

233

	of*Pharsalus*. Murder of Pompeius				
47	Alexandrine War. Settlement of Asia				
46	Battle of*Thapsus*. Death of Cato				
45	Caesar sole Consul. Battle of *Munda*(Spain)			PUB. SYRUS(*fl.* 45)	
44	**Murder of Caesar**				

IMPERIAL PERIOD.

43	**Second Triumvirate**(Lepidus, Antonius, Octavianus)	Herod the Great in Judaea	? 7-4	Pollio (*fl.* 40)	VERGIL (70-19)
42	Battle of*Philippi*(Brutus and Cassius)				
31	Battle of *Actium*(Antonius and Cleopatra)	**Egypt a Roman Province** (17)			HORACE (65-8)
27 B.C.-14 A.D.	OCTAVIANUS AUGUSTUS				TIBULLUS (54-19)
23	Death of**Marcellus**			LIVY(59 B.C.-18 A.D.)	PROPERTIUS (49-15)
20	Parthians restore standards	BIRTH OF CHRIST	] .C. 4		OVID(43 B.C.-18 A.D.
A. D. 9	Destruction of army under Varus (Arminius)		.D.	A.D.	A.D.

PERIOD III.—THE SILVER AGE, 14-117 A.D.

14 -37	TIBERIUS			V. PATERCULUS(*fl.* 20)	MANILIUS (*fl.* 12)
37 -41	CALIGULA				
41 -54	CLAUDIUS	Pontius Pilate in Judaea	? 6-36	VAL. MAXIMUS(*fl.* 26)	PHAEDRUS (*fl.* 30-40)
43 -51	Conquest of Britain	CRUCIFIXION	0		
		Boadicea in Britain	(1	SENECA (4 B.C.-65 A.D.)	PERSIUS (34-62)
54 -68	NERO Rome burnt 64			PETRON 9-65)	LUCAN (3

236

36 236368- 69	GALBA, OTHO, VITELLIUS			IUS (*ob.*66)	
70 -78	VESPASIAN. (Colosseum built)	Titus destroys Jerusalem	0	PLINY I. (23-79)	
79 -81	TITUS				
79	Eruption of Vesuvius (Herculaneum and Pompeii)			QUINTI LIAN (*c.* 35-95) FRONTI NUS (*c.* 41-103)	VAL. FLACCUS(*ob.* 90) STATIUS (*ob.* 95)
81 -96	DOMITIAN	Agricola subdues Britain	8-85	TACITUS (*c.* 55-120) PLINY II . (61-113)	SILIUS (25 -101) MARTIAL (*c.* 40-102)
93	Death of**Agricola**(father-in- law of Tacitus)			SUETON IUS (*c.* 75-160)	JUVENAL (*c.* 55-138)
96 -98	NERVA			FLORUS (*fl.* 137)	
98 -116	TRAJAN	*Greatest extent of Roman Empire*		JUSTINU S (*c.* 150) A. GELLIUS(*fl.* 169 .)	
11 7-138	HADRIAN	Hadrian 's wall	21		
13 8-160	ANTONINUS PIUS	Wall ofAntonine	40		
16 1-180	MARCUS AURELIUS				

PERIOD IV.—THE LATER
EMPIRE, FROM 117 A.D.

					NEMESIA NUS(*fl.* 284)
27 4-337	CONSTANTIN E THE GREAT	Council of*Nicaea*	25		TER. MAURUS(*c.* 300)
39 5-1453	**Byzantine Empire**	Romans leave Britain	09- 420		AUSONIU S(*fl.* 379)
40 8-410	**Alaric** the Goth at Rome (Stilicho)	Hengist and Horsa (Kent)	49	EUTROP IUS(*fl.* 375) Augusti ne (354-430)	CLAUDIA N(*fl.* 400) PRUDENT IUS(*fl.* 404) Rutilius (*fl.* 416)
45 1	**Attila** the Hun defeated at Chalons				
45 5	**Genseric** the Vandal at Rome				
47 6	**Odoacer** at Rome. **Western Empire ends**				
		Constan tinople taken by Turks	453		

Made in the USA
Las Vegas, NV
08 July 2023

74387208R00134